Queen Mary and her Lady in Waiting escorted by Sam Saunders outside his prefabricated house during the Royal Visit.

FROM SEA TO AIR

The Heritage of Sam Saunders

by A.E. Tagg
& R.L. Wheeler

Samuel Edgar Saunders
The founder of the Company; a portrait taken
in 1912 when he was 55 years of age.

PRINTED AND PUBLISHED BY CROSSPRINT
NEWPORT, ISLE OF WIGHT.

This book is dedicated
to the loyal workforce
without whom there would
be no story to tell.

© A.E. Tagg and R.L. Wheeler

First Published 1989

Published & Printed by
Crossprint, Daish Way,
Dodnor Industrial Estate,
Newport, Isle of Wight.

ISBN 0 9509739 3 9

FROM SEA TO AIR

The Heritage of Sam Saunders

CONTENTS

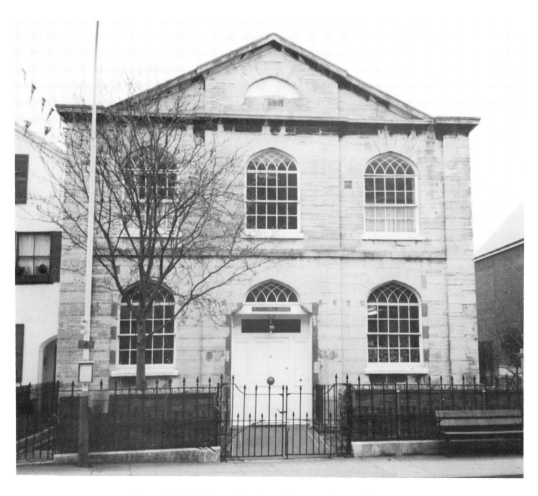

Alexandra Hall. Sam Saunders first premises at Cowes
Isle of Wight

FOREWORD

There are obvious similarities in the birth and growth of our automobile and aviation industries. Yet today one is languishing while the other is still reaching for the stars.

This book records the life of an aviation enterprise which after eighty years of success and failure in various directions has a fine reputation for the manufacture of advanced aerospace components and control systems. Through many vicissitudes and several changes of name and ownership shines the vision and determination of its successive leaders backed by a superlative workforce. And the secret of ultimate achievement may lie in Uffa Fox's tribute to the founder, Sam Saunders, as 'an exceptional man who collected the best craftsmen from all over Britain, splendid men who took great pride in all they did and inspired us apprentices with the will to do well'. That spirit has persisted and underpins some of our little Island's continuing triumphs. So Saunders-Roe trainees built Thrust 2, winner of the world's land speed record, and have helped to produce the famous Islander and Trilander aeroplanes, while their successors in Westland at East Cowes are working on a wide variety of high technology components for the worlds latest aircraft.

Posterity will be grateful to the authors for uncovering some of the foundations of a vital sector of modern British industry.

Sir John Nicholson, Bart, KBE, CIE,
Lord Lieutenant of the Isle of Wight
from 1980 to 1986,
Mottistone Manor,
Isle of Wight.
1989.

ACKNOWLEDGEMENTS

The authors and publishers wish to thank all those people who have assisted with advice and encouragement, which has enabled us to write and produce this book. It is impossible to mention all by name but first and foremost the directors of Westland Aerospace Limited, and their predecessors of the British Hovercraft Corporation Limited, deserve our special thanks for access to company records, without which, much of the background would be lacking. These records have principally been collected over many years by a senior company engineer, Charles Taylor, whose persistence and constant vigilance has ensured that much archival material has been saved for posterity. The company Works Engineer, John Line, has also assisted in the retention and storage of these precious records and has encouraged the authors in their efforts. Many other members of the staff, both past and present, and others with no direct company connection, have contributed their memories and memorabilia, all of which we gratefully acknowledge. Particular mention must be made of the collection of photographs, lectures and notes of Henry Knowler loaned to one of the authors by his widow.

Among those we would mention in particular: Sir Thomas Sopwith for his memories of Sam Saunders, Harald Penrose for his major works on British Aviation, which entailed much early research of great assistance to all who work in this field. Thanks go to Michael H. Goodall, who directed his efforts elsewhere and made available the results of his original research; to John D. Garrett, a Saunders-Roe ex-apprentice, whose father managed the Addlestone factory, for enlightening us on an hitherto obscure activity of the company in wartime and other earlier associations; to Sir Austin Robinson, Fred Pharoah, Philip Jarrett, Eric Morgan, Kevin Turner (who prepared the GA drawings of the major types) and others not mentioned who we trust will not be slighted by their omission.

The photographs have come from various sources. The large collection within the company at Cowes, ably preserved by Barry Elliott and Gilbert Hampton, provided the basis to which others have added their contributions, the use of which we acknowledge with our thanks for allowing them to be seen by a wider audience. We make particular mention of the old established firm of Beken of Cowes, who carried out the photography on behalf of the company in the early days in the Isle of Wight.

In certain cases it has been difficult or impossible to establish the original source of the photographs and in such cases we can only apologise for any lack of courtesy in not acknowledging.

We would however express appreciation of the help in providing illustrations from their collections, to Jack M. Bruce/G. Stuart Leslie and organisations such as the Quadrant Picture library (Flight Magazine), the Imperial War Museum, the Royal Aerospace Establishment and the Royal Air Force Museum. The bibliography lists many books and reports which have been consulted, and our thanks go to the authors where we have used them as a source of reference.

Finally, and by no means least, we would like to express our most grateful thanks to Margaret Tagg who typed much of the original draft and Paula Sheaf who painstakingly typed and repeatedly re-typed the text. Her interest and suggestions of text modifications which indicated that invaluable "extra-mile" were much appreciated.

FROM SEA TO AIR

The Heritage of Sam Saunders

Introduction

Originally this book was intended to cover the entire history of the company primarily known as Saunders-Roe. However as research and writing proceeded, it became abundantly clear that there was far too much interesting material for a single book. The authors decided, therefore, that this book should concentrate on the aviation story and that the marine history should form a separate volume.

In the aviation field the company, in its several forms, is probably best known for the manufacture of marine aircraft, which followed naturally from its original activities as a boat building concern which began in the Thames valley in the 1830s. In its time, the company pioneered methods of construction and hull design for high speed motor boats, which were applied to craft for skimming on the surface of the water and later used in the design of flying boat hulls. As the size and weight of flying boats increased, the use of wood was discontinued in favour of corrosion resistant aluminium alloys and the company changed accordingly to meet the new requirements. One ingenious method of construction evolved for boats, and known as Consuta, was not only used in early flying boats but also in car body and airship gondola construction.

In the course of its long history, its products included high speed craft which in their time were the fastest motor boats in the world and two notable types of flying boat, first the Princess which, to this day, is still the heaviest aircraft to be built and flown in Great Britain and only marginally smaller than the largest, the Brabazon land-plane, and secondly the SR.A1, the first jet-propelled flying boat in the world and the fastest flying boat at that time. Whilst these two aircraft were being test flown, the company's engineers were engaged in designing high speed fighters which could out-climb those of today and rocket launchers which ultimately became capable of launching the United Kingdom's only British launched satellite. Not much later the company was to design and manufacture helicopters and hovercraft until finally the helicopter activity was transferred to the Westland company and the hovercraft work was to continue at Cowes under a new name, the British Hovercraft Corporation.

The company's first production facilities were at its birthplace, as a boat-building establishment, on the Thames at Streatley and Goring and the move to larger premises on the Isle of Wight enabled this activity to be developed and for aircraft manufacture to commence. In Cowes, itself, a variety of premises have been occupied and wartime requirements, aggravated by bombing, caused operations to be dispersed, not only in the Island, but to various sites throughout the country. During and immediately following the Second World War the company had premises in many parts of the Isle of Wight, on the Island of Anglesey, at Eastleigh and at Addlestone on the outskirts of London. Contract cancellations, take overs, consolidation and rationalisation have reduced these locations to the Cowes area alone. Details of these premises are given in the text.

Although many personalities have been associated with the company, the one who is remembered as having the most influence on it and the town of East Cowes was Samuel Edgar Saunders, known affectionately as Sam, a grandson of the originator the the firm in Streatley.

From 1880, for nearly fifty years, he stands out as the personality responsible for seeing the company through many changes and difficulties until, in his later life, he was succeeded by pioneer aviator A.V. Roe, each in his time holding nominal status as President until their decease. They were the entrepreneurs who gave the company its well-known name of Saunders-Roe. Sam Saunders made his home in East Cowes, where he made generous gifts of property and became a notable and much loved Isle of Wight personality. No doubt he would be gratified to see the company developments in hovercraft as he was also making surface-skimming craft relying on air under the hull for their performance, including a crude form of hovercraft, in the early part of the century.

The company is now known as Westland Aerospace Limited and is one of the three companies which comprise the Westland Group plc. Westland Aerospace has three divisions, Westland Aerostructures Limited, British Hovercraft Corporation Limited and EEL Limited. The latter is a flourishing electronics company which is also responsible for the company's test facilities. Employing some fifteen hundred people, many of whom worked for the company when it was called Saunders-Roe Limited, it continues the tradition of forward looking diversification and is looking forward to many prosperous years of trading in the aerospace and marine fields.

The Swan Hotel at Streatley. Considerable changes had taken place to the old inn where S.E. Saunders was born. The picture was taken after 1890, the year when Harry Saunders was running the adjacent boatyard.

The Swan at Streatley. The inn where S.E. Saunders was born in 1857, a photograph taken many years later, with the steam launch 'The Flying Dutchman' moored at the bank.

The Swan Hotel in 1980.

Sam Saunders first boat works opposite the Swan at Goring. The premises still exist today.

The entrance to Sam Saunders first boat works which was also his home.

CHAPTER 1

S.E. SAUNDERS BOATBUILDER EXTRAORDINARY

The dominant character in this history of aviation centred at East Cowes on the Isle of Wight is a gentleman called Samuel Edgar Saunders. This man of remarkable energy, enterprise and ingenuity was born in the Swan Inn at Streatley beside the River Thames on the 29th May 1857. This inn had been the home of the Saunders family for two previous generations; his father Cornelius and his grandfather Moses. Samuel was the first son of Cornelius and his wife Ellen, who had been married earlier in the year in the parish church of Reading. The family, in addition to running the Swan Inn, had been responsible for the construction and maintenance of weirs and locks on the river since around 1830. This is often claimed to be the foundation of the company currently known as Westland Aerospace Limited, recently the British Hovercraft Corporation Limited, formerly Saunders-Roe Limited and originally S.E. Saunders Ltd. However, following several years of intensive research this can only be said to be the origins of the company rather than its foundation. This research has established that a company called Harry Saunders, Boat and Launch Builder was formally established in 1870. Harry could have been one of Samuel Saunders' older cousins. Local residents and boat builders have suggested that Harry Saunders was Sam's uncle, but a systematic check of local records shows that Sam had no uncle of this name. It is, of course, possible that the name of the company was changed after its foundation in 1870. It could have been founded by someone in the Saunders family and later became the company of Sam's younger brother Harry. Since it was not registered as a limited company, and the local records office can find no trace of its foundation, it is unlikely that we will ever know precisely who founded this first company of the Streatley Saunders family.

It is highly likely that very small boats, punts and dinghies were built by the family prior to the formation of this company. Indeed Samuel is said to have built a dinghy by himself at a very early age. Local villagers are supposed to have been so impressed with the standard of workmanship shown in this little boat that it was placed on a small carriage and paraded round the streets of the village.

Samuel was given a private education and then entered the family business as a boatbuilder towards the end of the 1870s. The main business at this stage was the hiring and repair of small Thames boats and the building of launches.

On Christmas Eve 1877, Samuel married Helen Baigent in St. Peters Church, Brighton. Their first child, Ethel Kate, who became the apple of Samuel's eye, was born a year later. Their son, Hubert Samuel, who was to be the last of their children, was born in 1881.

During the 1880s business prospered and the company established a reputation for high standards of workmanship. For example it was their proud boast that their punt poles were unbreakable and a £20 payment was offered to anyone who broke a pole whilst punting. This was a substantial offer, representing as it did very many weeks wages for the average workman at that time. There is no record that the £20 was ever paid.

In the mid 1880s a new idea for building boats occurred to Sam at the same time as efficient steam engines became available. This coincidence of time was to be the foundation of the future success of the business. Sam's idea was to use laminated wood for the hull of his boats. As the adhesives available in Victorian England were not suitable for immersion in water, Sam began his experiments of sewing the panels together with copper wire forming a strong, water-tight, but light hull. At the end of this decade contracts for the steam launches Thistle, Hera, Mariposa and Maritana were successfully completed and the significant expansion of the business had begun. By the early 1880s we know that two Saunders companies existed, the original Harry Saunders company at Streatley and S.E. Saunders Launch Builder & Engineer at Goring. In 1886 the family had purchased land on the north side of the Thames at Goring, directly opposite the Swan at Streatley. Almost as though Sam foresaw his future association with the Isle of Wight, he commissioned Percy Stone, FRIBA, an architect very well known to the Island, to design and supervise the construction of a large boathouse in 1894 on the riverside with first floor accommodation for the family. Covered storage of 6000 sq. ft. for 200 river skiffs or punts was provided together with some 4000 sq. ft. of wharfage on a private millstream branching off the Thames.

In his new premises Sam continued to develop his ideas for laminated wood construction and in 1896 a near neighbour, a Mr. Clutton, commissioned him to build a launch for the Umpire Committee of Henley Regatta. The launch was to be designed to produce minimum wash as the current umpires' launch had been producing an unacceptable wash at the Regatta. The resulting launch, named Consuta, which is Latin for "sewn together", was 51 ft. long and 7½ ft. in the beam, had a fine entry with a shallow run aft, and a rounded tunnel stern. The hull skin comprised four mahogany laminations hand sewn together with annealed 16 SWG copper wire stitches laid in approximately 40,000 inch long grooves in the outer lamination. Power was provided by a Desvignes steam engine which gave the launch a trials speed of 27.5 knots with so little wash that the Umpire Committee was fully satisfied and used Consuta for many years until she became the BBC's television commentary launch for the Oxford and Cambridge boat races. She is now being restored by Kew Bridge Engine Trust in a workshop near Kew bridge in London.

The success of Consuta size craft, combined with the general expansion of the business, required larger, more specialised, launch building premises. Furthermore, the branch water of the Thames at Goring was unsuitable for the testing of Sam's larger, fast launches due to the immediate presence of locks and weirs. He therefore sold his premises at Goring in 1899 to a Mr. G.A. Ellis, who planned to combine boat leasing with the continued utilisation of the millstream for the generation of electric

'Mariposa' at the Springfield Works.

Typical 19th Century S.E. Saunders River Launch.

Goring-on-Thames, The launch 'Arethusa' embarking for a river trip
from the lock at the new Goring boat-house in 1899.

'Consuta' – The steam launch built in 1898. With its copper wire sewn laminated construction and advanced hull form.
'Consuta' created a sensation in boating at the time and was the key to the major expansion of Sam Saunders' business.

power. The new premises were also built on the north side of the Thames at South Stoke, about a mile upstream of Goring, and were known as the Springfield Works.

Coincident with the completion of Springfield Works, and the success of Consuta, Sam was at last granted a provisional patent for his method of laminated boat construction and it was also, appropriately, named the Consuta system. The patent was dated December 31st 1898 and numbered 222 and was the first of a number of variations on the theme as well as many other original ideas. He was subsequently granted seventy-six patents, his last in 1930 at the age of 73 (see Appendix 7). The granting of the patent gave Sam, and several of his colleagues, the confidence to form a new company called the Saunders Patent Launch Building Syndicate which comprised, in addition to Sam, Sidney (Joe) Porter, the designer and draughtsman, Fred Goatley, the expert hull builder, Bill Attry, the mechanical and electrical fitter and Ted Smith, the blacksmith. Whether Sam's original company continued to operate following the formation of the Syndicate is not known, but we do know that the Syndicate continued until 1906.

In these early days of the century Sam built a craft which can only be described as one of the first sidewall air cushion craft. This boat was rectangular in planform, 33 ft. long and with an 8 ft. beam, described as having a flat bottom with a shoe shaped bow. The flat bottom had three shallow fore and aft walls, one on the centre line and one on each side of the craft. Between the three main walls were a number of fore and aft shallower fins between which were a large number of holes through the hull inclined aft. The boat's engine drove a compressor which forced air through these hull holes giving air lubrication to hull and forward propulsion from their aft inclination. There is a record of the hull being completed but no record of the success or failure of any trials. Uffa Fox, however, records that Sam Saunders built an unsuccessful air cushion craft which became known as the Bubble Boat!

Such trials and tribulations did not deter Sam who continued to build even faster boats.

In 1906 Saunders also opened a boat-building yard on the Seine, near Paris, and arranged for the construction, under his supervision, of a number of high-speed boats at yards near Genoa in Italy and Kiel in Germany. The "Legru Hotchkiss" was built in the Paris yard, the first "San Giorgio" in the Genoa yard and Baron Krupp was responsible for the Kiel yard. These arrangements fostered the Saunders' principle of construction, enabled the owners to compete in their own national races and contributed to the growth of the business. A full list of the racing boats built by the company is given in Appendix 1.

In a few short years came the most significant move in Sam's career. The Great Western Railway failed to make good a promise to build a spur to the Springfield Works and the Thames Conservancy Board began to rigidly enforce speed restrictions on the river which meant that fast launches could not be adequately tested before delivery.

No doubt Sam noted that, following the death of Queen Victoria in 1901, the new King, Edward VII, was taking a great interest in yachting, and boats in general, at Cowes. Since the Syndicate was also looking to expand the business, they decided to move to Cowes in that year, but

still maintained the business at the Springfield Works. Their first premises at Cowes were at the Alexandra Hall, in Birmingham Road, which was a former Wesleyan Chapel. The chapel was converted to showrooms and workshops and Sam and his family lived in the High Street at Seaview House, now part of the Island Sailing Club. Springfield Works continued to be used by the Syndicate, and then by Sam, until 1911, when it was sold to the Thames Launch Company of Hobbs & Sons. It was still in existence until well after World War II but the buildings have been pulled down and the site returned to mother nature. The Goring boathouse, however, Sam's first custom-built works, is still in first class order and continues in use as a boathouse.

The move to Cowes proved to be an inspiration, as the Syndicate built some 150 boats, a number of them some 75 ft. long, in the years up to 1906. The boats all utilized Consuta construction and were built both at Cowes and Goring. Among their many customers were the Admiralty, for whom they built the Navy's first motor boat, and Trinity House.

When the agreement to form the Syndicate expired in 1906, Sam decided that his future lay in setting up his own company unrestricted by the need to agree policy with his co-partners of the Syndicate. In 1907 he took over the almost derelict workshops of the Liquid Fuel Engineering Company in Columbine Road on the East Cowes side of the mouth of the River Medina. The company was called S.E. Saunders Limited, with a capital of £5000, part owned by the Wolseley Tool and Motor Company, then a subsidiary of Vickers, whose share holding was designed to promote sales of their internal combustion engines. The company held its first Board Meeting on 16th May 1908. The refurbished workshops became known as Columbine Yard. In his new premises Sam continued the development of high speed displacement motor launches, culminating in 1909 with a 50 ft. long racing boat, powered by two 360 HP 12 cylinder Wolseley engines, named initially the Wolseley-Siddeley II. In 1910 the craft was sold to the Duke of Westminster and renamed Ursula, or little bear, after the Duke's daughter. This powerboat won the Coupe de Nations at Monaco four years in succession reaching a top speed of 44 mph in 1910. Sam's granddaughter was named after this highly successful racing boat in the hope that her life would be just as successful.

In parallel with the design and build of more conventional hulls such as that of Ursula, Sam was investigating the development of planing hulls and in 1908 acquired the sole British rights to the Fauber principle of design of multi-stepped hulls with air fed in through tubes on the aft side of the steps to reduce hull resistance. Profiting by this experience Sam produced his own patented hydroplane design and his first boat, called Columbine, won fourteen British motor boat race meetings in 1910. This success led to the design and build of a 40 ft., five stepped, hydroplane of Consuta construction for Mr. E. Mackay Edgar called Maple Leaf IV, which won the British International (or Harmsworth) Trophy at 43 mph in 1912. It was significant for the future of Sam's company that the driver chosen was a young man called Tom Sopwith, then taking a considerable interest in aviation in addition to his boating activities. In July 1912 Maple Leaf IV raised the official

Springfield Works, South Stoke, near Goring. Built in 1899 to supersede the premises at Goring Lock.

Prefabricated House Designed by Sam Saunders and built by his company in the late 1920s still in normal use on the Isle of Wight.

The First Premises in Cowes. The syndicate built boats behind the Alexandra Hall in Birmingham Road.

East Cowes Waterfront 1931. The second Windhover is moored in the Medina off the Solent Works.
From left to right: The Esplanade and old Columbine building with the various buildings in High Street, Maresfield Road, Old Road and Union Street behind. Behind the Windhover is Seaholme House still in use as offices by Westland Aerospace and next is the White House where the Saunders family lived for many years.

world speed record to 46.5 mph and a year later retained the Harmsworth Trophy at a speed of 57.5 mph.

Before the onset of the First World War, not only had Sam built his first motor boat for the Admiralty, he had started building lifeboats for the RNLI, resulting in 63 being built between 1913 and 1932, received a Royal Warrant as launch builder to H.M. King George V and had been created a Chevalier of the Order of St. Charles of Monaco by the Prince.

As if Sam did not have enough to occupy his mind and his workforce in this period of almost frantic activity, he formally announced in 1909 that he had formed a new department within his company. This department was to design and build "everything required for aero-navigation". Initially this work was carried out in a small shed close to the Folly Inn on the east bank of the River Medina, where experimental work was undertaken for Sir Hiram Maxim and other early aviation pioneers. It is from this small beginning that the story of aviation recorded in this book unfolds. The full detailed story of the work Sam Saunders founded on boats continues to the present day and is more than sufficient for a separate book.

At the end of this period of highly successful technical and business activity tragedy struck Sam in his family. His only daughter Ethel, who had been his secretary and "right hand man", contracted meningitis and died on April 8th 1913 at only 33 years of age. Although Sam continued to throw himself into his business and local activities, that essential spark of enthusiasm seemed to die with his daughter.

He continued to encourage flying boat developments, through a number of chief designers, to obtain aircraft sub-contracts and to develop his existing businesses. In the mid-twenties he attempted to enter the business of prefabricated houses of octagonal planform, so that they could be erected to suit any site. One of these buildings still exists in the outskirts of Newport, but the business was ahead of its time and very few houses were made. His final fling, in 1927, was to change the name of the Gunville and Afton Brickyards he had acquired from the Prichett family in the early 1920's to the Carisbrooke Brick, Tile and Pottery Works and to install his son Hubert as its manager. The pottery was of a very high class and has become much sought after by collectors, both for its beauty and the fact that local clay from the Afton Down area was used in its manufacture. Sadly, this business failed to make profits and it closed in 1937, four years after Sam's death.

The full story of Sam's aircraft activities is told in subsequent chapters, coming to an end in 1929 when the company was reformed as Saunders-Roe Limited when Sam was 72. He was then made Life President of the company, taking no further part in day to day activities, and died in 1933 at the age of 76.

What of the character of this man who had such an influence on the marine and aircraft world of his day? Three quotations from men who knew him well should suffice. First, Fred Goatley, one of the Syndicate:

"He had built up his great reputation by always employing the best labour that he could possibly find, both in the drawing office and in the workshops, his great skill and enthusiasm, his untiring energy and his personal supervision. He had been a public benefactor in many ways, and I need only mention that period of industrial depression which followed the cessation of the war, when Mr. Saunders proved himself a gentleman and one who looked after his workmen. He put his hand very deeply into his pocket and built stock boats, which gave employment to hundreds of men. He must have spent about £30,000 in that way alone, and they were everlastingly grateful for his efforts in that direction, which had undoubtedly prevented much distress."

Second, Uffa Fox, the well-known yachtsman and boat designer who served his apprenticeship with Sam:

"Working in harmony in the Seaholme Shop was the finest set of craftsmen I've ever seen. No matter where you go you will find some wonderful men, but in his shipyard, S.E. Saunders had collected from London River, the Upper Thames, Cowes and from all over Britain, first rate craftsmen. Once you get together over twenty five men it is difficult to not include a few who are not so good, but S.E. Saunders was an exceptional man because he not only used the finest materials but collected the best craftsmen. All these splendid men took great pride in all they did, and were wonderful instructors to the apprentices as well as inspiring us with the will to do well."

Finally, Canon Judkins, speaking at the golden wedding celebration of Sam and his wife, Helen:

"He displayed a spirit of geniality, kindness and hospitality, which were the things that went down deep into the human heart. God had richly endowed him with those qualities and he held a warm place in the hearts of all."

Sam also played a full part in the social life of the East Cowes area and the Isle of Wight in general. When Sam's eventful life came to an end in December 1933 at the age of 76 the Isle of Wight County Press gave this record of his service to the community:

"Of a most generous and kind-hearted disposition, the late Mr. Saunders gave freely and liberally to many charitable and other deserving causes. He was a life vice-president of the Frank James Hospital and various funds in the district for the relief of the poor and suffering always found him a valuable supporter. He contributed most liberally to the East Cowes Soup Kitchen Fund. He gave the town a valuable strip of land for the extension and improvement of the eastern Esplande. A great lover of sport, he gave many trophies and contributions for its encouragement. He was the donor of the magnificent 100 guinea gold cup (the only one of its kind in the country) for annual competition to the the I.W. Football Association, of which he was an honorary vice-president. He also gave the association their junior challenge cup. The Cowes and District Billiard and Whist League, the I.W. County Bowling Association, and other organisations were also indebted to him for trophies. For about 15 years he was co-warden with Sir George Shedden at Whippingham Parish Church, where the beautiful adornment of the reredos and other improvements were largely due to his beneficence. Failing health caused his retirement from the warden-ship this year. He served for a short time on the East Cowes District Council. One of his last efforts for the public weal was the erection at Whippingham of a large and handsome Parish-hall. He was president of

Three Saunders Launches in the River Medina. A photograph taken around 1912.

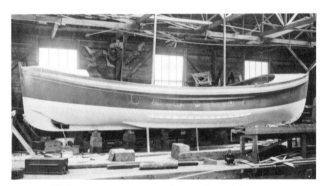

A lifeboat under construction at Cornubia Yard.

The building of the new sheds near the Folly Inn on the river Medina. Erected soon after Sam Saunders announced his entry into the field of 'aero-navigation' in 1909. The Ravaud Aero-Hydroplane in the foreground was a surface-skimming craft employing contemporary aeroplane features.

The Folly Sheds on the east bank of the Medina. The Sopwith Bat Boat is seen being readied for flight in May 1913. These sheds were destroyed by a gale the following year.

the Cowes Football Club and of the East Cowes Sailing Club, the latter from its start. An ardent Conservative and great patriot, Mr. Saunders was the esteemed president of the I.W. Conservative and Unionist Association during the war period until its reorganisation. He was a member of the Institute of Naval Architects, a Fellow of the Royal Society of Arts, a member of the Royal Motor Y.C., the British Motorboat Club, the Royal London Yacht Club, the Medina (Cowes) Lodge of Freemasons, and many other organisations. Among his most cherished possessions were a photograph of Princess Louis of Battenberg and a valuable cigarette case (the gift of the late King Edward to Admiral Prince Louis of Battenberg), which the latter gave Mr. Saunders in appreciation of kindness shown him during his residence at Kent House, East Cowes, after his retirement from the Navy in the early stages of the war."

Funeral of Samuel Edgar Saunders. The burial at St. Mildred's Church, Whippingham on the 21st December 1933. A special boat-shaped coffin made of mahogany Consuta was drawn on a carriage from his home at Padmore House to the church by his former employees and friends.

The Memorial at St. Mildred's, Whippingham. Sam Saunders had made a great contribution to local affairs as well as to the commercial life of the Isle of Wight for which he was well liked and greatly respected. This substantial but elegant memorial conveys something of the character of the man who will be remembered with affection.

Wellman Airship – America. The Saunders-built lifeboat.

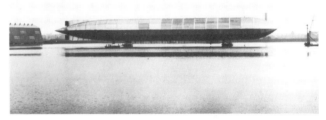

Airship H.M.A.I. The above two photographs show the Saunders built front and rear cars for Vickers of Barrow in 1910 using 'Consuta' in their construction.

Wellman Airship – America. The Saunders-built lifeboat can be seen suspended below the engine compartment, in the keel of the airship, just prior to the abandonment of the trans-Atlantic flight.

Wellman Airship – America. The crew of six and a cat were able to transfer to the lifeboat and were saved.

CHAPTER 2

EARLY FLYING DAYS AT COWES

Sam Saunders's outlook on the development of fast machines was to lead to an interest in flying machines and, as stated in Chapter 1, this led to the formation of an Aircraft Department in 1909. It was also to be expected that he would be keen to exploit his invention of rigid lightweight Consuta construction to the manufacture of aircraft components. The first major application was in 1909-1910 in the construction of the 25 ft. long open gondolas of the first British rigid airship, HMA.1, made by Saunders for Vickers Limited of Barrow. The gondolas housed the power plant and crew and were watertight to permit the airship to alight at sea.

An airborne lifeboat, to be carried by the airship America, in which Walter Wellman attempted to fly the Atlantic, was made in 1910 and served its intended purpose after the airship came down in the sea. This 27 ft. long lightweight lifeboat was constructed at Cowes of Consuta and was shipped on the White Star liner 'Teutonic' to America for Walter Wellman's third airship venture, in which he attempted to cross the Atlantic to Europe. The airship departed from Atlantic City on the 15th October 1910, trailing a device on the water called an "Equilibrator" intended to regulate the height at which the ship flew and containing additional supplies of fuel. The drag of this probably contributed to engine failure and after 69 hours the airship was forced to land in mid-ocean, the crew of six took to the lifeboat and were saved by the Royal Mail Steamship 'Trent' on passage to New York.

Among the early aircraft-related vehicles was a craft made at Cowes to the design, and under the supervision, of a Frenchman, M. Roger Ravaud, who was introduced, and possibly sponsored, by M. Henri Fabre, the first man to fly off water on 28th March 1910. Fabre was aware of the standard of Saunders' workmanship, for his father had purchased a fourteen foot cutter for use as a tender to his yacht. The Ravaud craft was completed by Saunders in 1910 and was intended for entry in the aeroplane and motor boat contests to be held in Monaco in the Spring of 1911, Ravaud no doubt hoping for greater success than achieved with his Aeroscaphe of 1909. The machine was intended to skim on the surface of the water, but not to fly, although it incorporated a number of aircraft features. It was supported at rest on two floats above which were short-span lifting surfaces, fore and aft, which must have been intended to support a significant portion of the weight of the craft and thus reduce water drag. Above these was mounted an aircraft-like fuselage with a 50 HP Gnome rotary engine driving a pusher airscrew. High speed directional control was by an air rudder on a post in the stem of the machine. Testing was carried out early in 1911 from a shed on the east bank of the River Medina at Folly near Whippingham. No information on its performance can be traced and it did not appear at Monaco, consequently it must be assumed that the craft was unsuccessful; nevertheless it represents a stage of development of surface-skimming craft leading to airborne flight over water.

The shed in which the Ravaud craft was housed was of timber construction with galvanised iron roofing and a similar building added in 1913 constituted two buildings 60 ft. long by 50 ft. wide which became known as the Osborne Yard. These two empty sheds were destroyed in a gale on the 16th March 1914 and were rebuilt later in the year.

During the first few years in the Isle of Wight, operations were extended to East Cowes in the Columbine works, enlarged in 1914 from premises previously occupied by the Liquid Fuel Engineering Company, manufacturers of 'Lifu' road transport vehicles and boats, and in various buildings adjacent to the Medina. In the High Street, which ran parallel to Castle Street, past Trinity Wharf, Seaholme House served as the main office and Sam Saunders lived nearby in the White House, Medina Road. New buildings were erected in Maresfield Road in 1915 to provide increased capacity for the aircraft work upon receipt of the Avro contract. These premises were completely destroyed by a disastrous fire on the 29th July 1916, together with all stocks and work in progress, the insurance claim totalling £13,700. Immediate steps were taken to replace these with two new enlarged buildings of 22,000 square feet area, built by the Fairby Construction Company, which were in commission early in 1917. The "Old Lifeboat Shop" in Albany Road served as a workshop until 1944 when it was destroyed by fire and was replaced in 1955 by new enlarged premises which continue in use to the present time. Workshops existed in Clarence Road, Columbine Road and Union Street which, with extensions, were to serve for many years until those in Union Street, known as the "Green Shed" and "Old Stables", together with the original Columbine and Sunbeam Yards were finally swept away to accommodate the new Columbine Works, built by Boulton & Paul and opened in 1935. In the course of this rebuilding, Union Street, which ran from the High Street to Castle Street, part of the High Street, and Medina Road, which ran from the junction of the High Street and Union Street to Albany Road, were absorbed into the area of the factory premises. Some half a mile further up the river, in Clarence Road, boats and aircraft were built and repaired in the Cornubia Yard from 1914 until this was destroyed by enemy action on the night of the 4th/5th May 1942, when in use for the repair of Walrus aircraft. In 1916, building of the Solent Works, with an area of 45,000 square feet in Medina Road, West Cowes, was commenced by the Building Construction Company on the site of the former Mitcham Boatyard. The constructors went into liquidation before it was completed, leaving other builders to finish and resolve the problems with the roof and structure of the building, which was not completed until 1919. The additional strengthening involved the use of bracings which limited the areas where large flying boats could be assembled. This shortcoming was of no great consequence in the early years after the war and in this period the Solent Works formed the most important part of the aircraft works until 1935 when the new Columbine

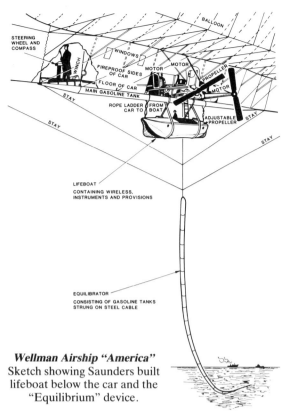

Wellman Airship "America"
Sketch showing Saunders built lifeboat below the car and the "Equilibrium" device.

Ravaud Aero-Hydroplane. A surface-skimming craft constructed at Cowes by Saunders in 1910-1.

The foreshore at the Folly Sheds. Launching the Mortimer Singer version of the Sopwith Bat Boat into the Medina June/July 1913.

The Solent Works 1929, West Cowes. Built in 1916 by the Building Construction Co., completed by F. Bevis Ltd., and destroyed by enemy bombing 4th – 5th May 1942.

Works at East Cowes in 1928. The old Columbine and Esplanade Buildings on the waterfront (centre). In the background the works in Albany and Maresfield Roads and in the foreground the Prefabricated House, White House, and the existing Seaholme building.

The Cornubia Yard, East Cowes, Used mainly for boatbuilding. Miss England II and Bluebird were built here. The buildings were destroyed in the bombing of 4th – 5th May 1942 when in use for repair of Walrus amphibians.

Works were built. The Solent Works were also destroyed in the bombing of the 4th/5th May, being a loss of more than twenty-five per cent of the floor area in use for aircraft work at the time.

Sam Saunders had been acquiring land along the Medina with the object of concentrating his aviation works at Whippingham, but in October 1914 this was not approved by the Home Office in wartime, under the Aerial Navigation Act of 1911. The area intended was at Padmore Farm, part of the Osborne Estate, adjacent to the existing sheds on the site where the Ravaud had been built.

These sheds, owned by Sam Saunders, were sold to the Company for £50 and dismantled in early 1916. Foreman Norris being reprimanded for breaking them thus preventing their re-erection, the timber remaining being suitable only for fencing round the Lifeboat Shed. This government ruling was presumably relaxed, for an aerodrome was in use later in the war in the vicinity of the Folly Inn when Avro 504 land-planes were being built.

A small biplane flying boat, originally sketched in 1910 by a Mr. Arthur D. Wigram of Sydney, Australia, was in the course of construction in 1913. He formed a company named Wigram Flying Boats Limited, of East Cowes, and entered into a sales agreement with Mossman Limited, of Carlton House, Regent Street, dealers in hydroplanes, hydro-aeroplanes, flying machines, airships, etc. Little is known of this company except that among its board members was Sir Brian B.M. Leighton, Bart., who learnt to fly at the Grahame-White School at Hendon and received his pilot's ticket No. 641 on 13th October 1913. It was reported that Wigram had entered the machine for the Daily Mail Circuit of Britain to be held in August. This machine was among several non-starters and finally the Sopwith Circuit seaplane piloted by H.G. Hawker, which had been assembled in the shed at Folly and test flown there from the Medina, was the sole competitor. The Wigram was a tandem two-seater with boat-shaped hull and an appendage for mounting the tail surfaces extending upwards and rearwards from behind the pilot's seat. This rear fuselage extension was shown as an open girder in the sketch of the machine published in the Aeroplane of 20th February 1913 but photographs of the hull under construction in the Medina Shop adjacent to Saunders' Columbine Yard show fully skinned surfaces. It is probable that funding problems arose causing work to be discontinued and the machine was never completed.

The construction of high-speed motor boats was a Saunders speciality and a Saunders hydroplane named Maple Leaf IV had been piloted by T.O.M. Sopwith for the Canadian financier Edward Mackay Edgar, on Sam Saunders' recommendations, in the Harmsworth International Trophy Contest of 1912 in which he was successful; as he was also to be in the contest of 1913. Sopwith's connection with Saunders arose from family holidays spent on the river at Streatley where be became acquainted with Sam's son, Hubert (Bertie) Saunders, and was to become an admirer of Saunders and his products. This led to an order for a similar but smaller hull made of Consuta ply for the first Sopwith Bat Boat which was to become the first successful type of European amphibian flying boat.

In February 1913 the Bat Boat was exhibited at the Aero Show at Olympia, before testing, where its workmanship was much admired, but the following month, during trials at Cowes, where it operated from the sheds at Folly, it suffered damage after stalling on to the water and, leaking badly, was left overnight on the beach where it was wrecked in a gale. However, the Consuta hull was repaired by Saunders and Sopwith replaced the Austro-Daimler with a Green engine to comply with the 'all-British' requirement for the Mortimer Singer contest. The new tail booms were extended in length and twin rudders fitted; at the same time the front elevator was removed. Upon completion of the rebuild at Kingston and after testing with a land-plane chassis at Brooklands the Bat-Boat was taken to Cowes and housed at the Folly Sheds from where trials were conducted. On the 8th July 1913, piloted by H.G. Hawker, it successfully contested the Mortimer Singer £500 Prize Contest, operating from a field between Lee-on-Solent and the mouth of the Hamble River to a buoy in the Solent off Cowes. A further machine, considerably modified, was already in hand for the Admiralty, No. 38, but this was being built completely in the Sopwith works with a similar Saunders-type hull.

Subsequently the Mortimer Singer machine was also accepted by the Admiralty as No. 118. The light weight and handling qualities of the Saunders type hull had made their contribution to an early Sopwith success.

A young apprentice who worked on Maple Leaf IV was Uffa Fox, who started his apprenticeship in January 1912 at the age of fourteen. A strong and unruly character, he was caught, with another apprentice, by Sam Saunders, stealing apples from the Saunders' orchard and was immediately suspended for one week without pay. His conscription into the Royal Naval Air Service in 1917 may have been viewed with mixed feelings for he was exhibiting the basic skills, to be further developed at Great Yarmouth, where he worked on flying boats, which were later to make him famous as a yachtsman and boat designer. His first attempt at boat building was a reconstruction of Saunders' first planing boat, Columbine, which he converted to become a sixteen foot sailing canoe, in 1925. Much later he was responsible for an air-sea rescue boat carried under Hudson aircraft in the Second World War, but he really came to public attention with his racing yachts and sailing with royalty in the post-war period.

Prior to the outbreak of war in 1914, Saunders provided facilities to other manufacturers for seaplane assembly and testing. Both the Sopwith Bat Boat and the Circuit seaplane had been assembled in the shed at Folly with initial flights made from the Solent after planing down the river, although alighting on the Medina near the shed after the flights.

In 1913 the Bristol Coanda biplane No. 120 was converted at Bristol to a single-float seaplane, using a Gnosspelius design of float. Attempts to fly the aircraft after assembly in the Saunders works showed the float to be so heavy and unsatisfactory that the aircraft refused to take off and a replacement was ordered from Saunders using Consuta ply and consequently was of considerably lighter construction. This enabled the aircraft to take off when flown by Harry Busteed on the 15th April, but the engine overheated, losing power, causing a heavy emergency landing in which the seaplane stalled on to the water when the float disintegrated, causing the loss of the aircraft although pilot Harry Busteed was rescued.

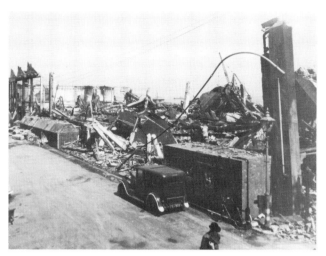

Blitz damage at Solent Works.

The bombing of Cowes 4th – 5th May 1942. A relatively small amount of damage was caused to the Medina works and offices adjoining the Columbine works in Castle Street.

The Sopwith Circuit Seaplane at East Cowes. After being brought across the Solent. The machine was unloaded by the quay and then towed up the Medina to the Folly works for assembly which was completed two days later. The machine was tested that evening by H.G. Hawker, who was to fly the aircraft in the contest. The date is the 9th August 1913.

Wigram Flying Boat. Shown during construction by Saunders in the Medina Shop, part of the old Columbine Works, this machine was not completed.

Maple Leaf IV. Commissioned by Canadian Financier E. Mackay Edgar from S.E. Saunders the 40ft long hydroplane had five steps and was powered by twin 380 hp Austin Engines. The hull was constructed of 'Consuta'. T.O.M. Sopwith won back the Harmsworth International Trophy in 1912 and successfully defended it again in 1913 piloting the boat.

Sopwith Bat Boat. Shown here in the form in which it was flown by H.G. Hawker to win the Mortimer Singer Prize. The hull was of Saunders design and construction.

Sopwith Bat Boat. In March 1913 after a frustrating day testing the first Bat Boat, Tom Sopwith and Harry Hawker left the machine outside overnight on the foreshore at Folly. It was badly damaged and overturned by winds during the night, seen photographed by Harry Busteed.

Bristol-Coanda No. 120. Bristol-Coanda central float hydroplane (No. 120) at the Folly Shed, Cowes, Isle of Wight, in April 1913. Standing beside the float is Harry Busteed, the pilot, and next to him, in white jersey, is his assistant, Ronald Kemp.

Bristol Burney X3 Hydroplane. A machine with hydropeds, and hydrofoils, the hull of which Saunders covered with 'Consuta'.

Capt. Ernest C. Bass. Son of wealthy parents, Bass was half of the Bass-Paterson partnership which sponsored the flying boat built by Saunders in 1914 and which was abandoned unflown.

E.W. Copland Perry. Born 4/2/1890. Killed in an aircraft accident 16/8/1914. Partner to the Perry-Beadle firm whose unsuccessful flying boat of 1914 was largely constructed by S.E. Saunders.

Bristol-Coanda No. 120. On River Medina at Folly Sheds.

Perry Beadle Flying Boat Type B.3. The aircraft was assembled at Cowes in the Columbine Works and included a hull, lower wings, tailplane and fin all covered with 'Consuta'. The machine is shown at Windermere where attempts at flight were finally abandoned.

White and Thompson No. 2. Saunders built a 'Consuta' hull for this machine which was basically a Curtiss design, it was entry No. 6 for the Seaplane Circuit of Britain of 1914 cancelled by the start of the war.

In the same year the Bristol X.3 aircraft was being built to demonstrate the application by Lieut. Charles Dennistoun Burney of hydropeds and hydrofoils to raise an aircraft hull clear of the water. The fuselage structure was passed to S.E. Saunders Limited for skinning with Consuta ply to provide a hull capable of floating on the surface of the water when the aircraft was at rest, but problems associated with the basic conception caused the whole project to be abandoned in June 1914 when the Admiralty refused further funding.

In 1914 Saunders produced the hull of the Perry-Beadle biplane flying boat in which the lower wing provided buoyancy to stabilise the aircraft at rest. The design of the hull was in the hands of Sidney E. (Joe) Porter, that little known specialist in hull design for boats, who had worked for Saunders as an original member of the Syndicate and who continued for many years to apply his knowledge to flying boat hull design. Designed by F.P. Hyde Beadle of Perry-Beadle & Company with works at Gould Road, Twickenham, this two-seater was exhibited in March 1914 at the Olympia Aero Show prior to testing, its finish and general quality being commented on most favourably in contemporary reports.

Evelyn Walter Copland Perry had learnt to fly in 1911 at Hendon, receiving RAe Certificate No. 130 in September, and then joined the staff at Farnborough where he carried out a considerable amount of flying of machines built by the factory, including testing the HRE.1 hydro-biplane on Fleet Pond. Later he joined Sopwith at Brooklands where, on an Henri Farman in July/August 1912, he instructed Major H.M. Trenchard to fly. Later that year he joined A.V. Roe for a short period and took an Avro machine to Lisbon. Upon inheriting wealth on his father's death, he set up the company with Beadle, also formerly on the staff at Farnborough. The partners had previously built a small tractor biplane with a 45 HP engine, which had been flown at Beaulieu with some success, reportedly reaching Cowes, and was taken over at Brooklands by the RFC on the outbreak of war, as No. 1322.

In April 1914, use was made of Saunders' facilities at the Columbine yard for assembly of the Perry-Beadle flying boat; this was recorded by the visiting impressment officer as a potential machine for service use, at that time fitted with a 90 HP Curtiss engine instead of the original ENV. The Perry-Beadle was taken to the Eastbourne Aviation Company in August 1914 and later by train to the Lakes Flying Company (subsequently the Northern Aircraft Company) premises on Lake Windermere for testing which was continued to July 1915, but without success. Proved to be impractical, the machine was discarded and broken up soon after at Borwicks boatyard where it had remained in storage, only a propeller still surviving as a reminder of this unsuccessful attempt to achieve flight from water.

By July 1914 the partners had separated, the company continuing as the Perry Aviation Company until wound up later in the year following the death of Copland Perry, whilst serving as a 2nd Lieutenant in the RFC. He was killed in the crash of the BE.8 No. 625 which he had flown to Amiens from Farnborough on the 16th August 1914. Beadle was to have further associations with Saunders and became chief designer in the immediate period after the war.

Another Consuta hull built in 1914 was that for the White & Thompson No. 2 single-engined flying boat based on Curtiss designs, intended for the Circuit of Britain, Entry No. 6, to be flown by Captain E.C. Bass. The contest was abandoned due to the war, but the aircraft flew successfully on 9th August 1914. The prototype was taken over by the Admiralty but modified versions, which saw service as the White & Thompson No. 3, were no longer fitted with Saunders-made hulls.

Captain Ernest Bass, a member of a wealthy family, travelled widely and, after service with the Texas Rangers, had learnt to fly in America with Curtiss, returning with the British rights for the Curtiss boats, one of which he imported and was operated at Brighton and along the south coast. An association with ex-Royal Navy Lieutenant J.C. Porte, later to be responsible for the development of the Felixstowe boats, was formed when Porte flew in the Curtiss at Brighton. Bass disposed of the rights to manufacture the Curtiss boats to the White & Thompson Company, retaining an interest in this and its successor, the Norman Thompson Flight Company. He also formed a partnership with Compton Paterson, who had designed and flown his own machines from 1910 and towards the end of 1914 the partners had arranged for Saunders to build a small flying boat. This was known as the Bass-Paterson Bat-Boat but, although known to be nearly completed in December 1914, it was not flown as it caught fire during the final stages of preparation in the hangar. When pushed out on to the road to prevent a major conflagration, it burnt itself out, leaving only the metal fittings, the engine and all the copper stitching of the Consuta hull. Bass was involved with the Norman Thompson Flight Company of Middleton, Bognor, for the remainder of the war years, a company whose aircraft were later also to be built at Cowes. Bass himself was not involved with aviation after the armistice and died in November 1939 after a long illness.

The BE.2 aircraft was designed by Geoffrey de Havilland at the Royal Aircraft Factory at Farnborough in 1912 and was used by the RFC and RNAS in many versions throughout the war. Initially produced at Farnborough, it was later sub-contracted to ten firms. It provided a sound basis for developing the capacity for aircraft manufacture in general industry, since the design had been largely proven and detailed drawings were available for tendering purposes. S.E. Saunders Limited was among the early suppliers of BE.2 type aircraft to the RFC, receiving an order for just one machine, before the outbreak of war, this being delivered to Farnborough on the 21st April 1914 unflown. The assembly of this machine at Cowes took place in the Medina Shop at the Columbine works in the same period as the Perry-Beadle.

The machine, BE.2a serial number 469, reassembled at the Royal Aircraft Factory, first flew on 1st August 1914 and was passed to the CFS at Upavon a few days later. In October it was taken over by the Military Wing and went to France on the 9th October 1914 for active service.

In the period following, having established a reputation for high quality workmanship, it was natural for small order for experimental floats to be placed with Saunders. One such order was for a float of the central pontoon type together with a tail float for a BE.2c. The main float was designed in such a way that it could be attached to the existing skid undercarriage thus facilitating reversion

B.E. 2a. This Royal Aircraft Factory type was subcontracted to a number of firms including Saunders. No. 469, the only machine built at Cowes is seen under construction in the Columbine Works with the Perry Beadle behind.

B.E. 2c Seaplane. The aircraft is being launched on Loch Doon after conversion by Saunders at Cowes.

Compton C. Paterson. Pioneer aviator and designer of the abandoned Bass-Paterson flying boat of 1914 built by S.E. Saunders at Cowes.

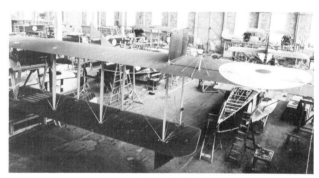

F.2A. Production in the Solent Works.

Curtiss H4 Flying Boat. One of the Airco-built machines serial No. 1235 with hulls by Saunders. In this case the hull differs from the 'Consuta' hulls of No's. 1231-2 and is probably the standard Curtiss type.

Curtiss H.12. Almost indistinquishable from the F.2A flying boat built in considerable numbers at Cowes. Saunders constructed many spare hulls and wing-tip floats for Curtiss and other flying boats during the war.

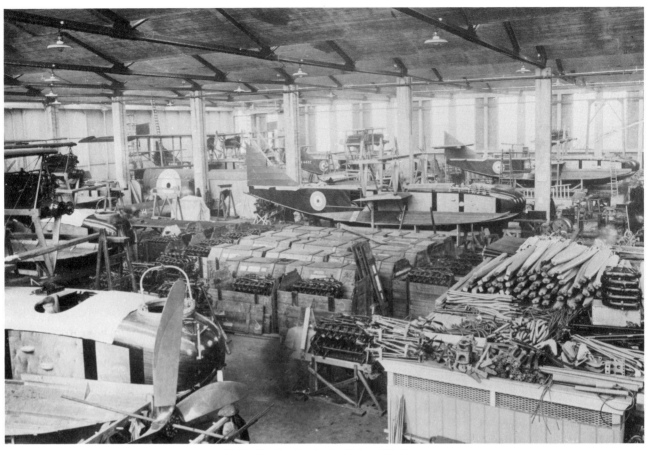

F.2A. Production in the Solent Works.

Short 184 Production. Final assembly of these aircraft took place in the original Folly Works.

back to a land-plane. The machine for conversion, Serial No. 4721, was received at Cowes late in 1916 and was intended for use at the School of Aerial gunnery, then being built at Loch Doon in Ayrshire. The machine was reassembled and tested on Loch Doon in November 1917, wing tip floats being added during the trials, but the Gunnery School was badly sited and the whole project was abandoned in January 1918, consequently 4721 was the only BE.2c seaplane built.

In 1915 and subsequently, there followed government contracts for a variety of aircraft and spares. Saunders became primarily a contractor to the Admiralty for marine aircraft, both for float seaplanes and flying boats, their pre-war experience in this field being no doubt of considerable value. Saunders assisted in the work being carried out at Felixstowe, under Sqn. Cdr. John Porte, on the Curtiss flying boats to improve their general strength and seaworthiness. At the outbreak of the war, the Admiralty had purchased the original H boat America, serial No. 950, intended for the proposed trans-Atlantic flight, for which Porte was nominated as the pilot, together with a sister ship, the H.2 No. 951. New wing tip floats were required as part of the major experimental work undertaken at Felixstowe and drawing No. SP126 was made at Cowes for floats to be fitted to No. 950. In addition to the large number of the developed version of these machines, the H4, known later as the 'Small America' purchased direct from Curtiss, a contract was placed with the Aircraft Manufacturing Company which included participation by Saunders in the manufacture of eight H.4 aircraft serial Nos. 1228 - 35. The extent of involvement in the manufacture of the Felixstowe improved standard type machines is not clear, but it is believed Saunders made the hulls at Cowes, AIRCO the wings at Hendon with final assembly being carried out at Felixstowe. Certainly Saunders designed and produced special hulls for two machines, Nos 1231 & 2 constructed of Consuta, which were possibly lighter in weight, but lacking buoyancy, lay low in the water, so were not produced in any quantity.

Felixstowe continued their experimentation on the H.4 boats until eventually a satisfactory type of hull was evolved, which, fitted to the U.S. built No. 3580, became known as the Felixstowe F.1, the first of a succession of types for British manufacture and with certain of which Saunders became deeply involved.

Curtiss had gone ahead with a larger, more powerful machine, which was also ordered by the British government. The first of these, the H.8, Serial No. 8650, delivered to Felixstowe in March 1916 was found to be still under-powered and unsatisfactory on the water. The work already carried out was applicable in many respects to the H.12 Large America which succeeded the sole H.8 and concentration on this resulted in the F.2 and succeeding Felixstowe designs.

Saunders was to be major contractor from 1916 to the immediate post-war period for the F.2A making use of Consuta in their construction. Deliveries of F.2As commenced in November 1917 and production of this useful flying boat was such that by the end of 1918 sixty-two had been delivered with another six passed inspection and awaiting collection by RNAS pilots. The completion of the remainder on contracts, totalling one hundred aircraft, was made post-war. In addition to the production

of complete F.2A flying boats, which averaged about five per month, the company made hulls for the F.2A and the F.3 against separate contracts - either for supply to major constructors or for replacement of hulls of aircraft in service. These machines were subjected to hard working conditions particularly in operations from the East Coast and damage to hulls frequently occurred. The changeover to the F.5 was taking place at the time of the armistice and of a contract for fifty, none was delivered.

In the early part of 1918, the company rebuilt two Curtiss H.12 flying boats, Serial Nos 8651 and 8690 for use at Calshot incorporting the changes brought about by service experience bringing the H.12 up to a standard similar to the F.2A.

Saunders production of Avro 504 aircraft commenced with a sub-contract from A.V. Roe & Company signed on the 30th June 1915 for 50 Avro 504A landplanes together with one machine built up from parts supplied for educational purposes. The success of the company in obtaining this and subsequent Avro contracts stemmed from the introduction made by Compton C. Paterson from his earlier contacts with both A.V. Roe and S.E. Saunders and warranted a special bonus voted to him by the board in April 1916. The first contract was followed by successive direct contracts for both the 504A and J versions to a total of 201 aircraft. This was the first association with A.V. Roe, the well known pioneer of flight, who experimented with models and then from 1907 with full size machines and was one the three earliest men to fly in Britain, until by 1913 he had successfully evolved the Type 504 prototype. The Avro 504 was to be the subject of much redesign over the years and the Types A and J were considerable improvements on the machine of 1913 for which, it is of interest to note, the drawings of the wings were produced by H.E. Broadsmith, for both Roe and Broadsmith were later to become senior members of the company at Cowes. Broadsmith is also credited with the redesign of the engine bay of the 504J to permit any of the current rotary engines to be fitted, a version which became known as the famous Avro 504K. The capability of the company in all forms of woodworking was applied to the manufacture of propellers for the Avros, of which at least one survives, and was doubtless extended to propellers for the other aircraft produced.

At about the same time as the Avro contract was placed, the Admiralty placed an order for 30 Short 184 seaplanes, the first of several contracts totalling 80 aircraft, for which the company had previously been a sub-contractor for the floats and had redesigned them to improve the construction.

Several firms were contracted to build the Short 184 for which working drawings were not available and each contractor undertook the preparation of these for separate sections of the aircraft and distributed them to the other contractors. Delivery of these machines commenced in February 1916 and continued to February 1918.

A building of wooden construction was erected for the assembly of the Short seaplanes on the bank of the Medina near to the original Folly sheds and was known as the Folly Works. The length of the building facing the river consisted of sliding doors allowing the launching of the seaplanes for testing from any position.

Avro 504.A. It was in better shape when it left the factory at Cowes.

The Folly Works. These buildings mainly of wooden construction were built in the early part of the 1914-18 war and were destroyed by fire on the 21st January 1960. Originally used for Short 184 seaplane assembly, later use included Cutty Sark wing manufacture and plywood production.

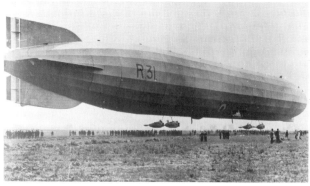

Engine Gondolas for Rigid Airships R31 and R32. These rigid airships were designed and built by Short Bros. at Cardington using wooden construction based on Schutte-Lanz principles. Six-engine gondolas were originally used on each ship but these were later reduced to five.

Engine Gondolas for Rigid Airships R31 and R32. A single 275 H.P. Rolls-Royce Eagle engine was mounted in each car and these were constructed of 'Consuta' by S.E. Saunders.

Norman Thompson N.T. 2.B Flying Boat. Final assembly taking place in the Columbine works in 1918. The large bay in the hulls in the foreground normally held the fuel tanks not the spare wheels.

In 1916 production was also commenced of the Norman Thompson NT.2B single engined flying boat against a contract received for 24 machines. The production of the NT.2B, which was mainly used for training purposes received low priority, continuing slowly to the end of the war, thereafter the contract was closed with no more than fourteen machines completed.

These were the major wartime aircraft contracts and it will be seen that aircraft manufacture had replaced boat building as the main activity of S.E. Saunders Limited although, of course, production of a wide range of boats and engines continued without cessation until the end of the 1950s. A typical boat and engine of the post 1914-18 war period is illustrated.

Short Brothers were contracted by the Admiralty, in 1916, to build two rigid airships of Schütte-Lanz wooden construction and Saunders became sub-contractors for the engine cars. Eight of these were made for the two ships R.31 and 32 and they were constructed in boat style of Consuta, each to house one RollsRoyce Eagle engine. R.31 flew in August 1918 initially with six cars, later reduced to five as a result of the trials. She saw little service and was decommissioned in July 1919. R.32 was commisioned in September 1919 and was finally tested to destruction at Howden in April 1921 after extensive use.

The first Saunders designed aircraft, the T.1, a two-seater shipboard biplane with detachable wings, had been built in prototype form in 1917 but was not made in quantity. Very little information can be traced on this aircraft which was not built to an official specification; the sole aircraft of the type being built under licence No. 13 under Defence Regulations in operation in 1917-1918. The aircraft was presumably aimed at establishing the company in the design field and to foster the use of Consuta in the monocoque fuselage of this material. Some resemblance to the Short 184 produced by the company is evident in the engine installation from the contemporary artist's impression and the only known photograph available. The aircraft was flown by RFC pilots Major Evans and Lieut. Sayers at Somerton aerodrome, but information on these flights is limited to the fact that performance was satisfactory although the engine overheated indicating that the aircraft was under powered. The chief designer was H.H. Thomas, who died in the 1918 influenza epidemic, and his small team of three men, two office boys and a tracer, was disbanded. The T.1 was dismantled and stored in the Solent works where parts of it remained for many years.

The number of aircraft produced had steadily risen with the resulting need for flight testing by the company; this requirement being met in July 1917 by the allocation of 2nd Lieut. H.S. Stevens by the RFC, and he remained with the company until the end of the war.

The T.1 was tested at Somerton, the aerodrome established by J. Samuel White & Company Limited, the Cowes ship, boat and aircraft builder. Testing of the Avro 504 landplanes was carried out at a company flying field established adjacent to the original seaplane sheds, known as Osborne Yard, on the east bank of the Medina above Folly Inn. Although some of the Avros were trailed to Somerton, the majority were collected by Service pilots from this field, among whom was Lt. Leslie S. Ash, who later was employed on the design of Spartan and

Saunders-Roe aircraft and became a company test pilot of many years standing.

With the coming of the Armistice, work on the Felixstowe flying boats was run down. In wartime, under Admiralty influence, except for lifeboat construction, Saunders had been solely engaged on aircraft manufacture thus there was a drive to revive the boat-building activities to meet stronger competition from the number of new firms which had entered the field. It was felt that a market existed for plywood products and justified the building and equipping of a specialised unit for manufacturing these at Folly, the expenditure being approved in March 1919. Many years later the Folly Works were destroyed by fire on the 21st January 1960, when in use for plywood production by the subsidiary company established later. Like other aircraft companies, Saunders was optimistic that commercial aircraft designs would help fill the gap left by the cessation of military work. Their marine background led Saunders to undertake the design of an amphibian flying boat, named Kittiwake, with the object of competing in the Civil Aircraft Competition, sponsored by the government, to be held in August 1920. Responsibility for the overall design of the Kittiwake rested with F.P.H. Beadle, who, in partnership with E.W. Copland Perry, had designed the Perry-Beadle flying boat of 1914, for which the hull had been made by Saunders. Percy Beadle had spent the war years at the Norman Thompson Flight Company (successors to White & Thompson Limited from the 4th October 1915) on flying boat design and came to Saunders in November 1919 after a period with the Gosport Aviation Company, holders of the Porte patents, so he had considerable experience of marine aircraft. He had also been responsible in 1915 at White & Thompson for the design of a landplane for the RNAS, nicknamed the "Bognor Bloater". The main claim to fame of this obscure aircraft was its advanced monocoque fuselage diagonally planked with Consuta, a small number of which were built by boat-builders H. Williams of Littlehampton.

Beadle and his assistant, H.W. Gravenell, made a concentrated effort and, with Porter's contribution, were able to complete the bulk of the design of the Kittiwake in three months. However, this was still not enough to enable the machine to be ready for the competition as it was not launched until the 11th September 1920. The Kittiwake had been inspected by King George V and Queen Mary during a tour of the Cowes works prior to its launching and trials in the hands of Captain Norman Macmillan whose personal recollections of the first flight on the 19th September and his subsequent experiences are described in Chapter 8. Further flights, including one of three-quarters of an hour with three passengers, were carried out in 1921 by F. Warren Merriam who spoke encouragingly of the machine. Nevertheless many technical problems remained to be resolved among which were the difficulties with the unconventional ailerons, independent of the wings, which were ineffective at small angles and suffered from reversal effects resulting in loss of control and damage to the aircraft in a crash when flown by an Air Ministry pilot, a former pupil of Merriam's. As a consequence of this, the only Kittiwake to be built was scrapped in July 1921 after considerable expenditure on its development.

Leslie S. Ash. As a lieutenant in the R.F.C. collected Avro 504s from Cowes in the 1914-18 war. Became a technician and part-time pilot for Saunders and Spartan aircraft and later full-time test pilot for Saunders-Roe.

F.P. Hyde Beadle. Designer of the Perry-Beadle and of Saunders' first post-war design, the Kittiwake, *centre.* *On the left* Gravenall, his assistant, *and right* Capt. N. Macmillan test pilot for the Kittiwake in August 1920

The Bognor Bloater. Designed by F.P.H. Beadle after leaving Saunders and when working for White and Thompson.

The Bognor Bloater. Twelve were built with Consuta fuselages made by Williams of Littlehampton.

S.E. Saunders Inboard Marine Power Unit. Developing 5 hp. Available post 1914-18 war.

Saunders Launches. Moored in the River Medina in the 1920s.

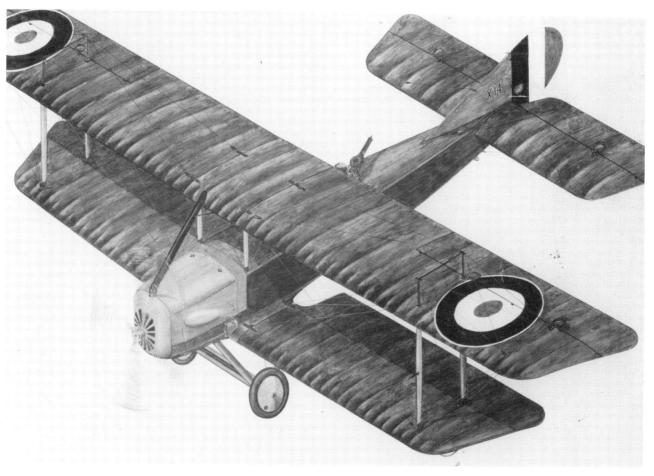

Saunders T.1. The artist's impression was the work of Alex W. Prickett,
then a junior member of the drawing office team.

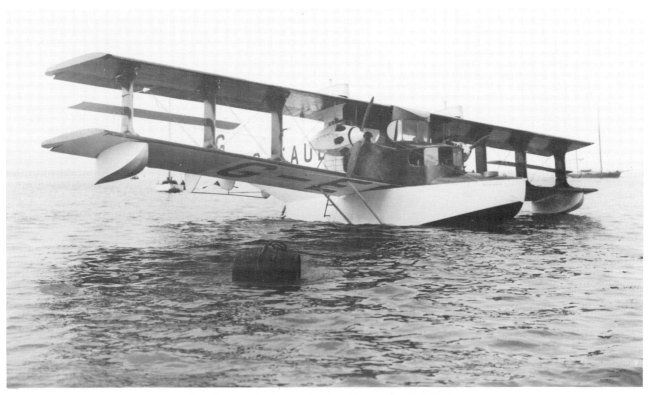

Saunders Kittiwake Amphibian. Moored in the Medina.

Vickers – Saunders Valentia BS.1. The third machine N.126 at the Isle of Grain.
The extensions of the ailcrons and elevators as fitted to the first aircraft have been removed.

As mentioned earlier the Wolseley subsidiary of the Vickers company had taken a small financial interest in the Saunders company in 1908. This was considerably increased in June 1914 at a board meeting held at Niagara Hall, York Street, Westminster, when the capital was increased from £5,000 to £12,000. In addition to Sam and his son Hubert, the board now comprised Mr. Edwin J. Smith, an accountant, who assisted Sam Saunders in financial matters and Mr. Arthur McCormack of the Wolseley company. Board meetings, which had previously been held only at the company offices at East Cowes, were later held at times at Adderley Park, Birmingham, the Wolseley head-quarters, as well as the Niagara Hall, their London office.

The financial holding in the company by Vickers had, by 1918, been increased until that company was now the majority shareholder with a controlling interest. The important change took place at a board meeting held on the 26th March 1918 at Vickers House, Broadway, Westminster, when a new agreement with Vickers, modifying the Wolseley agreement, was sealed. As a consequence, Sam Saunders vacated the chair and was replaced by Sir A. Trevor Dawson as Chairman. The board now comprised Sam Saunders, E.J. Smith and E. Hopwood, who had previously been a substitute for Hubert Saunders, A. McCormack, together with a new Vickers nominee Major Herbert Frederick Wood. Vickers directors Sir Vincent Caillard and Sir Francis Barker were named as substitute Chairmen. Sir Vincent himself later became a full-time director when Hopwood resigned in March 1920.

Wood, a retired officer, had been the leading light in establishing the Vickers Aviation Department and a strong military character with considerable ability but a reputation of being unpopular. He was soon pressing for the transfer of 'Joe' Porter, the Saunders boat hull designer, to the Vickers design office in London to take charge of flying boat hull design. Sam Saunders could not spare him entirely from Cowes and offered him in an advisory capacity, an arrangement that no doubt was the subject of controversy between the two men. Major Wood however died on the 11th September 1918 of meningitis and was followed by Capt. H.E.P.D. Acland who was elected to the board on the 7th March. The matter was not pursued, for Porter remained in the employment of S.E. Saunders Limited, although the board ruled that his services should be available to the Vickers design office as far as possible. No doubt the Consuta construction of the Viking stemmed from this arrangement and possibly the various flying boat and amphibian projects based on the Vimy which Vickers prepared in the early post-war period.

Three Valentia flying boats had been ordered from Vickers in May 1918 by the Air Board with the intention of utilising the capacity of the Vickers works at Barrow for their subsequent production. The design of the aircraft was carried out at Vickers' London office and was based initially on the Vimy. Construction of the wings and tail units was also carried out at Weybridge, but Saunders benefitted by an order to produce the hulls, for which Porter designed one of Consuta construction, and the wing-tip floats, examples of which were exhibited on the Vickers' stand at Olympia in 1920.

The Air Committee, a Vickers body under the chairmanship of Sir Trevor Dawson, met on the 17th October 1918 and proposed the transfer of the order for the three N.3 Flying Boats (Valentias) to Barrow. This caused concern when reported at the next board meeting on the 13th November, not helped by a report from Major Wood that the first hull, although partly constructed, was already out of date and work should be stopped. Problems of administration between Vickers and their various establishments as the contractor and government departments were resulting in Saunders receiving inadequate or incorrect instructions and it was necessary for the board to direct that a meeting should take place under the auspices of Sir James McKechnie, a Vickers director and General Manager of Barrow works, with experts from Barrow and others to resolve the problems. Some work on the prototypes was transferred to Barrow in November 1918.

Sam Saunders was concerned over the situation at Cowes and made a strong case for the manufacture of experimental hulls at Cowes in view of the experience there. It may have been the intention of the board to help the situation that they ruled that all future flying boats were to be known as Vickers-Saunders machines. The employees at Cowes were apprehensive about their future in the post-war period and disruption was being encouraged by union organisers. The war had brought considerable changes to industry and Sam Saunders was determined to be master in his own works and to this end resisted the introduction of union organisation of the workforce. The disruption that resulted from this was an added factor in delaying the prototype Valentia and continued throughout the period when the Valentias were being built, even into 1921 when the works were closed while non-union men were recruited, and they were only fully re-opened on the 14th April.

However, in the post-war reorganisation Vickers were returning the Barrow Yard to shipbuilding and subsequently the Valentia hulls were built in the Columbine works at Cowes. The contraction of the RAF in peacetime resulted in no production and eventually only three aircraft remained on contract and these were all built and flown at Cowes. The first Valentia N.124 flew from the Solent in 1921 in the hands of Vickers pilot Capt. Stan Cockerell and was accepted by the Air Ministry ex-works. When being flown to the Isle of Grain by the firm's pilot under cover of a delivery contract, on 13th March 1921, it was forced to alight and take refuge in Newhaven harbour. A letter from Newhaven Harbour Company to the Air Ministry on the 1st April reported that it was still there in a disabled condition and requested details of the passenger accommodation and volume for the assessment of a claim for harbour dues. The problems, both legal and technical, were presumably overcome, for a later report records the wrecking of the machine at the Isle of Grain on 15th June 1921, the propellers of N.124 being subsequently used on N.120, the Short Cromarty, the other contender to Admiralty Specification N.3, to improve that aircraft's rate of climb.

N.125 was also forced down on its delivery flight from Cowes to the Isle of Grain in the hands of Cockerell and Capt. Broome at midday on the 15th March 1922. The machine, reportedly tailheavy, struck the water heavily a mile and a half off Bexhill. The crew of three were taken

Vickers – Saunders Valentia BS.1. Engine nacelles and centre section being built onto a hull in the Solent Works Cowes.

Vickers – Saunders Valentia BS.1. On the hard standing at the Solent Works presumed to be N.124.

Schneider Trophy Contest at Bournemouth 1919. On the slipway of the Solent Works Cowes, S.E. Saunders with his hand on the shoulder of H.G. Hawker pilot of the Sopwith entry. Officials of the meeting in the group are from *left to right:* H.E. Perrin, Major Mayo, Alec Ogilvie and Frank McClean of the Royal Aero Club.

Schneider Trophy Contest at Bournemouth 1919. Sam Saunders with the French and Italian pilots at Cowes. *On left* in uniform Sgt. Janello, pilot of the Savoia S.13. *On right* Lt. Jean Casale and M. Sadi Lecointe.

Schneider Trophy Contestants 1919. Nieuport 29 pilot Lt. Jean Casale being launched at the Solent Works after major repairs were carried out by the Saunders workforce some now watching with interest the result of their efforts.

Schneider Trophy 1919. The Nieuport 29 undergoing extensive repairs including complete
re-erection in 48 hours in Solent Works at Cowes.

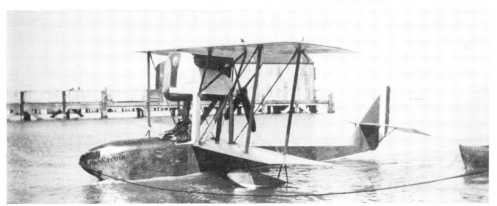

Schneider Trophy contestants 1919. Savoia. S.13 in which Jannello
completed the badly-defined course only to be disqualified.

Schneider Trophy Contestants 1919. SPAD-Herbemont after
reduction of the span of the top wing at Cowes under
instructions from the designer Herbemont. To be flown by
Sadi Lecointe the SPAD although flown to Bournemouth
was a non-starter.

Schneider Trophy Contestants 1919, Sopwith Schneider.
Harry Hawker leaving the slipway at Cowes. Due to fog he
completed only one lap in the contest.

Schneider Trophy 1919. Inside the Solent Works before the contest. Among the machines making use of the Saunders' facilities was the Italian Savoia S.13 in the foreground. In the left background is the Sopwith Schneider Racer to be flown by Harry Hawker and immediately behind the Savoia the dismantled Nieuport 29-C.1 of Frenchman Jean Casale undergoing major repairs.

Merriam-Newman Glider. Prior to the contest.

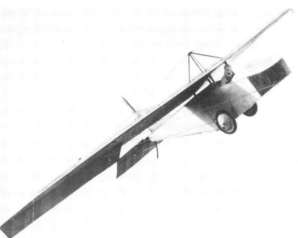

Constructors of the Merriam-Newman Glider adjusting the rudder of the Merriam-Newman glider before the 'Daily Mail' glider competition in 1922.
The glider was constructed as a spare-time operation in the Saunders Works by Newman. The Works Manager on the right and F. Warren Merriam the pilot, mainly responsible.

Merriam-Newman Glider. The mishap at the 'Daily Mail' Itford Hill meeting of October 1922. Capt. F.W. Merriam's monoplane tilting an an acute angle just before it came to the ground during an unsuccessful attempt to take off over the ridge of Firle Beacon. The nose of the machine was smashed, but the pilot unhurt.

off and the machine drifted unmanned on to the beach at Pevensey Bay, where the RAF collected the remnants.

The third machine N.126 was nearing completion in May 1922 when Vickers ordered further modifications to be embodied at Cowes. The changes included ailerons and elevators modified by the removal of the overhanging balance areas. This work was duly completed and the aircraft was delivered in February 1923 to the Isle of Grain where it served its useful life as a trials aircraft.

There was no great demand by the RAF for further aircraft of this type and so testing, which was to include trials with the 37mm Coventry Ordnance Work (COW) gun, and production was cancelled.

The determination and drive of Sam Saunders is exemplified by the incident when a French entrant for the 1919 Schneider Trophy Contest, the Nieuport 29.C1 flown by Jean Casale, arrived at dusk at Cowes after crossing the Channel to Brighton. To avoid the heavy waves of the Solent, the seaplane alighted in the estuary of the Medina but hit a buoy, severely damaging the floats and, with extensive damage throughout, the aircraft finished nose down in the water. The following morning a team directed by Sam Saunders raised the wrecked aircraft and took it into the works, where the Italian team and the Sopwith entry had also been provided with storage and servicing facilities. A new engine and floats were sent from France and by a superb effort of non-stop work the Nieuport was ready forty-eight hours later on the morning of the contest. The race was to start at Bournemouth but the floats were again damaged when alighting after its flight from Cowes. Ironically, it was all to no avail for the area was in fog and the contest was declared void after most competitors retired. The exception was Sgt. Janello flying the Savoia S.13 who was disqualified after completing the course, having mistakenly rounded a reserve marker boat at Studland instead of the correct one at Swanage.

So, despite Saunders's determination, the lack of demand and the setback of the unsatisfactory Kittiwake caused the aircraft design department to be closed at the end of 1920 and Beadle left the company. Vickers disposed of their interests in the following year but nevertheless made considerable use of Consuta in the construction of the forward fuselage of their bulbous nosed Vimy Commercial and Vernon aircraft. The Viking amphibian flying boat was a successful competitor in the Air Ministry competition, taking the first prize of £10,000, resulting in the manufacture at Cowes of a number of hulls of Consuta construction, which was some consolation for the failure of the Kittiwake.

In the post-war years there were few military orders. A contract to recondition ten F.5 flying boats and to manufacture spares for both the F.5 and the F.2A helped to sustain the aircraft department in the period from the middle of 1923 to March 1924.

Among the many automotive applications for Consuta was the streamlined body of a two litre DFP racing car made by Vickers for H.R.S. Birkin - later Sir Henry - the well-known racing driver, used at Brooklands in 1921. Six car bodies were made in 1922 for the FWL Propulsion & Traction Company which went into liquidation leaving Saunders with an unpaid debt.

The pioneer pilot and instructor, F. Warren Merriam, a farmer post-war on the Isle of Wight, who had participated in the testing of the Kittiwake at Sam Saunders' request, teamed up with Mr. G. Newman, Saunders' works manager, to build a glider in 1922. The Merriam-Newman glider, a 36 ft. span high wing monoplane, was built in the evenings in the Saunders' works and the tests at Merriam's farm were sufficiently encouraging to proceed with its entry, No. 18, in the Daily Mail Itford Hill Contest in October 1922. Inexperience with launching techniques caused the glider to crash at take-off. It was rebuilt and was last known to be in existence and ready for use in 1930 at Godshill on the Isle of Wight.

In the period of twelve years that the Saunders aircraft department has been operating, approximately 400 aircraft were built, the designs of almost all being those of other companies. (Appendix 2).

No doubt Saunders made a contribution to other aircraft produced during the war, although detailed records of the minor sub-contract work carried out are not available. It would appear from the serial numbers of parts of the surviving BAT Bantam, owned by the Shuttleworth Collection, that the cowling panels for the ABC Wasp engines of the twelve machines commenced in early 1918, but only partially completed in 1920, were Saunders products. One of the Bantams was flown to Cowes at Whitsun 1920 by BAT pilot Christopher Draper, possibly in connection with this work.

In March 1921 Sam Saunders bought the Vickers interest in the company and the Vickers directors resigned. He was now in charge again but at a time when trading was particularly difficult and the future would depend on the ability to attract orders from government and other sources. In August 1923 E.J. Smith resigned and Capt. D. Nicolson, an ex-Air Ministry official, took his place on the board to be based in London as the main company representative and negotiator of new contracts.

As with most other manufacturing concerns, the company had been profitable in wartime, but late demands for taxes on wartime production and the need for expenditure on new products, reversed the position in 1920 and it was not until 1924 that the company returned to profitability.

A Bentley with a 2 seater racing body. Built of Consuta for Sir H. Chiliott, of St. James's London in August 1922. The original columbine Yard and Medina Road in the background.

The Bentley from the rear.

Consuta body on D.F.P. racing car. Made by Vickers for H.R.S. Birkin. Seen here at the 1921 Easter Meeting with Woolf Barnato in a Locomobile behind.

CHAPTER 3

THE END OF AN ERA

In spite of earlier setbacks, Sam Saunders was determined to re-establish himself as an aircraft manufacturer and by 1923 he believed the time was right to re-commence operations. He engaged, as Chief Designer, Bernard Thomson, who had recently left H.G. Hawker Engineering Company after internal differences as a result of both the failure of the Duiker and the need to redesign the 2-bay version of the Woodcock. Thomson, with an assistant called Henry Knowler, began the design of the A.3 Valkyrie military flying boat to Specification R14/24, later amended to R22/24, for a general purpose patrol and reconnaissance flying boat with three engines and a crew of five. The hull was a type patented by Linton Hope (No. 127,067 of 22nd February 1918) which aimed at providing flexibility for shock absorption on rough water and was essentially a wooden monocoque of Consuta with multiple stringers and widely-spaced circular hoop-like frames, without transverse bulkheads. This hull, the weight of which was below the estimate, was severely criticised by the managing director at a board meeting on the 9th June 1925, when he described it as being weak and badly designed.

The prototype commenced flight trials in the hands of Frank Courtney in the spring and continued in the summer of 1926 and was delivered to Felixstowe initially on the 17th September. The Valkyrie was flying satisfactorily early in 1927 and was submitted to MAEE for testing in April. The General Report F/23 conveys the findings and criticisms made by the Felixstowe staff and is summarised in Chapter 10. A number of features were commented upon favourably but the fuel system and performance were criticised. However, sufficient modifications were made to permit the Valkyrie to be sent, on August 12th, on a 3,000 mile tour of the Baltic States in company with the Blackburn Iris, Short Singapore I and the Supermarine Southampton. Unfortunately the Valkyrie suffered engine troubles and consequent hull damage and was towed into Königsberg after a forced alighting, which delayed its return to Felixstowe and inevitably detracted from its prospects. Eventually improved versions of the other three types were ordered for the R.A.F., to the exclusion of the Valkyrie.

In 1923, while the design of the Valkyrie was proceeding the basic design of a three-seater fleet reconnaissance machine was prepared and an unsuccessful tender submitted. In the same period negotiations were in hand with the Chilean government for a twin-engined flying boat, which did not materialise.

Subsequent to the commencement of work on the A.3, work started on the design of the A.4 Medina ten-seater twin engined civil flying boat for the Air Council. Thomson was directed to give this aircraft priority but despite this the Medina was later than anticipated by the board, being reported nearing completion at the end of October 1926. Arrangements were made for Capt. F.J. Bailey to carry out the early flights and for Flight Lieut Sawyer to attend as an interested observer. Like the

Kittiwake, the Medina proved to be a disappointment for Saunders and resulted in Thomson departing from the company in July 1927. This left the way open for Henry Knowler to be promoted to Chief Designer and later to become a board member. He had previously worked on flying boat design at Vickers and English Electric and from this time until his retirement in 1956 he was to hold the major position of responsibility for technical direction within the company and was to become recognised internationally as a leading authority on the design and development of marine aircraft.

Other changes of personnel also took place at the end of 1924, when the services of 'Joe' Porter were dispensed with for reasons unknown and he went to Cowes boat-builders Groves and Guttridge where he remained until 1948. He had served Sam Saunders for many years, being one of the original syndicate who moved from the Thames. Later he was to work for Uffa Fox until 1964 when he died. To replace Porter at Cornubia Yard, Fred Cooper was appointed chief draughtsman, a position he held for a relatively short period for he resigned to work on his own as a free-lance designer. Further strength in hull design was brought to the company by the engagement of Capt. F. Shepherd, attached to the London office, and he was given the task of designing the Medina flying boat hull in June 1925.

The work on the flying boats was insufficient to occupy the large floor space available and Saunders again provided the accommodation in the Solent Works at Cowes for the competitors in the 1923 Schneider Contest. This time it was the Blackburn Pellet that required all night attention in an effort to overcome overheating and porpoising problems, but the undeveloped Pellet sank the following morning after stalling on the water at the mouth of the Medina when preparing to start the navigability trials. Pilot Kenworthy was saved and Saunders' works manager, Newman, and team recovered the Pellet at night but it was now beyond repair.

The period following the war was especially difficult and a number of firms were helped to keep going on rebuilding of surplus aircraft. The DH.9A was one of these types of which Saunders rebuilt eighteen; the amount of work varying with the condition of each aircraft but involving the manufacture of new components including wings. This work, however, was running down at the end of 1926 and with few contracts in prospect the working hours were reduced and the directors waived their fees and bonuses. The work situation in the aircraft industry was extremely serious and negotiations took place with Swan, Hunter Limited in regard to an arrangement to assist the deteriorating financial position. Sir John Hunter visited Cowes but declined to take any part. Further negotiations with Beardmores were broken off by Saunders because of reservations over their German connections with Rohrbach. Further support was obtained from finance houses who appointed Messrs G.G. Hans Hamilton and R.H.S. Abbott as directors in October 1926 with J.B. Close as an alternative to Abbott. Sam Saunders'

Saunders A.3 Valkyrie. Henry Knowler was largely responsible for the design of this the company's first major post-war military flying boat.

Saunders A.4 Medina. The second post-war commercial flying boat type and the last design by Capt. Bernard Thomson.

Schneider Trophy Contest 1923. The start and finish of the 1923 Contest was at Cowes and contestants used the Solent Works as their base. No.3 is the Curtiss CR-3 which finished second; No.7 the Supermarine Sea Lion III, third in the race and No.9 the C.A.M.S. 38 which retired after one lap.

D.H.9.A. Saunders rebuilt eighteen of these aircraft for the R.A.F. in the post-war years.

Parnall Peto. Floats of 'Consuta' were made for this small aircraft which was designed to be carried inside a submarine.

Westland Widgeon III Seaplane. Converted at East Cowes in 1929 with 'Consuta' floats. The 95 hp Cirrus engine gave insufficient power for a satisfactory performance and G-EBRL reverted back to a land undercarriage.

Felixstowe F.5 with Saunders Patented Hull. The shape of the planing bottom is well illustrated in this photograph taken at Felixstowe. The special beaching trolleys were also the subject of a Saunders Patent No. 229,409.

position was undoubtedly weakened at the time but at 70 years of age he was content to be elected chairman at the board meeting of the 5th November 1926.

A further change to strengthen the management took place with the engagement of G.H. Handasyde in March 1927 as aircraft superintendent. Handasyde had, with H.P. Martin, founded and built up the Martinsyde Company but left in 1920 during the post-war retraction. Subsequently he started Handasyde Limited, a small company, and built and experimented with gliders and light aircraft which found no market. Although reported to be something of a driving force, he made no progress at Saunders and in 1928 left to join the Desoutter Company at Croydon. Further personnel changes came with the resignation of Captain Shepherd of the London office in April 1927 and in December H.S. Abbott resigned. At the board meeting of the 11th January 1928 Lt. Col. W.A. Bishop, V.C., the well-known Canadian fighter pilot, was elected to the board in succession but he was to stay for only six months when, on the 25th July, both Bishop and Hamilton resigned.

The board decided on changes at the Cornubia Yard which they considered was slack and inefficient and in August 1928 dismissed the works manager. The yard had been building a 78 ft. long hydroplane, named Jack Stripes, for Miss Betty Carstairs for a planned record-breaking Atlantic crossing. This boat failed to match up to the requirements for such an attempt and was not accepted. As a consequence, on completion of the design work, F.P.H. Beadle, who was responsible, was discharged.

Minor contracts were obtained for the construction of seaplane floats for other companies, including alternative types made of Consuta for the Peto aircraft made in small numbers by Parnalls of Yate, and somewhat later for Westland's Widgeon III G-EBRL tested at Cowes in 1929. This work, although making a contribution to maintaining employment, was insufficient to keep the aircraft division occupied and, undeterred by the earlier failures, Sam Saunders recognised the need for change if he was to succeed in his ambition to build big flying boats.

A contract had been received in 1922 to convert a Felixstowe F.5 N.178 for investigation of the merits of a patent tunnel type wooden hull in comparison with an all-metal hull built by Short Bros. The aircraft was delivered to Felixstowe in September 1924 but its trials were short and it had been dismantled and scrapped by the middle of 1925. Inevitably the Short S.2 N.177 proved the durability of metal construction when tested at Felixstowe in 1925-26 and demonstrated that wooden materials, with their attendant watersoakage problem were no longer acceptable. The wooden A.3 Valkyrie, of course, had yet to reach Felixstowe for testing. So, despite the proprietory interest in sales of Consuta, Saunders' projects for military purposes would in future be basically of metal construction using duralumin and stainless steel fittings for the structure, entailing the need for large scale expenditure by the company for new metal-working plant and machinery.

The design was put in hand of a large biplane flying boat, to an Air Ministry specification for a general purpose requirement, which was designated the A.7. The hull was to be flat-sided with visible longitudinal corrugations stiffening the skin as an alternative to internal stringers. Weight was saved by this method of construction, inspired perhaps by the designs of Dornier and Rohrbach, which was initiated for ease of manufacture by the elimination of double-curvature skins and gave the added benefit of maximum internal hull space. The method, which was to be employed in the design of the company's flying boats in the future, had official backing. Supermarine was encouraged to convert a standard Southampton to utilise a Saunders-built hull, the A.14, and also built a similar hull for the experimental Southampton Mk.X.

There was an inevitably long period of gestation for the A.7 Severn which did not appear until early 1930. The aircraft was powered by three Bristol Jupiter IX 405 hp engines, had an all-up-weight of 22,000 lb, and a top speed of 130 mph. Subsequent testing at MAEE produced a number of criticisms, although confirmation that the water handling was good was given. The performance was down on specification requirements in most respects, particularly climb, operational height and cruising speed. There was general criticism of flimsiness of structure and fittings, such as wing ribs and walkways, and the ease with which damage to the external corrugations could be caused. The method of mounting the outboard engines across the wing joint, necessitating engine removal for a wing change, was particularly criticised. Nevertheless it was decided, after extensive repair and modification work had been carried out at Felixstowe, to take the Severn to the Middle East in 1931, in company with the Short Singapore II, for tropical trials. Both machines completed the trials and the flight from Felixstowe to Port Sudan and Lake Timsah and return, with Flight Lieut. P.H. Cahill piloting the A.7 and six crew members. The round flight of 8,324 miles from Felixstowe and back to Plymouth included the first non-stop flight from Gibraltar to Plymouth of 13 hours 40 minutes, the last two hours without one engine.

Although a number of problems arose, as was to be expected on such extended trials of a new type, these were overcome, albeit with considerable support, including the urgent supply of new parts from Cowes. Neither machine was considered acceptable for service without considerable expensive redesign and proposals made within the Air Ministry to fit Pegasus engines to improve the performance were not proceeded with.

Despite this performance by the single prototype, no production order was received for the Severn but much useful information was derived from the trials which was to be applied to later types, particularly the A.27 London.

After return from the Middle East, the Severn continued in use with MAEE and with No. 209 Flying Boat Squadron at Mount Batten, Plymouth. On 13th July 1932 she left Tarbet in Argyllshire for a flight to Northern Ireland when engine trouble developed and she came down in the sea off the Maidens group of rocks off the coast of Antrim. A Corporal and Aircraftman at work on the aircraft in a rubber dinghy were washed away and after drifting for five hours were washed ashore at Ballygalley in County Antrim. The Greek steamer 'Nicos' picked up the other six occupants, 3 officers and 3 airmen, from the wrecked Severn which afterwards sank.

Other projects were necessary for the design office and works and alongside the A.7, work had proceeded on the A.14, a duralumin hull for the Supermarine Southampton

Saunders A.7 Severn. The first Saunders flying boat with metal hull.

R.A.F. Flight to the Middle East 1931. The C.O., the crew and engineering personnel at
Felixstowe prior to the flight by the A.7 to the Middle East for tropical trials.

Saunders-Roe A.14 Hull. Constructed for experimental purposes and
fitted with Supermarine Southampton superstructure.

Saunders-Roe A. 10

Saunders-Roe A. 10 Fighter Aircraft.

N.251 which was rebuilt at Felixstowe. Fortunately a contract for a single-seater, single engined, fighter to specification F.20/27 was obtained which resulted in the A.10. Lt. Col. Bishop was invited to Cowes to inspect the mock-up but whether this transpired in his short period as a director is not recorded. The prototype was completed in 1928 and made its first flight at Somerton in January 1929 in the hands of H.S. Broad, well known as a test pilot for de Havilland. Manufacturer's trials continued until August when the aircraft was handed over to A & AEE at Martlesham for official trials in connection with both the interceptor and multi-gun roles (Specification F10/27). A number of significant flying and landing characteristics were criticised which resulted in the aircraft being returned to the company for action. Major modifications were put in hand and these included new tailplane and elevators, the lengthening of the fuselage by 1 ft 9 in. and repositioning of the undercarriage further aft. Although the aircraft was flying again by the middle of 1930, the Hawker Hornet, later renamed Fury, had by then been selected for the F.20/27 requirement by the RAF. Nevertheless, trials continued in competition with the Gloster SS.19 for the multi-gun role until late 1932. The sole Saunders-Roe A.10 being struck off charge finally in November 1933. The aerodrome at which testing of the A.10 was carried out was in the area of Northwood, but was known for a time as the West Wight aerodrome after Saunders acquired it in 1925 from J. Samuel White & Co., on a 5 year lease. Later it was referred to as Somerton, presumably named after the adjacent farm.

The contest for the Schneider Trophy was becoming something of an embarrassment to the Air Ministry after the American success of 1925 and Samuel Saunders and Col. W.A. Bristow, a well known consulting engineer, came forward with offers to produce contestants for the 1926 event. The Saunders machine, for which F.P.H. Beadle was engaged as designer in September 1925, was originally to be powered by a Rolls-Royce Condor VIII engine but an improved design using a higher powered Napier Lion was schemed but was not officially supported and did not proceed beyond the drawing board stage. The two proposals were both withdrawn at a Royal Aero Club meeting of 19th March 1926, both proposers being persuaded that their offers were futile in the light of the strength of the competition and the time available. Sam Saunders, a great patriot, was surprised by the attitude of some members of the committee and was most upset by the decision. The Bristow machine was to be revived for the 1927 contest as the Short Crusader.

Victor Isacco was an Italian who, after collaboration with de Pescara in Spain and France from 1919-25, designed and had manufactured in France between 1926 and 1929, to a French government contract, two versions of his Helicogyre machine with torqueless rotor drive. Interest in this was also displayed by the Air Ministry Directorate of Scientific Research who in 1928 placed an order with Saunders for the manufacture of one machine for testing at Farnborough as a result of the tender submitted early in the year.

The rotor was driven by four Bristol Cherub engines, driving four-bladed airscrews, mounted at the tips. The placing of the engines gave a gyroscopic effect which, in combination with hinged blades, was claimed to provide "stability of form", reducing the need for corrections by the pilot of attitudes of the machine caused by external forces, or perhaps, of its own shortcomings. A fifth engine was mounted conventionally in the fuselage nose for forward propulsion.

The controls were extremely complex and this was recognised by Isacco as a defect to be the subject of development.

The machine was delivered to Farnborough towards the end of 1929 but it is not known whether it was ever possible to persuade all five engines to run simultaneously or if the machine, which was overweight, left the ground. The centrifugal force adversely affected the lubrication of the horizontally opposed twin cylinder engines, the outer cylinders receiving an excessive supply of oil, neither could control of the fuel feed to the carburettors be achieved during the tests.

The Helicogyre No. 3 was scrapped in 1932 and Sr. Isacco departed for Russia where he was able to produce a further considerably larger example of his machine before being expelled in 1935 under the general edict for the expulsion of foreigners. Sr. Isacco went ahead with the design of Helicogyre No. 5 which was never built and he remains one of the names associated with helicopter development, whom success eluded. As late as 1947 he was experimenting with a telescopic rotary wing parachute device which was demonstrated on the back of a vehicle at Boreham Wood.

In 1928 Samuel Saunders was 71 years of age and for some time past had been taking a less active part in the day to day operation of the company. It so happened that another pioneer, A.V. Roe, at the age of 51 having sold out his interests in the Avro concern to J.D. Siddeley and now living near Hamble, was casting around for a firm in which to take a proprietorial interest. An arrangement was reached in November 1928 by which both A.V. Roe and John Lord, his colleague from Avros, became joint managing directors. They took over the reconstituted company on 12th December 1928, with S.E. Saunders, continuing as life president, no longer having an active role in any aspect of the company's operations, resigning as a director on 10th December 1928. The company name was changed to Saunders-Roe Limited at an Extraordinary General Meeting on 3rd July 1929 and confirmed at a further Extraordinary General Meeting on 18th July. The company's products were from then on identified by the new trade name of Saro. A.V. Roe received a knighthood in 1929 for his services to aviation and in future became known as Sir Alliott Verdon-Roe. Another ex-Avro employee, at one time assistant Chief Designer at the Hamble factory, Harry Broadsmith, also joined the company as a director and general manager. Capt. D. Nicolson, based in London, and Hubert S. Saunders (S.E. Saunders' son) retained their seats on the board, although Hubert Saunders resigned in May and became a director of Groves and Guttridge of Cowes who took over the lifeboat contracts. Since the hopes for the production of the A.7 Severn and the A.10 fighter were not fulfilled and the prospects for other orders arising from official sources were not good, the new management decided to embark on the production of small to medium sized amphibious flying boats, primarily for civil operations, as the main programme of work for the company.

Sir Alliott Verdon-Roe. Gave his name to the company in 1929 after acquiring a major share-holding. A director, managing director and chairman to 1937 when he became President, an honorary position he held when this photograph was taken in 1953. Sir Alliott died in 1958.

Isacco Helicogyre No.3. Completed in the Solent Works at Cowes.

CHAPTER 4

SAUNDERS-ROE FROM 1929 AND THE ACQUISITION OF SPARTAN

Sir Alliott's experience had convinced him of the importance of financial strength if major projects were to be successful and accordingly he concerned himself more with these aspects than with technical matters, although the success of the Avro 504 was still a matter of considerable pride to him and in his spare time he still designed various mechanical devices, including development prototypes of a motor scooter.

A major source of finance was the Canadian based Holt & Company who acquired a considerable holding resulting in Major Andrew Paton Holt becoming chairman from the 8th July 1929. The board was joined by Percy Waterman Pitt on the 16th August when the Aircraft Investment Corporation, a subsidiary of Whitehall Securities Limited of which Lord Cowdray was chairman and his son, the Hon. Clive Pearson, managing director, acquired 40,000 shares at £1 each. Holt resigned from his chairmanship in November and in the following June Sir Alliott was elected chairman in his place. Pitt remained on the board until the following January when he also resigned. It was inevitable that, with their considerable holding, the Aircraft Investment Corporation should seek greater representation on the board and consequently from the 6th February 1931 the board was reconstituted as follows:

Life President S.E. Saunders; Chairman and Joint Managing Director Sir Alliott Verdon-Roe; Joint Managing Director John Lord; General Manager H. Broadsmith; Directors Capt. D. Nicolson, A.E. Chambers, J. de C. Ballardie, Capt. H.H. Balfour, MC, the Member of Parliament for Thanet, a future Under-Secretary of State for Air from 1938 and an enthusiastic amateur pilot.

Sir Alliott resigned his joint managing directorship on 14th November 1934, a decision which was accepted by the Board at a meeting on 3rd December 1934 and thereafter John Lord was sole managing director.

The overall position of the company, which had not been profitable since 1925, was improved by the support of the Aircraft Investment Corporation. Its other interests, which included Blackburn, Spartan Aircraft from late 1929, and later General Aircraft, protagonists of the monospar principle, were of some considerable benefit since it resulted in arrangements for the provision of work for Saunders-Roe.

Sam Saunders was no longer active in the company but remained president until his death in December 1933 at the age of 76; Sir Alliott was to follow in this same position. John Lord, who was particularly active in improving the strength of the company, continued in his position as managing director until his death on the 25th January 1936. A great loss to the company, he was well-known through his positions in the SBAC and had many friends in the Isle of Wight.

Among the people subscribing to the company's finances was Leslie Irvin, the well known American parachute manufacturer, who was a resident in the country while establishing the English branch of his company, and who had a boat named 'Velda' built at Cornubia yard and

placed orders with the company for metal fittings for parachutes and for other uses.

With the object of raising more capital, it was proposed in June 1930 that the plywood factory be offered for sale to Hitchens Laminated Wood Products Limited for £40,000. This offer was not taken up and the option to purchase lapsed in June 1932. The plywood division was retained and several years later established as a successful subsidiary.

A review of the prospects of sales for flying boats resulted in a range of three types being considered and from early 1929 the design work proceeded apace. The initial emphasis was on the largest of the three types, which was to become the A.19 Cloud, but meanwhile a proposal was made that the smallest machine should be built for display at the next International Aero Exhibition. Since this was to be held in July and overtime was already being worked on the Cloud, a small team of three or four draughtsmen and technicians was given the task of scaling down the design, at home, out of office hours. By this means major drawings were available in four weeks and the machine was constructed in four months. This was the A.17 Cutty Sark, a cantilever cabin monoplane four-seater suitable for operation as a pure flying boat or amphibian. Power was provided by two Cirrus Hermes engines mounted on trestles above the centre section. The hull continued the flat-sided configuration and, after the prototype, incorporated the corrugations of the Severn and A.14 and was fabricated from Alclad - aluminium coated duralumin alloy for maximum corrosion resistance - but the wing was a wooden structure with plywood covering. The thick cantilever wing was designed to be buoyant in an emergency and was similar in principle to wings employed in Fokker aircraft and the Avro 5, 6 and 10 (Types 619, 624 and 618) which were based on Fokker designs, for which Avro had manufacturing rights and with which Harry Broadsmith was well acquainted. The A.19 Cloud and A.21 Windhover were larger aircraft based on similar construction. The prototype Cutty Sark flew as a pure flying boat in early July 1929 in the hands of Flying Officer Edward Chilton and was almost immediately dismantled to be displayed at the 7th International Aero Exhibition at Olympia held between the 16th and 27th July. The company's exhibition stand, still under the title S.E. Saunders Ltd., was of modest proportions compared to the adjacent Short and Bristol stands, was still larger than that of ABC Motors of Walton-on-Thames, who were showing the prototype of their ABC Robin single-seat high wing cabin monoplane, in front of which a placard advised that it was to be built by Saunders of Cowes, I.o.W. and Bush House, London. Perhaps it was ominous in that it was displayed on Stand 13 for it remained a prototype and no work for Saunders followed. However, the interest in the Cutty Sark was sufficient for the board to authorise the manufacture of three more.

The association with Blackburn resulted in an arrangement for the transfer of production in June 1929 of the Bluebird Mk.IV side-by-side two seater light

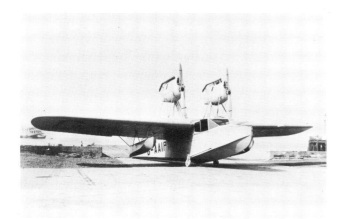

A.17 Cutty Sark. Prototype G-AAIP at Felixstowe in August 1929 for trials as a flying boat. The chassis is for beaching purposes only and the machine is fitted with Cirrus-Hermes engines.

Blackburn Bluebird Mk.4. The first Saro-built Bluebird on The Esplanade at East Cowes.

A.17 Cutty Sark.

M.V. Velda. Built at Cornubia Yard for Leslie Irvin the U.S.A. Parachute Manufacturer in the early 1930s.

A.B.C. Robin. This single seat sporting and utility aircraft appeared at the 1929 Aero Show at Olympia with a notice stating that it was to be made at Cowes by Saunders-Roe. There were no sales and the aircraft existed as a prototype only.

Saro A.19 Cloud. Launching the first machine from the Solent Works in July 1930. L.4 later G-ABCJ was originally fitted with Wright Whirlwind engines.

Saro A.19 Cloud. The prototype military Cloud K2681.

biplane to Saunders-Roe after three machines had been built at Brough. This was the all-metal version, the wings of which were sub-contracted to Boulton & Paul at Norwich; the remainder of the aircraft and components were produced at Maresfield Road Works, East Cowes, with assembly taking place in the Solent Works on the west bank of the Medina and flight testing at Somerton aerodrome. Under the overall direction of H.E. Broadsmith some redesign to facilitate production was made and subsequently fifty-five Bluebirds were built mostly at Cowes, output briefly reaching four per month. Although the contract was terminated before completion of the sixty-five aircraft originally envisaged, a number were completed at Brough when production ceased at Cowes in May 1931.

The Bluebird IV was used for a number of long distance attempts the most notable of which was that carried out by Mrs. Victor Bruce between September 1930 and February 1931. This was an eastbound flight round the world, except for the ocean crossings of the Pacific and Atlantic which were made aboard ship. The machine used was the 46th Saro-built Bluebird with Gipsy II engine, registered G-ABDS.

Receiving less publicity but nevertheless a noteworthy flight was that to Australia of Lieut. Cmdr. G.A. Hall in the 33rd Saunders-Roe built Bluebird. The machine, G-AAVG, was re-engined with a Hermes II for the flight which started from Croydon on the 8th August 1932 and reached Wyndham, Western Australia, twenty-four days later and included three days' delay searching in Burma for two missing aviators.

A Blackburn built seaplane version for Norway, registered N-40, was assembled and tested at the Solent works at the end of 1929.

Following the Cutty Sark, two larger amphibians on similar lines were completed. These were the much larger A.19 Cloud, powered initially with two Wright Whirlwind radial engines, and the intermediate sized A.21 Windhover with three DH Gipsy in-line engines. The Cloud and the Windhover went through extensive development trials in which an additional aerofoil, to improve lift and trim and reduce landing speed, was fitted across the engine nacelles. This was fitted to the second Cloud and both Windhovers, effectively making a biplane with a short span upper wing. Improvement of the elevator control was the subject of extensive test flying and wind tunnel tests with variations of nacelle fairings and narrow chord aerofoils fitted just above the wing centre section to certain of the early aircraft.

Capt. Scott flew the prototype Cloud, L.4 (G-ABCJ), from the water at the mouth of the Medina for four brief flights, totalling 32 minutes, in the early evening of the 15th July 1930. Flying continued on successive days and on the 19th the first airfield landing and take-off were made. Thereafter testing and development continued until February 1931, mainly with Scott piloting with R.V. Perfect as flight observer and Fred Pharoah flight mechanic. On the 21st February, Flight Lieut A.M. Blake, chief test pilot at Blackburn, was called upon to fly trials at overload conditions and his report confirmed "that with 900 lb overload, i.e. an AUW of 9,500 lb, the machine is equal to C of A requirements".

There was still much more development work to be done on alternative engine installations and general improvements. The second Cloud, G-ABHG, was flown initially as a three engined machine with Armstrong-Siddeley Lynx radials on the 18th February 1931 by Scott, with Leslie Ash as flight observer. Four flights were made in a period of 1 hours and a few days later Broadsmith and Knowler with Capt. Balfour separately sampled the machine as passengers. Flying in this basic configuration continued until the end of March, during which elevator and rudder control problems were experienced, Scott describing the aircraft as "crude and difficult to handle". The problems were thought to stem from the disturbed airflow from the engine installation and various flights were made with different combinations of Townend rings until, finally, the centre engine and ballast were removed and further wind tunnel tests were carried out. However, after a further series of four flights on the 6th May with new cowlings, nacelle fairings and wing floats, tail flutter and inadequate elevator control were again experienced. It was then decided to abandon the three-engined arrangement and the aircraft was converted to a twin-engined configuration with Pratt & Whitney Wasps.

Scott and Ash recommenced testing on the 2nd July, the first flight being without Townend rings, but these were immediately fitted with the bottom portions cut away, together with improved metal propellers, for the second flight. By the 11th the aircraft had been fitted with an aerofoil and three-bladed Hamilton propellers. Twin fins and rudders had been fitted above the tailplane with a trimming rudder fitted centrally below. Large and small versions of the trimming rudders and an adjustable centre fin were tried at various times. F.A. Kerry had now taken over as flight observer and S.G. Ford mainly carried out the flight mechanic's duties, although Pharoah and others appear at times in the flight reports. Townend rings of 16ins. and 20ins. chord were tried at various times and the original aerofoil was increased from 120 sq. ft. to 213 sq. ft. with incidence increased progressively from 3° to 7°05'. The engine thrust line was increased from 3° to 5° to the aircraft centre line. Small Townend rings of steel were eventually selected and spinners were fitted to the three-bladed Hamilton propellers. Flight testing continued until February 1932, clearing the aircraft for a loaded weight of 9,500 lb, increased to 10,000 lb after further testing in November 1932.

Despite this effort, few orders were received and two Windhover aircraft and four Clouds were all that found civilian employment. One Windhover was prepared with undercarriage removed for an attempt on a world flight endurance record by Mrs. Victor Bruce using flight refuelling.

The Cloud was eventually more successful, for in addition to the small number of civil orders, in 1930, the RAF became interested and the Air Ministry ordered the third production aircraft as a military prototype and this made an appearance as No. 12 in the New Type Park at Hendon in 1931 proceeding later to MAEE for preliminary assessment. The RAF under Spec. 15/32 later acquired sixteen with Armstrong Siddeley Serval engines for training of flying boat pilots and navigators at Calshot and Andover and for 48 Squadron at Bircham Newton. Not-withstanding the issue of a clearance on the civil Cloud in July 1931, albeit in a different configuration, Felixstowe experienced many problems and were critical of many features of the military version, involving several

Saro A.21 Windhover. The first machine in its original form as a flying boat, taken at Cowes.

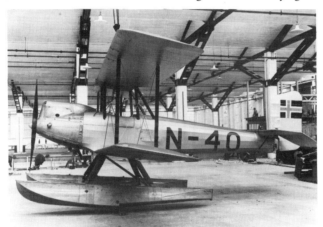

Blackburn Bluebird Seaplane. Trials of this Blackburn-built seaplane for Norway were carried out from the Solent Works at Cowes.

Moored in the Medina. Cutty Sark, Windhover and Cloud at anchor off the Solent Works in 1930.

returns to the works. The trials carried out with K2681, supplemented with K2894 in 1933, extended from April 1932 to March 1934 before the type was fully released for service. A substantial number of changes to strengthen the hull and to improve hydrodynamic and aerodynamic features were considered necessary and were embodied in subsequent production aircraft. The production programme was not helped by the placing of the contract in three separate stages, causing long breaks in continuity between the batches of aircraft.

Meanwhile the Cutty Sark was being made in small numbers but a total of twelve only were to leave the Cowes works. The three amphibian types met with limited commercial success despite the awareness of the board of the need to present the aircraft to potential customers, for which purpose both the Cutty Sarks G-AAIP and G-ABBC and Cloud G-ACGO were used on demonstration tours, the former to Yugoslavia in April/May 1931 and to the Stockholm Exhibition in March/April 1931 and the latter in July/August 1933 to the Baltic and other European countries. Tours were also made to Scotland and Ireland. The tour to Yugoslavia was described, presumably by Capt. Scott, in the 'Aeroplane' of 1st July 1931.

To attend the International Aircraft Exhibition held in Stockholm the Cutty Sark, G-ABBC, left Cowes on the 21st May with Capt. S.D. Scott, pilot; J. Lord, managing director; and S.G. Ford, flight engineer; making a stop at Lympne to clear Customs and then continuing to Amsterdam. On 28th May the machine left Amsterdam for Malmo making stops at Bremen, Hamburg and Copenhagen and on 29th May reached Stockholm after making a stop at Kalmar. During the week at the International Aircraft Exhibition a number of demonstration flights were given.

On 4th June the Cutty Sark left Stockholm for Kalmar, staying for the night and leaving the following day. After flying for about five minutes the pilot had to land and beach the aircraft due to engine trouble which, after investigations, proved to be a broken piston. The pilot and managing director returned to Cowes the following day by alternative means, the flight engineer remaining with the aircraft which was towed to Kalmar where a slipway was available to get it ashore. In due course the spare parts arrived and the replacement of the piston carried out and after a successful engine run, Cowes were informed that the aircraft was ready for flight. On 18th June, Capt. L. Cole, also a test pilot for SaundersRoe, arrived and flew the aircraft to Copenhagen. On 19th June they flew to Amsterdam, stopping at Hamburg and Bremen and on the 20th home to Cowes, stopping at Ostend and Lympne to clear Customs.

Extended sales tours were to become commonplace in later years but were extremely enterprising at the time and deserved greater success for few European sales resulted from these tours.

From 1930 the Japanese were attacking the Chinese mainland but negotiations for sales of the Cutty Sark resulted in orders from both nations. By September 1931 the agents representing the Kwangsi Air Force were sufficiently convincing for work to proceed on two special machines for military use, with the inverted Gipsy III engines. This contract was never fulfilled although the first machine was shipped and remained in store at Hong Kong, before being brought back after two years when it was refurbished and sold. At the same time as Chinese representatives were in the works, the Japanese pilot Yoshihara was present to accept the sole single-engined Cutty Sark specially built for long distance record flights. The hostility between the two sides was a source of concern to the genial John Lord who was able eventually to persuade them to shake hands. The Japanese machine was shipped to America and flown across the continent but crashed in Alaska and Yoshihara was badly injured.

In the year following the Stockholm exhibition, commencing on the 16th July, Cloud G-ACGO departed for a tour of the Baltic with Capt. S.D. Scott piloting and Mr. S.G. Ford as engineer. These two had just returned from Spain following the recovery of the Windhover from Gibraltar. (See Chapter 11). Saunders-Roe directors J. Lord and H. Broadsmith and Wallace Barr, managing director of Cellons were passengers. The flight was via Lympne to clear Customs to Amsterdam, on to Rotterdam for an overnight stop and then on the 18th to Copenhagen where demonstrations were carried out. On the 20th the Cloud left for Oslo where further demonstrations took place on the 21st and 22nd when they left for Stockholm. The 23rd to 25th were taken up with demonstrations and discussions including a flight to Cisby on the Isle of Gotland on the 23rd. The tour proceeded in this manner, flying on to Helsingfors (Helsinki) in Finland on the 26th, on the 28th to Tallin, Estonia, on to Riga, Latvia on the 29th and Kaunus, Lithuania on the 31st. After demonstrations on the 1st August they flew to Warsaw, staying there until the 4th when they flew to Breslau, passing on to Prague on the 5th giving demonstrations there till the 8th, which resulted in the only sale abroad of the Cloud, the actual machine on tour being later purchased by Bata. On the 8th they continued via Regensburg to Nuremburg then on the 9th via Cologne to Brussels. On the 10th demonstrations were given before returning to Cowes by way of Lympne to conclude a trouble-free tour.

In March 1928 Oliver E. Simmonds, a draughtsman with Supermarine, left to form his own company. His first design was a two and later three seater biplane of conventional style, but with interchangeable wing panels and tail surfaces for serviceability and economy of production. The first aircraft, G-EBYU, named Simmonds Spartan, was constructed in Simmonds' house at 65 Portsmouth Road, Woolston, and that of a fellow designer, George W. Garrett, who lived nearby and who joined in the Simmonds enterprise and later served in senior positions with Saunders-Roe. It was erected in premises known as the Rolling Mills, Archery Road, Weston. The test flight in July was made by Flt. Lieut. S.N. Webster of Schneider Trophy fame, at Butlocks Heath, Netley and resulted in minor damage which did not prevent entry in that month's King's Cup Race in which it was an unspectacular finisher. Simmonds was joined by Col. Louis A. Strange, MC, DSO, DFC, a well known pioneer and RFC pilot, forming Simmonds Aircraft Limited, with capital of £20,000. Production at approximately two aircraft per month proceeded at the Rolling Mill and erection and test flying by Strange and others was carried out from rented premises at Hamble under the supervision of W.D.L. Roberts. By late 1929 financial difficulties arose which resulted in reconsition

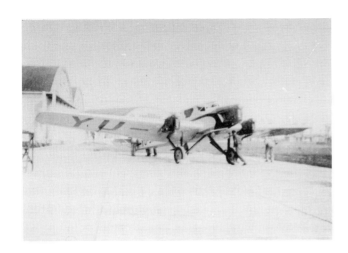

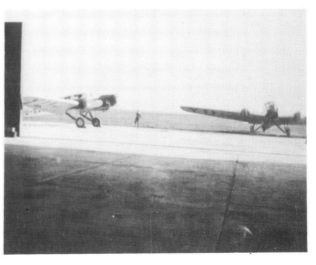

Yugolsav Spartan Cruiser Manufacture. The Yugoslav airline Aeroput purchased two Cruiser
Mk.II aircraft YU-SAN and YU-SAO in 1933-4 together with a manufacturing licence. Only
one machine YU-SAP was built by the Zmaj Company at Zemun near Belgrade and was
completed in six months, flying in December 1934. G.W. Garrett from Cowes, who supervised
the construction, carried out the first test flight and attended the religious ceremony (wearing
trilby hat) held later at the introduction of the machine into service.

Spartan Cruiser Mk.II. Assembling the first Cruiser Mk.II in the prototype shop at East Cowes.

Sir Henry at the controls of Miss England II.

Sir Henry O'Neal De Hane Segrave. Famous racing motorist and holder of the world land and water speed records. He was engaged as Aviation Adviser to the Aircraft Investment Corporation until his death in June 1930.

Spartan Aircraft Most of the Spartan types can be seen in this line of aircraft at Somerton. From the right they consist of two three-seater Mk IIs, a three-seater Mk.I, an Arrow, The Cruiser Mk I and the Mailplane when fitted with twin fins and rudders.

of the company as Spartan Aircraft Limited, refinanced by the Aircraft Investment Corporation, with Capt. H.H. Balfour, MC, a friend of Col. Strange on the board.

At this time, 1930, work was short at Saunders-Roe and it was possible to clear and then refurbish the old buildings, Columbine Works and Esplanade buildings, to make way for Spartan to operate as a separate unit. A further reconstitution of the company took place on 20th February 1931 when Spartan Aircraft Limited was removed to Cowes and O.E. Simmonds left the company to pursue his own developments and to become an MP. The new board comprised A.E. Chambers, MICE, Capt. H.H. Balfour, J. de C. Ballardie, W.D.L. Roberts, MICE, Col. L.A. Strange and Sir Alliott Verdon-Roe, later to be joined by John Lord, who became managing director, and Harry Broadsmith, technical director, who supervised design. Approximately fifty aircraft had been completed in two years when the change took place and now the premises at Hamble were given up and erection and test flying were transferred to a hangar at Somerton airfield, where variants of the biplane to a final total of 90 machines, known as the Arrow and the Three Seater Mk.I and II, were produced until 1935. The Spartan design team was absorbed into the Saunders-Roe office by January 1933 and the two companies had effectively merged.

Two Cambridge University Air Squadron pilots showed their confidence in the Spartan Arrow when they flew to Australia in the sixth Cowes-built machine G-ABHD. G.P. Fairbairn and K. Shenstone left England on the 19th December 1931 for a leisurely trip with no record-breaking intentions, reaching Darwin safely on the 19th April 1932.

At the time of the acquisition of Spartan Aircraft by the Aircraft Investment Corporation, Saunders-Roe was developing a three engined monoplane, as a high speed mailplane, to the design of E.W. Percival, later to establish his own company to produce a number of successful light aircraft. The design was taken over by the Saro design team as the A.24 and the sole aircraft, which was constructed at Cowes, was flying in 1931. Conceived as a high speed mailplane to carry 1,000 lb over distances of 1,000 miles, the Mailplane, finally designated a Spartan aircraft, found no market but formed the basis for a passenger version - the Cruiser. The Mailplane made a notable flight to India in June 1932 in the hands of Capt. Neville Stack, from Blackpool to Karachi in 5 days 23 hours 50 minutes with F.G. Taylor as flight engineer and William Courtenay, a well-known journalist and public relations man, as passenger, who described the flight in a light-hearted article which appeared in the magazine "Popular Flying" of March 1935. The later passenger-carrying version known as the A24M Spartan Cruiser was produced in Mk.I, II and III versions of which a total of sixteen were built at Cowes.

The method of entry to the cabin over the wing was soon seen to be impractical for normal passenger use and only a single Mk.I was built being replaced by the Mk.II with fixed cabin roof and side entry door. Twelve of this type were built and they played an important part in the development of air services in the British Isles and also served in parts of Europe and the Middle East. The Mk.III was an extended version of which only three were built. Two of the Mk.II Cruisers had been bought by

Aeroput of Yugoslavia who also acquired a manufacturing licence and a single Mk.II was built by Fabrika Zmaj of Zemun under this agreement. The construction of this machine in six months in the second half of 1934 was something of an achievement, for it included the time for tooling and was a great credit to the Yugoslav personnel and to G.W. Garrett, the technician from the parent company who supervised the construction throughout.

The board of Whitehall Securities formed a separate company, Spartan Airlines, on 2nd February 1933 to run internal airlines from Cowes to Heston or Croydon via Bembridge using the Cruiser as their standard type. This company was merged with United Airways on lst October 1935 as part of the re-organisation of companies controlled by Whitehall Securities and together with other subsidiaries the Group continued to operate internal airlines but not as Spartan Airlines from that date. Subsequently the various companies were amalgamated into Allied British Airways, shortened to British Airways, itself absorbed into British Overseas Airways Corporation (BOAC) under government control from September 1939.

Sales of the Cruiser were actively promoted by demonstrations and overseas tours, which began when Col. Strange took the first aircraft on a European tour to Greece and Yugoslavia, from which some sales did result. The use of Cruisers by Airwork in Egypt and Iraq, and delivery of aircraft to Yugoslavia, Czechoslovakia and India, further demonstrated the capability of the Cruiser over long distances, but the charter flight to Australia, flown by Spartan Air Lines chief pilot, Capt. Lynch-Blosse, at the end of 1933, was the most convincing proof of reliability of the aircraft.

Sir Alliott had faith in the commercial future for flying boats, and pressed the need for the construction of facilities for the manufacture and operation of machines suitable for long distance flights. These plans envisaged big aircraft and as a result the need to provide new assembly and machine shops at Cowes became apparent and this work was commenced in 1930. During the reconstruction, involving demolition of the old Columbine and other buildings, existing commitments necesitated the greater utilisation of the premises at West Cowes and on the aerodrome at Somerton where, from February 1935, the last few Spartan aircraft were being built. At East Cowes the new Columbine assembly building of 50,000 sq. ft., in use from 1935 and purpose-built by Boulton & Paul Limited for the building of large flying boats, provided access through doors measuring 40 ft. high by 150 ft. wide to hardstanding and a new slipway. Still retained alongside was a bay of the old Esplanade building on stilts above ground owned by the town, being part of the public open space presented by Sam Saunders in January 1929. Half a mile up the River, the Saunders shipyard, Cornubia Works, continued to produce a variety of power boats, among which was the Miss England II, powered by two Rolls-Royce 'R' type engines, as used in the Supermarine S.6 Schneider Trophy seaplanes, and built to the designs of Fred Cooper, by now a freelance boat designer. Sir Henry Segrave was to set a new World Water Speed Record at 98.76 mph on Friday, 13th June 1930, on Lake Windermere. The next day, on another high speed run, Miss England II hit a log and both Sir Henry and his mechanic lost their lives. After reconditioning at the Rolls-Royce works the boat, in the hands of Kaye Don, first took the record to 103.49 mph on 2nd April 1931 and then to 110.223 mph on the 9th July. The Saunders-Roe boat did not hold the record much longer for after overturning in September 1931, a new Miss England III with Rolls-Royce engines was built by Thornycroft and this raised the record progressively to 119.8 mph. Sir Henry Segrave had been engaged as an aviation adviser to the Aircraft Investment Corporation and had been involved with the design and development

of a high speed four seat twin engined monoplane landplane of wooden construction. This was the A.22 Segrave Meteor which made its first flight at Somerton Aerodrome on 28th May in the month before his death at Windermere. The later versions of this aircraft, produced by Blackburn were of metal construction, and known as the Segrave Mks.I and II but, although a very advanced design at the time, the type found no great market and only three were built.

Miss England II. Taking the World's water speed record.

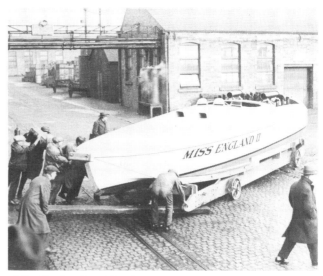

Miss England II. After being reconditioned at Rolls-Royce Derby, 13th January 1931 prior to further attempts on the World's water speed record by Kaye Don.

Miss England II. Capsized on Lake Windermere on Friday the 13th June 1930, the accident in which Sir Henry Segrave lost his life.

Saro A.22 Segrave Meteor. Preparing for engine run at Somerton.

CHAPTER 5

FLUCTUATING CONDITIONS IN PEACE AND WAR

The Air Ministry circulated in 1931 a requirement for a general purpose open-sea patrol flying boat to Specification R24/31. Incorporating the experience from the A.7, the design by which Henry Knowler prepared to meet this was a twin engined biplane with a crew of five, the A.27, later named the London. A contract for one prototype aircraft was received by the company in 1932 and the competitor firm Supermarine was also favoured with a prototype contract for a similar machine which became the Stranraer. Flight trials of the prototype K3560 commenced in March 1934 in the hands of Capt. S.D. Scott and these showed sufficient promise for an initial production contract for seven Mk.I aircraft to be placed in March 1935 with deliveries commencing in April 1936. The company received successive contracts, to a total of thirty-one aircraft, which endorsed the qualities of this rugged flying boat. The quantity of Londons produced was the largest of any Saunders-Roe flying boat and deliveries extended over a period of two years, with the last machine being delivered in April 1938. Ten of the original Mk.I version of this aircraft entered service in 1936. All were later converted to Mk.II standard by the introduction of uprated Pegasus engines and other minor modifications. The RAF received a total of thirty-one Mk.II Londons which served with 201, 202, 204 and 240 Squadrons, at home and abroad, until 1941, with some machines continuing in use for training purposes until the middle of 1942, some of the survivors being returned to Cowes for dismantling. Their reputation for reliability was established by an outstanding flight of 25,000 miles to Australia and back, between December 1937 and May 1938, by five specially equipped aircraft of 204 Squadron, of which further particulars appear later. Their operations in wartime were valuable, if not remarkable, and include at least one enemy aircraft, a Heinkel III, damaged believed destroyed on 19th December 1939. The London was certainly the company's most successful type of flying boat.

There were echos of the 1919 overnight effort to repair the French Schneider Cup entrant when in early November 1935 the RAF called on the help of Saunders-Roe. The Short Sarafand six-engined machine, the largest flying boat in existence at the time, was operating from Calshot with twelve crew aboard and made a heavy landing on a Monday afternoon off the entrance to the Medina. A large hole in the port side of the hull forced the pilot to beach the aircraft by the Esplanade at East Cowes at a point fortunately free of rocks thus avoiding further damage. Help could not have been nearer, in the form of a team from Saunders-Roe under works manager G.F. Anderson, who worked throughout the night to carry out temporary repairs which enabled the Sarafand to taxi back to base across the Solent at 5 am on Tuesday morning.

With the development of the London well in hand, consideration was being given to further reconnaissance flying boats with enhanced performance. Among the projects was a tail-less flying boat to Specification R1/33,

prepared in collaboration with Westland and proposed by G.T.R. Hill, which would have become the Pterodactyl Mk.VIII. It was inevitable, with the lack of success achieved with the land-based Pterodactyl types, that no firm commitment was forthcoming from government sources for the sea-going version. However, the Air Ministry did order a slightly more conventional prototype to Spec. R2/33 which was constructed as the Saro A.33. This was a large four engined monoplane incorporating a number of new design features. The balance of the aircraft on water was maintained by sponsons to which the wings were braced with no direct attachment of the wing to the hull. The wing was of monospar type based on the principles of H.J. Stieger, who pioneered this type of construction and now was chief engineer of General Aircraft Limited, at Feltham. In order to prove some of the features to be embodied in the A.33, the prototype RAF Cloud was fitted with monospar wing and sponsons and then became known as the A.29 Monospar Cloud. After initial tests at Cowes the aircraft was despatched to Felixstowe for official trials. The single prototype of the A.33, K4773, was under construction from 1936 and flew initially on the 14th October 1938.

With the responsibility for test flying the last of the Londons and this new A.33 and its successors falling on Leslie Ash, S.D. Scott had reached the end of his test flying career when he made a heavy landing after a routine test flight of a production London in 1938 which resulted in severe damage to the hull. To provide additional support, the veteran free-lance pilot Frank T. Courtney was engaged to share some of the flying, until the outbreak of war, and he took the A.33 on its first flight. He had flown the A.3 Valkyrie many years before for S.E. Saunders, but returned at a particularly difficult period when major problems with flying new types were experienced. Geoffrey Verdon-Roe, Sir Alliott's youngest son, also assisted with the test flying of the later Lerwick and continued flying throughout the war period.

After a few flights of the A.33 during which control was nearly lost due to severe porpoising, the monospar wing failed on the fifth flight during take off. The aircraft bounced three times, finally to 50 feet, without reaching flying speed, and was severely damaged.

Frank Courtney, the pilot at the time of the incident, reported on the circumstances as follows:

"..... but in the prototype tests of a large four-engined British experimental flying boat, the Saunders-Roe R.2/33, my luck ran out after several flights ...... The hydrodynamic experts had asked me to allow the porpoising to develop "a little" for study purposes. Unfortunately, true to its unpredictable nature, it developed much more suddenly and viciously than anyone thought possible. At the termination of the high-speed end of an attempted take-off run, with a warning so slight that I had no time to do anything about it, the plane left the water in a prodigious porpoising leap from which it crashed down completely stalled and out of control.

Saro A.27 London K.3560 The prototype Mk.1 on an early test flight.

Royal Air Force Londons in formation.

Short Sarafand. Saved by a working party from Saunders-Roe when damaged in the Solent in November 1935.

Saro A.27 London. Final assembly of Londons in the Columbine Works.

Pterodactyl XVIII Flying Boat. A model of a collaborative design by G.T.R. Hill of Westlands and Henry Knowler.

Saro A.33. Being towed in after a successful test flight F.T. Courtney standing at the pilots station.

Production in the Columbine Works. A variety of types on final assembly. Production of Londons is drawing to an end. The hull of the sole A.33 is on the left and on the right the first Lerwick.

Saro A.33. The result of the failure of the Monospar wing can clearly be seen. The test crew were not injured.

Saro A29 Monospar Cloud. K2681 in its final configuration with Monospar wing and sponsons and with wing-tip floats removed. In this form it enabled trials to be carried out of certain features used later in the larger A.33.

Saro A.33. The A.33 moored at the mouth of the Medina.

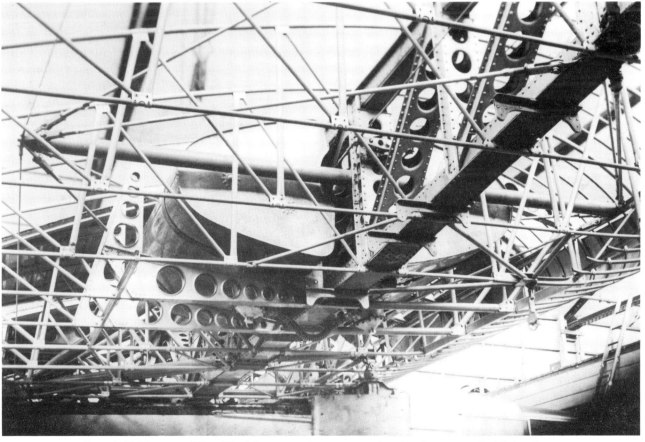

Saro A.29 Monospar Wing. The Monospar wing structure showing the system of cable bracing.

Nobody was much hurt, but the plane was wrecked beyond repair."

The A.33 was towed back to Cowes with the starboard wing failed in torsion and bending and with damage to the hull and sponson, both severely sliced by the starboard inboard airscrew. The damage was extensive and the craft was not rebuilt. Proposals for a later version to Spec. 21/36 were dropped, no doubt as a result of Short's success with their comparable aircraft, the Sunderland, which had been flying since October 1937.

The manufacture of boats mainly for civilian use continued to be an important part of the business but was overshadowed by the aviation activities on defence contracts in the years just prior to the outbreak of war. However, in 1937 a contender for the world speed record, named 'Bluebird', was constructed for Sir Malcolm Campbell. This used a single Schneider Trophy type RollsRoyce 'R' engine in a mahogany skinned hull and was constructed at the Cornubia yard. On 1st September 1937 on Lake Maggiore Bluebird set up a new water speed record of 126.33 mph and raised it again the next day to 129.5 mph. The following year on Lake Hallwyl the record was raised to 130.94 mph on the 17th September. Bluebird was to be the last high-speed aero-engined conventional planing boat made by the company at Cowes.

Fortunately for the company, while the design of the A.33 was proceeding, a Ministry contract was received in 1936 for ten long range general purpose flying boats to specification R.1/36. This machine, which was to be called the Lerwick, was a deep hulled monoplane powered by two Bristol Hercules engines, with an all-up-weight of 28,400 lb, and a maximum speed of 235 mph. An interesting feature was the requirement to jettison 90% of all fuel in one minute. Unfortunately, the tank vents were too small and on the first test of the system the fuel tanks imploded!

To assist production of the Lerwick, a building on Southampton Airport, Eastleigh, was acquired in 1937 for component manufacture, taking advantage of the pool of labour available in the area and replacing Adamant Engineering Limited of Luton which had been previously supported for this work.

Later, in 1939, to further help production of the Lerwick, a large hangar, known as the Medina Shop, was constructed on the southern side of Columbine hangar. The Lerwick programme was influenced by the impending war and the total order to equip two squadrons, placed in April 1938, envisaged development problems being resolved with the first three aircraft before entry into service.

The first Lerwick was launched and trials commenced one week after the A.33 at the end of October 1938. Initial trials revealed severe porpoising problems and therefore with no test tank available the full-scale craft had to be the experimental vehicle. The main step was moved either backwards or forwards, the hull made shallow, or a deep V, and the rear step was also moved. A total of a dozen modifications were incorporated before the porpoising characteristics were considered to be acceptable. The following March, the first aircraft was sent to Felixstowe for trials which revealed a number of shortcomings, including performance well down against specification. However, a limited release to service was given while the

company continued development, in conjunction with MAEE, to overcome the deficiencies.

By June 1939 aircraft were being delivered to 240 Squadron for operational training before transfer to operations around the northern isles. However, the Lerwick had proved to have difficult handling and flying characteristics, including a vicious stall, which proved a problem with the Squadron pilots. In addition the new Hercules engine was giving trouble with crankshafts and sleeves, resulting in breakages of both engine and mounting in the air. The following letter from Air Marshal Sir Sholto Douglas of the Air Staff to Air Marshal Sir Wilfrid Freeman (Air Member for Development and Production) sums up the position in the middle of September 1939.

"I have just been discussing the future of the Lerwick with Coastal Command. They have been actually trying it out in operations from Invergordon and the Shetlands, and the more they fly it, the worse they like it. The take-off is positively dangerous under certain conditions; it has no range to speak of; and they now say it is unpleasant and difficult in the air, which is contrary to previous reports. It is possible that we may even have to put all the twenty-one Lerwicks which are now on order on the scrap heap. However, I am trying to induce Bowhill to use them for a time from sheltered waters on short range jobs.

It is no use 'crying over spilt milk', but the moral of it all seems to me to be that you should get Saunders-Roe in production on Sunderlands as soon as possible. You said that you were thinking of doing this, but I am wondering whether you have actually taken any steps to that end as yet. If not, I think you should do so at once, since it seems a waste of time and money to go on producing the Lerwick there a day longer than is necessary to preserve the firm's labour force."

All work on the Lerwick contract was suspended for a brief period in October but operational presures were such that this decision was rescinded and work was allowed to proceed from the 1st November. A series of modifications to mitigate the difficulties was devised and an urgent programme for their embodiment prepared.

The various problems resulted in six aircraft losses before the eventual withdrawal of the Lerwick from operations in May 1941, although a few aircraft continued in use for training purposes with the RAF to June 1942 and the RCAF until September 1942, the latter service also carrying out a number of convoy patrols before disposing of their aircraft. Termination of production was possible, after 21 aircraft were built, by the greater availability of Sunderlands and of the American PBY.5 Catalina as a replacement for the Lerwick in Coastal Command from 1941, the last Lerwick being finally scrapped in March 1943. Although slower than the Lerwick, the Catalina had a remarkably long range for ocean patrol work and served with distinction with the RAF throughout the remaining war years.

The comparative failure of the Lerwick, although a blow to the company, brought home the need to provide more comprehensive test facilities to avoid such a repetition on any future project.

The production capacity made available was soon taken up mostly by the manufacture of the Walrus amphibian, not Sunderlands as suggested by Air Marshal

Bluebird. Sir Malcolm Campbell at speed in the first Bluebird boat used to create the World's water speed records in 1937/8.

Saro S.36 Lerwick Prototype

Saro S.36 Lerwick. The first aircraft L.7248 in its original form.

Saro A.37 Experimental Flying Boat. Seen here flying in its original form.

Saunders-Roe A.37. In its original configuration on the hardstanding outside the Columbine works late 1939.

Short Shetland. Short S.35 Shetland Mk.I DX 166 was the prototype of a very long range reconnaissance flying boat to replace the Sunderland.

The Military Shetland. In flight in 1945.

Short Shetland. Saunders-Roe designed and built the wings and engine installations for the two machines which were completed.

Short Shetland. Short S.40 Shetland II G-AGVD was built as a civil transport.

Douglas. The design department was engaged from February 1939 with the design of the rear fuselage and empennage of the Boulton Paul F11/37, the P.92 'cupola' fighter, a prototype set of units being manufactured for this aircraft which was never completed. As a safeguard against a possible shortage of aluminium alloy in wartime alternative wing-tip floats of wooden construction for the Sunderland were designed later but these did not go into production.

In spite of the design effort being expended on the A.33 and the Lerwick, the team had been able to begin studies of a four-engined long range passsenger flying boat to specification R.5/39 to replace the famous Short C class. In 1939 and 1940 this work included wind tunnel and structural tests of spars and ribs. As tendered by Saro, the specification was met with an aircraft weighing 55,000 lb, a top speed of 284 mph at 15,000 ft, and when overloaded had a range of 4,000 miles. This tender was made on 27th June 1939. This craft seemed to the designers to be too big a step in the state of the art and it was decided to build a scaled down aircraft. The availability of appropriate engines, Pobjoy Niagara III 95 hp engines were chosen, dictated a scale of 1 to 2.2, resulting in a machine of 6000lb all-up-weight and a top speed of 105 mph. Known as the Shrimp, it first flew, piloted by Leslie Ash, in September 1939, only seven months after start of design. This time hydrodynamic characteristics were excellent. In the meantime, the specification for the full-scale craft was progressively revised towards a larger machine and the relative scale to 1 to 2.5. In August 1940 the craft was delivered to MAEE, now at its wartime home at Helensburgh, for official trials.

While the work was proceeding on the Shrimp, constant air raid warnings at Cowes in the first months of 1940 were causing unacceptable interference with design and production. Much frustrating time was spent in air raid shelters adjacent to St. James' Church. The company, therefore planned dispersal of its facilities and in September the design department and its test facilities were transferred to Beaumaris on the Isle of Anglesey and the Head Office and Works Offices to Melchet Court near Romsey. Design work on the large civil flying boat, now designated SR.39, soon recommenced and was given new impetus early in 1941 by the issue of military specification R.14/40 for a four-engined machine with a range of 1500 miles at 5000 ft, 4000 miles with overload tanks, and a cruising speed of 220 mph. It was to have a crew of 11, a 20,000 lb bomb load and three powered gun turrets each fitted with two half inch Browning machine guns. It was expected to weigh up to 120,000 lb when overloaded. Both Saunders-Roe and Short Brothers tendered proposals to the government to this specification, the Saro design was numbered SR.41. The government response was to request the two companies to submit a combined proposal or no order would be placed. The companies agreed on a design and that Shorts should have the responsibility for the hull, including tail unit, and final assembly and SaundersRoe for the 150 ft span wings. Because of the success of the Shrimp, Saunders-Roe was also to be involved in the hydrodynamic design of the hull. The Saro design team subsequently carried out an intensive research and development programme into the further improvement of the hydrodynamic and aerodynamic characteristics of the hull and wing floats. The wings, the largest units made by

the company to that date, were made at Beaumaris and reduced to manageable sections for transport·by road. These, together with the nacelles, flaps and ailerons from Cowes and the wing tip floats from Eastleigh were despatched to Rochester where, due to their size, the aircraft were erected outside on hardstanding. The first aircraft, Shetland Mk.I DX.166, received its wings early in 1944 and was first flown in December. The machine, with a total weight of 130,000 lb and powered by four Bristol Centaurus 2500 hp engines, proved to have a highly satisfactory performance both on the water and in the air although rather ugly in appearance. However, with the end of hostilities, there was no longer a military requirement and there was a considerable delay while the second aircraft was redesigned as a civil transport.

Unfortunately, the Shetland was to have no great future either in military form or as a proposed passenger aircraft. The prototype, Mk.I DX.166, was accidentally burnt at moorings at Felixstowe on the 28th January 1946, while the second prototype, Short S.40 Mk.II G-AGVD, equipped to passenger layout, was not flown until September 1947, the last flying boat to emerge from Shorts' Rochester works. This aircraft was broken up at Queen's Island, Belfast, in 1951 having never carried a fare paying passenger.

The model A.37, Shrimp, received an extremely complimentary report in 1941 on its trials at the Marine Aircraft Experimental Establishment. It was used as a means for trying out various features for the Shetland. These included revised hull and float shapes and the single fin and rudder which replaced the original twin fins and rudders and dihedral tailplane. The A.37 continued in use for test purposes until the end of 1944, being finally scrapped in 1947 at Felixstowe.

During this period the successor to John Lord, Major J.W.S. Darwin, was appointed as managing director in February 1936. H. Broadsmith, appointed technical director instead of general manager in January 1935 with the termination of Spartan continued as a director with H. Knowler as director and chief designer of the aircraft department. The other directors continued in office. The Saunders Shipyard Limited, set up in 1937 as a separate company occupying the Cornubia Works in Clarence Road, was later to become the Saunders Engineering & Shipyard Company and its operations transferred, in late 1940, to Addlestone near Weybridge. In less than a year a further move was made to Edmonton and the Addlestone works were then employed by the parent company for aircraft work. These works provided a main office block and part of the facilities required, in premises which were formerly the works of Lang Propellers during the first world war.

The plywood division was also established as a separate company known as Saro Laminated Wood Products Limited, housed in the Folly Works. Boat construction continued at the old Cornubia Yard at East Cowes including lifeboats for the Royal National Lifeboat Institution. Also, although not generally known, one-man submarines were made there in secret in the war period. The manufacture of Consuta had been discontinued some years previously, superseded by glued laminations as a result of the advancements made with adhesives. A range of other materials was developed mainly with commercial applications but some, such as

Supermarine Walrus. An important wartime product of Saunders-Roe. The machine illustrated had been involved in nine air-sea rescue operations saving twenty personnel.

Addlestone Works near Weybridge, Surrey. The main office block with machine shop behind were originally the works of the Lang Propeller Co. in 1914-18.

Addlestone Works near Weybridge, Surrey. Wartime facilities. Separated buildings with external air-raid shelters. The right hand building was used for Walrus wing production.

"compregnated" wood, had aviation applications, its use for the main wing spars of the Heston-Napier J.5 Racer of 1939 appealing to the chief designer, George Cornwall, previously a technician of Saunders-Roe in the days of the London.

'Compregnated' wood spars for the wings and tailplane of the Armstrong-Whitworth Albermarle were supplied in considerable numbers by the subsidiary company for this bomber aircraft with wooden structure produced in wartime as an insurance against an aluminium shortage.

At a meeting in March 1937 at Parliament Street, the new London Office replacing Bush House, Aldwych, at which A.E. Chambers was in the chair, a new director, Capt. E.D. Clarke, MC, joined the board. Capt. Nicolson, who had been ill, was present and arrangements were made for his services to be terminated in the following September and he was thanked for his dedicated service from June 1929. At about this time a letter had been sent to Sir Alliott proposing that he relinquish his seat on the board in six months, to which he did not reply. An amicable solution was reached later in which he was appointed Life Pesident. Sir Alliott was not active in the running of the company, although he retained his honorary position until his death in 1958.

However, in March 1938 Major Darwin was relieved of his position as managing director, after a disagreement with the Hon. Clive Pearson of Whitehall Securities and the board then set up a management committee with a directive to meet every twenty days. This committee was under the chairmanship of Harry Broadsmith and included Messrs Clarke, Chambers, Balfour and Walsh. Capt. Balfour on his appointment as Under Secretary of State for Air tendered his resignation from the board in a letter dated the 16th May, his shares being taken by John Lister Walsh, who had been appointed to the board in the previous December. The Hon. H.N. Morgan-Grenville succeeded Capt. Balfour on the board in September and joined the management committee in December. Mr. de Ballardie relinquished his board position in October and Walsh withdrew in March 1939. A significant change to the board came in December 1939 with the appointment of Harry Broadsmith and Capt. Clarke as Joint Managing Directors; Broadsmith having responsibility for engineering, development and design with Clarke handling commercial and production matters. Although other directors were appointed, including Viscount Cowdray and R.V. Perfect in May 1941, and Arthur Gouge and others from Shorts later, Broadsmith and Clarke were to continue in their positions throughout the wartime period. At the end of the war Harry Broadsmith retired and Capt. Clarke became sole managing director and was to continue in this position until the absorption of the Saunders-Roe company by Westland in 1959. Morgan-Grenville became chairman in 1947 and was in this position also until 1959.

The wartime pressures at Shorts resulted in the departure from Rochester of their Chief Designer, Arthur Gouge, from his long-held position. He joined the board in 1943 and was appointed Chief Executive and Vice-Chairman at Cowes, considerably strengthening the company in flying boat experience and providing a measure of continuity when the Shetland design was shared with Shorts.

The re-armament programme had created a situation where the demand for the Spitfire compelled Supermarine to off-load the manufacture of the Walrus amphibian and in 1939 production was transferred entirely to Saunders-Roe. This extremely useful general purpose, training and air-sea rescue machine was produced in Mk.I form with a metal hull of which 270 were constructed, followed by a further 191 Mk.II versions with wooden hulls. Although Supermarine retained overall design authority, the Saunders-Roe design department, then at Beaumaris, undertook the design work for the wooden hull, five of which were constructed at Beaumaris. Provision of manufacturing facilities and vastly increased staff at Cowes was supervised by Lawrence Leach, typical of many wartime unsung heroes. In a few short months, in spite of repeated air raid warnings and the Battle of Britain taking place overhead, production rose to, and was maintained at, eighteen aircraft per month. The first flight of the prototype X.1045, which was assembled at Cowes, took place on the 2nd May 1940 in the hands of Leslie S. Ash. In addition to providing continuity at Cowes and Eastleigh, the manufacture and overhaul of Walrus aircraft created sufficient work for additional facilities to be needed. The subsidiary Shipyard Company's works at Addlestone was taken over and expanded for the production of the Walrus. Departments were established for the manufacture of all components, including tool-room, machine and press shops, and new erection and stores buildings were built after the bombing of Cowes in May 1942. The factory, an example of wartime improvis-ation, was managed by G.W. Garrett from Cowes and consisted of a number of buildings comprising a main works, hull assembly, erection shop, press shop and offices, all separately housed. The first six aircraft were taken to Brooklands for flight testing where they were housed in Vickers' flight shed. Later aircraft were towed with wings folded across the main Weybridge to Chertsey road to a new flight hangar, capable of housing two aircraft, on Chertsey Meads which served as an airfield adequate in size for the modest take-off requirement of the Walrus. The journey from the works to the flight hangar was not without its hazards being some half a mile along a narrow twisting track with the ground dropping away at the sides. There was a relatively small clearance to the high voltage cables humming away above the 15 ft. 3in. height of the Walrus and many shocks and sparks from the induced static.

Generally 40 minutes test flying sufficed before delivery to White Waltham but every fifth aircraft was flown to Somerton for more exacting flight and water tests at the mouth of the Medina. Geoffrey Verdon-Roe carried out much of the flying of Walruses at Cowes and Addlestone, as Chief Test Pilot after Les Ash transferred to Beaumaris, and he continued at Cowes on the later Sea Otter.

Take-off directions at Addlestone were restricted by the presence of electric power cables and pylons and in some circumstances left no margin in an emergency. The emergency inevitably arose on one Walrus in 1943 when Flt. Lieut Lamb, a 'resting' service pilot, with apprentice Ron Conway, attempted to turn back when the machine refused to climb and both were killed in the ensuing crash. It was later found that one half of the four-bladed propeller had been assembled in reverse and was unnoticed at final inspection.

The Addlestone works, which employed 600 personnel at peak, reached a production of eight aircraft per month

Walrus Production at Addlestone. Erection of both metal and wooden-hulled aircraft was carried out after the transfer from Cowes.

Addlestone Works near Weybridge, Surrey. Walrus wings and control surfaces in production.

Addlestone Works near Weybridge, Surrey. The newly constructed Erection Shop.

Addlestone Works near Weybridge, Surrey. Walrus aircraft outside the Erection Shop which is off to the left. The new stores building is under contruction. The confined nature of the site is apparent. The houses are part of the outskirts of Addlestone whilst the Weybridge to Chertsey Road passes through the trees on the right.

Addlestone Works near Weybridge, Surrey. Constructing a new Flight Hangar on Chertsey Meads for Walrus aircraft.

Melchet Court, Romsey. Main office of the Company 1941-45 after dispersal from Cowes.

Sea Otter. Wings folded, on "Saunders-Roe Type" jacking trestles

Supermarine Sea Otter. Typical of the 290 aircraft produced in the late years of the war at Cowes.

which terminated in January 1944, with 461 aircraft built by Saunders-Roe of the combined total of 746 built by the two manufacturers. In addition to the production of metal and wooden hulls at Addlestone, there were subcontactors also engaged on the manufacture of this major unit. At Eastleigh, Cunliffe-Owen Aircraft built metal hulls in the early war years that were supplied to Cowes or erected at Eastleigh, and Elliots of Newbury built some of the later wooden hulls for Cowes.

From 1936, Supermarine had been developing a successor to the Walrus, the Sea Otter, a similar type of small biplane amphibian flying boat but with tractor airscrew. Although able to handle the design, manufacture and flight testing of the prototypes, Supermarine again was forced by the problems associated with the bombing of their works and Spitfire production to pass production over to Saunders-Roe. It was not until early in 1942 that manufacturing commenced at Cowes, Eastleigh and Addlestone but, although complete hulls were made and supplied to Cowes, no Sea Otters were completed at Addlestone. The first aircraft was flown in January 1943 by Supermarine pilot Jeffrey Quill, and production terminated in July 1946, by which time 290 aircraft had been completed and a further 110 aircraft on contract were cancelled. Versions of the Sea Otter were supplied to both the RAF and the FAA.

A Repair Section of Saunders-Roe Limited had been created in 1935. At that time, Solent Works was allocated for this purpose and a combined staff of approximately 60 was engaged on this class of work, which primarily consisted of repairs and incorporations of modifications of Cutty Sarks, Windhovers, Clouds, Londons and a number of Stranraers. By the latter part of 1939, Walrus flying boats were being allocated to the Section for repair and embodiment of essential modifications. This aircraft was the chief source of repair work, which included the wooden hulls, although a small number of Vought-Sikorsky Kingfishers were also repaired.

During the early part of 1940, it was decided to give the Repair Section the title of Saro Aircraft Repair Works (commonly known as SARW).

It was soon realised that an increase of floor space would be necessary, and arrangements were made for the leasing of Cornubia Yard from Saunders-Roe Shipyards Limited. Upon completion of certain reconstruction work, this site was allocated for wing repairs, covering, doping, machine shop, detail fitters, etc.

It had also become necessary to use the buildings at Somerton Aerodrome as a receiving and dismantling depot. In addition, Northwood Garage was taken over about midway through the year and used for engine overhaul, nacelle repairs, etc. A couple of cottages and a store opposite Solent Works were taken over for additional offices and stores accommodation, the stores being converted into a canteen.

Later, when the top floor at Northwood Garage became vacant, some offices were transferred from Solent to make room for an increase of staff, as several new departments were being created, including production, progress, sub-contracts and ARP sections, Northwood becoming a central office for dispersal of records. Further dispersal action was taken by the acquisition of certain buildings in the West Wight, which included garages, a private school and a disused picture palace.

Four Dawney hangars were also erected on sites situated on the outskirts of Newport. During the early part of 1942 a sports pavilion in Newport was requisitioned for use as a dispersal store. By this time the combined staff had increased to approximately 1000.

An air raid on the night of 4th/5th May 1942 caused the total loss of Solent and Cornubia Works, offices, stores and canteen in Medina Road, together with the aerodrome buildings. Also lost at Folly Works were several million square feet of veneers representing 40% of the UK aircraft industry's requirements for plywood and many parts for boats and pontoons. Fortunately little damage was inflicted on the Columbine and Maresfield shops. The Repair Works used Northwood as a central clearing station and the pavilion at Newport was used as temporary accommodation for the office staff from the 6th May. On the 17th May, the staff was transferred from the pavilion to Medham House, Northwood, which had been taken over for this purpose, and the pavilion reverted to its original use as a store. Floor space also had to be found to accommodate the covering and doping department which was lost at Cornubia. After a general re-arrangement, space was allocated for this work to be done at Pinks Garage at Totland.

Repairs to hulls had to be carried out in the open on Somerton Aerodrome.

In this manner, SARW carried on production utilizing every square foot of floor space available and in very overcrowded conditions, which prevailed until the early part of 1943 when new factory buildings were erected on and around the aerodrome, two flight sheds to replace the ones lost on the night of 4th/5th May, a large hangar just off the aerodrome for use as a receiving and stripping shed and two "Robin hangars" on the outskirts of the aerodrome, for the accomodation of aircraft awaiting delivery, all these making up to some degree the floor area lost by enemy action.

Production continued uninterrupted until the aerodrome was sold in 1946, by which time major repairs had been carried out on 435 Walrus and Sea Otter Aircraft.

The facilities in Anglesey had been developed mainly to undertake the responsibilities of a "sister firm" for US aircraft operated by the RAF and RN. The RAF and FAA operated a number of different types of American aircraft in wartime which generally needed to be adapted to meet British operational requirements. To carry out the design changes and co-ordinate this with the general flow of US modifications and instructions, Saunders-Roe was given design approval on a succession of American aircraft starting with the Catalina. The design office, at Beaumaris since September-October 1940, functioned in three sections, one handling the US work, another the Walrus and the third Saunders-Roe designs. Capacity was also available in 1941 to design the tail unit of the Westland P.14 high-altitude fighter later known as the Welkin.

Initially the modification, repair and overhaul work on the Catalina aircraft was carried out by Scottish Aviation at Caird's yard, Greenock from December 1940. On the 6th May 1941 the yard was bombed, two Catalinas were burnt out and others had to be scrapped. Staff from both companies worked to re-establish the facilities and some of the operations were carried out on aircraft at Helensburgh. Meanwhile, a slipway had been established at Fryar's

Beaumaris, Anglesey. A general view of the site showing all of the major buildings.

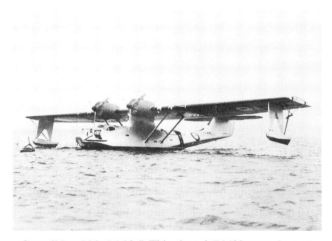

Consolidated Model 28-5. This aircraft P9630 was taken on charge by the Air Ministry in January 1939 and was the basis for the development of the Catalina for the R.A.F.

Consolidated PBY-5A Catalina IVA. A late version of this reliable American flying boat at Fryar's Bay, Anglesey. The Leigh Light installation was among the British modifications administered by the establishment in Anglesey.

Vought-Sikorsky OS.2.U-3 Kingfisher 1. One hundred of these machines were ordered for the Fleet Air Arm but only five were handled at Beaumaris.

Consolidated PB2Y-3B Coronado. The small number in R.A.F. service were handled at Beaumaris and subsequently supported in service.

Martin PBM-3B Mariner. Beaumaris serviced the aircraft which operated with the R.A.F.

Consolidated PBY-5A Catalina IVA. The machine on the right JX399 is a Mk IVB built by Boeing of Canada as the PB.2.B-1.

Spitfire Floatplane. This MK.VB Spitfire was converted by Folland Aircraft Ltd. and was one of the few built which carried out trials at Fryar's Bay.

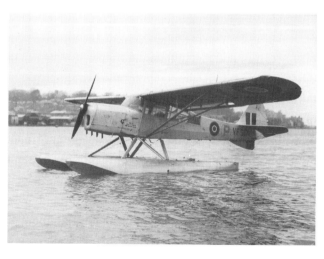

Auster MK.VI Floatplane. A set of floats were designed and manufactured at Cowes and a prototype converted and tested in 1946.

Bay, Beaumaris, and the first Catalina AM 266 was hauled ashore on 28th April 1941 for work to commence on a steadily increasing number of these extremely useful flying boats, totalling over 300 by the end of hostilities. An incident worth recording relating to the Catalina is that when one arrived fully loaded with much needed spares it was moored for the night in Fryars Bay. In the morning there was no Catalina to be seen. It was finally located, incredibly undamaged, sixty-five miles away in the mouth of the Mersey, driven thence by an overnight gale. A building known as the Red Hangar was transferred from Cowes aerodrome and by August 1941 was in use adjacent to the slipway.

Various other American aircraft types were handled but in considerably smaller numbers than the Catalina. In May 1941 work was started on the Vought-Sikorsky OS2U-3 Kingfisher float plane but the limited use made of this by the FAA, most of them being delivered direct to the Middle East or West Indies, resulted in only five aircraft reaching Saunders-Roe. The Consolidated Coronado PB2Y-3B and Martin Mariner PBM-3B flying boats saw little use by the RAF and only six and twelve aircraft respectively arrived at Beaumaris for attention. The Curtiss Seamew SO3C was even less popular with the FAA and the US Navy and only one of these floatplanes had a trial installation of one modification carried out at Beaumaris. From April 1944, as Catalina work was reduced, Saunders-Roe was appointed Control Firm for Boston and Dakota aircraft.

Repair, modification and overhaul work had been carried out from early 1941 with a labour force of some two hundred employed at peak in a variety of premises grouped round the main facility and slipway at Fryar's Bay.

A notable aircraft allocated to Saunders-Roe in January 1944 was the veteran Consolidated Model 28-3.NC777, named Guba, which had started life in 1938 operated by the Museum of Natural History in New Guinea. Following a survey flight in 1939 on behalf of the British and Australian governments of a route across the Indian Ocean from Australia, crossing Africa to Britain, Guba flew across the Atlantic to New York and continued the flight across America to the Consolidated works at San Diego. Purchased by the British Purchasing Commission for the RAF, it became AM.258 briefly but, being unsuitable for RAF operations, was transferred to BOAC as G-AGBJ. It was re-identified as SM.706 on transfer to Saunders-Roe for use for mooring trials and was sunk in a gale. The aircraft was raised for salvage purposes and then towed out to sea and finally sunk.

Among the aircraft housed at Beaumaris in 1943-4 were some of the prototype Spitfire seaplanes on test by Supermarine and MAEE. Trials of this famous fighter as a floatplane had been started in 1940 as a result of the invasion of Norway but were discontinued at the conclusion of this campaign. The trials were revived later for possible use in the Greek Islands and other versions of the Spitfire were converted. Supermarine was assisted in this work by Folland Aircraft of Hamble who made the floats and carried out the conversion of four of the five aircraft built. The trials were begun from Southampton Water using Folland's Hamble slipway but were transferred to Beaumaris after the army had fired many Bofors shells and small arms rounds at this unfamiliar aircraft,

fortunately without damage to man or machine. The third aircraft a Mk.VB, EP.751, was at Beaumaris in late 1942 and after test was sent to the Middle East with the second and fourth machines W.3760 and EP.754 for the Greek operation which was subsequently cancelled. The fifth machine was a Mk.IX, MJ.892, and this was tested at Beaumaris in 1943 and eventually passed to 6MU in September 1944 on completion of the trials for reversion to standard landplane fighter.

The performance of the Spitfire on floats was reduced compared to the standard fighter, as was to be expected, and handling on the water required special care particularly in rough conditions. Changing operational needs had caused the programme to receive varying degrees of priority until finally discontinued but water based fighters had become a particular interest of Saunders-Roe.

A floatplane at the lower end of the performance scale was the Auster VI for which floats were designed and manufactured in the immediate post-war period. The aircraft was assembled and tested at Cowes but remained a prototype, although a few years later an Auster for the Falkland Islands, with floats from another supplier, was flown on trials at Beaumaris by Geoffrey Tyson.

The Addlestone factory was handed over to Fairey Aviation in January 1944 and the buildings are currently part of the Weybridge Trading Estate. The flight hangar suffered a near-miss from a V.2 rocket during Fairey's occupation which blew off all the sheeting. The structure was later dismantled and now only the concrete base and a brick built shelter remain.

A device for the rescue of airmen forced down in the shallow coastal and estuary waters was designed and tested as a prototype at Beaumaris and took the form of a pontoon with wheels, powered by an aircraft engine and propeller mounted above. Hovercraft had yet to be invented.

During the period of hostilities Saunders-Roe had mainly produced aircraft to other firms' designs and had been sub-contractors for major components, which included Hurricane and Spitfire rudders and work for the Boulton Paul Defiant. The conclusion of hostilities now found the company with a need to re-establish itself in the field of flying boat design and manufacture. Since 1942 the management had authorised investigations to proceed into the aircraft types required for post-war civil aviation. These investigations favoured a large flying boat for certain routes, a type not included in the terms of reference of the Brabazon Committee, but for which the company campaigned strongly in official quarters, eventually receiving approval to proceed in 1946.

There had always been the boatbuilding side and plywood manufacture but the need for diversification into new products and for rationalisation of facilities provided for wartime need now presented a similar challenge to the board to that which faced S.E. Saunders a quarter of a century before.

The war years had seen considerable growth to a peak labour force of approximately 6,000. The need to expand, and the bombing of Cowes which had led to the dispersal of facilities to twenty small units now had to be reversed, although the site at Parkhurst Forest was retained until 1965.

Manufacturing continued at Eastleigh and the remaining premises at Cowes but the main offices, with a staff of some 400, located from 1941 at Melchet Court, and the Design Department, complete with wind tunnel and test facilities, at Beaumaris were to be returned to Cowes before the end of 1945 and steps were taken to close down some of the dispersal units. Those engaged on aircraft work were regrouped on the Isle of Wight and at Eastleigh.

The Design Department returned to Cowes in June 1945 having already prepared the basic design of the jet-propelled flying boat fighter, the SR.A1. The manufacture of the three prototypes was carried out at Cowes in accordance with the new general policy.

The offices and works at Beaumaris were now taken over by the Saunders Engineering and Shipyard Company which changed its name to Saunders-Roe (Anglesey) Limited in January 1951. This unit relinquished its aviation responsibilities and took over the work of boatbuilding, structural engineering and body building for buses and coaches previously undertaken by Saunders Engineering & Shipyard Limited at Edmonton.

In the immediate post-war period many surplus military aircraft became available, including of course Walrus and Sea Otters, produced by the company. A considerable number of each type appeared on the civil register, but few suitable commercial fields were found to justify their operational use. However a batch of six Walrus Mk 1 machines were purchased by United Whalers Ltd of London and these were returned to Cowes for refurbishing. The project was to employ the aircraft for Whale spotting in the Atlantic. operating from the factory ship Balaena. (A photograph of these aircraft appears in Chapter 12.)

Of the six machines four were modified and refurbished for the operation, the remaining two being cannibalised for spares. The changes to the aircraft involved the fitment of suitable radios and instruments, extra tankage, engine heating and provision of equipment for survival in the hostile environment in the event of a forced landing. The completion of the aircraft was marked by a handover ceremony in front of the Columbine hangar on the 20th July 1946 when the three aircraft selected to go aboard ship were christened and launched. The christening was carried out by the wives of officials involved in the venture, Mrs Stevenson, wife of a director of United Whalers naming G-AHFM Moby Dick, Mrs Grierson, wife of John Grierson, chief pilot for the whaling operation named G-AHFO Shark and Mrs Perfect, wife of Saunders-Roe director Robert Perfect christened G-AHFL Boojum. These three aircraft were flown to Belfast on the 13th September with two company engineers, to be taken on board the Balaena for the duration of the cruise. The whaling operation which lasted from November to April 1947 was very successful although the extent to which this was due to aircraft is not clear. Two of the aircraft were used in the Atlantic with undercarriages removed for maximum range, the third machine remaining in reserve at Cape Town. At the end of the whaling season the ship returned to home waters and the three aircraft flew back to Cowes from the ship in the middle of May, where they remained before being finally scrapped in July 1950, having been found no further employment.

The machine retained in this country, G-AHFN, had been flown in a two day race from Lympne by John Grierson, before the expedition embarked. On the 31st August he averaged 121.5 mph to win the final of the Folkestone Trophy race, beating among other faster machines a D.H. Vampire. It was, of course, a handicap event and handicappers had not previously come across the Walrus as a racing aircraft. This unnamed machine was eventually scrapped at Prestwick in 1955.

Civilian Walrus. In a field at Cowes prior to successfully competing for the Folkestone Trophy at Lympne August 30-31st 1946. Winning this handicap race at an average speed of 121.5 m.p.h.

CHAPTER 6

THE LAST SARO FLYING BOATS

Early in 1942 the Admiralty decided to request proposals from industry for a fighter aircraft which could land and take off from sheltered coastal waters and also be capable of short range fighter bomber performance. Initially the Blackburn Aircraft Company made a successful tender for the Ministry of Aircraft Production specification designated N2/42 drawn up for the Admiralty. This aircraft, however, was powered by a very heavy Napier Sabre IV engine with a main hull raised and lowered by a scissors jacking arrangement. The design proved to be very heavy and MAEE scientists, after comprehensive tests and calculations, decided that it was doubtful if the Blackburn proposal could take off and suggested that the specification required a gas turbine engine.

In July 1943 the Saro design department, under the guidance of Chief Designer Henry Knowler and company Vice-Chairman Arthur Gouge, produced their own proposal for a jet propelled flying boat fighter. The Saro design, which was largely based on MAEE suggestions arising from their investigations into the Blackburn proposal, had a 40 ft. wing span, was 35 ft. long and had an all-up-weight of some 7700 lb. The craft was to be powered by twin Metrovick F2/4 gas turbine engines. Following intensive work by the design team, a refined design was presented to the Ministry of Aircraft Production six months later, at the end of 1943. The aircraft had nearly doubled in weight to 13,500 lb, span had increased to 44 ft. and length to 45 ft. Presumably the design team had been promised more thrust from the Metrovick engines, since a speed at sea level of 525 mph was predicted. The company designated this type the SR.44 and design proceeded apace during the next year, 1944. In March of that year the company received notification of an order for three aircraft prototypes as a Directorate of Technical Development experiment. Two months later the contract was signed requiring the craft to be built to a new specification E6/44. The proposals for producing a hull design with minimum drag were comprehensively tested at the Royal Aircraft Establishment. The hull design was based on the successful A.37 Shrimp experimental flying boat with refined step design in both plan and elevation to reduce air resistance.

Following the end of World War II, the Saro design team, and the aircraft details already manufactured at Beaumaris, were transferred to the company's main factory at Cowes. At the end of 1945, the structure of the hull was nearing completion and the Metrovick engines had been bench tested to 4000 lb of thrust. However, progress now began to slip as the company's efforts were increasingly directed towards design and production of the SR.45 Princess flying boat. It was, therefore, not until July 1947 that the first aircraft to specification E6/44 was wheeled out on to the slipway at Cowes. By this time the company was using the SBAC system for designating military projects and the company's design team called the aircraft the A1 whilst the factory floor nicknamed it the Squirt.

The aircraft wheeled out for trials had a 50 ft long hull and a 46 ft. wing span constructed throughout of aluminium alloy. The hull followed typical Saro practice of the time with closely spaced frames and light longitudinal stringers. The wing was of single spar construction with skins stiffened only by transverse stiffeners. The pilot sat in a fully pressurised cockpit, with conventional manual controls, fitted with a Martin-Baker ejector seat, the first British aircraft to be so equipped. The two Metrovick engines now named the "Beryl" were completely buried in the hull below the high wing. Armament provided was four Hispano Mk V 20 mm cannon fixed mounted in the bow above the air intake. The floats could not be completely retracted into the wings and were therefore rotated through 90° about a fore and aft axis and then retracted inwards and upwards so that only the smooth upper surface of the float was exposed.

G.A.V. Tyson was now the company's Chief Test Pilot, having left Shorts in December 1946. He and J.O. Lancaster, who also had joined the company in 1946 from Boulton Paul, undertook all the early flight trials of the SR.A1. On July 16th the craft was towed out into the Solent just off the entrance to Cowes harbour for the commencement of taxi trials. After only three of four taxi runs Geoffrey Tyson took off at some 100 mph. After four more flights in July, he reported that the A1 suffered from roll instability. The problem was cured by fitting an "acorn" fairing at the leading edge of the tailplane and fin intersection. During subsequent trials the townsfolk of East and West Cowes were often disconcerted to find the SR.A1 on low level runs upside down, a manoeuvre repeated at Farnborough in 1948. The aircraft experienced the normal engineering problems of a new design, particularly one fitted with a new engine and, of course, all the associated systems. The second craft began trials in April 1948, primarily engaged on engine trials for the National Gas Turbine Establishment. At one stage in trials of the first aircraft both engines stalled when Tyson was several miles south of the Island and he just managed to glide back to Cowes from just above 25,000 ft.

Provision was made in the first aircraft for a sliding engine intake in the bow which was intended to avoid spray being ingested during take off and landing. However, trials showed that in waves up to 2 ft. the water ingestion was negligible.

By August 1949 flights at high subsonic Mach numbers at heights of 30,000 - 35,000 ft. had been made and flights above this were scheduled for the next few weeks. On August 12th the company had invited the very experienced service test pilot Lt. Cdr. Eric "Winkle" Brown to Cowes to fly the third prototype aircraft. After flying the aircraft at a Mach number of 0.82 in a dive he decided to land in calm water just off the mouth of the River Medina. Unfortunately, there was an object in the sea in the path of his landing line, which not only holed the hull but removed the starboard float. As a result, the aircraft yawed violently to starboard, broached and rolled over. Fortunately for Winkle Brown, Geoffrey Tyson, in the

Saunders-Roe SR. A/1. The prototype TG.263 at the point of unsticking during early trials.

Henry Knowler A.M.I.C.E., M.I.Mech., F.R.Ae.S
Born 2nd January 1891. Chief Designer 1927-52
and a Saunders-Roe Director from 1942.
Technical Director 1953-56.

SR. A/1. The first machine with acorn fairing introduced at the tailplane fin intersection.

Saunders-Roe SR.A/1. The first machine in flight before the acorn fairing at the fin/tailplane junction was fitted.

SR. A/1. Showing her clean hull and floats in the deployed condition·

Test Facilities at Osborne. The Ditching Tank is used for testing a model of the SR.A/1 in 1950. The wall behind is part of the building enclosing the Towing Tank.

company's launch, was very quick to see the problem and was able to rescue the unconscious pilot. No sooner had the rescue been completed than the aircraft sank and was never found, despite repeated searches by divers. Winkle Brown fully recovered for many subsequent years of test flying.

Only five weeks later a worse tragedy occurred which spelt the end of the SR.A1 programme. The flight commander at Felixstowe, Squadron Leader Peter Major decided to practice for the aerobatic display at MAEE open day, scheduled for the next day. Visibility was poor with no horizon and Squadron Leader Major, a former bomber pilot, inexperienced in jet aerobatics crashed in the second prototype, attempting a slow roll, and was killed. Again the aircraft was not recovered despite repeated searches by divers.

It was then decided that limited hydrodynamic trials should be undertaken by company test pilots and the first prototype was refurbished for this purpose. These trials, aimed at obtaining correlation between model and full scale data, commenced in October 1950. The conclusions drawn from the trials on the aircraft were as follows:-

"Throughout the trials the performance and handling characteristics of the aircraft, at altitudes up to 30,000 ft., has been very good. Pilots' test reports indicate that controls are light, positive and well harmonised, and that the SR.A1 has no disturbing vices during flight, or on the water.

Flight measured performance agreed extremely closely with design estimates, but unfortunately actual engine thrust from flight measurements, is still not available so that "brochure" figures have had to be used during the calculations.

The directional stability at high speeds and high altitudes, dealt with at some length in the text, might be improved. Modifications had been discussed and proposed, and further investigation of this point in flight is desirable.

Handling and manoeuvrability on the water has been well investigated and is satisfactory.

It is concluded that the problem of designing a modern jet fighter flying boat has been satisfactorily solved."

The Korean War had been in progress for several months and the company hoped to sell a developed version of the SR.A1 for use in this theatre of war. However, in spite of landing the aircraft on the Thames and mooring it off the Southbank Festival Site in June of 1951, the company was unable to convince the Air Staff of the concept. The SR.A1 returned to Cowes and was not flown again. The aircraft is now on display at the Imperial War Museum Duxford outstation.

In the same year, 1942, that the Admiralty decided to request proposals which led to the design of the SR.A1, the management of the company decided that some time could be spared from their considerable war effort to carry out a detailed survey of civil air transport. This survey was to cover current trends and probable post-war developments and was not limited to flying boats. It was primarily directed at the long range "Empire" air routes and non-stop flight across the Atlantic ocean. The study was completed in June 1943 with the publication of a printed brochure entitled "The Case for the Flying Boat". This brochure concluded by stating that the company's

market studies showed that there was "a definite and worthwhile place in post war aerial transport for the flying boat, particularly for long range work". The company discovered that flying boats were not included in the terms of reference of the Brabazon Committee, formed by the Government to advise on post war civil aviation, and therefore advised the Chairman of the committee of the conclusions of this study.

The market studies were followed by project designs first submitted to the Ministry of Aircraft Production in the summer of 1943. The flying boat was designed to fly at 250 mph at 25,000 ft. non-stop across the Atlantic, powered by six Bristol Centaurus engines, with a total all-up-weight of just under 190,000 lb. By the autumn of the same year, it was suggested that a better solution would be to increase the number of engines to eight, coupled in pairs, as proposed for the Bristol Brabazon 1, with the all-up-weight increased to 250,000 lb. At the end of 1944 the proposal had again been substantially modified. It was now proposed to power the craft with six Rolls Royce Eagle engines at an all-up-weight of 260,000 lb. More significantly, this proposal also suggested that gas turbine engines should replace the piston engines at a later stage in development. In the next four months the advantages of the higher speeds of some 370 mph at an altitude of 37,000 ft. offered by gas turbines in relation to the 90 mph head winds often occurring on an Atlantic crossing decided the company on this form of power. In August 1945 a preliminary specification was submitted to the Ministry of Aircraft Production for a 266,000 lb flying boat powered by six Rolls Royce Clyde gas turbines. In the ensuing months Armstrong Siddeley Cobra and coupled Rolls Royce Tweed engine units were also carefully evaluated. A great deal of serious work was carried out on this proposed Tweed powered aircraft.

It was nearly a year later, in May 1946, that the first draft of specification C10/46 was drawn up by the Ministry of Supply. Following many meetings, it was finally decided in January 1947, by the Ministry of Supply, the Ministry of Aviation and the British Overseas Airways Corporation that they would not complete the specification and that it was the "duty" of Saunders-Roe to prepare its own specification! The company took eight months to draw up a new draft specification, numbered P136/7, for an aircraft called the Saunders-Roe SR.45 long range flying boat, now to be powered by ten Bristol Proteus gas turbine engines with an all-up-weight of 315,000 lb. This was the final concept.

The aircraft was to have a true cruising speed of 350 mph at 36,000 ft., with a maximum operating height of 39,000 ft. Range was to be 3,450 miles, i.e. London to New York, against an average head wind of 89 mph carrying a payload of 20,000 lb.

It was at the commencement of this final phase of the preparation of the specification for SR.45 that a member of the Research Department (Seaplanes) of the Ministry of Supply visited the Managing Director at Cowes. He asked if the company would guarantee to fund all capital requirements themselves if it were awarded a contract to produce three aircraft. The Directors of the company gave the required undertaking and an Instruction to Proceed was issued by the Ministry of Supply on 7th May 1946.

Osborne Works, East Cowes. The long building houses the Towing Tank for testing models of flying boats and hull shapes. The tank is 618 ft long by 8ft wide and came into use in 1947. The large hangar at one time housed the Princess mock-up. The central buildings comprise the Technical College and Apprentice Training Centre.

East Cowes Waterfront 1951. The first Princess awaits fitment of wings outside the Columbine Works built in 1935. The surviving SR.A/1 nestles in the corner by the Medina shed and the original Seaholme buildings. Behind the Princess is the old Esplanade building closing off the hardstanding. The long narrow buildings extending from behind the Columbine Works to the left are the works in Maresfield Road.

Head Office and Design Department. Based on the Osborne House stables complex 1965.

Saunders-Roe SR.45 Princess. The first machine leaving the Columbine Works on 30th October 1951. The tail is held down by water ballast in tanks in the rear of the hull and further clearance under the hangar roof is provided by the omission of the upper fin and rudder. These units are mounted on platforms on the tailplane ready for fitment.

Princess. Roll-out nearing completion showing the enormous size of the aircraft.

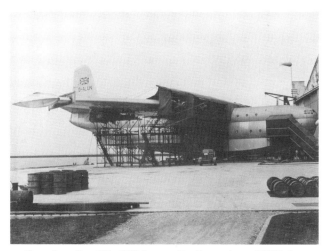

Saunders-Roe SR.45 Princess. By the spring of 1952 the wings and tail units had been rigged and much interior equipment fitted. Work in wintry conditions was aided by covered working platforms and an interior heating system using domestic radiators.

Saunders-Roe SR.45 Princess. The crew compartment, navigators station on the left behind which sat the radio officer facing aft. Up front the two pilots with the captain on the left side. An observer seat occupies the gangway for the initial trials with the flight engineers' station on the right.

Saunders-Roe SR.45 Princess. By late summer 1952 G-ALUN was ready for launching which was planned for the 19th August but abandoned due to a stiff breeze arising and this took place in the early hours of the next day. In the background is the second Princess G-ALUO, work on which had been 'postponed' by M.O.S. in March together with work on the third machine. The first SR.A/1 awaits its fate but, unlike the Princesses, manages to escape the breakers.

Two Famous Flying Boat Designers. On the occasion of the roll-out of the first Princess on 30th October 1951 Henry Knowler and Sir Arthur Gouge.

The Princess First Flight Crew. Standing, l. to r.: R.B. Stratton, 1st Engineer; S. Ingle, Powered Flying Control Observer; W.S. Worner, Flight Test Section; G.A.V. Tyson, Chief Test Pilot; J.S. Booth, Co-pilot; S. Welford, 2nd Engineer; H. New, Electrician; G. Jones, Flight Test Representative. Front Row, l. to r.: H. Palmer, Powered Flying Control Observer; M. Mabey, Radio Observer; A. Walker, Electrician; R.J. Wraith, Electrical Design.

Part of the intensive research and development work leading to the finalisation of the specification was concerned with the hydrodynamics and aerodynamics of the hull design. In addition to model test work at the RAE, the NPL, the MAEE and at Cowes, various hull planing surfaces had been tested on the Saro 37 Shrimp. Most of the test flying was carried out by Group Captain Frank Squire involving principally take-offs and landings in flat calm conditions checking the behaviour of a variety of flared hull steps. An auxiliary Ford V8 engine installed in the hull pumped air out of the hull immediately aft of the main step to avoid suction affecting take off. This suction was so serious with one flare design that all the plating in the step area was stripped from the hull. Much later, in 1953, Group Captain Squire was to fly the SR.45 itself. As a result of this prolonged intensive research and development work the performance of the aircraft was assessed at the time to be "seen to be at no disadvantage compared with contemporary landplanes".

Henry Knowler and his team designed many advanced ideas into the SR.45, later to be called the Princess. Without doubt the most advanced idea was the fully power operated flight control system, conceived by the Saro team and designed and built in conjunction with Boulton Paul Aircraft. The system was based on three twin electro-hydraulic power units each having a variable speed hydraulic motor supplied from a variable capacity hydraulic generator which in turn was driven by a direct current electric generator. These units were horizontally opposed and coupled into a central differential gearbox which transmitted power to the control surfaces by torque shafts and gear boxes, the final movement being executed by screw jacks. This new system was comprehensively ground tested and then flight tested in a Sunderland Mark V, Serial Number NJ265, in 1949. The flight tests proved that the powered flight control system was both practical and reliable. In the final event the powered control system proved one of the many successful features of the craft. The Marine Aircraft Experimental Establishment at Felixstowe reported as follows:-

"Flight experience generally proved that the controls were pleasant to operate, column and rudder bar forces being satisfactory" and

"The installation gave trouble free operation throughout the trials with two exceptions, both associated with the emergency control surface centralising gear."

All the other features of this ambitious aircraft project required major developments in the current state of the art of aircraft design. The structure, with its distributed flange two spar wing and "double-bubble" pressurised hull, required significant developments in stressing techniques and weight predictions as it was the largest metal aircraft of its day. The structure weight as a proportion of all-up-weight was only matched by the Bristol Britannia in spite of the disadvantage of planing hull weight. The electrical system pioneered the development of a high voltage, 120 volt, DC operation. Similar remarks can be made in relation to the pressurisation and air conditioning system, the de-icing system and the automatic pilot developed for the aircraft by Smiths Aircraft Instruments.

During the design of the aircraft an incident which caused considerable amusement to the design staff occurred when the Managing Director inspected the full-scale mock-up constructed at Osborne. On ascending the unusual spiral staircases between the two passenger decks he found that there were thirteen steps and immediately called for the staircases to be redesigned. Not only was this the only comment passed back to the design team, but the re-design proved quite difficult to achieve and finally the decision was made to have fourteen steps.

Although the Board of the early nineteen thirties had shown considerable foresight in their choice of the size of the Columbine hangar, even this very large structure was not quite big enough to house the complete Princess aircraft. However, by careful planning, it was possible to leave a minimum of work to be carried out on the specially extended hardstanding outside the Columbine hangar. Inside the hangar a major assembly fixture was positioned on the southern side, on which was built the major portion of the pressurised hull and this was transferred sideways and forwards on rails to an assembly station for fitting of the centre wing, rear fuselage section, fin less its top portion, two of the three rudder sections and fitment of equipment to the extent that was possible. In October 1951, the major move of the first aircraft out on to the hardstanding took place.

The second machine, already at the assembly stage, and the third, with the hull structure well advanced, were planned to follow at six-monthly intervals.

It was necessary to fit the power plants, the wings and top portion of the fin and upper rudder and to complete the erection of the aircraft, on the hardstanding but despite all the difficulties, particularly of outdoor working in winter, the work proceeded and the first aircraft, G-ALUN, was launched on 20th August 1952. After only two days of final preparation whilst moored at the company buoy in Cowes harbour, chief test pilot Geoffrey Tyson and his crew of eleven, mainly engineers of various disciplines, were scheduled to begin taxiing trials on the 22nd August. However, after only 28 minutes taxiing Geoffrey Tyson felt so comfortable with the craft that he took off for a 35 minute flight round the Isle of Wight. Flight trials continued until June 1954 when all work on this beautiful aeroplane was stopped. During the whole of this period it was unfortunate that the engines used were either prototype or substandard units requiring considerable effort to maintain them in a serviceable condition. Problems with the engines combined with the usual engineering development problems encountered in a new project of this nature meant that only 100 hours of flying were achieved in these two years. Perhaps the most interesting measurements made during the trials revealed that the lift to drag ratio of the complete aircraft was 18.9, a very significant improvement compared with 13.2 for the Sunderland II and 15.7 for the Shetland.

The whole project was so threatened by the delays in the development of the Proteus engine that alternative proposals were again investigated while flight trials continued. These included the Napier Double-Eland, the Pratt and Whitney T34, the Allison T40, the Wright TP51 and the New Bristol BE25 later called Orion. It was concluded that the only engine to receive support was the Orion which would not be available for fitment to the Princess until 1957. Accordingly it was decided in January 1953 to stop work on craft 2 and 3 and store them in plastic cocoons at Calshot. Similarly, when work stopped

Saunders-Roe SR.45. Taxiing trials in August 1952.

The Princess flying at Farnborough. An impressive sight well remembered by all who witnessed it.

The Princess flying above the Needles Rocks.

Saunders-Roe SR.45 Princess. Launched on August 20th 1952 with first flight on the
22nd August which lasted 35 minutes. Less than 10 hours had been logged when
the Princess flew over Farnborough runway on the 2nd September on V.I.P. day
of the S.B.A.C. Show 1952.

Saunders-Roe SR.45 Princess. The second and third machines stored at Calshot. The wings and tail units were assembled and
cocooning commenced at Cowes in January 1953. Thereafter the second machine was towed the six miles to Calshot on the
11th February and the third followed shortly afterwards.

Saunders-Roe SR.45 Princess. Flight testing of the first machine finished
in April 1954 and with engines removed, this also was cocooned at Cowes
and stored on the site of the Solent Works.

Saunders-Roe SR.45 Princess. G-ALUN, the first prototype, being towed
on her final voyage to Southampton to be scrapped. The day, appropriately
was a very gloomy one.

Princess Landplane Freighter Project.

Proposed Nuclear Powered version of The Princess for the
U.S. Navy, Nuclear Power units in the hull drove the
turbines in the two inboard nacelles.

on the first craft in June 1954, this aircraft was also co-cooned, this time on the company's Solent site at West Cowes. The air inside each cocooned aircraft was kept dry by a complex control system and eight tons of silica gel distributed throughout the aircraft in eighteen thousand bags.

It had been anticipated through most of the design, development and production of the Princess that BOAC would be the operator of the finished craft. The only doubt cast on this assumption was in 1951 when a press release announced that the three craft would be completed for the RAF as troop transports with the ability to carry out the task of nine troopships. However, later in the same year, a Capt. H.W.C. Alger of BOAC was seconded to the company. Capt. Alger was appointed a director of a company formed in January 1952 called the Princess Air Transport Company Limited, which was founded by Saunders-Roe Limited and Airwork Limited. Saunders-Roe bought-back the Airwork shares in October 1959. A few months after the successful first flight, in August 1952, Sir Miles Thomas, Chairman of BOAC, announced that the craft was now "out of date technically" and this could only be remedied by the fitment of the Orion engine. It was this announcement which caused the cocooning of the second and third craft. In November 1953 Aquila Airways offered to buy all three craft but for reasons never declared the Minister of Supply, Mr. Duncan Sandys, refused the offer.

Whilst the Princess aircraft were cocooned awaiting a decision on their fate, a number of interesting flying boat projects were investigated by the company even though the design team was now fully engaged on a new landplane fighter described in the next chapter.

The first of these related to a requirement for the Royal New Zealand Air Force. This project, numbered P176, investigated in 1953 was for an anti-submarine, maritime patrol and shipping strike flying boat. Proposed subsidiary duties were search and rescue, the carriage of troops and an emergency freighter. This 70,000 lb. boat was to have a radius of action of 750 miles at a cruise speed of 240 knots with a four hour patrol at this distance at a speed of 150 knots. Power was to be supplied by either twin RB 109 turboprops or two Napier Elands.

Three years later a consultant acting for the P & O shipping line requested a feasibility study into a 1000 passenger flying boat, the P192, for the route from England to Australia. It was concluded that the aircraft was indeed feasible at an AUW of 1,500,000 lb, a range of 1900 miles, powered by 24 Rolls Royce Conway bypass turbojet engines giving a cruise speed of 400 knots at 40,000 ft. The hull would be 318 ft. long, the span of the swept wing 313 ft.

In September 1957 the team investigated a land plane version of the Princess to be powered by six Rolls Royce Tyne turboprops for military transport duties as Project P.199.

This was a complex technical and logistics proposition involving the removal of the planing bottom with its buoyancy compartments. The lower pressurised section of the hull was modified to incorporate a main undercarriage consisting of two four-wheeled bogies retracting into fairings on the sides and a twin nose-wheel unit with power steering retracting into the hull. A massive loading ramp was to be incorporated in the rear fuselage for which

purpose the lower hull could be conveniently detached along the main construction joint.

This work was to be carried out at Cowes and it was proposed that the finished landplane would be floated some 20 miles with undercarriage retracted and temporarily sealed and, with beaching gear fitted, would be hauled ashore and prepared for flight at Thorney Island on the mainland.

The last major flying boat project was in 1958 when NATO initiated a medium range maritime patrol aircraft. With many similarities to the RNZAF project, the company submitted a flying boat of 73,000 lb. AUW, a cruise speed of 300 knots at 39,000 ft., powered by two Tyne turboprops. The hull was to be fitted with a retractable hydroski for landing in the open ocean in order to dip a variable depth asdic for submarine detection. The aircraft, the P208, would be capable of a radius of action of 1000 miles or an eight hour patrol.

Unfortunately none of these projects came to fruition.

The next potential customer for the Princess was the United States Navy who, in 1958, gave the company a substantial contract to investigate the feasibility of fitting the boat with nuclear powered engines. The design investigation showed this proposal with its obvious advantages for the testing of such engines was perfectly feasible. However, the development of the engines was cancelled by the U.S. government and in 1959 the project was abandoned.

In 1960 a newly created company called British Princess Flying Boats Limited was founded by a Mr. Halpin who wished to purchase all three boats, but only if the Government could guarantee route rights. Since this guarantee was not forthcoming he withdrew his offer.

Even in 1961, nearly ten years after the first flight, the Winder Corporation of Florida expressed an interest and, in co-operation with another company called Aero Spacelines, proposed to substantially modify these craft to carry Saturn V components across the United States. The proposal was to utilize the control cabin, the tail unit and the wings with a new fuselage to form a project called the "Super Guppy". In a complicated arrangement, another Bahamas registered company called Cargo Sales Limited of Cannon Street, London, acted on behalf of both these companies in the purchase of the craft. On 3rd January 1964 the company received a letter from the Director of Contracts at the Ministry of Aviation stating that a contract for the sale of the three Princess flying boats had been signed. The Super Guppy project required the support of NASA and by 1967 it became obvious that this was not forthcoming and the condition of the three craft had deteriorated. It was, therefore, reluctantly decided that the craft should be scrapped. The first craft was sold to Ferry Services and Supplies Limited, a Southampton scrap merchant, and was towed to Southampton in July 1967. The second two craft were dismantled at Calshot where they had been stored and were sold for scrap in 1965.

This sad end to the magnificent Princess marked the end of flying boat development in the United Kingdom and no boats of any significant size have been built anywhere in the world since this time. Henry Knowler had one final fling with the projected Duchess civil passenger craft, another beautiful flying boat, powered by pure jet engines but the die had been finally cast in favour of the landplane.

The P192 Project for P&O. A vast flying boat with 1000 passengers.

Saunders-Roe P.208. This medium-range maritime patrol aircraft to the NATO specification was the last major flying boat project for which a study in considerable detail was carried out.

The beautiful "Duchess", Henry Knowler's last flying boat design.

CHAPTER 7

ROCKET FIGHTERS TO SATELLITE LAUNCHERS

The company project and research team had continued to study high performance fighter designs following the completion of the SR.A1 design and the initiation of full detail design of the Princess. These studies and model tests included conventional hulls, hydrofoils, hydroskis and a hybrid of hydrofoils and hydroskis called skoils. This last system, for a water based fighter, seemed to lie in the improvement of retractable hydroskis. Ski efficiency was improved by the provision of greater area and a shorter lifting surface. The ski system proposed, with ingenious double hinges, retracted completely into the body of the aircraft. In order to provide full scale correlation of the theory and model tests it was decided to convert a standard production Auster J5G to a hydro-ski configuration. The trials in late 1954 and early 1955 proved that it was completely practical to operate the aircraft on hydroskis and good correlation between theory and experiment was obtained.

Whilst these studies continued, it was early in 1951 that the design team had substantially completed their work on the Princess and the company suggested to the Ministry of Supply that the possibility of a transonic water based fighter should be investigated. Obviously this would be a development of the SR.A1 successful aircraft. The suggestion was rejected by both the Services and the Ministry and the company decided to turn its attention to the design of a land-based rocket powered fighter capable of flight at 100,000 ft. After discussion of the project with the Services during the summer, the study concentrated on a fighter powered by both rocket and jet engines flying at an altitude of 80,000 ft. In February 1952 the Ministry issued specification F124T for a rocket powered interceptor, which was amended in May to include the possibility of adding a jet engine for additional power and permit the aircraft to return to base when the rocket fuel was exhausted. Clearly the company had a head start on its competitors and on 30th October 1952 was given an Instruction to Proceed with the design. To mark this outstanding success in a new field the company decided to immediately promote Henry Knowler to technical director and to appoint Maurice J. Brennan chief designer. The rocket was to be a de Havilland Spectre and the jet an Armstrong Siddeley Viper and the Ministry specification was now re-numbered F138D, the company allocated number being SR.53. On 5th May 1953 the formal Aircraft Design Conference was held at the Ministry of Supply and three days later the company was awarded the full contract for the design and construction of three aircraft. In January of the following year the number of aircraft was reduced to two.

The concept of mixed power units enabled the fighter to intercept a Mach 1.5 bomber at 60,000 ft. principally using the rocket engine and a subsonic Mach 0.97 bomber at 40,000 ft. primarily with the jet engine. The rocket was required to meet climb, turn and acceleration requirements and the jet the steady cruising Mach No. of 1.8 to safely exceed the anticipated speed of the supersonic bomber. It should be emphasised that the SR.53 was not, a research

project, but an aircraft designed to meet a full Royal Air Force requirement.

The completed aircraft had an all-up-weight of 20,100 lb, its delta wing had a span of 25 ft., the fuselage a length of 41 ft. and it had an all moving delta tailplane mounted on top of the swept fin. The phenomenal rate of climb at 50,000 ft. was 35,000 ft. per minute and its maximum speed 1,040 knots at 60,000 ft. The wing was of multi-web construction with four main spars and the fuselage of monocoque construction with skin and closely spaced stringers and four main bulkheads corresponding to the four main wing spars. The main armament of the fighter was to be two Blue Jay (the production version was known as Firestreak) air to air guided missiles one on each wing tip.

The ground crew had been warned of the hazards of handling High Test Peroxide, particularly in the quantities required for the operation of SR.53. Before the aircraft was completed and ready for flight trials the opportunity was taken to gain experience in the handling of this fluid and Saunders-Roe became the pioneers in the United Kingdom in this field. The refuelling crew was fully protected by specially designed Terylene clothing which was kept scrupulously clean as HTP in contact with dirt could start a fire. However, it needed only to be diluted with water to render it harmless. In addition, since it acts as a powerful antiseptic water pistols were included in special ground equipment so that any spillage could be washed away immediately. No difficulties were experienced with HTP tanks remaining fully fuelled for several days and nights. The team concluded, that refuelling presented no greater problem than handling other aircraft fuels and, that as a hazard inside hangars, in many ways, it was preferable to aviation gasoline.

The first aircraft, XD 145, was completed in the Columbine hangar in mid-June 1956. By the end of the month the wings had been removed, the aircraft loaded on to a Queen Mary transporter and conveyed to a special new hangar at the Aeroplane and Armament Experimental Establishment at Boscombe Down. The aircraft was re-assembled, all systems fully checked and the rocket engine first fired on 16th January 1957. Reliability checking of both engines followed enabling the first flight to take place on 16th May at the hands of the company's chief test pilot, Squadron Leader John S. Booth, DFC. The company had planned that most of the test flying of the SR.53 would be from Hurn Airport, where buildings had been leased and all necessary facilities installed including special storage buildings for HTP. However, the facilities were only used for a Meteor F Mk. 8 which was used for special instrument development tests such as the Rebecca 7 and Hannick Pitch and Roll Indicator. The longer runway at Boscombe Down was preferred for the SR.53 trials.

The second aircraft, XD151, successfully underwent its first flight on 18th December 1957. Unfortunately after eleven successful flights with this aircraft and thirty-one on the first aircraft, the second aircraft crashed on takeoff

Hydroski Development. The Auster J.5.G. modified by the
Helicopter Division Eastleigh carried out trials operating
from Bembridge aerodrome.

Hydroski Development. Water based trials took place from
the sands at Ryde initially with buoyancy canisters under
the wing-tips.

Hydroski Development. Landing in the Solent still fitted with buoyancy
canisters.

Hydroski Development. Operating from the River Medina in its final
configuration without buoyancy canisters.

Saunders-Roe SR.53. Ground test of the DH Spectre rocket motor provided a spectacular sight and sound, alleviated to some degree by the special detuner.

SR.53. Ready for a test flight at Boscombe Down.

Saunders-Roe SR.53. The first machine during an early test flight, in clean condition; wing-tip mounted missiles were flown later.

SR.53. At Farnborough on September 16th 1957, fitted with Blue Jay Missiles.

John Booth. Deputy chief test pilot from 1949 and chief test
pilot from February 1956 until his death in the accident to the
second SR.53 fighter on the 5th June 1958.

Saunders Roe SR177. Artists' impression of the SR.177 Interceptor
fighter with turbine and rocket propulsion.

killing John Booth on 5th June 1958. This accident was never satisfactorily explained, even after exhaustive investigations by the company and the RAE Accident Investigation Department. No fault was found with the aircraft, although impact with an airfield runway light pylon at the root of the wing resulted in considerable damage, nor could any evidence be found of pilot error on the part of Chief Test Pilot, John Booth. It was therefore concluded that test flying could be continued in the capable hands of new Chief Test Pilot, Lt. Cdr. Peter M. Lamb. The completion of the contract under Amendment No. 41 was now administered by the Aircraft Research Department of the Ministry of Aviation under Assistant Director R.A. Shaw. Fourteen further test flights on the first aircraft were undertaken bringing the total number to fifty-six with a total flying time of 22 hours 20 minutes, the last flight taking place in October 1959. During the trials the aircraft operated at speeds up to a Mach Number of 1.33, altitudes up to 55,000 ft. and achieved a phenomenal rate of climb of 29,000 feet per minute. Failure to achieve full performance was principally due to the reduction in performance of the Spectre 1A rocket engine from the specification of 8000 lb to 7000 lb. Peter Lamb ended his formal report on the handling qualities of the aircraft with this statement:

> "In conclusion it can be stated that the SR.53 is an extremely docile and exceedingly pleasant aircraft to fly, with very well harmonised controls within the flight envelope from sea level to 50,000 ft. and up to the present attained Mach number of 1.33."

On Friday, 29th July 1960, the company was informed by the Ministry of Aviation that the research programme had been abandoned and no further work was to be carried out on the aircraft. Later in the year the aircraft was prepared for transport by road to Rocket Propulsion Establishment, Westcott, where re-assembly was completed on 16th December 1960. The aircraft is now on display at the Aerospace Museum, RAF Cosford.

In parallel with the design and construction of SR.53 the company's engineers were continuing to investigate improvements in the operational effectiveness of the mixed power unit interceptor. Discussions with the Services and the Ministry of Supply and its Establishments determined that air to air radar, homing devices and associated electrical equipment independent of altitude were essential. Incorporation of these and other new equipment required a larger aircraft than the SR.53. Accordingly proposals were placed before the Ministry of Supply on 25th March 1954 and a design contract was placed with the company on the 18th May 1955. The aircraft was designated SR.177, the new numbering system being derived directly from that which had been used in the project office for some time. Maurice Brennan claimed that "the SR.177 is not just another fighter aircraft, it was designed as a weapon system in such a way that it could easily keep pace with systems developments and operational requirements of increasing severity. It was designed so that during each stage of development it could be a highly effective weapon capable of giving continuous protection against existing and anticipated threats."

The configuration of the SR.177 was basically the same as the SR.53 but the wing span was increased to just over 30 ft., the length to 50.5 ft. and the all-up-weight to between 26,000 lb. and 28,000 lb depending on the version. In the company's continuing investigations into the mixed unit concept its designers had come to the conclusion that a jet engine of much higher thrust than that proposed for the SR.53 would result in improved performance and give much greater flexibility of operation. To give this increased thrust the engine chosen was the de Havilland Gyron Junior DGJ.10-1 and the rocket engine was the latest version of the Spectre the DSPE 5. Armament was to be two Blue Jay missiles mounted on the wing tips as for the SR.53 with the alternative of two rocket batteries in cylindrical launchers. Two major versions of the aircraft were proposed, one for the Royal Air Force, and one for the Royal Navy for operation from aircraft carriers. In the case of the RAF version, alternative fuel tank arrangements were offered for normal warning sorties and for extended warning sorties.

Design proceeded apace to the satisfaction of the Ministry of Supply and on 4th September 1956 the company was given a formal contract to supply twenty-seven aircraft to specification F177D. The production of an initial batch of nine aircraft was authorised consisting of three basic development aircraft, three embodying RAF requirements OR.337 and three RN versions to NA.47. Twenty-three principal sub-contractors assisted with design and development, most of whom were also engaged on manufacture. New staff were engaged in all departments and a London design office was opened to ensure agreed programmes could be fulfilled. Nine foreign airforces expressed considerable interest in the aircraft and were given classified briefings on its performance. Most important of these was that of West Germany, where the outstanding rate of climb was obviously important in view of their proximity to the USSR. As a result of the Royal Air Force and Navy requirements combined with this important foreign interest serious discussions were commenced with Armstrong-Whitworth Aircraft Limited for the aircraft to be built under licence. Figures of two hundred aircraft for the German Air Force alone were being discussed at Ministerial level by both Governments.

In the midst of all this euphoria came the bombshell, the Government White Paper on Defence of April 1957. The Minister of Defence, Mr. Duncan Sandys, and his cabinet colleagues supported a policy that all British future fighter projects should be cancelled and defence against enemy air attack should be concentrated on guided missiles. The White Paper statement read "Fighter aircraft will in due course be replaced by a ground-to-air guided missile system".

Following the White Paper, the Ministry of Supply wrote to the company on 7th August 1957 cancelling the contract for the sixth and subsequent aircraft. In the next few months intensive discussions to save the project took place between the directors and senior staff of the company with the West German Air Force and high level government officials. These deliberations were actively assisted by the Minister of Supply Mr. Aubrey Jones, in discussions with the German Minister of Defence, Herr Strauss. On 16th December information was received from the Ministry of Supply that an official intent to purchase the aircraft would be received from the Germans. However, on 23rd December 1957 the company was advised that the German government had decided against

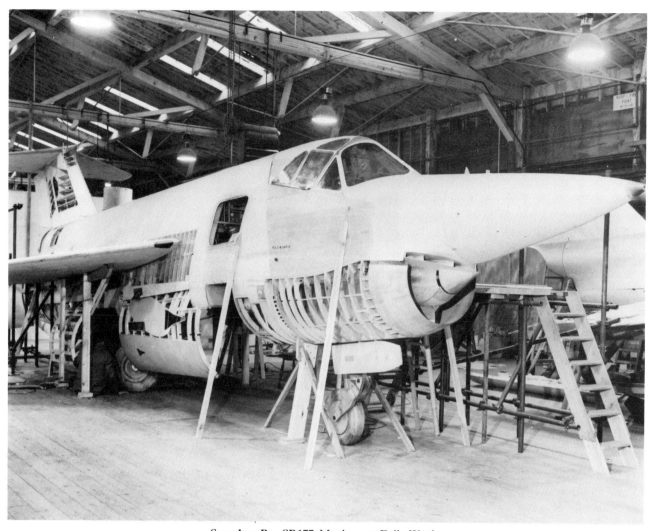

Saunders-Roe SR177. Mock-up at Folly Works.

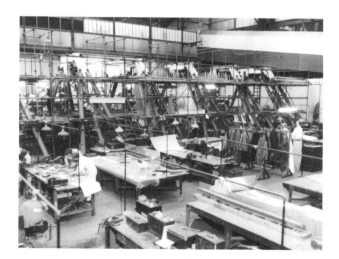

General view of SR.177 Wing Construction. 20th November 1957.

View of SR.177 Fuselage Construction 20th November 1957.

the SR.177. This was immediately followed on 24th December by cancellation of the Ministry of Supply contract for the first five aircraft. A most depressing Christmas present for the staff.

The last official statements by the company had indicated that design was 91% complete, some 8000 drawings having been issued, and that the structure of the first aircraft was approximately 50% completed. The first aircraft would be completed in November 1958. The employees were advised that 1470 members of staff were redundant. New techniques developed by the company, such as chemical etching, in full production in January 1956, were abandoned.

Project work on further developments of the mixed unit fighter concept, including new materials for the construction of this very high performance aircraft, was also abandoned never to re-start. Some details of these projects are given in Chapter 15.

Fortunately, this very serious blow was not the end of the company as other work was in progress. In the course of the design and development of the SR.53 and 177, the company's technical experts had worked closely and amicably with their contempories at the Royal Aircraft Establishment. This factor, combined with their knowledge of the Spectre rocket and high test peroxide, caused the guided weapons experts at RAE, led by Mr. J. Lyons, to invite the company, in March 1955, to design a guided weapons test vehicle. The directors expressed considerable interest and events moved so quickly that on 2nd June the company was given the instruction "to go full speed ahead" with a rocket powered vehicle to be called Black Knight. The vehicle was required in support of the British medium range ballistic missile, Blue Streak, to check atmospheric re-entry head materials and to gain experience in the design and development of large liquid fuelled rockets. On 29th July 1955 the full Instruction to Proceed was issued, under the reference "Super Priority"/6C.WPNS/627/CB.10(a), for the princely limit of liability of £125,000. This was increased, in February 1956, to £175,000 to cover design and development until completion, two prototypes for static tests, and the supply of six developed vehicles.

The vehicle would need the capability to reach an apogee altitude of 2000 miles, so that free fall would achieve an atmospheric re-entry speed similar to that to be achieved by Blue Streak. However, this would require a test range to cover a dispersion far greater than that available to the British Government. The range chosen was in Australia, with the firing point located at Woomera, some 250 miles NNW of Adelaide in South Australia. Black Knight was designed to achieve the demanded re-entry speeds of 12,000 - 18,000 ft/sec. within an apogee of 600 miles and a horizontal range of only 60 miles. This was achieved on the majority of Black Knight vehicles with two stages, the second stage arranged back to front so that its rocket nozzle lay just inside the tip of the vehicle nose cone. Following separation, as the second stage fell back to earth, the motor was fired, driving the head backwards into the atmosphere. For the flight of the missile during powered ascent, the basis of the control system was an autopilot with gyroscopes set to maintain a constant heading. To ensure that excessive dispersion around the desired impact point did not occur, a loose system of guidance by command link was provided.

Immediately following launch two ground controllers acquired and controlled the vehicle using information from four optical trackers equally disposed around the launch platform. At approximately 20,000 ft. a radar tracker took over from the optical system with the back-up of a powerful telescope. A radar transponder was housed in one fin pod and a lamp in another for the telescope after burn-out. Any serious dispersion from the desired trajectory was compensated for by a perturbation signal transmitted to the autopilot from a ground transmitter. This radio link between ground and missile provided for fuel 'cut-off' signals, should excessive malfunction of the missile occur, endangering personnel or instrumentation.

At the end of the following year, 1956, the basic vehicle design had been established and structural design completed. A month later construction work at High Down, near the Needles at the western end of the Isle of Wight, had been completed and the site was ready for static test firing of the vehicle. The early versions of Black Knight were single stage, nearly 33 ft. long, 3 ft. in diameter, propelled by four Armstrong Siddeley Gamma 201 rocket engines totalling 16,000 lbs of thrust and having a launch weight of 12,300 lbs. Control and stability were achieved by swivelling the four rocket chambers and the provision of four fixed fins at the base of the rocket. The main structure of the vehicle was principally formed by the outer shell of the fuel tanks which were thin welded aluminium alloy cylinders stabilised by tank pressurisation with no longitudinal stiffening apart from the first two vehicles which were of thinner tank material externally stiffened.

The first prototype vehicle was completed in remarkably short time and was test fired at the High Down site on 16th April 1957, three months less than two years after first receiving the contract. The firing was essentially successful and comprehensive further testing followed and was completed in June. The vehicle was then prepared for despatch, by air, to Australia and arrived there on 12th August. This prototype was used to ensure that all the facilities at Woomera were carefully checked before the launch of the first production vehicle. The launch facilities were essentially duplicates of those at High Down and were built by the company. The facilities were manned by staff of Saunders-Roe, RAE, de Havilland Aircraft Company and Armstrong Siddeley. The first production vehicle was successfully launched on 7th September 1958, just over three years from receiving the contract. It was at this time that the Chief Designer, Maurice Brennan decided to join a larger company and his deputy, Richard Stanton-Jones, took over the post.

The successful launches of Black Knight from 1958, which all took place under the clear skies of Woomera, had showed some unexpected spectacular optical effects as the test heads re-entered the atmosphere. Specialised US equipment was used in a co-operative programme called "Gaslight" to study these re-entry glows. In 1962 this programme was expanded into an agreement between the UK, the US and Australia known as "Project Dazzle". The UK led the programme and supplied Black Knight vehicles, the US provided special optical ground equipment and Australia the ground personnel and range equipment. The effect of various head shapes and materials was investigated in this important project which led to the

High Down Test Site, the Needles. This facility was established for the static testing of the Black Knight and Black Arrow rocket powered test vehicles.

Black Arrow. Assembling the separate sections of the first and second stages.

Test firing of the Black Arrow at High Down, Isle of Wight. 1967

Black Knight re-entry test vehicle. Two of these on the launching pads at the test site at Woomera in Australia. Various alternative heads for different weights and types of payload were carried. Extensive ground installations were needed including the servicing gantry between the two rockets which gave access to the various levels.

Black Arrow. Launch at Woomera, South Australia, on 28th October 1971 carrying the satellite Prospero into orbit.

Stanford Research Institute of California designing a special high power radar, with an 86 ft diameter dish, to study the head and its wake on re-entry to the atmosphere.

Eight more successful flights of the single stage Black Knight were made from the Woomera site, achieving an apogee of 600 miles with an impact point only 60 miles down-range but achieving the design re-entry speeds of 12,000 ft. per second. Some of these single stage vehicles were used for university space research on the ionosphere. The last of this Black Knight standard was fired on 17th October 1963.

Meanwhile design and development of a two stage version to achieve re-entry speeds of 18,000 ft. per sec. was proceeding apace. The second stage was to be powered by a Bristol Aerojet Cuckoo solid fuel rocket motor giving a thrust of 20,000 lb for four seconds. The first stage Gamma 201 had been upgraded to the 301 with over 20% more thrust. In addition, it was proposed to increase the first stage diameter from 36ins. to 54ins. and the all-up-weight would then rise to 14,000 lb. In the event, the design of the vehicle with increased diameter first stage was completed, but manufacture was indefinitely post-poned. Without this increase in diameter, the first of these two-stage versions was successfully launched on 24th May 1960, followed by a further thirteen launches, the last occurring on 25th November 1965. The re-entry pro-gramme was now completed. Thus a total of 22 Black Knights were successfully launched, without failure; an unequalled record for space launchers.

In the last few years of the Black Knight programme, the Government had decided to convert the Blue Streak ballistic missile to the first stage of a satellite launching vehicle. Included in the studies for the second stage of this launcher was a strengthened variant of Black Arrow. This combination, with a solid propellant third stage, was known as Black Prince. This project never came to fruition and the day was won by a design known as Europa 1. The Royal Aircraft Establishment, however, continued its studies of an all-British low cost satellite launcher based entirely on Black Knight which was to be called Black Arrow. The government order for this satellite launcher was placed in April 1966. This same month brought the appointment of a new Chief Designer, Raymond L. Wheeler, one of the authors of this book, Richard Stanton-Jones becoming Deputy Managing Director and Technical Director.

Whilst the Black Knight development programme may look relatively simple from the viewpoint of 1989, in fact it was a complex challenge for its time and broke much new technological ground ahead of United States launcher programmes.

Black Arrow was to be a three stage launcher based on Black Knight technology in order to give maximum reliability. The take off all-up-weight of 40,000 lb and 43 ft. long, was intended to enable the vehicle to put a 320 lb satellite into a low polar orbit. The total thrust at lift-off of 50,000 lb was to be provided by eight Rolls Royce Gamma 2 combustion chambers gimballed in pairs to give pitch, roll and yaw control in a similar manner to Black Knight. The first stage diameter was increased to just under 6 ft 7 in. from the 3 ft. of Black Knight, fuel remaining as high test peroxide and kerosene. The second stage was 4 ft. 6 in diameter and was powered by two

Rolls Royce Gamma combustion chambers with extended nozzles to give the higher expansion ratio required for optimum performance at high altitude. These two chambers were also gimballed to give pitch, roll and yaw control. Separation was achieved with explosive bolts and four "Siskin" solid propellent motors. Positive separation of the 1st and 2nd stages was necessary with the "Siskin" motors because of the long tail off of threat from the catalyst in the main propulsion engines. "All-burnt" of the second stage occurred out of the earth's atmosphere and the second and third stages now coasted for some $4\frac{1}{2}$ minutes. Attitude control in this period was provided by a combination of a Ferranti inertial platform and auxiliary nitrogen gas jets. The third stage, which was fired at apogee so that orbital velocity could be achieved, was propelled by a solid fuelled Waxwing rocket motor, developed by the Rocket Propulsion Establishment at Westcott, the motor case and nozzle being manufactured by Bristol Aerojet Limited.

As was usual for this enterprising company, design, development and manufacture of the vehicle, and parallel modification of the test site on the Isle of Wight and the launch site at Woomera, had been completed in only three years. Two development launches were planned and the first took place in July 1969. Both these development, sub-orbital launches, whilst substantially successful, revealed the necessity for modifications to the first production vehicle. On 28th October 1971 this first production vehicle successfully launched a technology satellite, Prospero, manufactured by Marconi, into a polar orbit. This satellite continued to function on command for many years and remains in orbit. The RAE planned significant developments of Black Arrow with use of four strap-on boosters and high pressure Gamma combustion chambers but government planners had other ideas. As one of the leading RAE space experts, H.G.R. Robinson, was to write in 1981:

"This great achievement in terms of cost effective technology was a bitter sweet affair for the contractors and the RAE, since the project had been cancelled shortly before the successful launching, ending the current UK capability for launching satellites."

The Black Arrow contract was not finally closed until June 1972 in order to clear the Isle of Wight and Woomera test and launch sites and store a completed Black Arrow, which is now on display at the Science Museum in South Kensington.

The experience of the company in satellite launchers led them to win a contract, in 1971, for satellite fairings for the French led Diamant B launcher programme. These were suitably modified Black Arrow steel capped magnesium alloy fairings using the simple and successful explosive bolts and separator springs. The fairings were also completely successful in the Diamant programme and the company hoped to continue this success in the Ariane developments which were to follow. Unfortunately, the United Kingdom funding of these early Ariane launchers was inadequate to support the company's bids and the satellite fairing technology was lost to the Contraves company of Switzerland.

Within a few months of the termination of the Black Arrow contract, in November 1972, the company was awarded a Ministry of Defence contract for the design, development and production of a space systems test

Falstaff launch imminent

Falstaff. One of the six successful firings during 1974/8.

vehicle. The company was to act as the Vehicle Design Authority and the vehicle, code named Falstaff by the MOD, was given the Project No. AP.135. The vehicle was based on a single stage solid fuelled rocket 17 ft. long and 3 ft. in diameter, called Stonechat, which was developed and supplied by the Rocket Propulsion Establishment, Westcott. Mounted on the nozzle end of the rocket were four large fins with a span of 14 ft. On the opposite end of the rocket was mounted the specialised equipment under test. This equipment was mounted on the rocket motor by means of a special adaptor bay and a payload separation bay which carried the attitude control units operating small control jets and the separation explosive bolts and rockets. The experiment was protected from the kinetic heating in the atmosphere by deployable fairing technology already developed on Black Arrow and Diamant B. Overall length of the vehicle was nearly 31 ft. and the all-up-weight some 15,000 lb. Falstaff could launch an experimental payload weighing 1200 lb to an apogee of fifty miles allowing the payload to free fall for at least 120 seconds. During the course of the programme, six vehicles were launched, each experiment being completely successful leading to the scrapping of four remaining reserve vehicles. In addition to the company's responsibility for the vehicle itself, it was prime contractor for the design, manufacture, installation and in-field support of the ground launcher, ground check-out and launch control equipment. This highly successful programme was completed and the contract closed in 1982.

The company, renamed Westland Aerospace in November 1985, made determined efforts to obtain work on significant items of the European Ariane 5 satellite launcher with the backing of the newly formed British National Space Centre. Unfortunately having won three major elements of the new launcher against fierce competition from major European Companies the Government decided in early 1988 to withdraw its support for the project.

Airborne Lifeboat Mark III under sail. Showing typical operation following a parachute descent from a Shackleton aircraft.

CHAPTER 8

DIVERSIFICATION LEADING TO HELICOPTERS, HOVERCRAFT AND REORGANISATION

In 1945 the company's aircraft activities had been returned from wartime dispersal at Beaumaris to the established premises at Cowes. The Beaumaris facilities were taken over by the company's engineering and boat-building subsidiary, then known as Saunders Engineering & Shipyard Limited, which was moved from Edmonton. Later this name was altered to Saunders-Roe (Anglesey) Limited. Many of the aircraft personnel had elected to remain at Beaumaris and this helped to decide the division to specialise in the application of light alloy construction in the light engineering, marine and general aviation fields. Patrol boats, motor torpedo boats, torpedo tubes, air transportable pontoons and motor tugs, and airborne lifeboats were built in this material for the Admiralty and the Ministry of Supply. The Mark III version of the airborne lifeboat was designed to be fitted to the Avro Shackleton aircraft and was produced in quantity to Ministry of Supply Specification AL/3 in the early 1950s. Work of this nature continued until 1959 when the division was sold to the Hawker Siddeley Group.

An interesting project (No. P.108) developed from the philosophy of the lifeboat work when, in 1949, the aircraft design team at Cowes carried out private venture studies on an airborne glider lifeboat which could jettison its wings and tail unit on landing on the water. It was realised that this idea could be developed for the transportation of personnel and equipment in time of war for raiding enemy coastal batteries and other shore facilities. The Government became interested in the concept and, in September 1951, the Ministry of Supply issued a Staff Requirement for an Airborne Raiding Craft. The requirement called for two designs, both capable of performing similar duties, the Mark 1 with a payload of 8 personnel plus 500 lb of stores and the Mark 2 with 35 personnel and 150 lb of stores. The project number was P.147 and the hull portion called the Sea Raider. The Mark 1 had a span of 60 ft, length 49 ft and an all-up-weight of 10,000 lb, whereas the Mark 2 had a span of 110 ft, length 79 ft and all-up-weight of 30,000 lb. The company also submitted a compromise design between the Mark 1 and 2, which they called the Flying Ant. This glider carried 17 personnel and 700 lb of stores, had a span of 77 ft, length 57 ft, an all-up-weight of 14,500 lb and power at sea was provided by two Rover V-6 engines. Unfortunately, after intensive design and tank and wind tunnel testing and further design proposals the Ministry decided not to proceed with the project.

In the immediate post-war years the company realised that in order to maintain the necessary high quality staff required by its increasingly complex business, its training facilities would need to be considerably expanded. Accordingly, under V.T. Stevenson as manager, a Saunders-Roe Group Technical College with full facilities, including accommodation, was set up at Osborne Works. It even had its own Chaplain, the first of whom was the Rev. R. V. Scruby. The college trained some three hundred apprentices annually drawn from all over the United Kingdom, encouraging technical apprentices to reach degree level. Company training continues to maintain a high reputation for quality.

In the early 1950s, when manufacture of the Princess flying boats had been completed and work on the SR.53 was far from sufficient to employ the total workforce, the company's long working relationship with the Vickers group was to prove of significant benefit. In 1951, the two companies agreed terms for the manufacture of Viscount wings. These were built in the Eastleigh factory, where 400 sets were completed by the end of the contract in 1959. On 30th March 1954 an order was accepted for the design and lofting of the Viscount fuselage. In the Cowes plant, 105 sets of pressurised crew cabins, bomb doors, elevators, rudders and ailerons for the Valiant bomber were manufactured and supplied to Weybridge between 1951 and 1956. A further major task was the design and manufacture of the rear fuselage and tail unit of the Vickers 1000. One set was supplied and the second partially completed when the project was abandoned in 1955. In the same period, tailplanes and other minor components were manufactured for the Supermarine Swift.

Another concern from which major sub-contracts were obtained at this time was the de Havilland Aircraft company, which became a major shareholder in December 1956 through its parent de Havilland Holdings Limited. The following year the Board elected F.E.M. St. Barbe as their representative. Some 300 sets of Vampire wings, tailplanes and elevators, followed by production of Venom tailplanes and elevators, were manufactured in the Eastleigh factory for de Havilland under contract from Folland. More important for the future, was the work carried out on the Comet aircraft directly for de Havilland. Various spares were manufactured for the Comet I and II and the pilot's cabin structure and outer wings for the Comet IV which involved considerable metal to metal bonding with Redux adhesive. Metal to metal bonding was to become a major activity of the company in the future. Aircraft sub-contract metal to metal bonding continues to the present day and all the company's hovercraft made substantial use of this method of construction. Complex ground test equipment for the Blue Jay air to air missile electronic system and the corresponding aircraft system was also designed and manufactured at Cowes.

Yet another aircraft company for which considerable sub-contract work was carried out was English Electric Aviation Limited, Guided Weapons Division at Stevenage and Luton. Structure for the early D3/D4 Thunderbird ground to air missiles was manufactured, but more important was the development and manufacture of the mobile ground support equipment for the in-service W1 Thunderbirds. This consisted of racks of electronic equipment plus hydraulic and pneumatic panels which were then built into the field workshop vehicles, the field

Vickers Viscount Wings. Production of wings for this very successful transport aircraft was carried out at Eastleigh for a long period in the nineteen- fifties.

Vickers Valiant front fuselage. The pressurised crew compartment as produced at Cowes ready for despatch to Weybridge.

Vickers V. 1000. Saunders-Roe designed and constructed the rear fuselage cone and tail fin for the prototype of this long-range jet transport which was abandoned in 1955 before it was completed.

DH. Vampire Wings under construction at Eastleigh. 27th July 1950

Supermarine. Swift Shop, Folly Works, Whippingham. 28th February 1955

Blue Jay Air-to-Air Missile Electronic ground test equipment.

De Havilland Comet. Control cabin under construction at East Cowes in the 1950s.

Cierva W.11 Air Horse. One of the two helicopter types under development when Saunders-Roe acquired the Cierva Co. in 1951. The prototype was lost in an accident in 1950 before the acquisition of the company by Saunders-Roe. The second machine WA 555 carried out a considerable tethered flying and ground running programme and a limited amount of flying before the type was abandoned in 1953.

Cierva W.14 Skeeter. The first of two machines built by the Cierva company and flown in 1948. Later machines had monocoque rear fuselages and many other changes were progressively introduced.

Saunders-Roe Skeeter. During Service Trials with company pilot Ken Reed at the controls the Mk.6 Skeeter XK.964/G-ANMI.

Skeeter Helicopters. Production at the Eastleigh Works.

assembly test point vehicles and the sensitivity test vehicles. The power supplies trailer was a 2 ton flatbed four wheeled trailer on which were mounted an electrical generator, an air compressor unit and a hydraulic pump unit, with their respective control panels, cable and hose reels, etc., to provide power to the missile during its test and pre-launch phases. At the firing site, the equipment in the vehicles obtained its primary power from an electrical generator on a second trailer.

Factory test equipment for the Blue Water ground to ground intermediate range missile and the Rapier ground launched anti-aircraft missile was produced. Work for English Electric Aviation Limited, later to become part of British Aircraft Corporation Limited, began in 1954 and continued into the 1970s. At its peak, it provided employment for 80 or more people and gave them valuable work experience in the electronics and mechanical engineering fields.

Apart from Saunders-Roe's entrepreneurial activities described in previous chapters, and the above aircraft sub-contract work, in the same period, the nineteen fifties, the company was engaged in many other diverse activities. These varied from the design and build of a hydrofoil boat, called Bras d'Or, for the Canadian Government to the manufacture of washing machines under contract! Other work covered the production of buses, bomb carriers and rotary bomb dispensers and even included golf clubs and hockey sticks! This account of a myriad of activity does not fully cover the activities at Beaumaris and makes no mention of Saro Laminated Products which was very active with both wood and plastic sheet materials. A summary of the diverse products outside the aircraft field manufactured by the company in this period is given in Appendix 9.

Early in 1958 the company was offered three major aircraft opportunities. Miles Aircraft Limited offered a licence to build their Caravan aircraft, later to be accepted by Shorts and to be built as the Skyvan and its developments the Shorts 330 and 360. The second opportunity was to build the Percival EP9 and the third a small agricultural crop spraying aircraft for Britten Norman Limited (Saunders-Roe Project P.204). However, it was decided at a board meeting on 22nd May 1958 that the investment required was "not justified by the prospects". The irony of this rejection is that the company has built the inner wings of the Shorts 330/360s for several years!

At the same Board Meeting, Saro Structures Limited was formed. This company undertook the construction of aluminium roofs, some domed, and a free standing three hundred and fifty foot high radio transmitter for the then British Somaliland. Also, on 23rd September 1958, Saro Nuclear Enterprises Limited was formed to exploit the growing national interest in nuclear engineering. This company still exists as Saunders-Roe Developments Limited making such components as Beta Lights, very low level nuclear lighting devices, which were first manufactured at Osborne Works.

Another significant development occurred in October 1948, when electronics came seriously into the activities of the company. The foil strain gauge was invented by this new department and was jointly produced by them and Technograph Printed Circuits Limited. By 1953 the department had achieved the status of a Division designing and manufacturing accurate displacement meters,

phase meters, vibration analysis equipment, electronic analogue computers and servo systems, amplifiers, special purpose oscillators, special generators and test instruments. An aircraft simulator for the SR.53 and automatic sequence ground equipment for Black Knight and Black Arrow were included in their work for the main activities of the company.

In the hectic period of activity in the late 1940s and the 1950s, board members, in addition to those already included mentioned, J.L. Walsh, W.A.F. Chambers, the Rt. Hon. Viscount Cowdray, H.F.R. Lubbock, D.N. Wyatt, Walter Browning, who was Works Director for much of the period, and P.D. Irons who was Finance Director for the last few years.

An event which was to be of great significance for the future of the Saunders-Roe group of companies occurred on the 24th January 1951, when the Cierva company at Eastleigh was acquired. This company, which was developing two types of helicopter was taken over together with the premises and two thirds of the work force. The two helicopter types were at opposite ends of the scale, the larger, known as the W.11 Air Horse, was a three rotor machine powered by a Rolls-Royce Merlin engine, the first prototype of which had crashed in 1950 after 69 hours flying, with fatal results to the crew. The second machine was completed in the early period of the takeover and carried out limited ground testing and tethered flying for basic information only. The project was then abandoned and the prototype dismantled and stored. The smaller machine, the Cierva W.14, had first flown at the end of 1948 and at the time of the takeover had reached the stage where a Ministry order for three prototype Mk.3 & 4 machines had been received and were in the course of manufacture, under the name of Skeeter. This was the beginning of a long period of development overcoming severe resonance problems and meeting the service requirements. Eventually ten development machines, including the two Cierva-built prototypes, were completed before it was possible to arrive at a suitable standard for service use. Various versions of this helicopter were built, mainly for the Army, with a few for civilian use and Mks 50 and 51 were versions supplied to the German Army and Navy, bringing the total to 78, in addition to the ten development aircraft, when production ceased in 1960. Design responsibility was initially with M.J. Brennan but later T.L. Ciastula was established as the Chief Designer of the Helicopter Division. The General Manager of the Division was Hugh Gordon who had joined the company from BEA in the summer of 1953.

In order to enhance the performance of the Skeeter in conditions of heat and high humidity, trials with a booster system were undertaken, with partial success, but this method was not adopted for service and the solution was found in the design of a new helicopter, the P.531. Two prototypes of this new helicopter were designed and built in seven months with considerable encouragement from the Director General of Aircraft Research and Development at the Ministry of Supply, Mr. Lewis Boddington. Limited production of this helicopter, to be known as the Sprite, was planned when Saunders-Roe was acquired by Westland in July 1959. Production was moved elsewhere so that this helicopter was to see long and successful service later with the Royal Navy as the Westland Wasp and as the Scout for the Army.

Eastleigh Works. The centre of helicopter operations with the prototype Skeeter Mk.5 above.

Saunders-Roe Pulse Jets P.J.1 and P.J.2. Two sizes of these power units were designed in 1953 with thrusts of 45lbs. and 120lbs. respectively. The illustrations show the larger of these mounted for trials as a tip-mounted booster for helicopters. Other applications were envisaged for guided missiles and as take-off units for sailplanes.

Close up of Pulse Jet, P.J.2.

Saunders-Roe P.531 Helicopter. The second machine G-APNV first flew in September 1958 was developed from Mk.0 to Mk.1 and as a Naval prototype.

The first Hovercraft. SR.NI was built for research purposes and was the subject of a number of changes in the course of the trials, from which basic design principles for future Hovercraft were evolved.

SR.N2 The second type of Hovercraft. The SR.N2 could seat 68 passengers and limited use was made of the type under operating conditions. This was carried out under the auspices of Hovertransport Ltd, before the craft was finally broken up.

SR.N3 Hovercraft. Operated by the Inter-Services Hovercraft Trials Unit, XS.655 was the sole example of the type. Used by the Royal Navy to prove the invulnerability of hovercraft to mine explosions.

SR.N5 Hovercraft. Designed for general purpose duties, search and rescue or for the carriage of fifteen passengers. In service in Canada.

SR.N6 Winchester Hovercraft. Stretched version of SR.N5 designed for patrol, search and rescue and to carry thirty-eight passengers. In service in Canada, Saudi Arabia and Iran.

SR.N6 Mark 1S the Super Six, with Twin Propellers.
Stretched version of the SR.N6 to carry fifty-eight passengers. Also used for patrol duties in Iraq.

SR.N4 Mark 2 Mountbatten. Large open-sea hovercraft designed to carry 282 passengers and 37 cars. Operates all-the-year-round across the English Channel.

The Queen, Lord Louis Mountbatten, Prince Andrew & Viscount Linley descending the steps of an SR.N4 during a visit to British Hovercraft Corporation on August 9th 1968.

In seeking new activities for the company, in 1953 the helicopter division built the Medina outboard motor for small boats and designed and tested pulse-jet units and produced schemes for a 50 passenger tandem rotor helicopter. At the other extreme, the one-man Hiller Rotorcycle XROE-1 was brought over from the United States by Helicop-Air, the European agents for Hiller, in 1958, and after investigations at Eastleigh the company's tender for the manufacture of ten YROE-1 machines for the US Marine Corps was accepted. The first of these was flown on the 19th October 1959 by Phil Johnston of Hiller, all ten being completed early in 1960. Sales of the Rotorcycle for civil operations, as evidenced by the tentative registration of G-APYF, did not follow.

The Defence White Paper of 1957 had included the requirement that the aircraft industry should re-organise itself into small groups. The Westland Aircraft Limited board reacted by negotiating to take over the nation's helicopter interests. As this coincided with the wish of Sir Arthur Gouge, a major shareholder, to realise his assets it was finally agreed to sell the whole company. The Board Meeting of 23rd July 1959 records that agreement had been reached between Westland Aircraft, the Gouge and Pearson interests and Saunders-Roe Limited on the one hand and de Havilland and Saunders-Roe on the other. Under this agreement de Havilland acquired Saunders-Roe (Anglesey) Limited and Saro Laminated Wood Products Limited and Westland Aircraft Limited the remainder of Saunders-Roe Limited, including, of course, the helicopter division. Although helicopter manufacture continued at Eastleigh for a time, eventually the work was transferred to their Fairey Division at Hayes and White Waltham and the Eastleigh facility closed down. At the next Board Meeting on the 18th August, Mr. Eric Mensforth and Mr. E.C. Wheeldon, both of Westland Aircraft, were made chairman and deputy chairman respectively and Captain E.D. Clarke was made a director of Westland Aircraft limited; an appointment from which he resigned on 1st March 1960. Another Saunders-Roe director at the time of the take-over, Henry (Harry) W.D. Winkworth, was to become a Westland director on 6th June 1962 resigning on 30th September 1966. Subsequent meetings were routine to keep the name of the company alive.

After the takeover, Maurice Hugh Charles Gordon (Hugh), who had been General Manager at Eastleigh was appointed General Manager of the newly formed Saunders-Roe Division of Westland Aircraft Limited. He held the post until 9th October 1961, when he was appointed Sales Director of Westland Aircraft. He was followed by Eric F. Gilberthorpe, who became Works Director when British Hovercraft Corporation Limited was formed in 1966, retiring on 30th September 1969. The next works director was Arthur N. Street, who resigned on 1st May 1975, his place being taken by John McGarity who remained on the board for twelve years until his retirement.

In 1950, whilst the company was engaged in the incredibly varied activities described earlier in this chapter and in the previous chapter, a gentleman by the name of Christopher Cockerell decided that he needed a change from radio engineering, with Marconi. He acquired a boatyard on the Broads and his active inventor's mind soon decided that boats could be designed to use much less power if an air cushion was created under the craft.

Subsequent events have been described by many authors and need not be repeated here, sufficient to say in this context that after much experiment and walking of the corridors of power in Whitehall an Assistant Director -Aircraft Research in the Ministry of Supply, Mr. R.A. Shaw, decided to investigate Cockerell's invention by awarding a study contract.

Saunders-Roe was chosen to be the first contractor because of its considerable hydrodynamic and aerodynamic experience and test facilities and a contract was placed in 1957. Later in the same year NRDC decided to purchase Cockerell's patent rights and Saunders-Roe was awarded a contract in 1958 to build the first hovercraft, later designated the SR.N1.

Cockerell's principle which created a full air cushion under the vehicle enabling it to operate over both water and land was regarded at the time as an exciting new form of transport with much promise for the future. Only eight months later, on 11th June 1959, the craft was launched and, incredibly, only some five weeks later on the 50th Anniversary of Bleriot's first cross-Channel flight, 25th July, the SR.N1 made the Channel crossing from Calais to Dover. The SR.N1 (Saunders-Roe Nautical No. 1) was powered by an Alvis Leonides radial engine driving an axial fan for both lift and thrust and weighing 3 tons. The machine was extensively modified as the technology developed including the fitting of a Bristol Siddeley Viper pure jet engine with which it achieved a speed of 66 knots with the weight having doubled.

The full story of this crossing and subsequent technical developments will be part of a separate work dealing with the company's marine history and only matters affecting the company itself will be dealt with in this volume.

In the next six years, the company developed the SR.N2 passenger craft, the SR.N3 military craft, the SR.N5 and 6 general purpose craft which were produced in quantity and began development of the SR.N4 cross-Channel passenger/car craft, still the world's largest hovercraft.

Meanwhile the NRDC had decided to actively promote hovercraft development and formed a subsidiary company called Hovercraft Development Limited which owned all Cockerell's patents with Christopher Cockerell as its first managing director. This company expanded very quickly with extensive facilities and engineers who designed and built experimental craft.

Also active in the field at this time was the Vickers Supermarine company who also designed and built craft. However, the Government in its wisdom decided that the market for hovercraft was not large enough to sustain these three companies and encouraged them to merge. Hence, on 6th December 1966 British Hovercraft Corporation was formed from the Saunders-Roe Division of Westland and the hovercraft activities of Vickers Supermarine and the Government decided to wind down the activities of Hovercraft Development Limited.

This new company was 65% owned by Westland Aircraft Limited, 25% by Vickers Limited and 10% by NRDC and was formed by changing the name of a Vickers subsidiary, Vickers (Aviation) Limited, to British Hovercraft Corporation Limited. Christopher Cockerell was vehemently opposed to this decision and resigned from his position with Hovercraft Development Limited. Subsequently Westland began to buy the interests of their two partners and by 1971 wholly owned the company.

BH.7 Mark 4 Wellington Military Hovercraft. Used for logistic support by the Iranian Navy.

Central Electricity Generating Board On-the-road Air Cushion Assisted Transporter. Used to convey generating equipment weighing up to 400 tons across country bridges.

SR.N4 Mark 3 Mountbatten, the Super Four. The world's largest hovercraft. Stretched version of the Mark 2. Capable of carrying 418 passengers and up to 60 cars. Also operates all-the-year-round across the English Channel.

AP.1-88. Diesel engined hovercraft designed to carry up to 100 passengers. Seen here operating over ice between Malmo and Copenhagen. Also operates across the Solent and in Australia.

AP.1-88. Open-decked version designed for the Canadian Coastguard on maintenance of marine navigation aids, search and rescue and ice breaking duties.

Shorts Belfast Military Aircraft Freighter. The rear fuselage and tail designed by the company. The ramp was manufactured at East Cowes.

113

Further new craft were designed and built accompanied by very active and original research and development of the hovercraft principle, particularly the complex technology involved in the flexible "skirts" surrounding and under the vehicle. A new military design, the BH.7, was funded by the Ministry of Technology in 1967 and also bought by the Imperial Iranian Navy. At the same time the cross-Channel 200 ton SR.N4 was completed and in the next few years six were operating across the Channel. Later, in February 1976, the company received a contract to stretch the SR.N4 to 300 tons and equip it with a new skirt system. The hovercraft team, at Cowes was honoured by the 1978 Award for Innovation in Transport of the Worshipful Company of Coach Builders and Coach Harness Makers. This distinguished award was given for the outstanding increase in performance and comfort in the design and development of the SR.N4 Mk.3, or Super 4, cross-Channel hovercraft. A Seaspeed Super 4 sailed to the Pool of London to mark the presentation ceremony. The company was also honoured, in this period of intensive hovercraft and space launcher development, by two visits by Her Majesty the Queen. The first, accompanied by the Duke of Edinburgh and Lord Louis Mountbatten, took place on 26th July 1965. On the second, on 9th August 1968, she was accompanied by Lord Louis, Prince Charles, Prince Andrew and Viscount Linley.

The company has played a considerable part in the development of amphibious hovercraft in the United States. Through it licencees, the Bell Aerospace, Textron Company, the U.S. Army developed the L.A.C.V. 30 (Lighter Air Cushion Vehicle - 30 tons) logistic support craft carrying a thirty ton payload from ship to shore was developed directly from SRN.6 technology. The U.S. Navy L.C.A.C. (Landing Craft, Air Cushion) tank landing craft utilizes SRN.4 Mk.3 skirt technology in order to carry a main battle tank from inside large amphibious support ships across the beach several miles inland.

The latest hovercraft, a new diesel powered craft, the 40 ton AP.1-88, was initiated in April 1981 with an unusual tripartite contract between NRDC, Hovertravel, a company operating hovercraft across the Solent, and British Hovercraft Corporation. Subsequently, eight of these craft have been completed and are operating in six countries.

Even during these years of intensive effort to develop hovercraft the company continued with sub-contract aircraft work. In 1960 the company undertook the major task of the design of the complete rear fuselage and tail unit of the Shorts Belfast military freighter for the Royal Air Force. This large aircraft, with an enormous cut-away in the rear fuselage to accommodate a loading ramp for tanks, presented considerable structural problems for analysts and designers. The task was completed in 1964 and the company manufactured thirteen loading ramps for the craft delivered to the RAF.

Britten Norman Limited was struggling to build adequate numbers of their Islander aircraft in 1967/68 and in March 1968 contracted with the company to build the aircraft with Britten Norman providing the internal trim and the product support. By the time Britten Norman's financial collapse came in July 1972, 363 aircraft had been completed and kits for 29 more were ready for assembly. Unfortunately the new owners, Fairey SA of Belgium, transferred production to Belgium and Rumania.

The company was also fortunate that following the take-over by Westland in 1959 considerable manufacturing work on details and sub-assemblies and detail design work on all their helicopters was obtained at an early stage and has continued to the present time. The most important helicopter work was given to the company in 1970, when Westland decided that responsibility for all Ministry of Defence support work on the Wessex helicopter should be transferred to Cowes. This was agreed with the MOD and all Wessex support contracts have been held at Cowes ever since. This has included all post design work on modifications, including new avionic fits, but excluding responsibility for support and spares of rotating components.

Over most of the years covered by this chapter, fibre reinforced plastics formed an increasingly important part of the company's business. Many large components for all the hovercraft were made in glass reinforced plastic, including sandwich construction. Cowes acquired the reputation in the late 60s as being the Westland Group experts in reinforced plastic construction, making many helicopter components.

In 1983 the company and Westland Group boards made the far sighted decision to convert the main factory building at Falcon Yard into a modern, high technology, reinforced plastics and bonding plant for aerospace components. Ironically this site had been acquired in 1966 when the famous Cowes shipyard of John Samuel White & Company Limited was forced into liquidation. The yard had been purchased immediately following the formation of British Hovercraft Corporation to build 90 knot hovercraft frigates, a project which, sadly, never materialised. This new facility is now complete, although further improvements are continually being added, and manufacturing of components for many customers in the United Kingdom, Europe, Canada and the United States proceeds apace.

In 1985 the Westland Group found itself in severe financial difficulties and was financially restructured with a major investment by the United Technologies Corporation of the United States and Fiat of Italy. The new main board decided that the Group should be reorganised. All the varied work at Cowes is administered by a company called Westland Aerospace Limited. Under this administrative company are three operating companies. Mr. Christopher C. Gustar, who joined Saunders-Roe as an apprentice in 1962, was appointed the Managing Director of the new company.

The largest of these is called Westland Aerostructures Limited engaged in the manufacture of Shorts 330 and 360 inner wings, de Havilland Canada Dash 8 engine nacelles, Boeing Vertol fuel pods, much of the detail structure for the Group's new large helicopter the EH.101 and many other components for such companies as British Aerospace and Rolls-Royce.

British Hovercraft Corporation Limited continues to support all its operating hovercraft and delivered a new version of its diesel powered AP.1-88 craft to the Canadian Coastguard in 1988.

EEL Limited has developed from the electronics division described earlier in this chapter. This is a flourishing small electronics company manufacturing such diverse items as very accurate torquemeters, laser communication and cable marking devices and emergency flotation gear for helicopters.

In November 1987 Westland Aerospace acquired a 65% interest in Marex, a computer software company based in Cowes.

Since the take-over of Saunders-Roe by Westland in 1959, Saunders-Roe Limited continued to exist as a paper company with regular nominal board meetings carefully and meticulously recorded. But on the 8th April 1987 the name of the company was legally changed to Westland Aerospace Limited. However, with the logic known only to legal departments the admirable name has been preserved for future use by changing the name of another Westland company to Saunders-Roe Ltd.

Britten Norman Islander in the final assembly stage. All structural components were manufactured by the company in aluminium alloy.

Shorts 330 Light Transport. The company at Cowes has built the inner wing for this aircraft for several years.

Shorts 330 Inner Wing. These major units are built in several assembly fixtures at the Cowes Works.

115

De Havilland Canada Dash 8

De Havilland Canada Dash 8. Engine nacelle cowlings partly assembled on master inspection fixture.

Boeing Vertol Chinook.

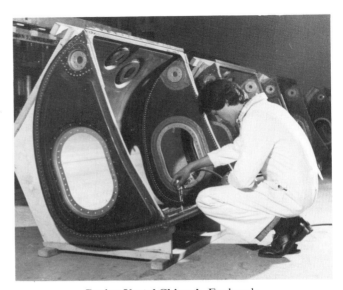

Boeing Vertol Chinook. Fuel pods.

Westland Agusta EH.101. On early flight trials in 1988

EH.101. Glazing bar structure for the control cabin manufactured in kevlar and carbon fibre epoxy composite construction.

CHAPTER 9

AIRCRAFT PRODUCTS OF THE EARLY DAYS 1910 - 21

In the early years prior to 1914 a variety of aircraft types were produced and tasks carried out on types which were not specifically identified as Saunders designs but to which undoubtedly Saunders contributed much in the way of techniques of construction and design. In wartime the main emphasis was on large scale production of other companies' established designs (see Appendix 2) which encouraged Sam to embark on the T.1, the only Saunders design to appear before the Armistice. This aircraft like the second Saunders type, the post-war Kittiwake, did not proceed beyond the prototype stage. In the period of Vickers control, Saunders contributed much to the design and construction of the Valentia flying boat usually identified as a Vickers aircraft but again only prototype machines were built.

The wartime records refer to the manufacture of 116 hulls for Felixstowe flying boats, in addition to contracts for complete aircraft. Separate contracts for fifteen Felixstowe F.3 hulls were received, six of these were completed by December 1917 and the remainder at the rate of one or two a month by the middle of 1918. Contracts for separate F2A hulls totalling sixty-seven have been identified of which five a month would have taken deliveries well into 1919 and then liable to cancellation. It is possible that the Air Board were placing contracts for hulls with the object of allocating these to major contractors or as replacements for hulls damaged in service and some may have been absorbed into Saunders production of complete F2A aircraft, which averaged five per month and continued into 1919. Despite this uncertainty, it is clear that Saunders were in receipt of contracts for large numbers of hulls on separate orders and it does not detract from the firm's massive wartime achievements. The company records also show the manufacture of 389 seaplane floats, which included those for the Short 184, the Sopwith Schneider, the Hamble Baby, the Fairey N.9 and Curtiss wing tip floats. The main floats for the Hamble Baby were redesigned in 1917 by Saunders to increase the length by nearly 3 ft. to 13 ft 1 in. with a slight increase in beam. A set was fitted for trials to N.1190, the first Baby built by Parnalls on a sub-contract from Faireys, but the remaining fifty-five seaplanes on Parnalls' contract were fitted with Sopwith-type floats.

It was common practice in many cases to re-draw the drawings received from other sources to amplify the information contained, particularly the lines of hulls and floats which eventually needed to be drawn accurately to full scale for standardisation of manufacture.

This and the succeeding chapters include descriptions outlining the changing nature of the aircraft of both Saunders' and other companies' designs, with which the company was associated, to convey in simplifed form the tasks facing the company at various times. The data, particularly for the early types, is far from comprehensive and performance, for many reasons, is notably imprecise but nevertheless an indication of the capabilities of each type is given.

The Fairey N.9 Seaplane. This early Fairey seaplane was fitted with floats designed and made by Saunders.

Sopwith Baby. Floats for the earlier Schneider and the later Hamble Baby version of the basic Sopwith design were made at Cowes for other contractors.

RAVAUD AERO-HYDROPLANE   1910-11

TYPE — Surface-skimming craft.

ENGINE — 50 H.P. Gnome driving a pusher airscrew by extension shaft.

DESCRIPTION — No detailed information on the machine survives but photographs provide a good guide to the general layout. The overall length of the body was 20 ft. approximately and was constructed of Consuta. The engine installation was at the aft end, the pilot was positioned amidships and an air-rudder was carried on a post at the bow. The single surfaced wings were of unequal span, approximately 9 ft. overall, and were contoured matching the underside of the body and stiffened externally. The machine was borne on the water by steamlined section floats with the maximum depth aft and well clear of the water on an undercarriage of struts suitably braced by cables.

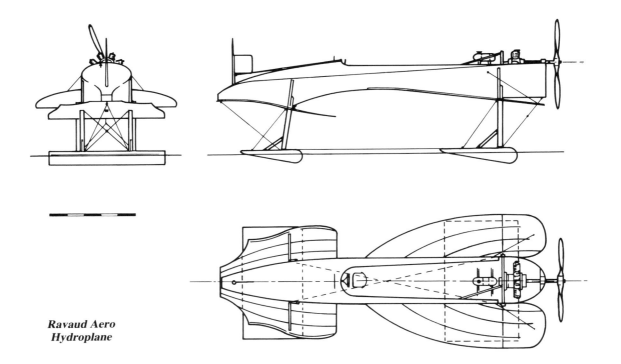

Ravaud Aero Hydroplane

Sam Saunders and Roger Ravaud discuss the Aero Hydroplane in the Folly shed.

M. Ravaud in the Aero-Hydroplane at Cowes, Isle of Wight.

SOPWITH BAT BOAT TYPE NO.1   1912-13

Type — 2 seat flying boat or amphibian.

Engine — 90 HP Austro-Daimler 6 cylinder in-line water cooled driving a two-blade pusher airscrew direct.
100 HP Green Type E.6 6 cylinder in-line replaced the Austro-Daimler for the Mortimer Singer Contest.

Hull — Single step hull with V entry seating two side by side. This was 21 ft. long with a 3 to 4 inch step 12 feet from the stempost. The hull for the first aircraft was built by Saunders of Consuta.

Wings — Two-bay wings of equal span and parallel chord mounted on short struts above the hull immediately behind the cockpit. The original bracing wires to the forward part of the hull were soon replaced by substantial struts to the engine mounting structure. Wing warping was originally employed but was superseded by the fitment of ailerons to the rebuilt first and to the second machines. Cut-outs in the trailing edges provided clearance for the propeller.

Tail Unit — Various forms of tail surfaces were fitted at different times, all mounted on twin strut and wire braced booms extending from the inboard interplane struts. Initially without a fin, a curved single rudder and tailplane with angled leading edge mounted on the top boom were fitted together with an additional elevator on the bow of the hull. This elevator was discarded, the tail booms were lengthened by one bay to four bays to compensate and twin rudders, below the tailplane, were fitted to the second version of the machine at the time of the Mortimer Singer attempt. This machine eventually became R.N.A.S. No. 118. The second machine, No. 38 was fitted with a single rudder aerodynamically balanced top and bottom but no fin was fitted initially. After major repair this machine was fitted with a triangular shaped fin and oval rudder.

Wing Tip Floats — These were of cylindrical form with conical ends and were made of light gauge copper sheet and provided with bicycle valves to permit inflation for the removal of dents occurring in service use.

Power Plant — Radiators of tubular construction were carried on either side of the engine mounting structure. For the Green engine a handle for hand starting from the cockpit was operated by chain to the forward end of the crankshaft. This was direct on the crankshaft on the Austro-Daimler.

Undercarriage — Mounted on the hull adjacent to the cockpit, it was designed to be raised by a lever in the cockpit and to fall under its own weight. The two wheels were 2 ft. diameter with 4 inch wide tyres and were unsprung and the hull was supported at the rear by a tail skid when at rest on the ground.

(The undercarriage was not fitted when exhibited at Olympia and was later removed before delivery of the aircraft to the Navy.)

Span		41ft. 0ins.
Length	30ft. 4ins. later	32ft. 0ins.
Height		11ft. 6ins.
Chord		5ft. 6ins.
Gap		5ft. 6ins.
Dihedral		2°
Incidence		4°
Wing area		400 sq. ft.
Track		4ft. 6ins.
Forward Elevator Span		8ft. 0ins.
Chord		2ft. 0ins.
Hull Length		21ft. 0ins.
Beam		4ft. 0ins.
Weights —	Basic	1,200 lbs
	Gross	1,700 lbs
	Hull	180 lbs
Performance —	Maximum speed	65 m.p.h.

Production — Saunders built one hull only for the first machine, later hulls were built by Sopwiths to Saunders basic design but not of Consuta.

Sopwith Bat Boat. The original machine being assembled in the Sopwith works; the Skating Rink at Kingston. The hull had been supplied by Saunders. The machine is depicted early in 1913 just before being dismantled for despatch to the Aero Show at Olympia.

Sopwith Bat Boat. In flight over Cowes Harbour.

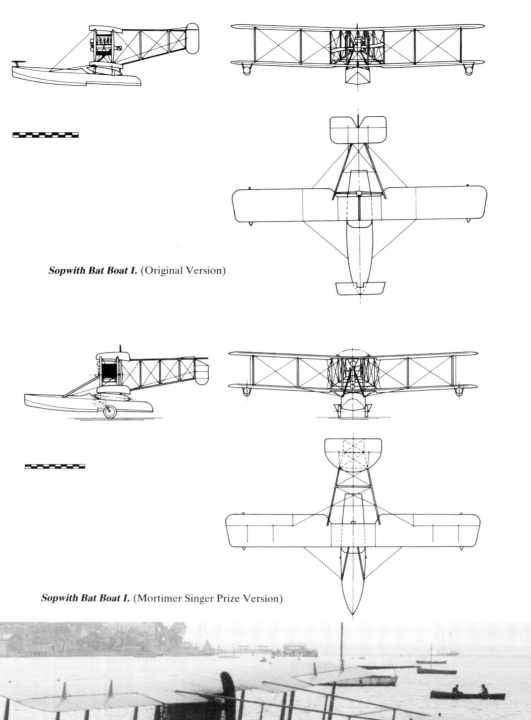

Sopwith Bat Boat I. (Original Version)

Sopwith Bat Boat I. (Mortimer Singer Prize Version)

Sopwith Bat Boat. Shown here in the form which it was flown by H.G. Hawker to win the Mortimer Singer Prize.
The hull was of Saunders design and construction.

WIGRAM FLYING BOAT   1913

The following is a description of this aircraft from "The Aeroplane" of February 20th, 1913:

"The Wigram hydro-biplane is the result of the development by Mr. Wigram of Sydney, Australia of a design originally sketched by him in 1910. It is now in the course of construction at Cowes. The biplane consists of a stepped hydroplane in which are placed the engine and pilot's and passenger's seats arranged in tandem. A fuselage springs upwards and backwards from the boat and bears the tailplane and rudders. The main planes are stayed in the usual way, the lower plane springing from the boat and having stabilising floats at the wing tips."

Photographs exist of the aircraft under construction, by which time the hull extension was completely enclosed with plywood. The fabric-covered tail surfaces were fitted and adjacent wings in the workshop are fabric covered and evidently the aircraft was nearing completion but no record exists of its completion or eventual use. It was intended that a 100 H.P. Green engine should be installed in the hull driving a pusher airscrew by chain. Mr. Arthur Wigram formed Wigram Flying Boats Limited of East Cowes and optimistically entered the machine for the Circuit of Britain Contest.

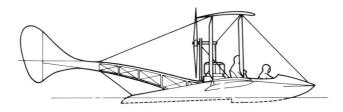

Wigram Flying Boat.

Wigram Flying Boat. Shown during construction by Saunders in the Columbine Works, this machine was not completed.

Wigram Flying Boat. Shown during construction by Saunders in the Columbine Works, this machine was not completed.

Wigram Flying Boat. Shown during constuction by Saunders in the Columbine Works, this machine was not completed.

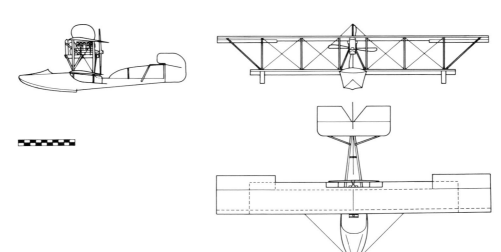

White and Thompson - Seaplane No. 2.

White and Thompson Seaplane No.2. The hull, more elegant than those of contemporary Curtiss flying boats, no doubt benefitted from Saunders' boat-building experience.

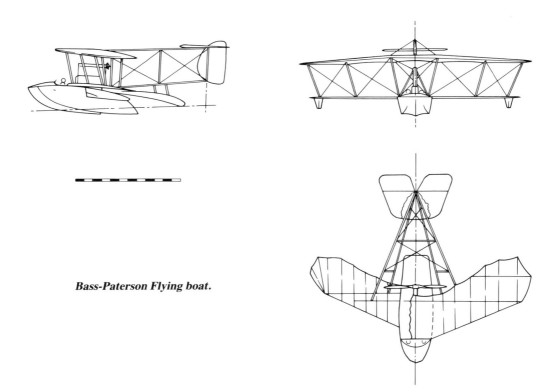

Bass-Paterson Flying boat.

WHITE AND THOMPSON SEAPLANE NO. 2   1914

Type — 2 seat flying boat.

Engine — 120 H.P. Austro-Daimler built by Beardmore, four-blade pusher aircscrew direct.

Hull — A single-step hull seating two side by side was constructed by Saunders using mahogany Consuta with ash and spruce frames.

Production — 1 hull only supplied to White & Thompson of Middleton, Nr Bognor, for a machine based on Curtiss designs for which the firm held a licence. Entered as No. 6 for the Circuit of Britain Contest which was abandoned, it was taken over by the R.N.A.S. as Serial No. 882.

Dimensions -		
	Hull length	24 ft. 0 ins.
	Span	45 ft. 0 ins.
	Length	27 ft. 6 ins.

BASS-PATERSON FLYING BOAT   1914-15

This can best be described by the Report No. 6/70/A of the 14th December 1914 to the Inspecting Captain of Aircraft R.N.A.S. by the C.O. of Calshot -

'Submitted, I have visited the Seaplane in question and examined it most closely.

It is ready for the engine, but it is not quite finished, and it appears that there is about three weeks' work still to be carried out on it.

It is a well constructed job.

The following are the claims made by the designer, Mr. Compton Paterson:-

(1) The pilot and passenger sit near the front of the boat and thus do not get wet, as the spray is thrown clear.

(2) The wings are back swept which gives a certain amount of fore and aft stability and at the same time gives a very wide arc of vision from the seats, viz: about 30° abaft of the beam.

Construction — The engine is placed in the boat, and the latter is closed in with a streamlined bonnet similar to a motor car, thus being protected from the wet.

The propeller is driven by a chain and is placed behind the planes.

The tail is of the open type.

The ribs are similar to those employed in the Caudron, but owing to the way they are bound, they are more springy.

The hull is built on the well known Saunders sewn principle, and is very light and strong. The step is a false one, so as to avoid the possibility of leakage.

Two bulkheads are provided.

No provision has been made for an axle and wheels or for slings for hoisting, although both these could be added.

The control is by foot steering and lever.

The machine is expected to weigh complete about 1,500 lbs with 4 hours fuel. At this weight the loading works out to be about 3 pounds per square foot.

Double main lift cable wires are provided, attached to separate fittings.

Mr. Compton Paterson, the designer, has been flying for 4 years and has made five or six machines in that time, all of which he has flown himself.

His idea in constructing the machine, was to experiment with this type of machine for Service purposes. He is quite willing to provide force diagrams of the structure and any information with regard to material employed in the construction of the machine.

I consider that, if the machine fulfils its designer's claims, it will be of value to the Naval Air Service. Private constructors find it extremely hard at the present time to obtain engines, and as we have two spare 100 H.P. Green engines, it is submitted that one of them could not be put to better use than for this experiment.

A rough sketch of the seaplane is attached.

(Sgd) J.L. Travers
Flight Commander R.N.A.S.
(Commanding Officer)

Calshot   14th December 1914

General — Apart from Saunders' drawings SP.137 and 217 of the hull and SP.218 of the wing tip floats, no other technical data has come to light on the Bass-Paterson Bat Boat. It is known to have reached the final stages of preparation for trials to commence, when it caught fire in the hangar at Cowes and was completely destroyed in early 1915.

PERRY-BEADLE FLYING BOAT TYPE B.3   1914

Engine — 60 H.P.E.N.V. Type 'F' mounted in the hull and driving two tractor airscrews by chains. 90 H.P. Curtiss fitted from April 1914.

Dimensions —		
	Span	35 ft. 0 ins.
	Chord: Top	6 ft. 0 ins.
	Bottom	4 ft. 0 ins.
	Gap	6 ft. 0 ins.
	Wing area	285 sq. ft.
	Length	26 ft. 0 ins.
	Height	9 ft. 0 ins.
Weight —	Basic	950 lbs
	Loaded	1,600 lbs

Performance — Maximum speed 64 m.p.h. (not proved in flight).

Description — The hull was constructed of two skins of mahogany Consuta and had one deep step. The aircraft laid low in the water with the lower wings partly immersed. The lower wings were to act as sponsons and were covered by Patent No. 4634 of 1914 by Perry-Beadle; the tailplane also rested on the water. The engine was mounted in the nose and drove, by means of an extension shaft and chains, twin propellers supported between the planes by the interplane struts and bracing wires. Behind this is a single open cockpit in the rounded top decking housed the passenger in front and pilot behind. The fin and tailplane were built integrally with the hull.

Production — 1 aircraft without identification. May have been entirely constructed by Saunders.

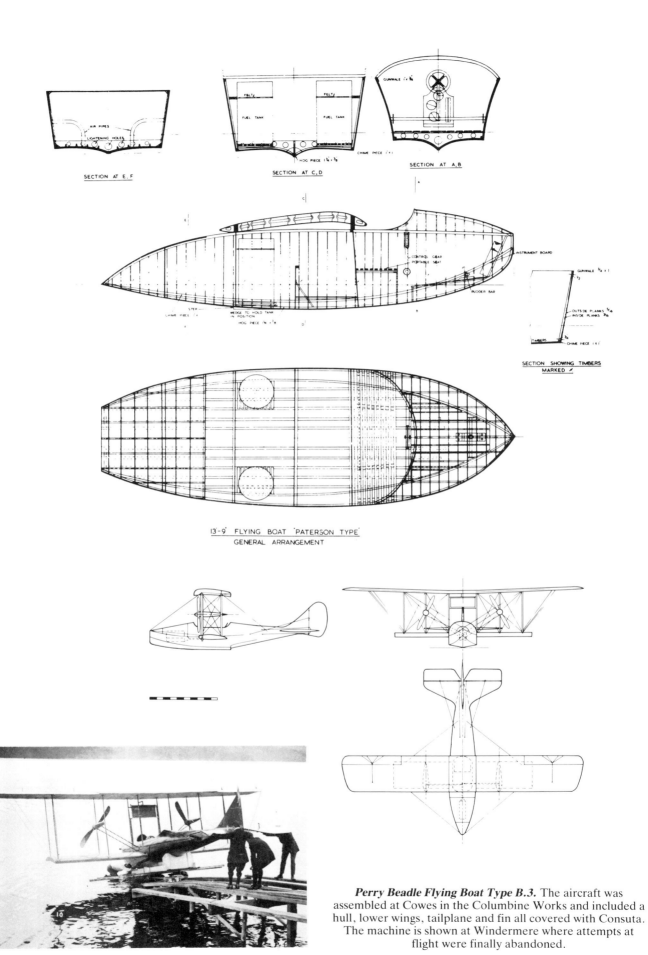

SECTION AT E, F

SECTION AT C, D

SECTION AT A,B

SECTION SHOWING TIMBERS
MARKED

13'-9" FLYING BOAT 'PATERSON TYPE'
GENERAL ARRANGEMENT

Perry Beadle Flying Boat Type B.3. The aircraft was
assembled at Cowes in the Columbine Works and included a
hull, lower wings, tailplane and fin all covered with Consuta.
The machine is shown at Windermere where attempts at
flight were finally abandoned.

B.E.2a 1913-14

Type — 2 seat biplane for observation and general duties.

Engine — 1 - 70 H.P. Renault air-cooled V.8.

Fuselage — A wire-braced wooden girder structure with fairings on the upper surface and the whole fabric-covered. Separate cockpit openings accommodated the pilot in the rear and observer in the front cockpits.

Wings — Two bay, unstaggered biplane of two-spar wooden construction with fabric covering. Small dihedral angle. Lateral control by warping.

Tail Unit — A large tailplane with elevator in separate halves. No fin was fitted and the rudder pivoted on a vertical sternpost. The units were of welded light steel tubular construction and fabric covered.

Undercarriage — A steel tubular axle was rubber mounted on a pair of ash skids which were carried on a pair of struts below the engine mounting and a pair of V-struts below the wing. A sprung tail-skid operated in unison with the rudder.

Power Plant — The air-cooled engine was uncowled but provided with a central air-scoop. Exhaust pipes on each side were carried vertically down in front of the lower wing and along the underside of the fuselage. A four-bladed propeller of 8 ft. 10 ins. diameter was fitted.

Dimensions —		
	Span	36 ft. 11⅛ ins.
	Chord	5 ft. 6 ins.
	Area	376 sq. ft.
	Length	29 ft. 6½ ins.
	Height	10 ft. 2 ins.
Weight —		
	Gross	1530 lbs
	Basic	1100 lbs
Performance —		
	Maximum speed	72 m.p.h.
	Stalling speed	42 m.p.h.

Production — One aircraft Serial No. 469.

B.E.2a. The machine illustrated, although built at Farnborough, was identical to 469 built by Saunders.

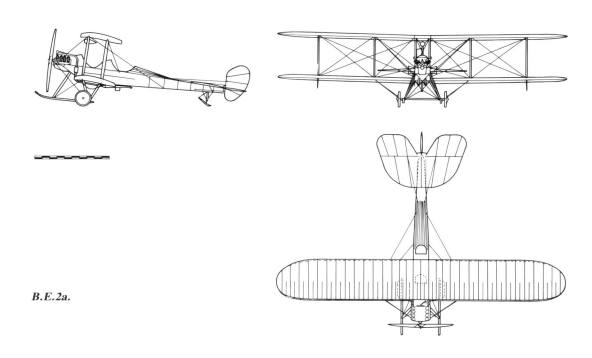

B.E.2a.

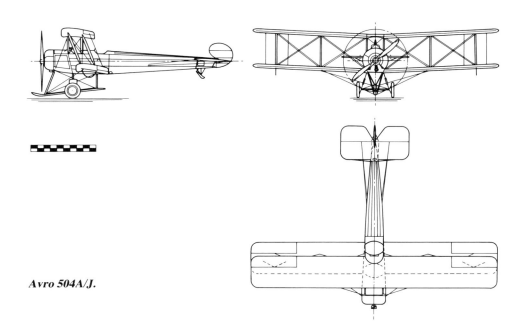

Avro 504A/J.

Avro 504.J. The last of two hundred of these machines built by Saunders.

Airship R.31 Engine Gondola. Built by S.E. Saunders for Short Bros. Assembly at Cardington.

Short 184. 8014 225 HP Sunbeam engine. The fourteenth machine on Saunders first contract. N1616 HP Renault engine. Saunders 57th machine.

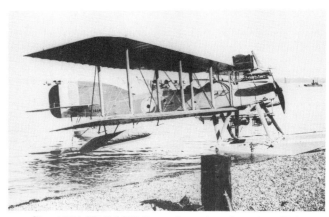

Short 184. N1616 HP Renault engine. Saunders 57th machine.

AVRO 504A and J   **1915-17**

Type — 2 seat dual-controlled training biplane.

Engine — 80 H.P. Gnome   (Type 504A)
           100 H.P. Gnome Monosoupape (Type 504J)

Fuselage — The fuselage comprised a deep tapered wooden girder structure with curved plywood decking around the cockpits, aft of which the shape was maintained by stringers and formers, and was wholly fabric covered. This main girder consisted of four ash longerons with spruce vertical and cross struts and was extensively cross-braced with piano wire with adjustable turn-buckles. The stern post consisted of a vertical steel tube and brackets which attached to the top and bottom longerons. At the forward ends of the longerons a fitting of steel tubes and plate served as the forward engine mounting; behind the engine a steel mounting bracket carried by diagonal fuselage side struts supported the rear engine bearing. Fuel and oil tanks were mounted on the top longerons behind the engine. A circular aluminium cowling, cut away at the lower quarter, enclosed the rotary engine and this was faired into the fuselage sides with aluminium panels. The cowling was enlarged in the Type 504J to accommodate the increased diameter engine. Dual controls were provided with full instrumentation only in the rear cockpit.

Wings — These were conventional two-spar wooden construction and fabric covered. The two-bay structure had noticeable stagger and dihedral and carried hoop-shaped skids below the outer interplane struts.

Tail Unit — The tail units were of mixed construction with wooden ribs and spars but with light tubular members forming the periphery. In the case of the rudder the main member was a steel tube which pivoted in the sternpost, the characteristic shape providing aerodynamic balance. The tailplane was made in separate halves and was attached to the upper longerons and carried separate elevators. The tailplane attachment was by extensions of the tubular leading edge which fitted into a socket fitted across the fuselage and was ajustable for incidence on the ground by a choice of positions at the rear spar attachments.

Undercarriage — The wheels were carried on a steel tubular faired axle and were sprung by rubber-cord housed in fairings in the vertical struts. The reinforced ash central skid was carried on V struts front and rear, the rear being rubber mounted. The axle and telescopic struts were wire-braced to the V struts against loads in all directions. A sprung pylon-mounted tail skid was fitted.

Dimensions —

Span	36ft. 0ins.
Length	29ft. 5ins.
Height	10ft. 5ins.
Wing area	330 sq. ft.
Chord	4ft. 9½ins.
Gap	5ft. 6ins.
Stagger	2ft. 0ins.
Incidence	4°
Dihedral	2½°

Weight —

Gross	1,700/1,800 lb.
Basic	1,050/1,100 lb.

Performance —

(100 H.P.)	
Maximum speed	82 m.p.h.
Service ceiling	13,000 ft.

Production —

201 aircraft.
Serial Nos. 7740 (ex. Avro contract)

2890 - 2939	
A.412 - 461	Type 504A
A.3355 - 3404	
A.9763 - 9813	Types 504A & J

17 aircraft were delivered in 1915. Production continued throughout 1916 and is believed to have terminated early in 1917.

General — This well-known aircraft, originally designed by A.V. Roe, was produced by the Avro company in the years before the war but evolved into a number of versions of the same basic design by the use of various engines and improvements. Although adapted for many purposes, its primary use was for training and the two versions manufactured by Saunders were used by the R.F.C. for this purpose and differed only in respect of the engine installation. A small number of 504A machines produced in early 1916 were transferred to the R.N.A.S. In addition to the main production contracts for 200 of the current Type 504A and J aircraft, an additional machine was produced "ex Avro contracts" and was completed from a set of sample units supplied by Avro to Saunders for educational purposes.

ENGINE GONDOLAS FOR AIRSHIPS R31 & R32   **1916-18**

R31 and R32 were built by Short Brothers at Cardington and were of wooden construction based on Schütte-Lanz design practice and the engine gondolas were sub-contracted to Saunders. The airships were originally designed with six gondolas, later reduced to five, each containing one Rolls-Royce Eagle engine with forward mounted radiator and pusher airscrew. The gondola contained an engineer's station with instruments and controls operated on instructions from the main control cabin.
The main structure of the car was built in boat style of Consuta plywood with a raised wooden windscreen and roof structure glazed with celluloid panels and covered with fabric.

SHORT 184   **1915-16**

Type — 2 seat torpedo and bomb-carrying seaplane suitable for operation aboard carrier ships.

Engine —

225 H.P. Sunbeam
240 H.P. Renault
260 H.P. Sunbeam Maori I

Fuselage — This was a conventional wire-braced girder structure of four spruce longerons, spindled for

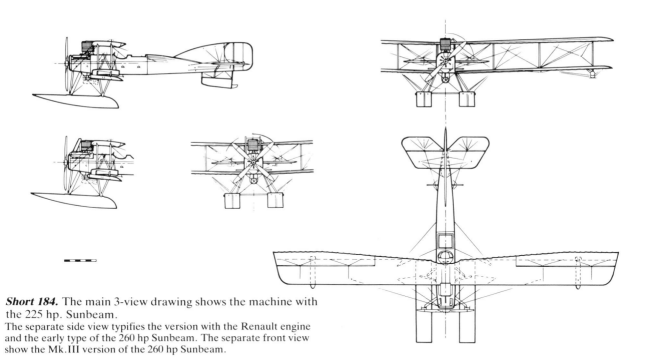

Short 184. The main 3-view drawing shows the machine with
the 225 hp. Sunbeam.
The separate side view typifies the version with the Renault engine
and the early type of the 260 hp Sunbeam. The separate front view
show the Mk.III version of the 260 hp Sunbeam.

Short 184. Towards the end of Saunders' production the 260
H.P. Sunbeam engine was supplied for the Short 184. N.1621
was the first of these, Saunders' 62nd machine, and is here
seen on the ramp outside the Folly Works.

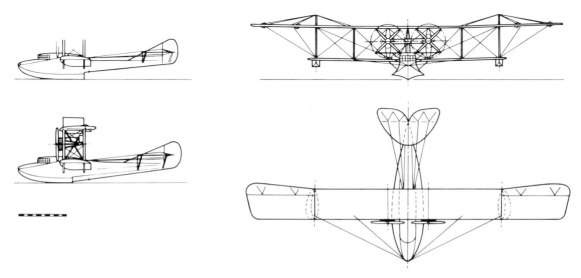

Curtiss H.4 Flying Boat. Upper view depicts Saunders type
hull as fitted to aircraft Serial Nos. 1231-2.

lightness with high tensile steel fittings at joints. Rounded fairings on the upper longerons provided apertures for the crew consisting of the pilot in front and rear gunner. Below the cockpits the fuselage sides were plywood covered with inserted footsteps; to the rear the fuselage was fabric-covered.

Wings — The wings comprised three bays and were equal in span. The upper wing consisted of a centre section the same width as the fuselage, followed by a tapered section on the trailing edge outboard of the second bay, where the chord then became parallel. Wide span ailerons were fitted to both top and bottom wings. The lower wing was parallel and of narrower chord. Cylindrical air-bags hung below the outboard inter-plane struts. The whole wing assembly could be folded and locked and employed ingenious means of controlling the complicated bracing system to keep it clear of the tail unit and to provide for single-handed operation by the pilot from the cockpit. The wing structure was a conventional two spar wooden structure with closely spaced nose-ribs; the interspar and trailing edge ribs were wider spaced and the wire trailing edge produced a scalloped appearance to the fabric covering.

Tail Unit — The tail surfaces were similar to those fitted to previous Short machines. The long curved fin was shaped to match the aerodynamically balanced rudder and was extended to provide a top rudder pivot point. The tailplane was in one piece attached to the top longerons and a divided elevator gave clearance for the rudder. Stranded bracing cables, as used elsewhere in the aircraft, stabilised the tail unit.

Undercarriage — Faired steel tubes formed the mounting of the twin main floats which consisted of a pair of single struts at the front and a pair of V struts at the rear attached to cross-tubes and braced by cables. The floats were attached to the cross-tubes by rubber cords and were slotted to allow vertical movement. The tail float was also sprung by rubber cords and had a water rudder actuated by the main rudder control. The floats were parallel box structures, at some stage redrawn by Saunders to facilitate manufacture and increase the buoyancy. The length was increased from 16 ft to 18 ft 11 in and the beam from 2 ft 10 in to 3 ft.

Power Plant — The three different engines fitted at Saunders were of V.12 type, exhausting between the cylinder blocks, the exhaust pipe extending upwards forward of the radiator block and top wing on the machines with Renault and 260 HP Sunbeam engines. The radiator was raised to be well clear of the engine and fuel tank on later production aircraft and a twin side-mounted installation was tried but believed not on Saunders-built aircraft. A radially slotted nose cowl and aluminium panels enclosed the engine installation back to the leading edge of the lower wing and the front cockpit. The two-bladed propeller was replaced by one with four blades when the 260 H.P. Sunbeam was fitted; the later Mk.III version of this engine had exhausts on the outboard sides.

Armament — Initally intended to carry the 14 ins. Whitehead Naval Torpedo, this proved to be operationally unsuccessful and the curved cross-tubes in the float chassis and attachments for the torpedo were not embodied in Saunders aircraft. The prime duty of the Short 184 became bombing for which purpose a centre line rack mounted below the fuselage could carry a variety of loads up to 500 lbs weight. The rear cockpit could mount a Lewis gun on a Scarff or Whitehouse mounting and could include a transmitting and receiving radio.

Dimensions —		
	Span	63 ft. 6 ins.
	Chord: Upper	6 ft. 6 ins.
	Lower	5 ft. 0 ins.
	Gap	5 ft. 6 ins.
	Wing area	688 sq. ft.
	Folded span	6 ft. 4¾ ins.
	Height	13 ft. 6 ins.
	Length	40 ft. 7½ ins.
	Length folded	44 ft. 2 ins.
Weight —	Gross	5100/5600 lbs
	Basic	3500/3700 lbs
Performance —	Maximum speed	75 - 88 m.p.h.
	Duration	2¾ - 5 hours
	Service ceiling	5500/9000 ft.
Production —	80 aircraft -	
	30 Serial Nos.	8001-30
	31 Serial Nos.	N.1140-49
		N.1600-20
	19 Serial Nos.	N.1621-24
		N.1760-74

General — Saunders were among the first sub-contractors, of which eventually there were nine, including the Cowes firm of J. Samuel White. The first batch of 30 aircraft, Serial Nos. 8001-30, was ordered in June 1915 and were fitted with the 225 H.P. Sunbeam, deliveries of these commenced in February 1916. Subsequent contracts were for the "Improved 184" with 240 H.P. Renault and later 260 H.P. Sunbeam engines. Delivery of the fifty aircraft on the second and third contracts commenced in May 1917 and was completed in February 1918.

CURTISS H.4 - SMALL AMERICA   1914-15

A contract was placed with the Aircraft Manufacturing Company of Hendon (CP.65070/14) for eight of these flying boats (Serial Nos. 1228-35) which were developed from the machine built pre-war by the Curtiss company for a trans-Atlantic flight. Saunders built special hulls of Consuta for at least three of these machines (Serial Nos. 1230-2) and may have constructed the remainder of the hulls. The H.4 was the basis from which the Felixstowe series of flying boats were developed and major changes, particularly to the hull, were made at Felixstowe, as a result of service use. The 90 H.P. Curtiss OX water-cooled engines were discarded almost from the outset and were replaced by two air-cooled Anzani radial engines of 100 H.P. Saunders made redesigned wing-tip floats for the original American-built machine used by the R.N.A.S. and it is probable that these were also constructed as

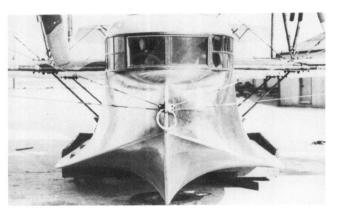

Curtiss H4. Built by S.E. Saunders and Aircraft Manufacturing Co.

Curtiss H4 Flying Boat. The aircraft Serial No. 1231 seen
here at Felixstowe was the first of two machines with
redesigned hulls made of 'Consuta' by Saunders.

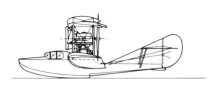

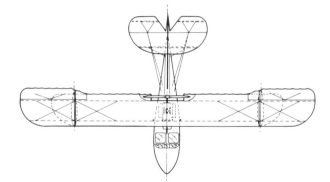

Norman Thompson NT.2.B Flying Boat.

replacements for the latter machines. The Curtiss design of wing structure remained unchanged.

The Curtiss H.4 machines were purchased for long-range patrol duties off the east coast of Britain but were superseded by improved types and eventually relegated to training duties.

Few performance and other specific details for the A.M.C./ Saunders type machines are available and the data quoted is based on the Curtiss machine of 1915 with OX engines. The small amount of additional data on the "Small America Improved Type with 2 Anzanis" is extracted from official records, as is the report on machine No. 1230.

Dimensions —		
	Span: Upper	75ft. 9¼ins.
	Lower	46ft. 0ins.
	Chord: Upper & Lower	7ft. 0¾ins.
	Gap	7ft. 6ins.
	Length	37ft. 0ins.
	Height	14ft. 0ins.
Weight —		
	Gross	4750 lbs
	Basic	3350 lbs
Performance —		
	Maximum speed	60 m.p.h.
	Minimum speed	40 m.p.h.
	Endurance	12 - 17 hours
	Fuel capacity	206 gallons

SMALL AMERICA - IMPROVED TYPE WITH 2 ANZANIS

Equipped with 1 Lewis gun and ammunition and 2 - 100lb bombs.

Full range at full power	192 miles
Speed at full power	48 knots
Full range at cruising speed	225 miles
Reasonable cruising speed	45 knots
Time to climb to 3000 ft.	25 mins
Time to climb to 6000 ft.	60 mins
Landing speed	34 knots

The following quotation from the official Felixstowe RN Air Station report is of interest:—

"The Saunders Boat Machine No. 1230. Drawing No. H402

This machine was English built, with thin fins of less width but carried further back. In getting off she was less successful than the American hulls, largely on account of the rounded underside of the tail being a much worse hydroplaning surface than the previous flat bottoms. This also caused a suction which was difficult to break away in smooth water.

She was not good at landing and did not last very long -a saving of 300 lbs weight had been made, but at the expense of considerably weakened construction."

General — Machines Serial Nos. 1232, 1233 and 1235 were in use at Killingholme in 1917, for training second pilots for the larger H.12, by which time the hulls were severely waterlogged and proving difficult to lift from the water and even more difficult to achieve a height where turns could be carried out safely.

No. 1235 was in use at Felixstowe and appears in company with the Porte Baby prototype, probably in 1916, with a hull which may be the standard Curtiss, but is certainly not the Saunders type as seen in photographs of No. 1231

NORMAN THOMPSON NT.2B   1916-18

Type — 2 seat light flying boat for training purposes.

Engine — 200 H.P. Sunbeam Arab.

Fuselage — The hull was built of two layers of planking with oiled calico between, over a structure of formers and stringers. The V-shaped entry changed to an angular shaped section with raised cabin for the crew, seated side by side, aft of which was housed a 60 gallon fuel tank. Dual controls with aileron control by wheel were fitted. Behind the single step the shape of the hull became circular and tapered to the stern, carrying below it a small skid at its extremity.

Wings — The two-bay wings were of conventional two-spar wooden construction and of unequal span. The upper wing extensions were braced to fins mounted above the outer interplane struts and carried the ailerons which extended aft of the scalloped trailing edge. Separate centre sections, the lower integral with the hull, terminated adjacent to the unfaired interplane struts and provided strong points for the attachment of beaching gear. The wings were rigged without stagger with 1° only of dihedral.

Tail Unit — These were wooden structures with fabric covering, except for the lower portion of the rudder which was plywood covered and served as a water rudder. The tailplane was made in two halves and was mounted high on the fin and braced by pairs of streamlined struts to the lower portion of the hull. The rudder and the divided elevator were unbalanced.

Power Plant — The V.8 water-cooled engine was mounted slightly to starboard to offset torque reaction, on a tubular trestle structure above the centre section and drove a four-bladed wooden pusher airscrew. The narrow radiator nearly filled the gap between the upper wing and the cabin top. A gravity fuel tank was attached to the underside of the upper centre section. No starting handle was fitted with the Arab engine, which was the only type fitted to Saunders-built machines.

Dimensions —		
	Span:	Upper 48ft. 4¾ins.
	Lower	28ft. 6¾ins.
	Chord	5ft. 6ins.
	Gap	5ft. 6ins.
	Wing area	453 sq. ft.
	Length	27ft. 4½ins.
	Height	10ft. 8ins.
Weight —		
	Gross	3169 lbs
	Basic	2321 lbs
Performance —		
	Maximum speed	85 m.p.h.
	Service ceiling	11,400 ft.
Performance —		
	24 aircraft. Serial Nos. N.2500-2523 (at least 14 completed).	

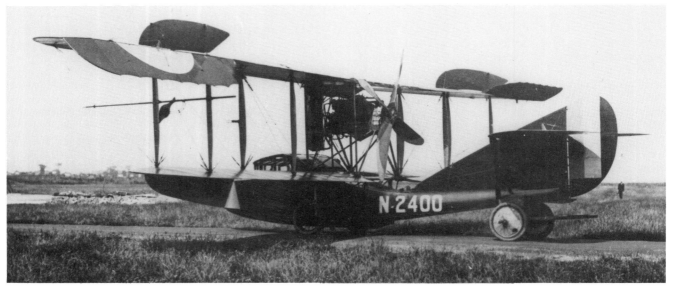

Norman Thompson NT.2B Flying Boat. This machine N.2400, although
built by the parent company, is virtually identical to the Saunders
machines. Its origins in the Curtiss types are apparent.

Norman Thompson NT.2B Flying Boat.
The NT.2B in flight.

Norman Thompson NT.2B Flying Boat. When at rest the
NT.2B laid well down in the water. N.1185 was an early
product of the Norman Thompson works near Bognor.

Norman Thompson NT 2B. After the war these NT2B's, stored in the Medina shop, were some of those remaining uncompleted.
N2518 is identifiable. Some boatbuilders made conversions of the hulls into river boats.

FELIXSTOWE F.2A & F.5   1917-19

Type — Flying boat for sea patrol and offensive operations with crew of 4/5.

Engines — 2 x 360 H.P. Rolls-Royce Eagle VIII.

Fuselage — The hull structure was based on a tapering cross-braced box-girder of ash longerons with diagonals in side elevation in the forward section and elsewhere braced by wires and tie rods. The lower cross-bracing was planked over much of its length to provide substantial floors to support the crew and equipment and extending below, at each station, was a triangular frame section, cut away on the centre line to accept the heavy keel member, which extended the full length of the hull. The flared side fins and planing bottom were built on to the hull and incorporated steps at the rear spar and at the station two bays aft. These surfaces were planked with two skins of cedar and mahogany with a fabric interlayer. The upper surface of the hull was covered with veneer from the nose to aft of the front gunner's cockpit. The pilot's cockpit was initially a partially enclosed cabin but later reverted to an open cockpit and deletion of the fairing behind for improved vision. Rearwards the top surface was fabric-covered over stringers and included a hatch for access to the engines for starting and servicing purposes. Behind the wings a second gunner's position was supplemented by hatches on either side, the hatches normally being closed by fabric-covered sliding doors. The fabric covering extended to the sides of the rear portion with shallow vertical mahogany washboards along the lower longerons. Later Saunders-built machines employed Consuta ply-wood panels to the full depth of the sides of the rear fuselage, in addition to the wooden panelling of the sides from the nose to the wing. Sections of the spars of the lower centre section were integrated into two main frames.

Wings — The wing structure derived from the Curtiss H.12 and consisted of three bays outboard of the engine mountings. The top wing, having considerable overhang, was built in five sections consisting of a short centre section extending to the engine support struts, two long parallel intermediate panels followed by two shorter outer panels, the trailing edges of which comprised the unbalanced ailerons with extremely tapered rear outlines. The upper wing extensions were braced by wires over kingposts which were covered with fabric to form fore and aft vertical surfaces. The lower wing was built in four sections consisting of two separate stub wings built on to the sides of the hull and braced by pairs of struts, which passed through the top of the flared fins to the lower longerons. The outer panels were parallel in chord and carried balancing floats, made of birch ply screwed to wooden formers positioned against the underside below the outer interplane struts. Construction was based on two main spars with continuous stringers and trailing edge member. The stub wings and the leading edges were covered with plywood, all other surfaces being fabric covered. The wings were rigged without stagger and with only 1° of dihedral.

Tail Unit — These all consisted of wooden structures generally similar in construction to the wings. The fin was integrated with the rear of the hull. The tailplane was braced to both upper and lower longerons by two pairs of struts each side. All units were fabric covered.

Power Plant — The two engines, which were handed on aircraft delivered from April 1918, N.4291 being among the earliest, were mounted conventionally on braced structures of wooden streamlined struts between the wings and drove four-bladed tractor airscrews in opposed directions outwards at the top. The engines carried front mounted radiators and hand starting gear on the outboard sides and were uncowled. A small gravity fuel tank was mounted on the centre line of the top wing and was fed from four main tanks in the hull necessitating a complex fuel system.

Armament — The crew and armament could be varied to suit the particular type of operation and could include bombs or depth charges carried on racks below the lower wing at the engine mountings. Gun armament could be varied but Scarff rings were provided at the front gun position, accessible by folding the port control column, and rear position and could mount twin Lewis guns in front and a single Lewis gun at the rear position. Additional Lewis guns could be carried on the port side above the second pilot's position, accessible for use by a folding seat, and at aft positions on swinging arms extended outside of the port and starboard sliding hatches.

Dimensions —		F.2A	F.5
Span:	Upper	95ft. 7½ins.	103ft. 8ins.
	Lower	68ft. 5ins.	74ft. 2ins.
	Chord	7ft. 1ins.	8ft. 0ins.
	Gap	7ft. 1ins.	8ft. 6ins.
	Wing area	1,333 sq.ft.	1,409 sq.ft.
	Length	46ft. 3ins.	49ft. 3ins.
	Height	17ft. 6ins.	18ft. 9ins.
Weight —			
	Gross	10,978 lbs	12,682 lbs
	Basic	7,549 lbs	9,100 lbs
Performance —			
	Maximum speed	95 m.p.h.	88 m.p.h.
	Service ceiling	9,600 ft.	6,800 ft.
	Endurance	6 hours	-

General — The operational experience with the F.2A resulted in many changes being embodied in production machines. The Felixstowe team produced a new design, the F.3, which was not made by Saunders, although at least 15 hulls were built. In 1918 on the last contract, F.2A production was to be switched to the later type F.5 but this type had not reached production at the time of the Armistice, subsequent to which the contract was cancelled. The F.2A shipped a great deal of water in the rear of the hull due to the inadequate shallow washboard and fabric covered upper portion. Saunders designed and produced one experimental machine 'constructed on the Consuta system' which was the subject of a letter dated 27 August 1918 from Capt. Leckie. HQ RAF Great Yarmouth advising the firm 'that the machine is in every way superior to the ordinary F.2A type'. Soon after the firm received a contract from the Air Board for 42 sets of

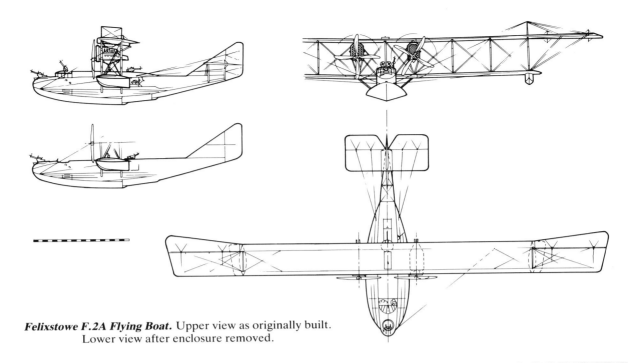

Felixstowe F.2A Flying Boat. Upper view as originally built.
Lower view after enclosure removed.

Felixstowe F.2A. N4287 is typical of the early Saunders built machines with enclosed and
faired crew compartment. N4297 shows this partially removed in service. N4465 and N4477
are examples of later Saunders production with open cockpit and were delivered post-war.

Felixstowe F.2A Flying Boats. On the Medina awaiting collection by naval pilots at the end of 1918.

Consuta sides for retrospective modification of existing aircraft and future aircraft were built to this design. The F.5 followed the same general configuration of the F.2A but was larger and heavier, which did not enhance its performance. Nevertheless, it was to continue in use with the R.A.F. in the post-war years and this resulted in some refurbishing work for Saunders, returning stored aircraft into service. The F.5 served also for experimental purposes which included one machine with a special Saunders tunnel hull which appeared in 1924.

Production —
F.2A — 100 aircraft.
Serial Nos. N.4080-99
N.4280-309 } Contract No. AS.14154
N.4430-79 Contract No. AS.4498/18
By November 1918, 62 aircraft had been completed including 6 still to be delivered. The 38 outstanding aircraft were completed and delivered after the war.

F.5 — 50 aircraft.
Serial Nos. N.4580 - 629 Contract No. 38A/550/C563
Work was in hand at the time of the Armistice but no aircraft had been built and the contract was cancelled. These aircraft were to have Consuta hulls and were estimated at a cost of £6125 each by the firm.

SAUNDERS T.1   1917

Type — Two-seat military tractor biplane for use on both wheels or floats.

Engine — 150 H.P. Sunbeam Nubian fitted in prototype. Intended engine 200 H.P. Hispano-Suiza.

Fuselage — Constructed mainly of Consuta plywood eliminating internal bracing and metal fittings.

Wings — Unequal span single-bay. Upper wings only fitted with ailerons. Detachable for shipboard stowage.

Armament — Fixed forward firing Lewis gun mounted externally. Observer's Lewis gun on Scarff ring.

Dimensions —		
	Span: Upper	37ft. 5ins.
	Lower	24ft. 9ins.
	Chord	5ft. 6ins.
	Gap	5ft. 6ins.
	Dihedral	2°30′
	Incidence	2°15′
	Span: Tailplane	14ft. 0ins.
	Area: Wing	314 sq.ft.
	Ailerons	21 sq.ft.
	Tailplane	33.5 sq.ft.
	Elevators	22 sq.ft.
	Fin	5.5 sq.ft.
	Rudder	8 sq.ft.
	Fuel Tank	35 gallons

Production — 1 aircraft only. Serial No. X.14

Service — Test flying only.

General — The original artist's impression and the three-view drawing shows a central exhaust stack-pipe,

whereas the photograph shows outside stub exhausts, indicating the initial planned use of a different type Sunbeam engine from that actually fitted.

The T.1 was retained by the company in the Solent Works for many years before being scrapped.

SAUNDERS KITTIWAKE   1920

Type — Passenger biplane amphibian flying boat for civil operations.
2 crew, 6 - 7 passengers.

Engines — 2 x 160-200 H.P. A.B.C. Wasp II 7 cylinder radials mounted in nacelles on the inboard interplane struts.

Fuselage — This was built as two separate units. The lower portion consisted of a hull with V-shaped bottom and two steps and contained the main undercarriage which could be retracted into slotted housings and a combined water-rudder and tail-skid. A deep super-structure was mounted on top of the hull and contained both the crew and passenger compartments and was extended aft of the hull to provide the mountings for the tail surfaces. The fuselage was constructed largely of Consuta plywood, mahogany for the hull bottom and cedar elsewhere, attached to a wooden structure. The pilot controlled the aircraft from a position in the lower glazed cabin, on the starboard side, in the roof of which was an emergency escape hatch; the engineer, on his port side, being able to go forward to a hatch for mooring operations and was available to assist with the manual undercarriage retraction and could reach the engines when required through the passenger cabin via the exit/entrance doors in both sides.

Wings — These were very original in concept at the time and included a patented system of camber variation (No. 163,853) as a lift improvement device. The basic wings were a biplane structure attached to the top and bottom of the cabin superstructure. Each wing structure consisted of front and rear spars built into a box structure by Consuta cedar plywood skinning top and bottom between the spars minimising the need for internal ribs. Forward and aft of the spars were separate hinged units capable of being lowered to provide the increased camber. These hinged units consisted of the complete leading and trailing edge portions of the wings and were constructed of duralumin ribs mounted on tubular spars with Consuta covering. The control by wheel at the pilot's left side was taken by rods terminating in racks at housings mounted externally at four positions on each wing. In each housing left and right hand screws operated external tubular rods and cranks mounted on the spars of the hinged units.

Interplane struts were provided at four positions and were of I sections enabling incidence wires to be dispensed with. The inboard struts were of duralumin construction for mounting the engine in a seven-sided nacelle which also contained the oil tank. The remainder of the I section interplane struts were of wooden construction, the two outboard providing mountings for aileron hinges, the ailerons being displaced from the main wings by the hinge camber flaps.

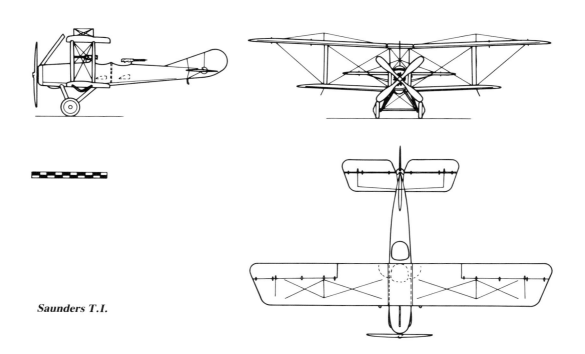

Saunders T.I.

Saunders TI. The only known photograph of the machine.

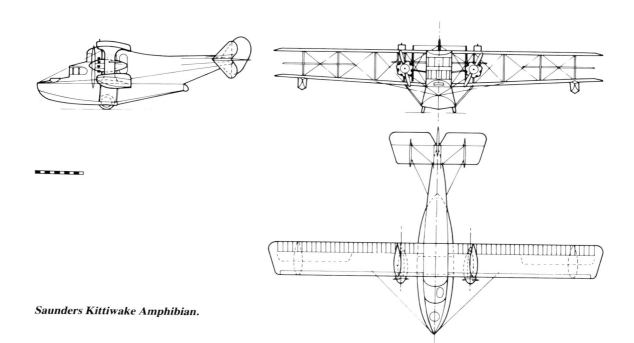

Saunders Kittiwake Amphibian.

Sanders Kittiwake. At her moorings in the Solent.

Saunders Kittiwake Amphibian. Lifting off from the Solent.

Saunders Kittiwake Amphibian. Launching at the Solent Works.

Tail Unit — The adjustable tailplane carried small fins, extending above and below, towards the tips and these were braced by horizontal struts and diagonal wires to the fuselage mounted central fin. A single balanced rudder was fitted.

Wing Tip Floats — Made of Consuta, these were fitted flush to the underside of the wing below the outboard interplane struts and were angled to clear the lowered leading and trailing edges.

Fuel System — Two tanks mounted externally above the top wing contained a total of 108 gallons. Fuel was fed to the engines by gravity and was estimated to give 4 hours duration of flight.

Dimensions —		
	Span	68 ft. 3 ins.
	Chord	7 ft. 0 ins.
	Length	43 ft. 8 ins.
	Height	14 ft. 9 ins.
	Wing area	864 sq.ft.
	Wheel track	6 ft. 0 ins.
Weights —	Basic weight	3840 lb.
	A.U.W.	6000 lb.
Performance —	Maximum speed	105/110 m.p.h.
	Alighting speed	42 m.p.h.

Production — 1 aircraft only.

Constructor s Number — 101

Registration — G-EAUD

Service — Development flying from September 1920 to July 1921.

A very interesting article by Captain Norman Macmillan entitled "Testing an Amphibian" appeared in Shell Aviation News and provides a first-hand account of the problems encountered in the early trials of the Kittiwake. The concluding paragraphs make a chilling forecast of problems to be encountered some thirty years later with the Princess flying boats:-

"There we obtained a calibrated tachometer and fitted it to the port engine. Its full throttle rpm read 1440. The same instrument was then connected to the starboard engine. Its rpm were 1575. Here was the source of our troubles. The starboard engine, made by ABC Motors, was virtually a hand made pre-production motor. The port engine came from a sub-contractor as a production model and was consistently down in power, and lost yet more power after brief use. Until this primary fault was corrected there was no purpose in flogging Kittiwake further. It meant, as I reported to Saunders, an engine overhaul at the makers, or fitting another Wasp engine or alternatively two engines of a different make.

Six months passed before Kittiwake was again ready to fly. Four months after that she was scrapped. Despite novel design features she failed to find a place in civil aviation, partly because she was too experimental, partly because her power units were unable to give her what later became established practice - cruise at half power or less to obtain the dual advantages of fuel economy and reliability, plus an ample reserve for take-offs in adverse conditions. Kittiwake had no power reserve and that was her chief defect."

VICKERS-SAUNDERS VALENTIA B.S.1 BOAT SEAPLANE   1918-21

Type — Flying boat for sea patrol and offensive operations with crew of 5 to Admiralty Specification N.3.

Engines — 2 x 650 H.P. Rolls-Royce Condor IA.

Description — The design of the Valentia was initiated by Rex Pierson of Vickers and when it finally emerged was seen to be loosely based on the layout of the Felixstowe F.5 but was considerably larger and heavier and with a Saunders design of flat-sided hull with two steps, covered with Consuta plywood. It was powered by two Rolls-Royce Condor engines mounted on V-struts between the wings in six-sided nacelles somewhat similar to those of the Vickers Vimy. The two-bay wings had flat rectangular fabric-covered panels above the outboard interplane struts and wire-braced upper wing extensions. Ailerons were fitted to the top wings only and initially these were aerodynamically balanced and extended beyond the wing tip and the trailing edge. On N.126 the balance portion was removed and the outline blended to the wing shape. The biplane tail had triple rudders but a single central fin only was used, which resembled the style of unit used on the Vimy and other Vickers aircraft of the time. The elevator balance areas were also removed in line with the tailplane tip on N.126. The wing tip floats were fitted below the outer interplane struts with bracing struts inboard. On the first machine the floats were originally flush to the underside of the wing but were soon lowered on four short struts with lengthened bracing struts on all aircraft.

Armament — Forward mounting for 37 mm C.O.W. gun for anti-submarine use. 1 Lewis gun on starboard side of pilot's cockpit. 1 Lewis gun amidships. Bombs carried under bottom wing below engine mountings.

Radio — A telescopic aerial mast was housed in the hull just forward of the amidships gun position and this could be extended to a height of 34ft. 6ins. to raise aerials from the tail and each wing panel, when the machine was afloat.

Dimensions —		
	Span: Top wing	112 ft. 0 ins.
	Bottom wing	83 ft. 0 ins.
	Chord	10 ft. 6 ins.
	Gap	10 ft. 0 ins.
	Length	58 ft. 0 ins.
Weights —	Basic	10,000 lbs
	Gross	21,300 lbs
Performance —	Maximum speed	105 m.p.h.
	Climb to 5,000 ft.	12 minutes
	Endurance	4½ hours

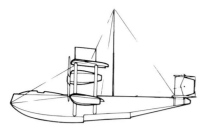
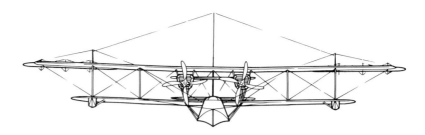

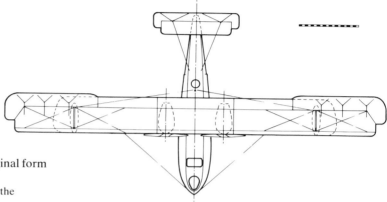

Vickers-Saunders Valentia BS.1.
The main 3 view drawing shows the aircraft in its original form before the deletion of the balance areas.

The separate front elevation shows the equal-span wings of the projected version.

Vickers – Saunders Valentia BS.1. N.124 The first machine on the Medina.

Vickers-Saunders Valentia BS.1. The third machine N.126 finally afloat at Cowes early in 1923. Although reported complete in August 1922 further modifications were specified which delayed delivery. These included the removal of the extensions of the ailerons and elevators as fitted to the earlier aircraft.

Vickers-Saunders Valentia BS.1. N.126, by now the sole survivor of the three Valentias, spent its working life on trials at the Isle of Grain and is believed to have been scrapped with the closure of the establishment when experimental marine aircraft testing was transferred to Felixstowe in 1924.

Production — 3 aircraft. Serial Nos. N.124,5,6.
N.124 Despatched from Cowes 13.3.21. Wrecked at Isle of Grain 15.6.21.
N.125 Despatched from Cowes 15.3.22. and dismantled at Pevensey Bay during delivery flight to Isle of Grain.
N.126 Although reported complete in August 1922 further modifications were requested by Vickers. Finally delivered in February 1923 and served as a trials aircraft at Isle of Grain.

General — Variously referred to as either a Vickers or a Vickers-Saunders type, the design was the responsibility of R.K. Pierson of Vickers and was contributed to by Henry Knowler, at that time employed by Vickers at Weybridge, and evolved by stages from the Vimy bomber. Schemes for amphibian, civil and military versions, some with Napier Lion engines, were further stages in this development. The specification N.3, to which the Valentia was submitted, permitted the use of the liquid-cooled Armstrong Siddeley Tiger engine as an alternative.

In the immediate post-war period Vickers offered an alternative civil version capable of carrying 17 passengers and 2 crew or 2.3 tons of freight and mail.

The design finally intended by Vickers was for a three-bay wing structure of equal span top and bottom and with overhanging aerodynamically balanced ailerons. The wing tip floats were further outboard below the new outer interplane struts and there were no fabric panels above the top wings.

HULLS FOR VICKERS VIKING AMPHIBIANS
1919-21

Vickers built a total of 31 Vikings and a number of hulls for these were constructed by Saunders, using Consuta plywood, during the period when Vickers were in control. Some later hulls for this type were changed to S.C.T. (Securely Cemented Together) plywood supplied by the Tucker Armoured Plywood Company of Crayford when Vickers withdrew from the Saunders company.

The aircraft was supplied for both civil and military purposes, housing 3 or 4 passengers and crew in open cockpits or an enclosed cabin. Variants of the aircraft from Mk. I to IV were built with overall lengths of 30 to 34 feet.

Vickers Viking Amphibian.

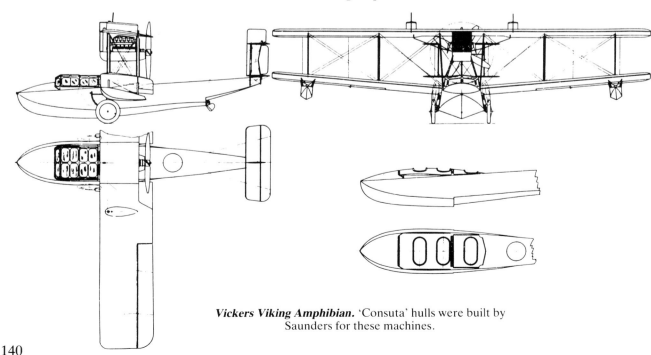

Vickers Viking Amphibian. 'Consuta' hulls were built by
Saunders for these machines.

CHAPTER 10

THE AIRCRAFT OF 1923 - 29

This was a period of experimentation and building of prototypes, mainly of flying boats, but with one attempt at a fighter. Construction in both wood and metal was tried and resolved in favour of metal for large flying boat hulls, although wooden construction of wings continued into the future. The Isacco Helicogyre was not a success, although a quarter of a century later the manufacture of helicopters was an important part of the company's activities.

S.E. Saunders remained the head of the company, and the aircraft types designed by the company continued to be identified by his name, although he had now reached a good age and was approaching his retirement. The reconstitution of the firm under A.V. Roe and others took place at the end of this period, from which time the use of the Saunders-Roe name, often abbreviated to Saro, ensued.

Previously there was no basic system of type numbering in use, although the first design was identified as T.1, but during this time type numbers prefixed with 'A', for aircraft, were used, commencing with the A.3, Valkyrie. The use of A.5 to identify the Valentia was presumably made retrospectively for administrative purposes.

SAUNDERS PATENT TUNNEL HULL ON FELIXSTOWE F.5 SERIAL NO. N.178

Apart from proving the relative merits of wood and metal construction in comparison with the Short S.2, the hull of the special Felixstowe F.5 N.178 was made to prove the principle of the Saunders Patent No. 230196. This overcame the U.S. "Sea Sled" Patent of a plain inverted V by providing an additional channel section tunnel through the hull intended to collect the bow wave and pass it along. It was very effective in its clean running, providing freedom from spray, but the large area of immersed side made control on the water very difficult. Also the hull was inevitably much heavier than previous conventional types.

The aircraft was tested at Felixstowe in 1924 and a relevant extract from Report No. F/A/8 on the performance and comparisons with a reconditioned F.5 are recorded below. This was one of the early reports by the Marine Aircraft Experimental Establishment operating at Felixstowe from the 1st April 1924, previous experimental work having been carried out by a unit at the Isle of Grain, now transferred to Felixstowe.

N.178 was reported scrapped by May 1925.

Felixstowe Report No. F/A/8 December 1924

Tests of Saunders Patent Hull with F.5 Air-structure No. 917

1. The above aircraft was tested under the following conditions:-
   (a) Taking off tests by gradually increasing loads up to a maximum at which the aircraft would not leave the water. A standard re-conditioned F.5 Boat Seaplane being tested under similar conditions for the purpose of comparison.
   (b) Air tests with 150 gallons of fuel and crew of four, which was the maximum load for which strength approval had been given.

2. The Saunders aircraft consists of a Saunders Patent Tunnel Hull fitted with a standard F.5 air-structure. The general arrangement being in every way identical with the Service F.5 Boat Seaplane, with the exception of slight modifications in the arrangement of the internal petrol tanks, necessitated by the shape of the hull.

3. **Weight** — The tare weight of the Saunders aircraft with fixed military equipment is 10,037 lb which is 384 lb above the weight of a F.5 Boat Seaplane with similar fixed load. Both these weights include soakage obtained in service; the aircraft being weighed after trials.

4. **Mooring** — During the mooring out a number of ribs were damaged in the trailing edge of the outer bay of the starboard bottom plane; this trouble has never been experienced here with F.5 Seaplanes. The F.5 moored out at the same time, and at a buoy close to the Saunders, was undamaged by the sea. This is probably due to the Saunders having a larger submerged keel surface and tends to lie more "head to tide" than the F.5.

5. **Taxiing** — At low speeds, control of the water is inferior to the standard F.5. The hull, forward of the trailing edge of the lower plane, is very clean at all speeds.

6. **Taking Off** — On opening up the engines the aircraft tends to trim down by the tail and considerable pressure on the elevator control is required to overcome this. During the time when the aircraft is running tail down, it becomes very unstable directionally and tends to turn out of the wind. Unless this tendency is checked immediately it becomes too great to be overcome by rudder and aileron control. The tendency to swing disappears when the aircraft is hydroplaning on the steps.

It was found, during the take off trials that by moving the load carried further forward, the take off was improved, the centre of gravity being not so far forward under these conditions as to make the aircraft noticeably nose heavy in the air. The difficulty in taking off the Saunders boat lies entirely in the time required to trim the hull forward on to its step. Once it is planing on its step the aircraft takes off easily.

With the maximum load attempted (13,750 lb all-up-weight) the aircraft could not be trimmed forwards, although several attempts were made, including changes in the disposition of the load.

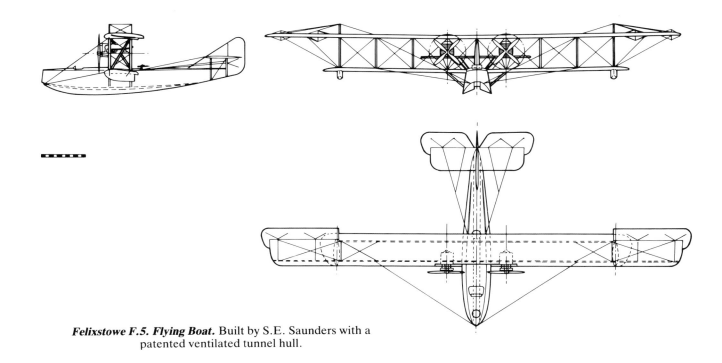

Felixstowe F.5. Flying Boat. Built by S.E. Saunders with a patented ventilated tunnel hull.

Felixstowe F.5 with Saunders patented hull. N.178 was built with a wooden hull incorporating a special design of planing bottom.

No tendency to porpoise was observed at any speed. The weight was increased by taking on board two extra men between each run. Only a short straight flight was attempted after each take off run, on account of the increase over the approved stressed load. The greatest weight at which the Saunders aircraft could be taken off was 13,485 lb at which the length of run was 734 yards in 56 seconds. The F.5 under similar conditions as to weight and wind required a run of 1483 yards, taking 1 minute 21 seconds. The F.5 was however, taken off later at a total weight of 14,100 lb after a run of 1856 yards in 1 minute 53½ seconds.

7. **Air Trials** — Flown at 12,827 lb total weight the aircraft handled in the air similar to a standard F.5. No peculiarities due to the increased keel surface forward were noticed.

8. **Conclusions** — It is considered that the hull performance might be improved by modifications to the steps bringing both further aft. In its present form the water performance is unsatisfactory, owing to the great difficulty in taking off the water.

December, 1924

A.3 SAUNDERS VALKYRIE   1927

Type — General purpose patrol and reconnaissance flying boat with a crew of 5. To Specification R14/24, later amended to R22/24.

Engines — 3 - 685 H.P. Rolls-Royce Condor IV (at 1900 rpm as tested at MAEE).
3 - 650 H.P. Rolls-Royce Condor IIIA.

Fuselage — The hull was of wooden construction, covered with two layers of Consuta copper-sewn plywood laid diagonally with a calico interlayer. Of Linton Hope style, it was designed with a V-shaped entry changing to a well rounded form. The planing bottom incorporated two steps, the main step being ventilated, and there were chines built externally on the main hull. Forward of the wings two pilots sat in tandem raised cockpits with dual controls and separate windscreens, in front of which was the forward gun position. Aft of the wings two gunners were placed in staggered positions, all being fitted with Scarff mountings. Radio and navigation equipment, engineer's station and crew facilities were provided inside the hull.

Wings — The high-aspect ratio biplane wings were visually unstaggered and of equal span and chord and provided with ailerons on both surfaces. The structure was of wood with fabric covering, apart from plywood skinning of the leading edges and the lower centre section. The outer wings comprised two bays outboard of the centre section; the lower wing centre section carried in one piece across the hull to which it was attached below the centre engine mounting and in addition by N-strut bracings from below the outboard engine mountings to the lower portion of the hull below the waterline.

Control Units — The adjustable monoplane tailplane, strut and wire braced to the hull, was mounted at

one-third of the height of the single fin, on which was pivoted the rudder with Flettner-type servo-tab. The rudder was operated by cables exterior to the hull from aft of the rear gun position, but inside the hull all flying controls, including those for the ailerons, were operated by rods. The tail units were of wooden construction and fabric-covered with plywood leading edges to the tailplane.

Power Plant — The three engine nacelles were mounted on pairs of inverted V-struts betwen the centre sections and each accommodated within the cowlings an 18 gallon oil tank and a 98 gallon service fuel tank behind. On either side were externally mounted underslung, cylindrical Lamblin-type radiators. Two-bladed metal Fairey-Reed propellers 9ft. 8⅝ins. diameter were fitted, their axis tilted upwards at 4° to datum. The main fuel tanks originally consisted of four 138 gallon tanks inside the hull, later changed to two 460 gallon tanks in the upper centre section.

Dimensions —		
	Span	96ft. 0ins.
	Chord	10ft. 6ins.
	Gap at centre section	9ft. 2ins.
	Length	65ft. 6ins.
	Hull	56ft. 0ins.
	Depth	7ft. 10¾ins.
	Beam	10ft. 0ins.
	Height (off trolley)	18ft. 5½ins.
	(on trolley)	19ft. 6½ins.
	Wing area	1967.5 sq.ft.
	Tailplane area	185 sq.ft.
	Elevator area	86.88 sq.ft.
	Fin area	59.875 sq.ft.
	Rudder area	52.1 sq.ft.
	Servo area	5.6 sq.ft.

Weights — Refer to Part 1 of Report F/23.

Rigging —		
	(Datum horizontal)	
	Incidence	4°
	Sweepback	4°
	Stagger	3° backwards.

Performance —		
	Maximum speed	125 m.p.h.
	Stalling speed	60 m.p.h.
	Ceiling	15,000 ft.
	Endurance	10 hours.

Armament —	
	3 Lewis guns.
	1000 lb. bombs carried below the wings.

Production —	
	Contract No. 543186/25
	A3/1 - 1 Prototype N.186 only.

MAEE TESTS ON THE SAUNDERS VALKYRIE

The contract for the Valkyrie had been placed in 1925 but by April 1927, when the aircraft was tested at Felixstowe, it was evident that wooden hulls were unsuitable for flying boats for military purposes and the Valkyrie proved to be the last Saunders-built machine using this form of construction. By 1927 MAEE had been established for four years at Felixstowe and had

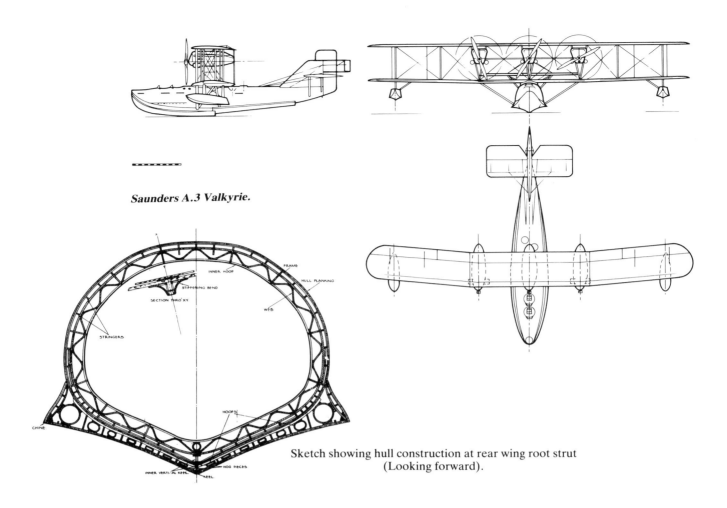

Saunders A.3 Valkyrie.

Sketch showing hull construction at rear wing root strut
(Looking forward).

Saunders A.3 Valkyrie. Henry Knowler was largely responsible for the design of this the company's first major post war military flying boat.

developed the system of testing and reporting in a methodical way.

Two extracts from Part 1, Performance Trials, of the very comprehensive MAEE Report No. F/23 of April 1927 on the Valkyrie are as follows:

1. **Sections 1 - 7** — These sections contain basic data and descriptive matter already mainly covered but the following data, applicable to the time of testing is extracted.

Weights —

Tare		17,851
Light		17,506
Fixed military load		345
Service load		2,819
Fuel load		4,330
Flight weight on trials		25,000
Fuel		846 gallons
Oil		54 gallons
Bombs		1,100 lb
Crew		5

Aircraft floats in 2ft. 11¾ins. of water at full load

Performance —

Maximum Speed		Time to Altitude	Rate of Climb
Sea level	102 m.p.h.	0	585 ft./min.
2,000 ft.	100.8 m.p.h.	3-45 mins	483 ft./min.
5,000 ft.	98 m.p.h.	11-9 mins	331 ft./min.
10,000 ft.	85 m.p.h.	38-36 mins	79 ft./min.

Service ceiling   9,600 ft.
Take-off run 729 yards in 39.2 secs, wind 9.5 knots.
Landing run   229 yards, speed 56.5 knots.

2. **Section 8, para 5, Flying Qualities**

On the water the seaplane handles poorly at low speeds, owing to lack of thrust and because the rudder does not become effective unless the centre engine is at fairly high RPM. This should be much improved by fitting geared engines.

In the air, it handles well except laterally. There is a tendency to fly left wing low which cannot be cured by rigging adjustment. This occurs when gliding and more markedly with engine on. Also the aileron control is heavy in spite of being balanced to a point where the ailerons are liable to take charge in bumps.

Except for these two faults the aircraft is free from vice and the elevator and rudder controls very good. The servo rudder is a definite success - it is adequate mechanically and aerodynamically and a great relief to the pilot. Its only fault is a tendency to be soft at low speed.

There is no turning tendency.

With any one engine stopped, the aircraft remains controllable and is not difficult or tiring to fly.

At full load, it is not possible to get off the water with two engines functioning. But once in the air, the aircraft can maintain height with one outboard engine idle and can climb 80 feet per minute at 1000 feet with the centre engine idle.

The aircraft is considered a good bombing platform.

A.4 SAUNDERS MEDINA   1926

Type — Passenger carrying flying boat for 6 to 10 passengers and 2 crew.

Engines — 2 - 450 H.P. Bristol Jupiter VI.

Fuselage — The hull was of all wood construction covered with Consuta plywood, the V-shaped entry changing to flat sides, the flared planing bottom incorporating two steps. The two flight crew were accommodated side by side in an open cockpit with the pilot on the port side. Access to a mooring hatch and to the passenger cabin was on the starboard side. Luggage and radio compartments were inside the forward section of the hull and a further luggage and toilet compartment aft of the cabin. The prototype was furnished with seats facing inwards for six passengers with a separate seat forward of the cabin for a cabin attendant. Access to the cabin was by companion-way and ladder from a hatch to port in the roof of the hull.

Wings — The wing structure was unconventional with 5° dihedral on the top outer wing which was of shorter span than the lower. All wing bracing was by steel struts of fixed length to simplify rigging. Balancing floats were fixed directly to the lower wing and rod-operated ailerons were provided on both surfaces. The structure was built of wood with fabric covering, except for walkways covered with Consuta plywood, and was of a thick high-lift section (RAF 33). The top centre section was mounted on a vertical strut to the hull at the front spar and on the engine mounting structures, with diagonal struts at the rear spar from the centre-line to the lower centre section. The lower centre section was integrated to the hull and braced with struts to main bulkheads above the chine.

Tail Unit — A single fin and monoplane tailplane mounted on top of the fin were of wooden construction with fabric covering. The fin was built integral with the hull. The tailplane incidence was adjustable by screw-jack at the leading edge and was braced to the hull by struts attached at the tips. Both rudder and elevators were provided with aerodynamic balance areas and were operated by push-pull rods.

Power Plant — The Jupiter engines were faired into the under-surface of the upper wing and were mounted on an assembly of struts between the upper and lower centre sections. 200 gallons of fuel, together with oil tanks, were contained in the nacelles. Two-bladed wooden airscrews, 9 ft. diameter, were fitted.

Dimensions —

Span: Top		52 ft.
Bottom		58 ft.
Chord		9 ft. 4 ins.
Length		49 ft.
Height		16 ft.

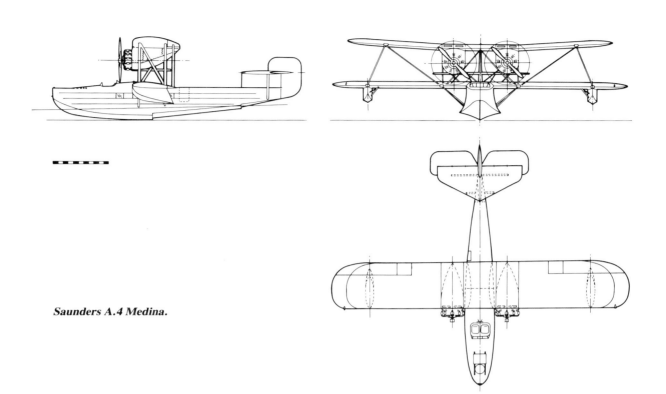

Saunders A.4 Medina.

Saunders A.4 Medina. The only one of the type moored on the Medina.

Weights —	Basic	8,060 lb.
	Gross	11,560 lb
	Wing loading	11.5 lb per sq. ft.

Performance —	Maximum speed	115 m.p.h.
	Cruising speed	90 m.p.h.
	Duration	4 hours

Production — A4/1 Prototype only, G-EBMG, also N.214 allocated.
The aircraft was ready for flight in November 1926 and Capt. F.J. Bailey, an experienced civil pilot was invited to carry out the flight trials on behalf of the Air Council, who sponsored the machine, with Flight Lieut Sawyer in attendance.

General — The Medina was retained at Cowes for development purposes but performance proved to be unsatisfactory and the aircraft was dismantled in 1929.

A.7 SAUNDERS SEVERN   1927-30

Type — General purpose reconnaissance flying boat with crew of 5. To Specification R4/27.

Engines — 3 - 485 H.P. Bristol Jupiter IX & XIFP.

Fuselage — The hull was of metal construction using duralumin with corrugations for stiffening of the exterior skinning and with a planing bottom of Alclad. Above the V-shaped planing bottom with two steps, the sides of the hull were flat and tapered back to the wedge-shaped rear section. Forward of the wings an open cockpit provided accommodation for two pilots side by side and further forward were a front gunner's position and mooring station. Gun positions were located amidships and at the tail end. The interior of the hull provided generous cabin space for navigation and radio operator and crew facilities.

Wings — The biplane wings were of unequal span and chord and of thick high-lift section. The lower wing was attached direct to the top of the hull with no additional bracing and was parallel in chord and mounted with a dihedral. The upper wing consisted of a centre section with separate tapered outer panels mounted with dihedral and sweepback on the leading edge. The wings were of metal two-spar construction with fabric covering. The balancing floats were of similar construction to the hull with visible external corrugations were were mounted below the outboard interplane struts by a complex arrangement of struts with shock absorbing devices.

Tail Unit — A monoplane tailplane, strut braced to the hull, was mounted on the swept-up rear fuselage. Twin fins and rudders with Flettner servo-tabs were carried at the tips of the tailplane. Construction was all metal with fabric covering.

Power Plant — The centre section contained 6,220 lb. of fuel and oil and carried the three engine nacelles mounted directly underneath, the outboard engine mountings being attached to both the centre section and the outer wing. Hand turning gear for engine starting was mounted externally on the interplane struts. Two-bladed wooden airscrews, 12ft. 6ins. diameter, were fitted at 12ft. 8ins. centres although a four-blader was fitted later to the centre engine.

Dimensions —	Span: Top	88ft. 0ins.
	Bottom	51ft. 0ins.
	Tailplane	25ft. 7¾ins.
	Chord	Top 15ft. 0ins. max.
	Bottom	8ft. 8ins.
	Tailplane	9ft. 7ins.
	Gap	8ft. 9ins.
	Stagger	2° 5'
	Length 64ft. 6ins. Beam	9ft. 6ins.
	Wing area	1,567 sq. ft.
	Height (off trolley)	19ft. 3ins.
	(on trolley)	21ft. 6ins.
	Sweepback: Top wing 3° 49' at L/edge	
	Bottom wing	Nil
	Dihedral: Top wing	2° 0'
	Bottom wing	2° 0'
	Incidence	2° 0'

| Weights — Gross | 22,153 lb as tested at MAEE but increased to 22,503 prior to Middle East cruise. Overload 26,000 lb as tested. |
| Basic | 14,803 lb. |

Performance — At 22,153 lb.

Maximum Speed	(125 m.p.h. at S.L.
	(120 m.p.h. at 5,000 ft.
Cruising speed	97 m.p.h.
Stalling speed	62 m.p.h.
Alighting speed	69 m.p.h.
Service ceiling	8,930 ft.
Take-off time (0 wind)	24.5 secs.
Range	870 sea miles
Climb to 5000 ft.	11 m 21 secs.

At 26,000 lb

Cruising speed	94 m.p.h.
Take-off time (0 wind)	57 secs.
Range	1,410 sea miles

NOTE   Further strengthening and redesign was estimated to add an additional 650 lb. to the basic aircraft with further reductions to the performance figures which already were below the specified requirements. Details of the itinerary of the cruise and the aircraft's performance follow.

1931 MIDDLE EAST CRUISE

Saunders-Roe A.7 in Company with Short Singapore II

Date	Distance Miles	From - To	Flying Time
Aug. 15	319	Felixstowe - Plymouth (Positioning)	
Aug. 17	457	Plymouth - Hourtin	4.29
Aug. 18	356.5	Hourtin - Berre (Marseilles)	3.36
Aug. 19	750	Berre - Malta	7.25

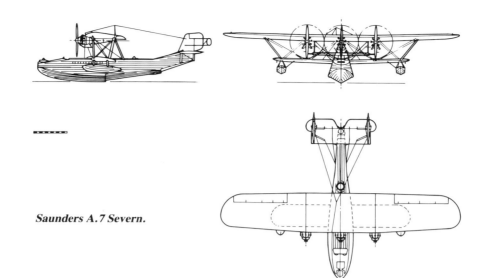

Saunders A.7 Severn.

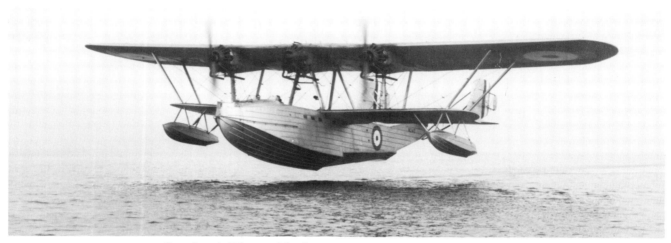

Saunders A.7 Severn. The first Saunders flying boat with metal hull.

R.A.F. flight to the Middle East, 1931. The crew of the A.7 at Felixstowe prior to the flight to the Middle East for tropical trials. Flight Lieut Cahill was the Captain, and Flying Officer Sturgiss his co-pilot. A four-bladed propeller was fitted to the centre engine at the time.

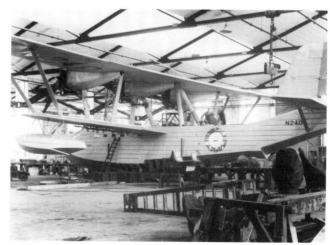

Saunders A.7 Severn. Undergoing maintenance between flights in the Solent Works.

Date	Distance Miles	From - To	Flying Time
Aug. 22	966	Malta - Aboukir	9.20
Aug. 28	1,073	Aboukir - Port Sudan	9.45
Aug. 31	883	Port Sudan - Lake Timsah	10.45
Sept. 8	201	Ismailia - Aboukir	2.15
Sept. 9	966	Aboukir - Malta	13.02
Sept, 11	655.5	Malta - Algiers	9.56
Sept. 15	467	Algiers - Gibraltar	3.50
Sept. 16	1,230	Gibraltar - Plymouth	13.40

Plymouth return -

Totals	8,005		88.03

Average flying speed 91 m.p.h.

A.10 SAUNDERS-ROE UNNAMED FIGHTER 1929

Type — Single seater intercepter fighter. F20/27.
Multi- gun single seater fighter. F10/27.

Engine — 1 - 480 H.P. Rolls-Royce F.XI.

Fuselage — The structure of the fuselage was all-metal, being basically made of tubular members of both steel and duralumin with suitable fittings at the bolted joints. The forward portion, consisting of the engine, radiator and armament bays back to the cockpit, was covered by aluminium alloy panels, the majority of which were readily detachable for access purposes. Aft of this, the fuselage covering was of fabric over metal formers and stringers.

Wings — The single-bay biplane wings of R.A.F. 31 section consisted of an aluminium alloy structure with fabric covering. Dihedral was provided on the upper wing which also contained the inset ailerons and was built with a separate centre section, reduced in thickness and slightly arched for improved forward vision. Separate outer panels contained the two gravity fuel tanks. Both wings were parallel but of unequal span and chord with well rounded tips, the trailing edge of the lower wing and the centre section having cutaways for improvement of the pilot's view.

Tail Units — These were conventional metal-framed structures with fabric covering. The tailplane was braced to the fuselage by struts and wires and wirebraced to the fin.

Dimensions —

Span	32 ft.
Length	24 ft. 5 ins.
	modified to 26 ft. 2 ins.
Height	9 ft. 9 ins.
Wing area	273 sq.ft.

Weights —

	F20/27	F10/27
Basic	2,674 lb.	2,694 lb.
Gross	3,467 lb.	3,598 lb.

Fuel — 49 gallons.

Performance —

Maximum speed	200 m.p.h.
Landing speed	70 m.p.h.

Armament —

2 Vickers guns with 600 rounds each.   F20/27.
4 Vickers guns with 500 rounds each.   F10/27.

Production — 1 Prototype only, initially unmarked, later with Class B marking, L.2 and finally K.1949 from February 1931 when taken on charge a A & AEE.

A.14 HULL FOR SUPERMARINE SOUTHAMPTON 1929-30

A contract was placed with Supermarine, No. 826424/28 dated 5.4.28, for the supply of a Southampton Mk.II aircraft with metal hull designed by Saunders, the object being to prove the hull concept in comparison with a machine of known performance. Saunders, as sub-contractor, built the hull and despatched it to Felixstowe where it was erected by MAEE personnel with assistance from a Saunders representative. For convenience, a Mk.I superstructure with Mk.II centre section and standard Southampton tail units were fitted.

Hull — The design of the hull was generally similar in style to that being designed for the A.7 Severn and the later successful A.27 London with flat sides and parallel external corrugations designed to save the weight of internal stringers and avoid drilling and sealing of all the attachment rivets. Similar skinning was used on the upper and lower surfaces, where appropriate. The whole concept was to provide a roomy hull of light weight and simplified construction avoiding the use of double curvature.

Experience at Felixstowe showed it necessary to provide more light to the interior of the hull by the fitting of additional scuttles and reinforcing the main step to avoid local buckling of the skins. Also the width of the hull prevented the use of a standard Southampton beaching chassis and it was necessary to use an improvised trolley.

Weights —

A.14 Southampton	Basic	8,870 lb.	
	Overload	18,000 lb.	
Southampton Mk.I (wooden hull)	Basic	9,320 lb.	
S.1231 Mk.II (metal hull)	Basic	9,160 lb.	

Performance —

A.14 Southampton

Maximum speed at sea level	90.3 knots
Rate of climb at sea level	590 ft. per min.
Service ceiling	10,400 ft.
Take-off run	250 yards } In 9.5
Take-off time	15.5 secs. } knot wind.

Mk.II (metal hull)   S.1231

Maximum speed at sea level	92.8 knots
Rate of climb at sea level	660 ft. per min.
Service ceiling	11,150 ft.

Mk.I (wooden hull)   N.9896

Take-off run	217 yards } In 8.5
Take-off time	15 secs. } knot wind

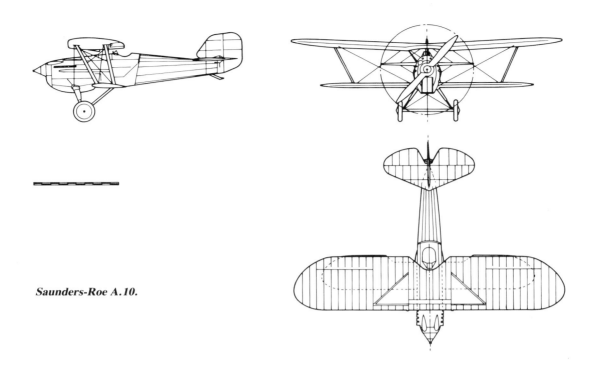

Saunders-Roe A.10.

Saunders-Roe A.10 Fighter. The only piston-engined single seater fighter
built by the Company. Many years later the Company re-entered this field
with turbo-jet and rocket-propelled prototypes.

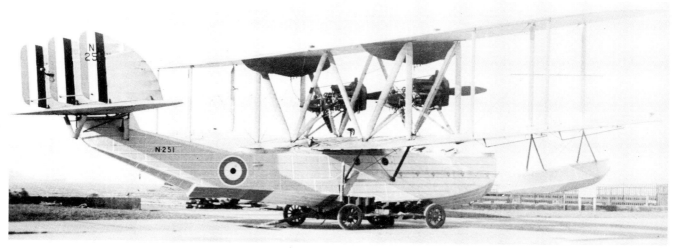

Saunders-Roe A.14. The experimental metal hull fitted with
Supermarine Southampton superstructure

NOTE The A.14 hull being lighter allowed greater payload at the same all-up-weight. Felixstowe also commented that a standard Southampton take-off time in a 10 knot wind was about 17 seconds. At large overloads the A.14 hull behaved better on the water than the standard Southampton and could be taxied easily to speeds of 25 knots and take-off was easier and cleaner. (M.A.E.E. -Report F/63 of 22.10.30. refers).

Production — 1 aircraft N.251 for comparative trials only.

General — The aircraft was launched on 13th March 1930 and by October had flown 77 hours, much of it at full throttle. The slight reduction of performance from the standard Southampton, due to the larger cross-section of the hull, was balanced by the increased hull space and crew comfort and by the better behaviour on the water.

Although the Felixstowe report No. F/63 of 22.10.30. was generally favourable, insufficient advantage precluded further production. A hull of similar general design but with stainless steel planing bottom was also made by Supermarine for the Southampton Mk.X, an aircraft comparable to the A.7 Severn, which proved heavier than design estimate and down on performance and like the Severn was not produced in quantity.

ISACCO HELICOGYRE NO.3   1929

Type — Helicopter for research purposes.

Engines — 4 - 32 H.P. Bristol Cherub.
1 - 100 H.P. A.S. Genet Major.

Fuselage — This was a tubular structure of rectangular section with a vertical post for mounting the rotor, braced by struts to the top longerons, just ahead of the pilot's cockpit which was protected by a hoop-shaped enclosure. Metal panels covered the engine compartment, whilst the remainder of the fuselage was fabric-covered. The rigid undercarriage was mounted well forward and the axle was

sprung by rubber chords. The tail-skid was pivotted well below the fuselage maintaining the machine in a horizontal attitude on the ground.

Power Plant — The four tip-mounted engines drove the rotor by small four-bladed wooden tractor airscrews and thus provided the lift. The engine for forward propulsion drove a two-bladed tractor airscrew through an extension shaft. Fuel for all engines was contained in the fuselage.

Rotor — The four-bladed rotor embodied lift and drag hinges and consisted of tubular spars with a series of ribs and sub-spars and was fabric-covered. Flaps along the full length of the trailing edge of each blade, inboard of the engines, controlled the vertical movement. Small trimming flaps were provided behind the engines to regulate the incidence of each blade separately, to overcome the vibration resulting from the inaccuracies of setting of the blades and flaps plus the play in the controls. Separate flaps on a tubular spar rigidly joined to the pylon above the rotor were differentially operated during each revolution to equalise lift. The pylon above the rotor hub provided the anchorage for support cables to the tip of each blade.

Flying Controls — A balanced rudder and normal type elevator were provided for directional and pitch control in forward flight. The elevator was in one piece hinged to the tailplane which was attached to the underside of the fuselage and braced by struts to the top longerons.

Length — 28 ft. 4 ins.

Rotor Dia. — 48 ft. 2 ins.

Rotor Speed — 50 r.p.m.

Weights —	Basic	2,400 lbs.
	Gross	2,920 lbs.
Production —	1 machine, Serial No. K.1171.	

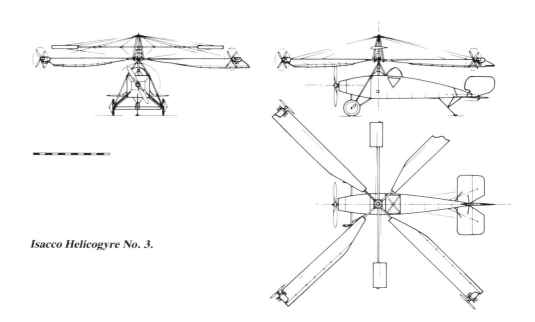

Isacco Helicogyre No. 3.

Isacco Helicogyre No. 3. At R.A.E. Farnborough in the original Airship Shed A. Prophetically facing east, for Isacco moved to Russia to build No. 4.

In the open air if not in the air!

CHAPTER 11

SARO, SPARTAN AND OTHER AIRCRAFT OF 1929-35

A.V. Roe was now in a senior position on the board of a company whose title and products were from now on identified by the names of the two famous pioneers of the aircraft industry, Saunders-Roe, generally abbreviated to the trade name of Saro.

Initially the workload was augmented by the manufacture of the Bluebird and Spartan biplanes while success to a limited degree was reached with the Cutty Sark and Cloud amphibians and the Spartan Cruiser landplane. Production of these machines for both civil and military requirements was the major activity in the factory during this period, whilst the design and manufacture of a prototype to Specification R24/31, which became the London, was proceeding, also preliminary design of the larger R2/33.

A.17 SARO CUTTY SARK   1929

Type — Light 4 seater cabin flying boat or amphibian.

Engines —

(1) 2 - 105/115 HP Cirrus Hermes I.
    F.B. version A.17A.
    Amphibian A.17B.
(2) 2 - 120 HP D.H. Gipsy II.
    F.B. version A.17G & P.
    Amphibian A.17H & Q.
(3) 1 - 240 HP A.S. Lynx IVC.
    F.B. version A.17E.
    Amphibian A.17F.
(4) 2 - 130 HP D.H. Gipsy III.
    F.B. version A.17N.
    Amphibian A.17O.
(5) 2 - 140 HP A.S. Genet Major I.
    F.B. version A.17L.
    Amphibian A.17M.

Sales brochures stated that other engine installations were possible, such as 3 Pobjoys or 3 Genets A.17J & K, but these were not employed.

Fuselage — The hull was of Alclad construction throughout with a V-shaped planing bottom and single step. For ease of production most of the hull panels were flat, stiffened by corrugations, except for the prototype which was without the corrugations, relying on interior structure. The section of the hull provided a roomy cabin for four, including the pilot, with opening windows and transversely sliding roof section on the starboard side for access by ladder. A folding hatch in the foredeck, for mooring purposes, could be reached from the cabin and a triangular hinged panel in the roof enabled the pilot to stand, also for mooring purposes. A luggage compartment was accessible from the roof behind the wing. The hull was compartmented to minimise flooding in the event of damage. Dual controls, the starboard being removable, were fitted. Twin flaps mounted on the sides of the hull, forward of the step, served as water rudder and brakes but were not very effective.

Wing — The tapered cantilever wing was of wooden construction based on Avro-Fokker practice as introduced into the company with the arrival of A.V. Roe, J. Lord and H. Broadsmith. It contained the main fuel tanks and was also compartmented for buoyancy and carried balancing floats at one-third of the span which were of metal construction similar to the hull.

Tail Unit — The fin was of "Alclad" and constructed integrally with the hull. The aerodynamically balanced rudder was fabricated by welding from steel tube and sections as were the tailplane and divided elevator. The tailplane was mounted on top of the fin to which it was braced by struts and wires. The forward struts attached to the front spar which formed the tailplane leading edge, to which the bracing wires were also attached and carried down to the base of the fin. The rear struts went from the rear spar to a kingpost in a vertical slide in the fin enabling the tailplane to be adjustable pivotting about the front spar.

Power Units — The engine installation consisted generally of two engines mounted on struts above the wing giving adequate propeller and spray clearance. One aircraft was built with a single engine only, mounted in a similar manner but on the centre-line. Gravity fuel tanks for $\frac{1}{2}$ hour of flight were incorporated into each nacelle and were fed from the two main tanks of 25 gallons each in the wing. Heywood compressed air unit for starting the engines from inside the hull could be provided. The in-line engines were fully cowled and the radial engined machines were fitted with Townend rings. The twin engines were positioned at a small angle to the centre-line to facilitate handling on one engine.

Undercarriage — Most machines were supplied as amphibians although the prototype first appeared as a pure flying boat as was the single-engined machine for the Japanese pilot. The undercarriage radius arms pivotted on the sides of the hull with the oleo legs attached to a screwed cross-shaft just below the wing. The rotation of this shaft caused the top of the legs to be drawn inwards, behind the cabin, thus swinging the wheels upwards to clear the water. Retraction was by manual means by the pilot. Some aircraft incorporated wheel-brakes. The tailskid was positioned below the rear fin post.

Dimensions —

	Span	45ft. 0ins.
	Length	34ft. 4ins.
	Height	11ft. 2ins.
	Length of Hull	32ft. 0ins.
	Beam	4ft. 0ins.
	Wing Area	320 sq.ft.

Weights —

	(Subject to engine type)	
	Basic	2246 lb to 2744 lb
	Gross	3200 lb to 3900 lb

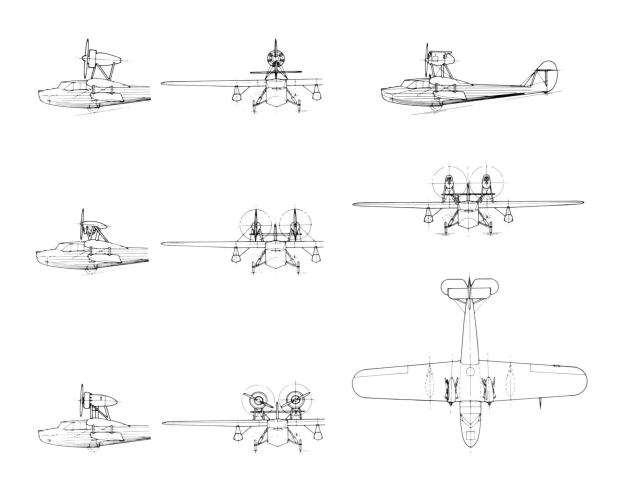

Saro A17 Cutty Sark Variants.

Saro A.17 Cutty Sark. The only single-engined version built was for Japan. Here seen moored outside the Solent Works with the East Cowes frontage behind on the opposite side of the Medina.

A.17 Cutty Sark. *Carrying out pleasure flights from the beach at Falmouth.* The first machine G-AAIP operated by Kirsten and Mace.

A.17 Cutty Sark. The fourth machine takes to the water at Cowes.

A.17 Cutty Sark. The sixth machine. The only R.A.F. Cutty Sark.

A.17 Cutty Sark. The first of two military Cutty Sark amphibians ordered in 1932 for the Kwangsi Air Force. Although despatched to Hong Kong the machine was not handed over and eventually returned to Cowes. The inverted Gipsy III engines were replaced by Genet Major radials and the aircraft were then used by Air Service Training for training flying boat pilots for the airlines.

Cutty Sark in flight.

Cutty Sark wing manufacturing at Folly Works.

Saro A.19 Cloud. The prototype military Cloud moored in the Medina.

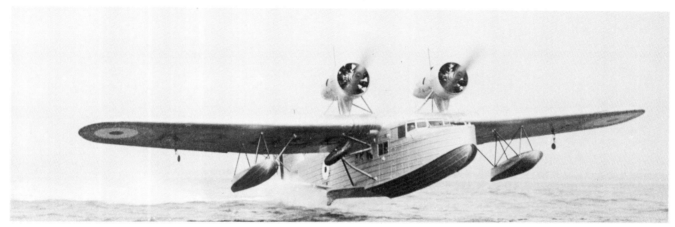
Saro A.19 Cloud. The third production Cloud K.2896 for use as a training aircraft by the R.A.F.

Performance —

	A.17A	A.17.P	A.17.Q	A.17E	A.17M
Maximum Speed (mph)	105	110	100	112	107
Cruising Speed (mph)	85	88	80	90	85
Range miles (4 hours)	340	300	300	-	315
Ceiling (feet)	9,500	9,500	9,000	10,000	9,000

General — The prototype first flew as a flying boat on 4th July 1929 and was then taken to Olympia for the 1929 Aero Show. The Cutty Sark was primarily intended for civilian operation by small airlines and for private and business operators. G-AAIP was tested at Felixstowe in August 1929 and certificated for civil use (Felixstowe Report F/45 of 5.9.29 refers). However, one machine was taken on to the strength of the RAF for use by the Seaplane Training Flight at Calshot and three were used by Air Service Training Limited. For RAF use the crew was restricted to two, by weight considerations, after S1575 was tested at Felixstowe early in 1931 (Felixstowe Report F/69 Feb. 1931 refers) and precluded more general Service use. The board authorised the design and manufacture of a metal wing in January 1932 but this was not completed.

Production — 12 aircraft.

Constructor's No. A17.1 (Engine types 1 & 2)
Registration/Serial No. G-AAIP
  Originally built as a flying boat with Cirrus Hermes engines later converted to amphibian and engines changed to Gipsy II. Extensively flown for demonstration purposes before being sold but soon bought by Kirsten & Mace and named Silver Bat. (Resold to Isle of Man Air Service in January 1932.) Scrapped in 1935.

Constructor's No. A17.2 (Engine type 2)
Registration/Serial No. VH-UNV
  Originally flew with Class B identification L.1. Sold to Matthews Aviation of Melbourne, Australia. Written off in April 1938.

Constructor's No. A17.3 (Engine type 1)
Hull No. S2/1611
Class B Identification L.3
  This machine was supplied to the New Zealand Permanent Air Force as a flying boat. First flown at Cowes by S.D. Scott on 3.3.30, it received a C of A on 18.3.30. and was then dismantled and shipped to Auckland. The aircraft was reassembled in a seaplane hangar at Hobsonville and was flown on 14.6.30. for the first time by Sqn. Ldr. L.M. Isitt, later to be Chief of Staff of the RNZAF The Class B identity L.3 was retained under the wing tips together with roundels and rudder stripes throughout its service life, which included familiarisation flying, photographic and search missions and general transport duties including carriage of the Governor-General and other VIPs. A total of 221 hours 5 minutes flying was recorded to 23.11.36. when the aircraft was written off.

Constructor's No. A17.4 (Engine type 2)
Registration/Serial No. G-AAVX (VR-SAA)
  Built as a flying boat for the Hon. A.E. Guinness but transferred to Royal Singapore Flying Club 1930 as an amphibian. Scrapped 1935.

Constructor's No. A17.5 (Engine type 2)
Registration/Serial No. G-ABBC
  Sold to Mr. Francis Francis in July 1930. To Kirsten & Mace later British Amphibious Air Lines 1932-35. Named Progress. Returned to Cowes and destroyed in bombing May 1942.

Constructor's No. A17.6 (Engines type 2 and 4)
Registration/Serial No. S.1575
  The only RAF Cutty Sark was delivered in December 1930 for trials at Felixstowe and potential use as a training aircraft at RAF Calshot. The type was not accepted owing to severe trim change at low throttle settings and loss of elevator control prior to the stall.
  In January 1934 the aircraft was flown from Calshot to Somerton by S.D. Scott for overhaul by the Company. The following day on take-off the machine hit a telegraph pole and landed in a field behind houses in upper Newport Road near the reservoir. The port wing and undercarriage were smashed necessitating dismantling and then transfer to the Solent Works for repair. To improve performance the engines were replaced with Gipsy IIIs. Further testing at MAEE ensued, when major structural faults occurred which precluded the further possibility of service use of the type.

Constructor's No. A17.7 (Engine type 4)
Registration/Serial No. VR-HAY
  Operated by the Far East Aviation Company in Hong Kong.

Constructor's No. A17.8 (Engine types 4 & 5)
Registration/Serial No. L.5 G-AETI
  Originally for use by the Kwangsi Air Force. Shipped to Hong Kong unregistered for sale to China which was not concluded. The only Cutty Sark equipped with armament, a machine gun on a movable mounting in the nose position. L.5 was returned to UK in 1936 and rebuilt for Air Service Training Limited. In use February 1937 to February 1940.

Constructor's No. A17.9 (Engine type 3)
Registration/Serial No. G-ABVF
  To Japan in 1932. Single engined flying boat for Yoshihara. Crashed in Alaska.

Constructor's No. A17.10 (Engine type 5)
Registration/Serial No. G-ACDP
  Air Service Training Limited April 1933 to April 1939.

Constructor's No. A17.11 (Engine type 5)
Registration/Serial No. G-ACDR
  Air Service Training Limited April 1933 - 1938.

Constructor's No. A17.12 (Engine type 5)
Registration/Serial No. G-ADAF
  To R.H. Kulka Limited of San Domingo February 1935

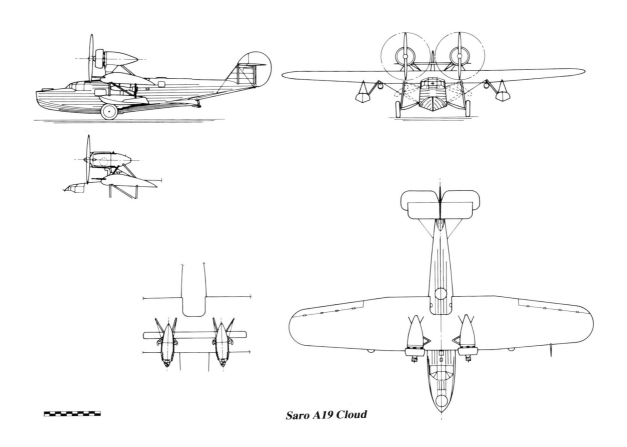

Saro A19 Cloud

Saro A. 19 Cloud. G-ABCJ in its original form with Wright Whirlwind engines.

Type —   A.19 - Passenger amphibian flying boat for
                civil operations 2 crew, 7/8 passengers.
            A.29 - Military version for pilot and navigator
                training, 2 crew, 6 pupils, to
                Specification 15/32.

Engines —   (1) 2 - 300 HP Wright Whirlwind J-6.
                    FB version
                    A.19.A, Amphibian A.19.B.
            (2) 3 - 255 HP A.S. Lynx IV C. FB
                    version
                    A.19.G, Amphibian A.19.H.
            (3) 2 - 425 Pratt & Whitney Wasp C.
                    FB version
                    A.19.Q, Amphibian A.19.R.
            (4) 2 - 340 HP Napier Rapier IV.
            (5) 2 - 340 HP A.S. Serval III & V.
                    (Originally named Double
                    Mongoose). FB version
                    A.19.N, Amphibian A.19.P.
            (6) 2 - 300 HP Walter Pollux.

Construction — The constructional features of the Cloud
were the same as for the Cutty Sark for it was a larger
version of the same basic type. The layout of the aircraft
was identical except for the positioning of the combined
tail-skid and water rudder at the additional second step.
The enlarged cabin was entered through a forward
folding door in the side of the hull just aft of the wing.
Inside were luggage compartments forward and a toilet
compartment aft. The mooring point in the foredeck had
a sliding panel. Although changes were made in the
course of development, all machines were built as
amphibians with wheel brakes but various engine types
were fitted, including one machine fitted with three
engines which later reverted to the standard twin-engined
arrangement. This same machine was also non-standard
in other respects and was given an aerofoil above the
engines and twin fins and rudders with central trimming
rudder for reduction of landing speed and improved
controllability.

Power Units — The engine mountings of the radial
engined machines were unlike those used on the A.17 and
A.21. The front support consisted of a vertical member,
enclosed in tapered fairings which contained the controls
and services to the nacelle. The front mounting was
completed by a diagonal stabilising strut inboard,
although additional outboard struts were fitted to some
aircraft. The rear mounting consisted of splayed struts
without fairings. The Rapier engined machine reverted to
splayed strut mountings without fairings.
   The first machine was uncowled originally but Townend
ring cowlings were adopted later on radial engined
machines after extensive trials with various types of these.
Electric starting was employed.
   RAF aircraft carried an oil cooler and an aerial mast on
the top of each nacelle.

Tail Units — In the course of development the overhanging portion of the rudder was cut back and replaced
by a small trimming fin of similar construction mounted

on the tailplane. Improved airflow over the tail to
improve elevator control was investigated by the addition
of narrow chord aerofoils just above the wing centre
section.

RAF Version — This was fitted with dual controls for two
pilots and the cabin was equipped for six pupils to
undergo navigation and radio training. Gun positions
with sliding hatches were provided in the bow and
amidships for the carriage of Lewis or camera
guns. A bomb load of 200 lb could be carried below the
wing. During development changes were made to the hull,
which increased its length and depth at both the bow,
which was deepened forward of the cabin, and aft along
the top, forward of the fin. The planing bottom and the
steps were also modified to improve the handling on the
water. These changes were introduced at stages in production and carried out retrospectively where possible.
The Cloud was introduced in the RAF in August 1933 at
Calshot and was later used at Andover and by No. 48
Squadron at Bircham Newton.

Dimensions —

Span	64 ft. 0 ins.
Length	47 ft. 9 ins. (1st-3rd)
	49 ft. 9 ins. (4th & 5th, early
	RAF and 1st modified
	later)
	50 ft. 1½ ins. (Later RAF)
Height	19 ft. 0 ins. (over
	propeller arc)
(Later RAF dimns	17 ft. 6 ins. aerial)
at ground angle)	15 ft. 8 ins. (over cowlings)
Wing Area	650 sq. ft.
Aerofoil Area	120 sq. ft. increased to
(2nd aircraft only)	213 sq. ft.

Weights — (Subject to engine type)

	Gross	From 8,100 to 10,000 lb
	Basic	5,240 to 6,970 lb

Performance — (Subject to engine type)

Maximum Speed	118-125 mph
Cruising Speed	94-102 mph
Take-off Speed	55 mph
Landing Speed	50 mph
Endurance	4 hours
Ceiling	10,000 ft.

Production — 4 Civil aircraft
17 RAF aircraft to Specification 5/32 after prototype.

Constructor's No. A.19/1 & 1A (Engine types 1 & 4)
Registration No. G-ABCJ (CF-ARB)
   Prototype flew originally on 15.7.30. with Class B
registation L.4. C of A issued 1.8.31, then went to Robert
Holt agent for Canada in December 1931. Subsequently
brought back by the Company at the end of 1932 when
Holt relinquished the agency and from 1934 used for
Rapier engine and general development. A narrow-chord
aerofoil was fitted just above the centre section for a time.
Loaned to Jersey Airways in 1935 and use discontinued in
December 1936.

Saro A.19 Cloud. The second Cloud in early form with three Armstrong Siddeley Lynx engines.

Saro A.19 Cloud. The second Cloud after conversion to two Pratt and Whitney engines and the fitment of the overhead aerofoil.

Saro A.19 Cloud. The second machine built for the Hon. A.E. Guinness and orignally had three engines. After conversion to twin engines it later reverted to a single vertical tail unit and the aerofoil was discarded.

Saro A.19 Cloud. After a period in Canada G-ABCJ was returned to the Company and fitted with Napier Rapier engines.

Saro A.19 Cloud. The fifth Cloud was the last civil machine. Fitted originally with Armstrong Siddeley Double Mongoose (Serval) engines the aircraft was re-engined with Walter Pollux after sale to Czechoslovakia.

Constructor's No. A.19/2 (Engine types 2 & 3)
Registration No. G-ABHG

Built in 1930 with three engines and registered in December. First flown 18th February 1931. Reverted to two larger engines and fitted with aerofoil and twin fins and rudders. C of A issued July 1931. Sold to the Hon. A.E. Guinness and named "Flying Amo". To BOAC in 1940 for crew training. Written off in June 1941. Hull used as a caravan.

Constructor's No. A.19/4 (Engine type 5)
Registration No. G-ABXW

Completed in July 1932. Operated by British Flying Boats Limited and later Guernsey Airways when lost with all passengers in July 1936. Named "Cloud of Iona" when delivered in May 1933.

Constructor's No. A.19/5 (Engine types 5 & 6)
Registration No. G-ACGO (OK-BAK)

First flight 16th July 1933. Separate narrow chord aerofoils below and behind each engine mounting. Acquired in 1934 by Bata of Czechoslovakia and from 1936 operated by CSA to the Adriatic coast. Hull used as a motor boat post-war, later retained for preservation.

Constructor's No. A.19/3 (AS Double Mongoose II)
Serial No. K.2681. Military prototype.
No. 12 in New Type Park, Hendon 1931.

Constructor's No. A.29/1-16 (Engine type 5)
Serial Nos. K.2894-98, K.3722-29, K.4300-02

The third machine of the initial batch of five constructed was purchased by the Air Ministry as the prototype of the RAF version, a further sixteen of which were ordered in stages from the end of 1932. The first production machine, K.2894, was flying in 1933. All Clouds were despatched from the works as amphibians although a pure flying boat version had been envisaged.

Ordered in three batches of five, eight and three and delivered to the RAF between August 1933 and June 1933, December 1933 and May 1935 with final deliveries in December 1934/January 1935.

A.21 SARO WINDHOVER   1930

Type — Flying boat or amphibian for civil operations for 2 crew and 4/6 passengers.

Engines — The type was offered as either a pure flying boat or as an amphibian with a variety of alternative engine installations and was then identified as follows:

	F.B.	Amphibian
2 - 135 HP A.S. Mongoose	A.21.C	A.21.D
3 - 120 HP D.H. Gipsy II	A.21.J	A.21.K
1 - 340 HP A.S. Double Mongoose	A.21.L	A.21.M

(The two aircraft built were both Type A.21.K.)

Construction — The constructional features of the Windhover were the same as for the Cutty Sark, it being a larger version of that type and intermediate in size with the Cloud. To facilitate transport, the wing of the machine for New Zealand was made in three sections. The overhead aerofoil became a basic feature of the Windhover to preserve weight and balance conditions. A Heywood starter could be fitted.

Dimensions —	Span	54ft. 4ins.
	Length	41ft. 4ins.
	Height	14ft. 5ins.
	Wing Area	562 sq.ft. (including aerofoil 112 sq. ft.)

Weights

	Flying Boat	Amphibian
Basic	3,650 lb	4,245 lb
Gross	5,500 lb	5,700 lb

Design Performance

(Achieved on test)	Flying Boat	Amphibian
Maximum Speed	110 mph	102 mph (95 mph)
Cruising Speed	90 mph	85 mph (80 mph)
Stalling Speed	60 mph	62 mph (57 mph)
Endurance 4 hours	650 miles	650 miles
Ceiling	10,000 ft	9,000 ft

Production — 2 Civil aircraft.

Constructor's No. A21.1
Registration/Serial No. ZK-ABW (VH-UPB)

The first aircraft flew, piloted by S.D. Scott, on 10.10.30., as a pure flying boat and without an overhead aerofoil in which form it was flown to Felixstowe for C of A trials. It had been sold to Dominion Airlines Limited of New Zealand for use on a proposed route from Wellington in North Island across the Cook Strait to Blenheim and Nelson in South Island. Type-approved after attention to defects at Cowes by MAEE, the Windhover was shipped in November by way of Auckland, reaching Hobsonville seaplane base by mid December. The aircraft remained in its crates as Dominion Airlines ceased operations as a result of a crash which occurred on 23.12.30., causing liquidation of the company and the sale of the Windhover to Matthews Aviation Pty Limited of Melbourne in November 1931. Converted to an amphibian and with an overhead aerofoil, the aircraft was used for charter work around the region and after one of these flights to King Island the aircraft was unable to anchor in heavy seas and was destroyed on the rocks on 14.5.36.

Constructor's No. A21.2
Registration/Serial No. G-ABJP

The second aircraft, without overhead aerofoil, was used for C of A trials at Felixstowe and Martlesham in early 1931, receiving its C of A on 8.7.31. The aerofoil was fitted for further trials before being sold to private owner Mr. Francis Francis who resold in September 1931 to Gibraltar Airways who named the aircraft "General Godley". Mrs Victor Bruce acquired the aircraft in May 1932 and travelled by airline to Gibraltar with Capt. S.D. Scott and S.G. Ford to prepare the Windhover for the flight home. They left Gibraltar for Alicante on 1st June where they stayed overnight, but on take-off in the morning all three engines cut out and the machine was severely damaged in an emergency landing. The aircraft was dismantled with the help of local labour and shipped to Cowes via Gibraltar. After repair at Cowes and renamed

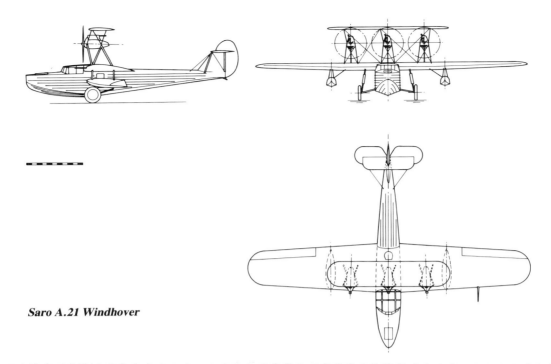

Saro A.21 Windhover

Saro A.21 Windhover. The first machine now with undercarriage and aerofoil fitted at Melbourne in company with the Cutty Sark VH-UNV also operated by Matthews Aviation.

Saro A.21 Windhover. Illustrating some of the difficulties of servicing on open beaches. The Second Windhover named 'General Godley' during its short period of service with Gibralter Airways.

Saro A.21 Windhover. The first Windhover ZK-ABW being launched at the Solent Works in 1930.
The Cloud G-ABCJ is inside the hangar.

Saro A.21 Windhover. The second Windhover complete with undercarriage and overhead aerofoil.
The notice below the cabin limits the maximum permissable weight to 4224lbs.

Saro A.19 Cloud. The hull of the Czechoslovakian Cloud OK-BAK after use as a cabin cruiser prior to restoration for display at the Prague Technical Museum.

Saro A.19 Cloud. Cloud wing under construction at the Folly Works.

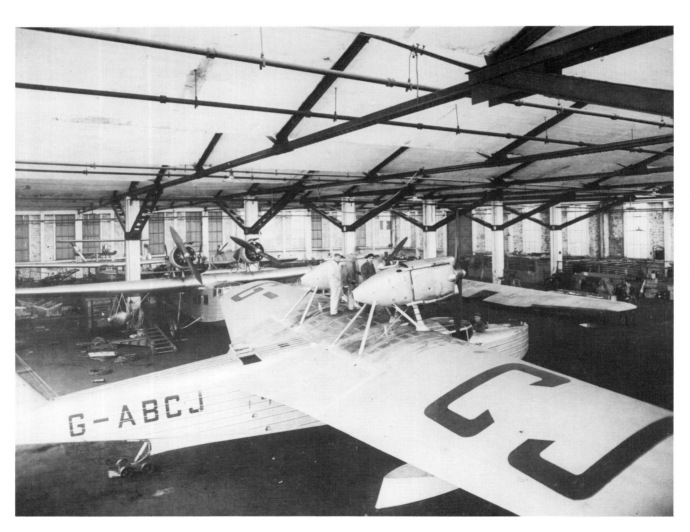

Saro A.17, A.19 and A.21. All three types appear in this scene in the Solent Works in 1933. Two Clouds with the Napier engined machine prominent; in the background a Windhover and two Cutty Sarks, one of which has the inverted Gipsy engines and displays rudder stripes showing its intended military purpose.

"City of Portsmouth", Mrs Bruce made an unsuccessful attempt on the world endurance record on the 22nd July. Starting from Cowes she was forced to alight at Ventnor after 16 hours due to failure of the aircraft generator. On the 6th August the Windhover, operating with undercarriage removed and increased tankage, took off from Cowes for a further attempt at the record. By the use of in-flight refuelling by a Bristol Fighter, aided by a Gipsy Moth, a British record of 54 hours 13 minutes was created. Failure of an engine oil pipe terminated the attempt with the additional hazard of severe fog in the Solent causing the aircraft to land in the Ipswich area.

The aircraft was subsequently operated by Jersey Airways from May 1935 to 1938.

General — The Martlesham Report M/583/CA Trials for C of A of Windhover G-ABJP dated 16.7.31. (Ref. AVIA.18/1098) is an indication of the flying characteristics of the Windhover, which were obstacles to its success:-

Introductory. Trials for C of A have been carried out on G-ABJP an amphibian flying boat with 3 Gipsy II engines. The aircraft underwent trials before but was rejected on account of poor control at low speeds and bad take-off characteristics. Modifications have now been incorporated to improve these features. They consist of alterations to the mainplane and the addition of a small upper mainplane above the engine nacelles. (The tests were carried out at 5,700 lb gross weight and wind speed of 5 mph giving the following recorded take-off, climb and landing performances.)

Climb	1 minute	380 ft.
	2 minutes	800 ft.
	3 minutes	1200 ft.
Take-off run		295 yards
Landing run		278 yards

Handling Report. Satisfactory with CG forward or aft. Very sensitive to bumps and under these conditions initial climb is adversely affected. The controls are poor at 65 mph and below. Aircraft tends to land itself and pilot appears to have little control with the elevator. The view on approach to landing is bad. The glide with engine throttled back is very steep. Stalling speed 57 mph; the aircraft is steady when stalled, but falls out of control if a bump is encountered.

Report on Structural Details. Complies with C of A requirements. Only a single bracing wire to the top plane -if one broke, all lateral stresses on spar would be taken by internal drag bracing and anti-drag bracing. Take additional care on inspection.

A.22 SARO SEGRAVE METEOR I   1930

Type — 4 seat high performance twin engined monoplane for civil use.

Engines — 2 - 120 HP D.H. Gipsy III

Fuselage — Monocoque of oval streamlined shape with enclosed cabin with sliding windows and access panels in the roof on the port side. All wood construction using Consuta plywood extensively. Fixed tail skid.

Wing — Entirely of wooden construction mounted below and well faired into the lower fuselage. The narrow track undercarriage was of divided type using rubber in compression. Fuel and oil tanks on each side could serve both engines.

Control Surfaces — Welded tubular steel structures with fabric covering. The tailplane was wire braced to the fin and fuselage and was adjustable for incidence.

Dimensions —	Span	39 ft. 6 ins.
	Length	27 ft. 6 ins.
	Height	7 ft. 9 ins.
	Wing Area	230 sq.ft.
Weights —	Basic	1948 lb
	Gross	2948 lb
Performance —	Maximum Speed	132 mph
	Cruising Speed	110 mph
	Service Ceiling	14,000 ft.
	Range	340 miles

Production — One prototype G-AAXP first flew on 28th May 1930 in the hands of Stuart Scott and was in use until September 1932 in the ownership of the Aircraft Investment Corporation and various individuals.

A.24 SPARTAN MAILPLANE   1931
(Originally SARO-Percival Mailplane)

Type — Three engined long range mail carrying monoplane. Crew of one.

Engines — 3 - 120 HP D.H. Gipsy III.

Fuselage — Constructed of wood with plywood covering. Pilot in enclosed cabin behind centre engine and large mail compartment occupying remainder of available space. The mail compartment was later modified to accommodate two passengers for a special long distance flight. Fixed narrow track undercarriage with tail wheel.

Wing — Low wing of wooden construction with plywood covering. Outboard engines forward of leading edge faired to centre section which contained fuel tankage.

Tail Unit — Monoplane tailplane with single fin and rudder, later twin fins strut-braced to fuselage. Rudders aerodynamically balanced and cutaway to clear elevators. The units were of conventional duralumin construction and fabric covered.

Dimensions —	Span	56 ft. 0 ins.
	Length	41 ft. 6 ins.
	Height	9 ft. 0 ins.
	Wing Area	470 sq.ft
Weights —	Basic	4,425 lb
	Gross	5,645 lb
	Payload	1,000 lb

165

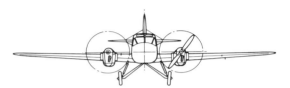

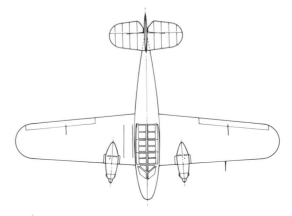

Saro A.22 Segrave Meteor

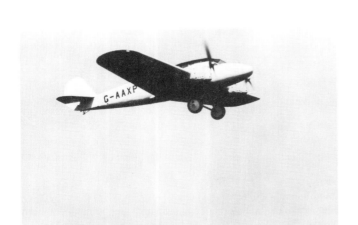

Saro A.22 Segrave Meteor. Airborne from Somerton.

Saro A.22 Segrave Meteor. Three quarter front view.

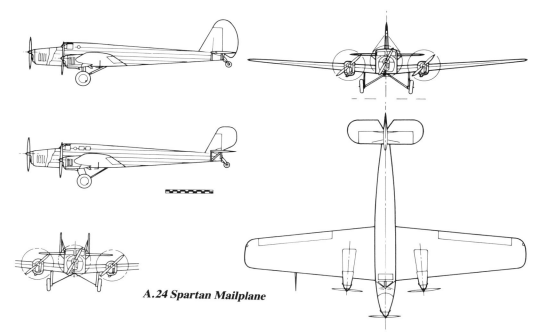

A.24 Spartan Mailplane

Spartan (originally Saro-Percival) Mailplane. The mailplane was adopted
by Spartan in 1931 and acquired twin fins and rudders early in 1932.

G-ABLI

Spartan (originally Saro-Percival) Mailplane. The Mailplane on engine run at Somerton is seen here
in its original form with single fin and rudder.

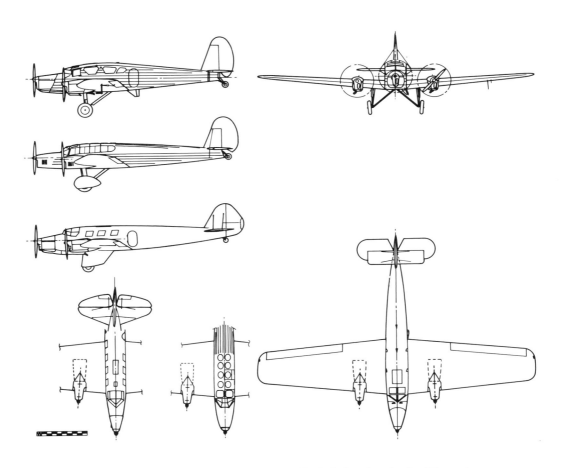

A.24M Spartan Cruiser 3KS. I, II & III. Basic 3 view drawing is of the main production version the Mk II. Side elevations and partial plan views show the differences for the Mks I and III.

Spartan Cruiser Mark I. The prototype was the only cruiser with entry to the cabin from over the wing.

Performance —

	Maximum Speed	122 mph
	Cruising Speed	105 mph
	Range	1000 miles.

Production — One aircraft G-ABLI flown in 1931 received its C of A 24.2.32 and was scrapped in February 1933. Named 'Blackpool' for the flight to India.

General — Basically conceived by Capt. E.W. Percival and absorbed into the Saunders-Roe design system. The Mailplane was already being built in the Saunders-Roe works when Spartan Aircraft became an associated company and development continued under Spartan control.

An interesting account of the flight of a Spartan Mailplane to India appeared in "Popular Flying" for March 1935 under the title "My Most Thrilling Flight". The article was written by William Courteney, Air Correspondent of the London Evening Standard.

A24.M SPARTAN CRUISER MKS I, II & III   1932

Type — Three engined passenger monoplane for 2 crew and 6/8 passengers.

Engines —

3 - 120 HP D.H. Gipsy III	Mk.I
3 - 130 HP D.H. Gipsy Major	
3 - 130 HP Cirrus Hermes IV	} Mk.II
3 - 130 HP Walter Major 4	
3 - 130 HP D.H. Gipsy Major	Mk.III

Fuselage — The fuselage was flat sided with a slightly curved top panel and with stiffening corrugations following Saunders-Roe practice. It was cut away below the forward portion of the cabin to allow the wing to be offered up and this was attached each side at two positions at the main spars to the lower longerons and also at a mid-chord position. The structure was of 'Alclad' with substantial frames and light gauge corrugated skins. On the Mk.I, entry to the cabin was gained over the wing. The roof was provided with transparent panels and the cabin was extensively glazed and windows could be opened. Two sections of the side and roof panels on the port side were hinged at the centre-line and opened upwards for access. On the Mk.II and III versions the cabin top was integrated structurally, with a consequent reduction of vision area because of the need for the windows to follow the shape of the diagonal members in the structure. Access to the cabin on these versions was by a door at the rear on the port side with emergency exit through the forward roof. The cabin for either one or two crew members was entered from above by access through the aperture provided by a sliding canopy which ran forward on rails over the fixed glass windscreen on the final Mk.II versions. Earlier Mk.II and the Mk.III machines had folding side and roof panels for crew access. The centre engine mounting was a tubular structure mounted at four points on a sloping bulkhead forming the front of the main fuselage shell. The Mk.III fuselage was completely redesigned and lengthened, losing some of its flat sided appearance, and now accommodated eight passengers, pilot and wireless operator. The redesigned monocoque of oval section extended from the forward engine bulkhead to the bulkhead aft of the cabin door and flat panels superseded the corrugated skins. The rear fuselage was a welded tubular structure with stringers and fabric covering.

Wing — The wing was of tapered cantilever type of wooden construction, basically as used on the A.21 Windhover. The leading and trailing edge portions were cut back at the centre to clear the fuselage.

Tail Unit — Single fin and rudder with monoplane tailplane, adjustable for incidence, mounted at the top of the fuselage. Strut bracing between fin and tailplane on the Mk.III replaced wire bracing of the earlier versions and the struts below the tailplane to the fuselage. The fin and rudder shape was changed and were reduced in height on the Mk.III also the outline of the tailplane and elevators was changed. The units were of conventional duralumin construction and fabric covered.

Undercarriage — The tall main members of the divided undercarriage embodied coil springs and were hydraulically damped. These were mounted midway between the outer engines and the fuselage and gave a pronounced tail-down appearance but this was somewhat reduced on the Mk.III by the lengthened fuselage and extended tail wheel leg. Wheel brakes were a standard fitment. Wheel fairings on the Mk.I were discarded from the second Mk.II and reappeared as fully trousered fairings on the cantilever undercarriage of the Mk.III.

Dimensions —

	Span	54ft. 0ins.
	Length	39ft. 2ins. Mk.I & II
		41ft. 0ins. Mk.III
	Height	10ft. 0ins.
	Wing Area	436 sq.ft.

Weights —

	Basic	3,400 lb Mk.I
		3,600 lb Mk.II
		4,010 lb Mk.III
	Gross	5,500 lb Mk.I
		5,600 lb Mk.II
		6,200 lb Mk.III

Performance —

	Maximum Speed	135 mph Mk.I & III
		140 mph Mk.II
	Cruising Speed	110 mph Mk.I
		118 mph Mk.II & III
	Range	660 miles Mk.I
		650 miles Mk.II
		550 miles Mk.III
	Ceiling	13,000 ft Mk.I
		15,000 ft Mk.II & III

Production —   16 aircraft as follows at Cowes.
1 aircraft built under licence.

Spartan Cruiser Mk.II. In service with Spartan Air Lines. The third Cruiser G-ACDW later saw service in Eygpt.

Spartan Cruiser Mk.III. The third and final Mk. III. showing the means of entry to the cabin.

Spartan Cruiser Mk.III. The second Cruiser Mk III in flight over Cowes.

Mk.I

Con. No.	Engine Type	Reg. No.	C of A	
(A)24M	D.H. Gipsy III	G-ABTY	8.32	S.A.L. to 2.35. Lost in Channel 11.5.35 when operated by Channel Air Lines.

Mk.II

Con. No.	Engine Type	Reg. No.	C of A	
2	Cirrus Hermes IV	G-ACBM	2.33	Operated by Iraq Airwork Ltd., as YI-AAA on Bagdad-Mosul service till returned to UK in 9.34 and operated by British Airways Ltd., and the Straight Corporation. Scrapped 1937.
3	D.H. Gipsy Major	G-ACDW (Faithful City)	5.33	Flew to Australia and back at end of 1933. Sold to Misr Airwork 4.34 as SU-ABL.
4	D.H. Gipsy Major	G-ACDX (Hampshire)	6.33	Crashed at Gosport 9.10.35. Operated by B.A.L.
5	D.H. Gipsy Major	G-ACJO	9.33	To Aeroput, Yugoslavia as YU-SAN 9.33.
6	D.H. Gipsy Major	G-ACMW	3.34	To Aeroput, Yugoslavia as YU-SAO 4.34.
7	Cirrus Hermes IV	G-ACKG	11.33	To Maharajah of Patiala as VT-AEQ 11.33.
8	D.H. Gipsy Major	G-ACNO (Cape of Good Hope)	2.34	To Bata, Czechoslovakia as OK-ATQ 4.34.
9	Walter Major 4	G-ACOU	7.34	To Bata, Czechoslovakia as OK-ATM 8.34.
10	D.H. Gipsy Major	G-ACSM (Sussex)	6.34	SAL to BAL and N & SA until 4.40. Impressed RAF.X.9433. Scrapped 7.40.
11	D.H. Gipsy Major	G-ACVT	8.34	SAL to BAL 1.10.35. Crashed Ronaldsway 23.3.36.
12	D.H. Gipsy Major	G-ACYL	10.34	SAL to UAL, BAL and N & SA 4.35 until 4.40. Impressed RAF as X9431.
14	D.H. Gipsy Major	G-ACZM	12.34	UAL to BAL and N & SA 10.35. Destroyed 5.42.
-	Walter Major 4	YU-SAP	12.35	Built under licence in Yugoslavia for Aeroput by Fabrika Zmaj.

Mk.III

Con. No.	Engine Type	Reg. No.	C of A	
101	D.H. Gipsy Major	G-ACYK	4.35	SAL to BAL and N & SA 10.35. Crashed at Largs, Ayrshire 14.1.38.
102	D.H. Gipsy Major	G-ADEL	4.35	SAL to BAL and N & SA 10.35 until 4.40. Impressed RAF as X9432.
103	D.H. Gipsy Major	G-ADEM	6.35	SAL to BAL and N & SA 10.35. Crashed at Blackpool 20.11.36.

SAL	=	Spartan Air Lines
UAL	=	United Airways Limited
BAL	=	British Airways Limited
N & SA	=	Northern & Scottish Airways

Type — 2-seater cabin monoplane for private ownership.

Engine —   75 HP Pobjoy 'R' later.
                       90 HP Pobjoy Niagara III.

Fuselage — Side by side two seater originally with a sliding cabin top. The windscreen and enclosure were later modified to provide panels that opened upwards on hinges at the centre of the roof to provide access. The fuselage was mainly of wooden construction built on to a central tubular keel forming the primary structure to which the wings, undercarriage and engine mounting were attached.

Wings — Outer wings, similar to those of the Monospar ST.4, designed and made by General Aircraft Limited at Croydon as Type ST.5 were used. These were based on the Stieger system of construction with a single main spar with pyramidal bracings.

Dimensions —   Span   34 ft. 0 ins.
                     Length   28 ft. 2 ins.

Weights —   Basic   770 lb
                     Gross   1,300 lb

Performance — Maximum Speed 110 mph

Production —   1 aircraft only. Constructor's No. 201.
                     Class 'B' registration S.3, later G-ACEG.

General — The original helmeted cowling was discarded and a longer chord cowling of neater design fitted. In 1938 the more powerful Niagara engine was installed.

TYPES DESIGNED BY OTHER FIRMS

BLACKBURN BLUEBIRD MK.IV   1929-31

Type — 2 seat side by side light biplane for club and private owner use.

Engine —   (1) 95 HP A.D.C. Cirrus III
                     (2) 100 HP D.H. Gipsy I
                     (3) 120 HP D.H. Gipsy II
                     (4) 130 HP D.H. Gipsy III
                     (5) 130 HP A.S. Genet Major I

Fuselage — This was made in four sections: engine mounting, cockpit section, rear fuselage and tail bay and was fabricated throughout from steel tube of uniform gauge connected at the joints by steel plates using bolts and tubular rivets. In section the fuselage was rectangular based on the four main longerons and to this were added light alloy curved members to form the top decking shape and posts on the side and bottom surfaces on to which light alloy stringer sections were sprung into position. The stringers formed a streamlined shape to which the fabric

covering was applied but which could be easily removed for inspection and repair of the primary structure. Bucket seats, suitable for parachute use, and dual controls mainly using rods were fitted. Fold-down doors facilitated access to the cockpit behind which a luggage compartment with a port side access door was provided. The various engines installed were closely cowled but made readily accessible by hinged and removable aluminium panels.

Wings — The wings were conventional single-bay braced structures capable of being folded for storage purposes with the aid of jury struts. The upper centre section was a fuel tank with integral front spar of 22 or 30 gallons capacity, removable with the wings folded. The wings were metal structures employing high-tensile steel strip sections, two of which were rivetted together to form the two I section main spars. Ribs fabricated from duralumin sheet and rolled sections together with a small curved section nosing and flattened tubular trailing edge constituted the structure which was fabric covered but reinforced adjacent to the cockpits. A small amount of sweepback and dihedral angle were employed.

Ailerons, constructed as the tail units described below, were fitted to the lower wings only, their nosings operating in shrouds.

Automatic slots were fitted to the leading edges of the top wings.

Tail Units — The tail units consisted of an adjustable tail-plane, divided elevators and aerodynamically balanced rudder but no fin was fitted. These were based on tubular steel stars with simple formed duralumin sheet ribs with flattened tubular trailing edges and fabric covering.

Undercarriage — This was of divided type consisting of compression struts employing steel springs with oil-dampening and high-tensile steel radius rods and split axles. The non-steering tail skid was sprung by a steel spring enclosed in the tubular sternpost. An alternative twin-float undercarriage was fitted to a few aircraft.

Dimensions —   Span   30 ft. 0 ins.
                     Span Folded   8 ft. 10 ins.
                     Length   23 ft. 2 ins.
                     Wing Area   270 sq.ft.

Weights —   Gross   1,496 lb
                     Basic   960 lb

Performance —

	Cirrus III	Gipsy I
Maximum Speed	107 mph	109 mph
Cruising Speed	82 mph	84 mph
Service Ceiling	15,000 ft.	15,000 ft.
Range	300 miles	340 miles

Production — Serial Nos SB.200-254 (Saro Bluebird) were allocated at Cowes for 55 aircraft some of which were completed at Brough.

Con. No.	Registration
SB.200(1)	G-AAOA
201	To USA unregistered
202(2)	G-AAIR

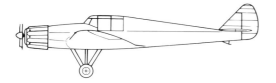

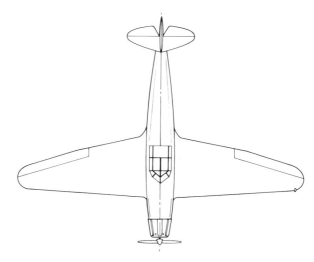

Spartan Clipper

Spartan Clipper. The modified Clipper after receiving its
C. of A. was a competitor in the Kings' Cup Race of 1933.

Spartan Clipper. Built at Cowes and seen here at Somerton before type approval. Only one Clipper was built and considerable
changes were made later to the cabin top, the engine cowling and the undercarriage.

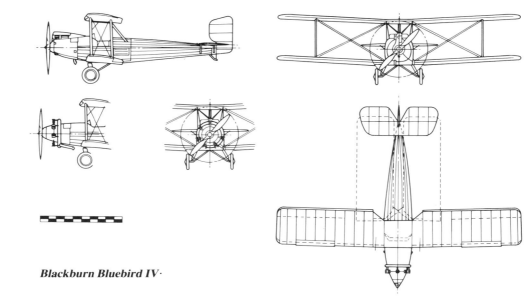

Blackburn Bluebird IV·

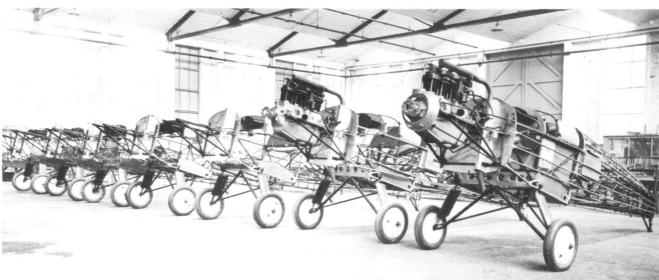

Blackburn Bluebird Mk IV. Under construction in the Solent Works.

Blackburn Bluebird Mk IV. The collection of the first six Saunders-Roe built Bluebirds from Somerton by the uniformed pilots of the National Flying Services for delivery to Hanworth.

Con. No.	Registration
203(1)	G-AAJE/G-AAOB
204(1)	G-AAOC/EC-UUU
205(1)	G-AAOD 206(1) G-AAOE
207(2)	G-AAJC/VP-YAI
208(2)	G-ASSU
209(1)	G-AAOF/TF-LOA
210	G-AATE
211(2)	G-AASV
212(2)	VH-UNS
213(1)	G-AAOG
214(1)	G-AAOH
215(2)	G-AATS
216(5)	VH-UOC
217(2)	G-AATM
218(2)	G-AATN/VH-ACR
219(2)	G-AATO
220(2)	G-AATP
221(1)	G-AAOI
223(2)	G-AAUF
224(2)	G-AAUG
*225(2)	G-AAUT
226(2)	G-AAUU
227(2)	G-AAUV
228(2)	G-AAUW
229(2)	G-AAUX
230(2)	G-AAUY
231(2)	G-AAVF
232(2)	G-AAVG/VH-UQZ
233(2)	G-AAVH
234(2)	G-AAVI/VT-ADI
235	G-AAVJ) To Japan
236	G-AAVK) unregistered
237(4)	G-ABOT
238	G-ABPN
239	VT-ADK
240(3)	G-ABVZ/D-2536
241	G-ABZX/G-ADXG/B.10
242	No information
243	No information
244	No information
245(3)	G-ABDS
246(2)	G-ABEU/CH345/HB-ULU
247(2)	VT-ACP
248(4)	CF-AUP
249(3)	G-ABJA/E1-AAO
250	VT-ADD
251(4)	CF-ALN
*252(4)	G-ABGF
253(3)	G-ABPV
254(4)	G-ABMI

* These aircraft flown as seaplanes.
( ) Engine type.

SPARTAN ARROW AND THREE SEATER
MK.I & II   1930-33

Type —   ARROW - 2 seat light biplane for club and
private owners' use.
THREE SEATER - 3 seat development for
joy riding and air taxi operations.

Engine —
(1) 100 HP D.H. Gipsy I.
(2) 120 HP D.H. Gipsy II.
(3) 95 HP A.D.C. Cirrus III.
(4) 105 HP Cirrus Hermes II.
(5) 115 HP Cirrus Hermes IV.
(6) 160 HP Napier Javelin III.

Fuselage — A conventional wooden structure of spruce internal members and plywood covering. Cockpits, particularly large for this class of aircraft, were entered by fold-down doors on the starboard side. The three-seater Mk.I had the passenger cockpit in the forward position under the centre section; in the Mk.II these positions were reversed.

Wings — Constructed conventionally of wood with two spars and fabric covering, with high-lift Clark 'Y' aerofoil section for improved control near the stall. Aerodynamically balanced ailerons fitted to all four wings except for the last six aircraft where only the lower wings had ailerons. Interchangeability of wings, top to bottom and port to starboard, which was an original feature of Spartan design, was only retained by the use of detachable trailing edges and wing tips and was further restricted by the aileron change. The upper centre section constituted the main fuel tank, the lower, consisting of stub wings braced by struts to the upper longerons, provided mountings for the undercarriage and permitted the wings to fold close to the sides of the fuselage.

Tail Unit — These were simple wooden structures with fabric covering. The three seaters generally retained the interchangeable principles of the original Spartan where the fin and outboard thirds of the tailplane were identical and similarly the rudder and elevator halves. As part of the search for improved handling near the stall, the Arrow had new tail surfaces. The tailplane was built in one piece with large aerodynamically balanced divided elevator. A new shaped fin and increased area rudder were fitted. The test machine for the Napier engine was unique in the shape of its fin and large rudder, which had curved profiles.

Undercarriage — The sprung legs of the undercarriage were mounted on the stub wings thus providing a wide track divided unit. Most machines were supplied as landplanes but at least two were flown on twin floats, the first production Arrow, G-ABBE, being flown on trials at Felixstowe to clear the seaplane version.

Dimensions —

	Arrow	Three Seater
Span	30ft. 7ins.	28ft. 10ins.
Length	25ft. 0ins.	26ft. 3 ins.
Height	9ft. 6ins.	9ft.8ins.
Wing Area	251 sq.ft.	240 sq.ft.

Weights —

	Arrow	Three Seater	
		Mk.I	Mk.II
Gross	1,850 lb	1,030 lb	1,150 lb
Basic	965 lb	1,680 lb	1,850 lb

175

Performance —

| | Arrow | Three Seater | |
		Mk.I	Mk.II
Max. Speed	106 mph	103 mph	107 mph
Cruising Speed	92 mph	90 mph	95 mph
Range	430 miles	300 miles	260 miles

Production —

ARROW - 13 aircraft (inclusive of 2 aircraft built prior to the move to Cowes).

THREE SEATER Mk.I - 19 aircraft.

THREE SEATER Mk.II - 7 aircraft.

ARROW

Con. No.	Registration
*75(2)	G-ABBE/ZK-ACQ
76(1)	G-ABKL
77(2)	G-ABGW
78(4)	G-ABWP
79(4)	G-ABWR/OY-DOO
80(2)	G-ABHD/VH-UQD
81(3)	G-ABHR
*82(4)	S.1/G-ABMK/LN-BAS
83(2)	G-ABOB
84(4)	G-ACHE
85(2)	G-ACHF
86	G-ACHG/OY-DUK/SE-AFR
87(6)	G-ABST

THREE SEATER MK.I

Con. No.	Registration
53(2)	G-ABAZ
54(2)	G-ABET
55(2)	G-ABKJ
56(4)	G-ABJS/VH-UUU
57(4)	G-ABKT
58(4)	G-ABKK
59(2)	G-ABLJ
60(4)	G-ABPZ/ZS-ADP
61(4)	G-ABRA/EI-AAT
62(4)	G-AABRB/VR-TAJ
63	VH-URB
64(2)	G-ABTT
65(4)	G-ABTU
66(4)	G-ABWO
67(4)	G-ABWU
68(4)	G-ABWV
†69(4)	G-ABWX
70(4)	G-ABYG
71(4)	GABYH

THREE SEATER MK.II

Con. No.	Registration
†101(4)	G-ABTR
102(5)	G-ABYN/EI-ABU
103(5)	G-ABZH
104(5)	G-ABZI/YI-AAB
105(5)	G-ACAD
106(5)	G-ACAF
107(5)	G-ACEF

* These aircraft flown as seaplanes.
( ) Engine type.
† Cabin tops fitted over passenger cockpit.

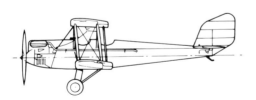

Spartan Arrow.

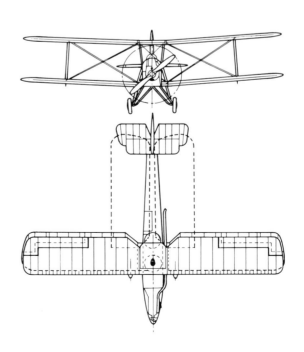

Mark I

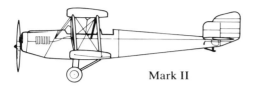

Mark II

Spartan 3-Seater

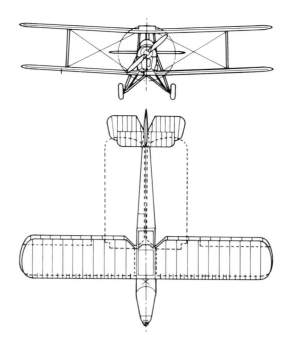

Spart 3-seater Mk.II. Back in Britain after a spell in Iraq. The fourth of the type built at Cowes is seen at Hanworth in use by 601 Sqn. A.A.F. based.

Spartan 3-seater Mk.I. Typical of the Cowes-built with Cirrus Hermes Mk.II engine.

Spartan Aircraft. The first Mk II 3-seater was later fitted with a cabin top over the passenger seats for use by Spartan Air Lines.

Spartan Aircraft. The last Arrow constructed was used to test the Napier Javelin engine. It operated as a single-seater and had redesigned vertical tail surfaces, and ailerons fitted to the lower wings only.

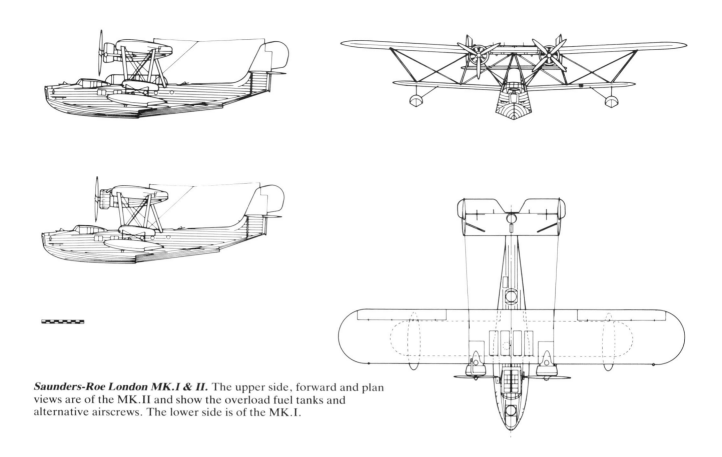

Saunders-Roe London MK.I & II. The upper side, forward and plan
views are of the MK.II and show the overload fuel tanks and
alternative airscrews. The lower side is of the MK.I.

Saro A.27 London Mk.I. K.3560 on test at Cowes carrying bombs.

CHAPTER 12

AIRCRAFT OF 1934 - 45: SARO AND SUPERMARINE

The London flying boat gave the RAF reliable service in the early war years but was already obsolete for operational use. Neither of its successors the, A.33 and the S.36 Lerwick, fulfilled the company's expectations consequently the major wartime production effort was of aircraft to another firm's designs. The Supermarine Walrus and Sea Otter amphibians were both produced in considerable numbers. The research aircraft A.37 appeared in the early months of the war and was used for a variety of trials for proposed flying boat types until after the war.

A.27 SARO LONDON   1934-5

Type — General purpose reconnaissance flying boat with crew of 5.

> Mk.I to Specification R.24/31
> Mk.II to Specification R.3/35

Engines —   Mk. I 2 - 875 HP Bristol Pegasus IIIMS
                Mk. II 2 - 1055 HP Bristol Pegasus X

Fuselage — The hull was an all metal structure using corrugated Alclad for the external surfaces. Double curvature was avoided to simplify manufacture and repair, which resulted in the flat sides and generally angular appearance of the hull. The planing bottom had a V-shaped entry and two steps. The pilots were seated side by side with dual controls in a raised cabin forward of the wing and a gangway between them gave access to the forward gun and bomb aimer's position. The gun ring could be slid aft when necessary for mooring purposes. Aft of the pilots' cabin was the crew accommodation with navigator's station on the port side; further aft were the radio operator, port side, and the engineer's station on the starboard side, followed by galley and workbench and midships gun position. The remainder of the hull provided stowage space for equipment and provided access to the rear gun position behind the tail unit.

Wings — These were of biplane form of unequal span and parallel chord. The lower wings were attached at the root ends near the top of the hull and were built in four sections, with a break at the outer interplane struts, thus simplifying replacement in the event of damage. The upper wing was built in three sections; the centre section, housing the 550 gallon fuel tank and with oil tanks in the leading edge, was mounted on interplane struts forming three substantial pylons also providing the mountings for the engine nacelles. Ailerons were fitted in the upper wing only and were operated by cables which ran externally along the underside of the top wing. The wings, partly designed and made by Boulton Paul Ltd., were two spar structures mainly of high tensile rolled strip and stainless steel construction with duralumin ribs and with fabric covering except for the lower centre section where a metal surfaced area formed a platform for maintenance and handling. Wing tip floats of similar construction to the hull were mounted below the outboard interplane struts. Originally without a step, a single step was introduced.

The construction and shape of the floats were modified and the mounting struts improved after trials with the prototype. Handley Page slots were fitted to the top wings of one aircraft, K.5910, but were not adopted for production.

Tail Unit — A braced monoplane tailplane carried twin fins and rudders at the tips. The tailplane was adjustable and the rudders incorporated twin tabs replacing the Flettner tabs used initally on the prototype. Horn shaped aerodynamic balance areas were employed. Construction was of duralumin and steel with fabric covering.

Power Plant — The Pegasus engines were faired into the underside of the upper centre section and on the Mk. I were fitted with Boulton Paul type polygonal cowlings with built-in exhaust collector rings exhausting above the wing. On Mk. II aircraft fitted with Bristol designed engine installation the collector rings formed the whole of the cowling which was of circular shape. Propellers were originally 2-blade 13ft. 6ins. diameter on the Mk. I, 4-blade 11ft. 6ins. diameter on the Mk. II, although 3-blade were later used on the long range aircraft. An ABC auxiliary power unit, housed in the starboard lower wing, was a source of electrical power and enabled bilge pumps, refuelling pumps and air compressor, for starting purposes, to be available independently of the main engines. The engines could be changed with the aircraft afloat with the aid of special slinging gear and platforms capable of being stowed in the hull. Two cylindrical overload fuel tanks were fitted above the hull on five aircraft for the Australian flight, this position providing mountings for alternative carriage of equipment such as a spare engine carried horizontally or an aerial torpedo.

Dimensions —		
	Span: Top	80ft. 0ins.
	Bottom	56ft. 0ins.
	Chord: Top	13ft. 0ins.
	Bottom	8ft. 9ins.
	Length	56ft. 9ins.
	Height	18ft. 9ins.
	(less propeller arc)	
	Wing area	1,425 sq.ft.
Weights —		
	Basic	12,000 - 12,800 lb
	Gross	18,400 - 19,300 lb
	Military load	2,810 lb
	Overload	22,000 lb

Performance —

Maximum speed		(Mk. I) 145 mph
		(Mk. II) 155 mph at 6,250 ft.
Cruising speed		100 - 105 mph
Range	1100 - 1700 miles with 544 gallons of internal fuel increased to 2600 miles with 318 gallons in overload tanks.	
Duration	8 hours to 13½ hours with overload tanks.	

Saro A.27 London. London hulls in production at Maresfield Road Works.

Saro A.27 London. K5262 aircraft modified from a Mk.I in
service with the R.A.F.

Armament — 3 Lewis guns.
2,000 lb bombs or depth charges carried under wings.

Production — Following the single prototype a contract for seven aircraft was placed in March 1935 and this was progressively increased to a total of 31 aircraft inclusive of the prototype. The prototype K.3560 and ten production aircraft were built to Specification R.24/31. The prototype was later modified to Specification R.3/35 with Pegasus X engines and circular cowlings. Subsequent production was of this version and all Mk. I aircraft were modified progressively to Mk. II standard.

	Mk. I	Mk. II
K.3560	1	-
K.5257-63	7	-
K.5908-13	3	3
K.6927-32	-	6
K.9682-6	-	5
L.7038-43	-	6
Total	**11** +	**20** = 31

FELIXSTOWE TRIALS
REPORT F/129 LONDON I K3560 2 PEGASUS III MS

This is a voluminous report covering trials which over several years beginning with the prototype K3560 in which praise was given to the flying qualities and ease of maintenance of the London.

F/129 (Part I) London K5258 May 1937 2 Pegasus X
Summary of Flying Qualities

In this summary the flying qualities are considered only in so far as they differ from those given in Report 129 which describe the tests on the prototype K3560 with Pegasus III M.3 engines.

The flying boat is not stable longitudinally either with engines on or off and is not so pleasant to fly as the prototype London K3560 which was stable. This instability is difficult to explain as there does not appear to be any significant difference between the two flying boats. Repeated tests have, however, confirmed that it is unstable. It was not possible to check the prototype in its original form as the Pegasus III engines, had, in the meantime, been changed for Pegasus X engines. Check tests were, however, made with the flying boat in its new form and with the same centre of gravity position and it was again found to be stable.

The loads on the controls in flight remain approximately the same. The rudder is light; the elevator control is reasonably light; the aileron control is distinctly heavier than either of the other two and this heaviness affects, to some extent, the manoeuvrability. The aileron control is particularly effective at low speed and is retained after the elevator control becomes ineffective; lateral control is therefore retained at any speed down to which it is practicable to fly.

There is evidence of overbalance of the elevators when they are at large angles during take-off. This is shown by a tendency of the flying boat to hunt unless it is trimmed approximately correctly. During take-off there is no indication of overbalance except at extreme positions.

The prototype London was very pleasant to fly and could be flown for long periods without the pilot experiencing undue fatigue. This good quality has, to some extent, been reduced by the loss of stability and, in bumpy weather, it is necessary to use the controls continuously. The production London K5258 differs very little from the prototype K3560. The weight has increased about 650 lb and the climb performance is therefore slightly inferior to that of the prototype. There is little alteration in top speed.

The production London is unstable, although the prototype was stable. There is no obvious reason for the difference and the instability may be caused by a slight overbalance of the elevators for small angular movements.

The oil cooling does not appear to be adequate for tropical conditions. (This latter point was to be the subject of much development and testing prior to the Australia flight).

The Australia Flight of 1937-38

The following was the itinerary laid down for No. 204 Squadron:-

			Sea Miles	Duration Hours
December	2	Mount Batten - Berre	705	9¼
	3	Berre - Malta	658	8¾
	5	Malta - Alexandria	808	11
	6	Alexandria - L. Habbaniyah	704	9½
	9	L. Habbaniyah -Bahrein	580	7¾
	10	Bahrein -Dubai	265	3½
	11	Dubai -Karachi	649	8½
	13	Karachi -Allahabad	812	11
	14	Allahabad - Calcutta	452	6
	15	Calcutta - Rangoon	635	8½
	18	Rangoon - Penang	740	10
	20	Penang - Singapore	370	5
January	10	Singapore - Batavia	416	5¾
	12	Batavia - Sourabaya	384	5⅛
	13	Sourabaya - Koepang	681	9⅛
	15	Koepang - Port Darwin	479	6½
	17	Port Darwin - Karumba	665	9
	18	Karumba - Bowen	487	6½
	21	Bowen - Brisbane	545	7⅛
	26	Brisbane - Sydney	425	5¾
February	7	Sydney - Melbourne (Point Cook)	580	7¾
	17	Melbourne -Launceston	260	3½
	19	Launceston - Hobart	290	4
	23	Hobart - Melbourne	400	5½
	25	Melbourne - Adelaide	480	6½
March	2	Adelaide - Ceduna	340	4½
	4	Ceduna - Albany	840	11⅛
	7	Albany -Perth	360	5
	12	Perth -Carnarvon	420	5¾
	14	Carnarvon - Port Hedland	570	7¾

Saro A.27 London. The Mk.I prototype at Felixstowe.

Saro A.27 London. K.5257 the first production aircraft originally built as a Mk.I re-emerged as a Mk.II in 1937.

Saro A.27 London. Bomb carrying arrangement.

Saro A.27 London MkII. One of 204 squadron aircraft for the Australian flight with overload fuel tank and three bladed propellers.

Saro A.27 London. The tenth production aircraft K.5913 was fitted with 3-bladed airscrews and other modifications in readiness for the flight to Australia.

			Sea Miles	Duration Hours
March	16	Port Hedland - Derby	432	5¾
	17	Derby - Bima Bay	580	7¾
	18	Bima Bay - Sourabaya	375	5
	21	Sourabaya - Batavia	384	5⅛
	23	Batavia - Singapore	416	5¾
April	21	Singapore - Penang	370	5
	22	Penang -Rangoon	740	10
	23	Rangoon -Calcutta	635	8½
	25	Calcutta -Allahabad	452	6
	26	Allahabad -Karachi	812	11
	29	Karachi -Dubai	649	8½
	30	Dubai -Bahrain	265	3½
May	1	Bahrein -L. Habbaniyah	580	7¾
	4	L. Habbaniyah - Alexandria	704	9½
	6	Alexandria - Malta	808	11
	9	Malta - Berre	658	8¾
	10	Berre - Mount Batten	705	9½
		Totals	25,565	344

This itinerary was calculated on an average speed of 95 knots against a 20 mph wind which perhaps would sometimes be favourable. Each boat carried 850 gallons of petrol and 44 gallons of oil, for the longer stages, enough for 11¼ hours flying. In normal conditions they cruised at a height of from 1,000 to 1,500 feet.

The crews of the five boats were as follows:-

Flagship K6930

Wing Cdr K.B. Lloyd, AFC (Sqn Cdr)
Flt Lt W.S. Jenkins (Sqn Navigator)
FO E.L. Hyde (Pilot)
Sgt Lawry, W.G. (Senior W/Telegraphist)
A/C.1 Hooper, E.H. (Rigger)
A/C.1 Browning, A.W. (Fitter)
L.A/C Machin (Clerk)

Boat K5912

Sqn Ldr V.P. Feather (Sqn Technical Officer)
P/O J. Barrett (Pilot)
Sgt Wheeler, A.E. (Sgt Pilot)
Cpl Moore, C.E.H. (NCO i/c Fitters & Riggers)
Cpl Harrison, A. (NCO i/c Fitters & Riggers)
Air Cmdre S.I. Goble, CBE, DSO, DSC (RAAF)

Boat K5908

Flt Lt W.A.J. Satchell (Cdr)
P/O F. Phillips (Sqn Adjutant)
P/O R.P.A. Harrison (Navigator)
A/C.1 Roberts, A.F. (Fitter)
A/C.1 Jenkins T.H. (Rigger)
A/C.1 Bickle, F.G. (W/T)

Boat K6927

Flt Lt H.M.T. Neugebauer (Cdr)
P/O H.B. Johnson (Navigator)
P/O R.G.C. Lovelock (2nd Pilot)
Cpl Chapple, C.E. (Fitter)
Cpl Sayers T.G.B. (Rigger)
A/C.1 Pannel, P.A. (W/T)

Boat K6929

Flt Lt B.M. Cary (Cdr)
P/O S.R. Gibbs (2nd Pilot)
Sgt Godwin, R. (Navigator)
Cpl Linfoot, G.H. (Instrument Maker)
A/C.1 Terrill, F.T. (Rigger)
A/C.1 Parsons, A.H. (Fitter)
A/C.1 Hoskins, R.B. (W/T)

A.29 SARO MONOSPAR CLOUD   1934-6

Type — Research aircraft embodying two of the major features of the A.33 flying boat built to Specification R2/33.

Wing — This was designed with a single main spar with pyramidal bracings in accordance with the basic monospar principles of H.J. Stieger. It was of all-metal construction with fabric covering and was of equal span to the original Cloud wing but revised plan shape and with dihedral on the outer portions

Sponsons — These were 24 ft 6 inch span overall and attached to the sides of the hull which was reinforced and provided with suitable external attachment points.

General — The wing was designed and built by General Aircraft Ltd of Feltham as Type ST.7 and fitted to the prototype Cloud K2681 for trials at Cowes and MAEE Felixstowe. The aircraft was flown initially with both wooden sponsons and standard Cloud stabilising floats, which were removed after confirmatory tests. Development flying was curtailed when A.33 development was discontinued.

A.33 SARO UNNAMED FLYING BOAT   1938

Type — Long range reconnaissance and patrol flying boat, to Specification R.2/33 with a crew of 7.

Engines — 4 - 830 HP Bristol Perseus XII sleeve-valve radial engines.

Fuselage — The hull of this unusual machine was of all metal Alclad construction incorporating all the latest military requirements. The pilot's cabin was a raised structure resembling that of the London and the hull provided internal accommodation for navigator, radio operator and general crew facilities. Defence was to be provided by four gunners' stations, those at the nose and extreme tail to be in hydraulically powered turrets (the rear turret was not installed on the prototype). The remaining gunners' positions were manually operated beam stations in a dorsal fairing extended forward from the base of the fin. The nose turret could be retracted aft to facilitate mooring operations. The planing bottom had two main steps and terminated below the fin in a further V-shaped stern.

Sponsons — Sponsons were provided for balancing purposes and these, mounted at anhedral angle on the hull sides, were of aerofoil section and tapered in plan to square cut tips. The sponsons were sealed to constitute the

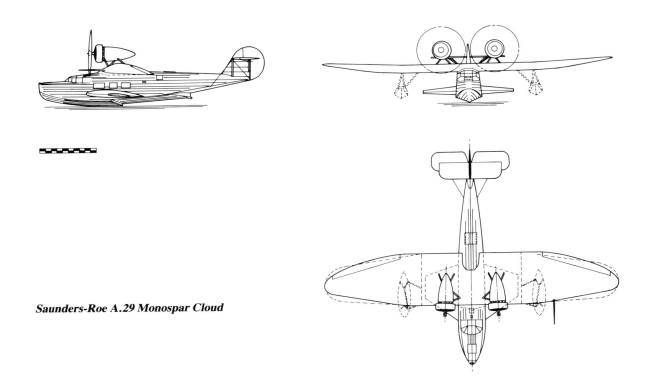

Saunders-Roe A.29 Monospar Cloud

Saro A29 Monospar Cloud. K2681 in its final configuration with Monospar wing and sponsons and with wing-tip floats removed. In this form it enabled trials to be carried out of certain features used later in the larger A.33.

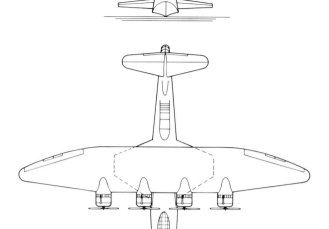

Saunders-Roe A.33.

The Saro A33. Showing details of the wing failure.

Saro A.33. Being towed back after structural failure caused by a heavy impact with the water.

A.33. before the disaster. The A.33 outside the Columbine works in 1938.

main fuel tanks which was one of the earliest applications of sealed integral tanks and were largely constructed using the sytem of de Bergue rivetting carried out by machines where the flush rivet head fitted into a depression with a shallow countersink. These tanks remained fuel tight after the eventual crash.

Wing — The parasol wing was mounted on N-struts raised at an angle from the sponsons to the outboard engine nacelles with no direct connection of the wing to the hull other than streamlined wires from the outboard nacelles to the top of the hull. The wing was of monospar type (Stieger system) and was of metal construction with fabric covering. It comprised a parallel centre portion carrying the four engine nacelles and separate tapered outer portions with eliptical trailing edges with dihedral. The single main spar took care of the bending loads and a pyramidal arrangement of wires from top and bottom booms to points at the leading and trailing edges resisted the torsional loads. This unconventional structure intended for lightweight construction was extremely flexible, the centreline moving up and down about 3ins. in normal flight, and necessitated extensive full-scale ground testing of specimens for which the "Elephant Test Rig" was installed in the Solent Works.

Tail Unit — The swept-up portion of the hull terminated in a large single fin and rudder with monoplane tailplane and elevators at the base. A model was tested with twin fins and rudders but this configuration was not employed for the aircraft.

Power Plant — The four Perseus engines were mounted at equal intervals along the leading edge of the centre wing and drove three-bladed variable pitch propellers. The engines were close cowled with leading edge exhaust collectors and trailing edge gills. Fuel and oil tanks were housed in the centre wing.

Dimensions —		
	Span	95 ft.
	Length	75 ft.
	Span of Sponsons	32 ft. 3 in.
	Height	22 ft. 6in.
Weights —	Gross	41,500 lb
Performance —	Maximum speed	200 mph
	Endurance	12 hours.

Armament — Not finalised. Multi-gun turrets front and rear with .303ins. Browning guns. Vickers 'K' guns on pillars in beam positions.

Production - One aircraft K.4773. Development to Specification 21/36, for which a batch of 11 aircraft, serial Nos L.2147-57, was allocated, was not proceeded with.

S.36 SARO LERWICK   1938

Type — High performance general reconnaissance flying boat to Specification R1/36 with a crew of 6 or 7.

Engine — 2 - 1375 HP Bristol Hercules II or IV. (IM on first four aircraft)

Fuselage — The hull, although clean in shape, was exceptionally deep throughout. The planing bottom was unusual in that the rear of the two steps was positioned well back below the fin. Three gun positions, in hydraulically powered turrets, were conventionally positioned in nose, tail and amidships, the forward being retractable to assist mooring operations. The raised pilot's station was faired into the centre wing and the hull interior provided crew accommodation, radio and navigator's stations with fuel tanks holding 675 gallons built above the rear cabin. Access for the crew was by a door in the port rear fuselage. Hard points for the attachment of beaching gear were built in.

Wing — The all-metal wing, built in three sections, consisted of a parallel centre section carrying the engine mountings and fuel tanks. Tapered outer wings with rounded tips were built as separate units and carried electrically operated landing flaps and fabric covered manually operated ailerons. The wing was notably small in area for a machine of the size and weight of the Lerwick and particularly so compared with previous designs of flying boats. Wing tip floats were mounted on V-struts cantilever fashion. An additional 2° incidence was introduced on the last 9 aircraft. Some earlier aircraft were also modified.

Tail Unit — Unbraced monoplane tailplane and single fin and rudder mounted directly to the top of the hull. On the prototype, L.7248, a taller rudder and auxiliary shield-shaped fixed fins were added near the tailplane tips in the course of development. Later on L.7252 the original rounded fin was increased in area along the leading edge and the rudder increased in height and squared off; this was the design adopted on all subsequent aircraft and applied retrospectively. A proposed scheme with twin shield-shaped fins and rudders fitted to the tips of the tailplane, for which it was proposed to raise the mountings in the hull, was not proceeded with. Both control surfaces were fabric covered and manually operated.

Power Plant — The sleeve-valve Hercules engines were carried on tubular mountings containing also the oil tanks and were fitted with rounded cowlings incorporating exhaust collector rings and cooling gills. The lower portions of the fairings formed the bomb bays. Propellers were 3-blade DH Hamilton Standard constant speed type; 12ft. 6ins. and later 13ft. 6ins. diameter.

Dimensions —		
	Span	80ft. 10ins.
	Length	63ft. 7½ins.
	Height	22ft. 6ins.
	Wing Area	845 sq.ft.
Weights —	Gross	28,400 lb.
	Overload	33,200 lb.
Performance —	Maximum speed	215 mph
	Cruising speed	165 mph
	Range	1,500 miles
	Service ceiling	15,000 ft.

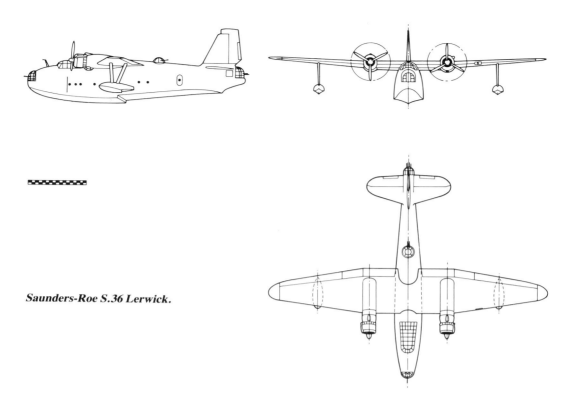

Saunders-Roe S.36 Lerwick.

Saro S.36 Lerwick. The second Lerwick L.7249 showing the addition to the top of the rudder.

Saro S.36 Lerwick. Testing time for Lerwicks. L. 7248 is seen with the temporary auxiliary fins.

Saro S.36 Lerwick. An unidentified Lerwick on test from Cowes.

Saro S.36 Lerwick. L.7257 the tenth machine was in service with No. 209 Squadron, but sank at its moorings after transfer to No.4 (C) O.T.U. at Stranraer on 10/11th November 1941. This shows the enlarged rudder finally adopted.

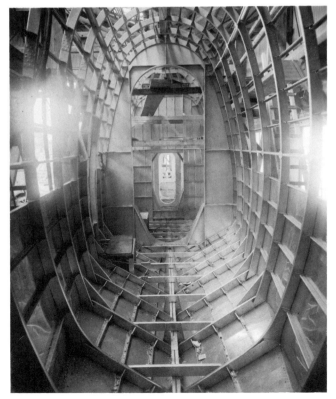

Interior of Lerwick hull.

Lerwick rear gun turret.

Armament —

1 -.303 ins. Vickers 'K' gun in nose
2 -.303 ins. Browning guns amidships
4 -.303 ins. Browning guns in tail
(All Frazer Nash power operated turrets built by Parnall Aircraft)

2,000 lb. of bombs or depth charges enclosed in the engine fairings.

Production —
Contract 636200/36

21 aircraft S.36/1-21 Serial Nos L.7248-68. A proposed batch of 30 aircraft was not proceeded with. 10 aircraft were completed by the end of 1939 and a further 10 in 1940, the last aircraft being completed early in 1941.

General

The first aircraft, L.7248 was flown at the end of 1938 and went to MAEE in March 1939 as a trials aircraft, being followed at various times by L.7249, L.7252 and L.7254.

The prototype L.7248, when fitted with the auxiliary fins, suffered severe corrugating in flight of the upper wing skins at Helensburgh on the 26 - 27th December 1940 and was subsequently struck off charge.

L.7254 saw limited operational use being mainly engaged in trials, finishing up for ground/water handling purposes as 3300M at Wig Bay until March 1943, when this machine, the last Lerwick to survive was dismantled.

A.37 SAUNDERS-ROE SHRIMP   1939

Type — 2 seat monoplane for flying boat research in connection with Specification R3/38 and later R5/39 and R14/40.

Engines — 4 - 90 HP Pobjoy Niagara III.

Fuselage — The hull was of Alclad construction reproducing the step positions, planing bottom and general form of the large flying boat project. The pilot and test observer were housed in tandem in an enclosed cabin. Later the hull was modified to reproduce the planing bottom of the Shetland.

Wing — The tapered cantilever wing was of wooden construction with plywood and fabric covering. Tubular steel engine mountings supported the four engines which were housed in long chord cowlings and well streamlined nacelles. The wing tip floats were of Alclad construction and although fixed on the model, would have been retractable on the full scale aircraft. Later the floats were changed for those proposed for the Shetland.

Tail Unit — These were also of wooden construction with plywood covering and comprised initially a monoplane tailplane with twin fins and rudders at the tips. Later a single fin and rudder, a scaled down version of the Shetland tail, were fitted.

Dimensions —

Span		50ft. 0ins.
Length		42ft. 3¼ins.
Height		12ft. 8¾ins.
Wing area		340 sq.ft.

Weights —

Basic		4,360 lb.
Gross		5,700 lb.
Overload		6,200 lb.
Wing Loading 18.25 lb. per sq.ft. (Overload)		

Performance —

Maximum speed	130 knots
Cruising speed	100 knots
Stalling speed (flaps up)	54 knots
Stalling speed (flaps down)	45 knots
Endurance	3 hours
Time to height	4.95 mins to 5,000 ft.
	16.50 mins to 8,000 ft.

Production — 1 aircraft A.37/1 G-AFZS later TK.580.

MAEE Helensburgh   Report No. H/158

Issued to cover the handling trials on the Saunders-Roe A.37 scaled down version of the R5/39 flying boat.

"TAKEOFF is easy except for the slight tendency to swing to starboard. This swing can be easily corrected by means of the rudder. Throughout the trials no tendency to porpoise was discovered in any conditions.

Some experiments were made in the best use of the flaps for take-off and very interesting results obtained particularly one method of lowering flaps at the point of take-off. These experiments will be reported separately.

LANDING at a small angle is particularly easy but if landed tail down the boat almost invariably comes off the water again. The best speed for the approach is about 80 knots ASI with flaps fully down; the best landing speed is 60 knots ASI.

TAXIING. The behaviour taxiing is very good. The hull is clean, very seaworthy for its size and the handling qualities excellent. The turning circle is small.

VIEW. The view taxiing, taking-off, in the air and landing is good.

THE FLYING QUALITIES of this aeroplane are very good. The controls are light and fully responsive over the speed range. The elevator control is particularly light and effective. The aileron control is slightly heavier, the rudder is still heavier and not quite so effective as the other controls. The differences are, however, small and the controls can be regarded as reasonably well harmonised. When the aircraft is stalled without flaps, a wing invariably drops before the nose drops in the dive. This tendency to drop a wing is the one undesirable feature of this aircraft."

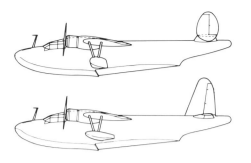

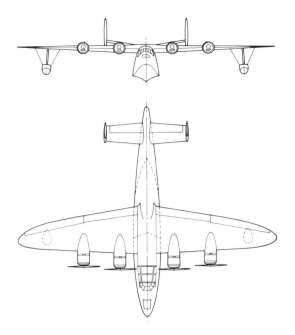

Saunders-Roe A.37. The lower side view shows the Shetland configuration.

Saro A.37 Experimental Flying Boat. In its final form representing a scaled down version of the Shetland (Spec. R14/40) in respect of the planing bottom, wing tip floats and tail surfaces.

Saunders-Roe A.37. In its original configuration on the hardstanding outside the Columbine works late 1939.

WING AND ENGINE INSTALLATION FOR THE SHORT SHETLAND   1940-44

Type — Mk.I (Short S.35)
Very long-range reconnaissance flying boat to Specification R.14/40 capable of carrying bombs, mines and depth charges. Crew of 11.
Mk.II (Short S.40)
Civil flying boat for 40 passengers plus crew.

| **Engines** — | 4 - 2500 HP Bristol Centaurus VII (military prototype) |
| | 4 - 2600 HP Bristol Centaurus 660 (civil prototype) |

Wing — The wing was designed with a swept leading edge and straight trailing edge and was attached to the sides of the hull to fittings built into the top of the frames. A front spar at quarter chord and thick leading edge skins formed a strong torsion box. The auxiliary rear spar was straight and provided mountings for the ailerons and parallel slotted flaps. An 80 gallon oil tank for each engine was housed in the torsion box.

Between the spars were three welded magnesium fuel tanks on each side totalling 2,928 gallons. Between the inner tank and the two outer tanks was a weapon bay behind the inboard nacelles utilised on the civil machine for housing further fuel tanks totalling 6,112 gallons.

The wing of 150 ft 4 in overall span was constructed and delivered in sections.

Production — 2 aircraft sets.

| Mk.I | DX166 | Wings supplied in March 1944. Aircraft burnt out at Felixstowe 28.1.46. |
| Mk.II | G-AGVD (DX171 originally) | Wings supplied in mid 1945. Aircraft scrapped at Belfast 1951. |

SUPERMARINE WALRUS   1939-44

Type — General purpose, reconnaissance, training and air-sea rescue amphibian with crew of 3/4 to Specification 37/36.

Engine — 1 - 750 HP Bristol Pegasus VI.

Fuselage — The Mk.I hull was a flat sided structure of Alclad frames, longitudinal members and skins. The planing bottom with a flared V-shaped entry met the sides at a hard chine and continued to the single step; the V-section of the underside extending aft to the sternpost. The crew of pilot, navigator and radio operator were normally accommodated in the raised cabin forward of the wings. Open gun positions, which could be covered by hatches, were provided in the bow and amidships. The Mk.II was fitted with a wooden hull of the same general configuration, but nearly 600 lb. heavier than the Mk.I and was designed by Saunders-Roe.

Wings — The single bay wings of parallel chord were mounted on top of the hull, with noticeable sweepback but with little stagger or dihedral and were capable of being folded for shipboard stowage. The lower wing was built in halves and attached direct to the sides of the hull. The upper wing consisted of a small centre section mounted on struts above the engine nacelle, which itself was carried on four streamlined struts above the hull, and two main outer panels. Ailerons were provided on top and bottom wings, the latter having at the inboard ends sections of the trailing edge capable of being folded upwards for clearance from the hull when the wings were folded. The whole was suitably braced with streamline wires and in addition a pair of removable jury struts was provided to support the main wings at the inboard leading edge when folded. The aircraft was frequently flown with these struts in position. Wing tip floats were mounted below the interplane struts. Construction was based on two main spars made from rolled sections of high-tensile steel forming tubular booms and corrugated webs. The ribs were made of spruce and plywood and the whole was fabric-covered.

Tail Unit — The fin was built integrally with the hull and carried the tailplane near the top and this was braced by pairs of struts to the top longerons. The tailplane was of similar construction to the wings and was fabric-covered.

Power Plant — The Pegasus engine was mounted in a stremlined metal nacelle and drove a four-bladed wooden pusher airscrew. Fuel was carried in tanks in the upper wing outboard of the centre section and totalled 155 gallons. The nacelle was set at 3° to starboard to counteract yaw.

Undercarriage — The main undercarriage was pivotted on external fittings on the sides of the hull and was retracted hydraulically enabling the wheels to be flush in bays built into the lower wings. A sprung tail-wheel was pivotted on the sternpost and an enclosed fairing served as a water rudder. The original metal wheel was replaced in Saunders-Roe production by one with a rubber tyre.

Armament — Vickers 'K' gun mounted on Scarff rings at fore and aft positions could be retracted and the cockpits covered by hatches. The rear hatch locked in a raised position formed a screen against the slipstream for the rear gunner. Bombs or depth charges could be carried on external racks outboard of the retracted wheels.

Dimensions —		
	Span	45 ft. 10 ins.
	Length	37 ft. 7 ins.
	Height (on wheels)	15 ft. 3 ins.
	Wing area	610 sq. ft.

Weights —		Mk.I	Mk.II
	Basic	4,900 lb.	
	Gross	7,200 lb.	7,716 lb.

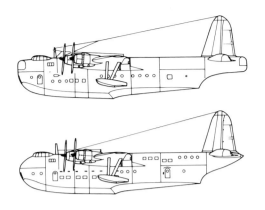

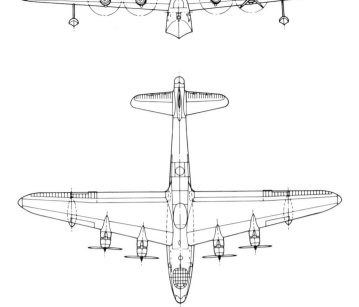

Short S.35 and S.40 Shetland.
Upper view S.35 Military version.

Short Shetland. S.35 Shetland Mk.I DX 166 was the prototype for a
very long range reconnaissance flying boat to replace the Sunderland.

Short Shetland. S.40 Commercial version.

Performance —

	Mk.I	Mk.II
Maximum speed	135 mph at 4,750 ft.	126 mph
Cruising speed	92 mph	
Alighting speed	57 mph	
Range	600 miles	
Service ceiling	18,500 ft.	15,900 ft.
Rate of climb	1,080 ft/min.	970 ft/min.
Take off	20 secs.	23.4 secs.

Production —   Total 461 aircraft.
Contract No. B43393/39.

Mk.I aircraft supplied to the RAF, FAA, RNZAF, RAN and RCN - 270 aircraft.

Serial Nos   R.6582-91
W.2670-89
W.2700-29
W.2731-60
W.2766-98
W.3005-51 (less W.3010, 3047 & 3051)
W.3062-101 (less W.3076 & 3078)
X.9460-84
X.9498-532
X.9554-58

Mk.II aircraft supplied to the RAF, FAA, RNZAF and RCN - 191 aircraft.

X.1045 Prototype
W.3010
W.3047
W.3051
W.3076
W.3078
X.9559-93
Z.1755-84
Z.1804-23
HD.804-37
HD.851-78
HD.899-939

Aircraft refurbished for United Whalers Ltd in 1946

G-AHFL	Boojum.	Scrapped at Cowes in 1950.
G-AHFM	Moby Dick.	
G-AHFM	Not named.	Won Folkestone Trophy at 121.5 mph on 31.8.46. Scrapped at Prestwick 1955.
G-AHFO	Snark.	Scrapped at Cowes 1950.

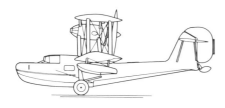

Supermarine Walrus.

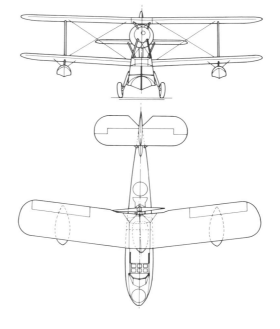

Walrus Production at Addlestone. Nearing flight test. The flight hangar
was half a mile away on an improvised airfield on Chertsey Meads. The
aircraft were towed with wings folded across the main road from
Weybridge to Chertsey.

Civilian Walruses. Three Supermarine built MK.I machines prepared by
Saunders-Roe for United Whalers Ltd. Seen here at Cowes on July 1946.
G-AH FO and G-AH FL were used in operations in Antartica during the
1946-7 whaling seasons.

SUPERMARINE SEA OTTER 1943-46

Type — General purpose, reconnaissance (ABR Mk.I) and air-sea rescue amphibian (ASR Mk.II) with crew of 3/4 to Specification S12/40.

Engine — 1 - 965 HP Bristol Mercury XXX.

Description — In general layout and construction the Sea Otter followed closely the style of the Walrus Mk.I with the notable change from pusher to tractor propulsion. In the preparation of the design the opportunity was taken to clean up the aerodynamic and hydrodynamic shape of the hull and to align the thrust line of the engine nacelle which now drove a three-bladed constant speed airscrew and was integrated with the centre section of the upper wing. Flaps were fitted to the top wing and an arrester hook was provided on Fleet Air Arm machines. The outward splayed interplane struts, the rounded wing tips and shallower wing tip floats, supported by two pairs of struts, made significant changes to the external appearance.

Armament —   (ABR 1) 1 - Vickers GO gun forward
2 - Vickers K guns aft
10000 lb bombs on
external racks.

Production —   Total 290 aircraft.
Contract No. AIR/1806/CB20(b)

ABR Mk.I for the RAF   241 aircraft
Serial Nos JM 738-773 (JM 739 civil registered as G-AKWA)
          796-837
          861-885
          905-922
          943-989
      JN 104-142
          179-205
          242-248
ASR Mk.II for the FAA   49 aircraft
      JN 249-257
      RD 869-898
          913-922

Supermarine Sea Otter.

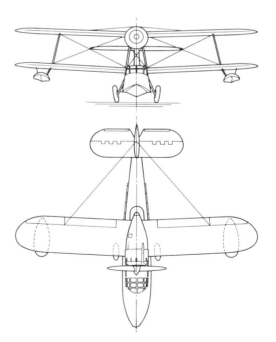

Vickers Supermarine Sea Otter Mk.I. The second Saunders-Roe built aircraft was used for trials at RAE., MA.E.E. and aboard ship. Later civil registered as G-AKWA.

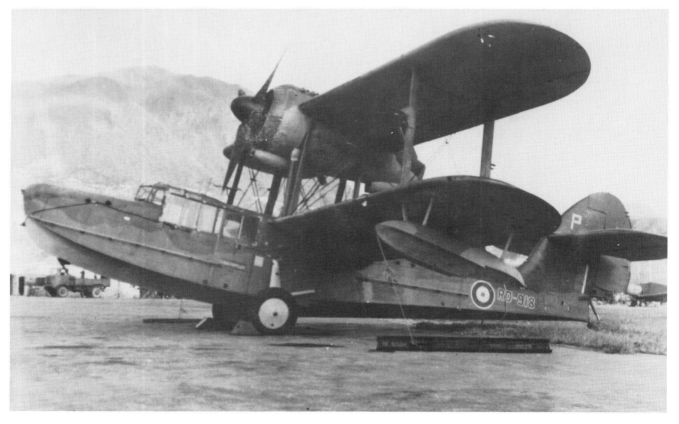

Supermarine Sea Otter. An ASR Mk.II from the last batch built by Saunders-Roe seen here at Gibralter.

Supermarine Sea Otter. A number of Sea Otters were civil registered. G-AIDM was a four-passenger conversion by Supermarine of Saunders-Roe built aircraft known as Type 503.

Supermarine Sea Otter. Final assembly of production aircraft in the Columbine Works.

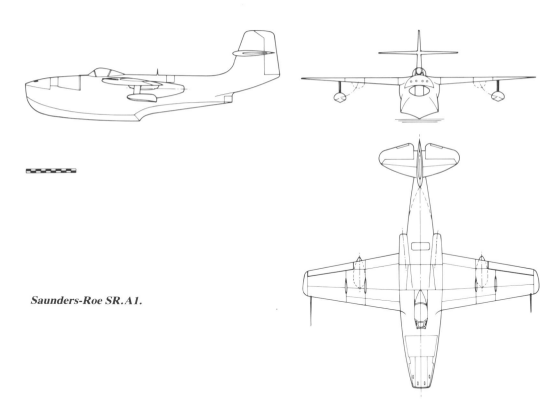

Saunders-Roe SR.A1.

Saunders-Roe SR.A1. Trials with the overload fuel tanks fitted. This is the third aircraft TG. 271, complete with bullet fairing which was lost in the Solent on the 12th August 1949.

198

CHAPTER 13

PRINCESS AND JET-PROPELLED FLYING BOATS

From June 1943, when a report was issued entitled "The Case for the Flying Boat", the company fought hard to maintain continuity of design and manufacture of the aircraft type with which it was most familiar and was best equipped to provide.

Two widely different types of flying boat resulted from development work carried out by the design department over a long period, both of which appeared post-war.

In both the civil and military fields the concentration on landplane operations limited the support for development of marine aircraft and inevitably resulted in the SR.A1 and the Princess being the last of their class, although Henry Knowler, until his retirement, continued to investigate a number of projects.

SR.A/1 UNNAMED JET FIGHTER FLYING BOAT
1947

Type — Single seat jet fighter for operation from sheltered or inland waters, to Specification E6/44.

Engines — 2 - 3,850 lb. thrust Metropolitan Vickers F2/4 Beryl axial-flow turbojets.

Fuselage — The hull was a conventional Alclad structure with closely spaced frames and stringers. The V-shaped planing bottom incorporated a main step at half distance along its length and terminated in a knife edge and water rudder at the tip. The lower portion of the fin was integral with the fuselage. The upper part of the forward fuselage contained a four-cannon gun installation forward of the pressurised pilot's cockpit, which was in a raised position at the leading edge wing junction and was provided with an ejector seat. A single air intake with retractable lip to avoid spray ingestion, divided below the guns and was carried down below the cockpit to the two engines mounted below the wing centre section. The main wing attachment was at a single heavy frame at the forward face of the engine bay, the top of which consisted of removable panels for access purposes.

Wing — The unswept wing, tapered in plan and section, was based on a single main spar with additional span-wise members and stringers. It was built in halves and attached at shoulder height to the hull. Conventional ailerons and landing flaps were supplemented by dive brakes along the trailing edge and dive recovery flaps below the inboard main spar. The balancing floats retracted inwards under hydraulic power and rotated through 90° to be stowed inverted when retracted. Internal fuel was stored in four integral tanks forward and aft of the main spar. A pair of 141 gallon overload fuel tanks could be mounted inboard between the retracted float and the hull.

Tail Unit — The upper fin and tailplane were provided with a streamlined fairing after buffetting was experienced on initial test flights. These units, together with the rudder and divided elevator, were conventional light alloy structures.

Power Plant — The SR.A/1 was the only British aircraft designed to use the axial-flow Beryl engines which were buried in the hull and mounted with a 5° angle from the aircraft centre line. Access for assembly and servicing was provided from the top of the bay which was extensively lagged against heat transfer.

Dimensions —

Span		46 ft.
Length		50 ft.
Height		16 ft. 9 in.
Wing Area		415 sq.ft.

Weight — Gross 16,255 lb without overload tanks.
Basic 11,262 lb.

Performance —
Maximum speed 512 mph (Mach 0.81)
Endurance 2½ hours with 2 - 141 gallon overload tanks.

Armament —
4 - 20mm Hispano cannon with 240 rounds each.
2 - 1000 lb. bombs or 8 rocket projectiles.

Production —
3 prototypes -
TG 263 First flight 16.7.47. Later G-12-1. Aircraft still in existence at Duxford.
TG 267 Crashed fatally at Felixstowe 1949.
TG 271 Damaged on alighting off Cowes and lost in the Solent 12.8.49.

SR.45 SAUNDERS-ROE PRINCESS 1952

Type — Large long-range civil flying boat for 100 plus passengers.

Engines — 10 - 3,200 SHP/800 lb thrust Bristol Proteus 600 propeller-turbines.

Fuselage — The upper hull was of figure eight section and was pressurised back to a bulkhead at the base of the fin to contain crew and passenger compartments and all facilities on two levels. Below the lower deck was the planing bottom compartment for buoyancy, which extended aft to a point below the leading edge of the fin, where it tapered to a knife edge and curved into the swept-up underside of the tail-end. The planing bottom was V-shaped with a well flared entry and single step which blended smoothly into the underside. The structure was mainly of aluminium alloy and conventional, but on a scale in keeping with the size of the project.

SR.A1 in flight. Showing the clean lines of the hull.

Saunders-Roe SR.A1. The wing tip floats of the SR.A1 rotated as they folded inwards for partial stowage in the wing.

Saunders-Roe SR.A1. Trials with the overload fuel tanks fitted. This is the third aircraft TG. 271, complete with acorn fairing which was lost in the Solent on the 12th August 1949.

Wing — The wing was built in five sections and consisted of a centre section of 27 ft. span and 30 ft. 9 ins chord, built into the upper level of the hull extending to a rib inboard of the innermost engine installation. The next section continued basically parallel with spars at 12 ft. apart and contained the three engine bays and four integral fuel tanks together with mountings for the slotted trailing edge flaps which were divided into three sections on each side. This section of inner wing was 40 ft. 3 ins long and with a chord of 30 ft. and was built with two main spars and intermediate stringers with multiple attachments to the centre section and outer wing. The outboard wings of 51 ft. span were tapered in plan and section and attached to provide a horizontal underside and downward slope on the upper surface. The wing was cut square at the tip to match the balancing floats when these swung into the raised position where they formed end plates. A scheme to retract the floats inboard and to stow them in the thickness of the wing by splitting them along the vertical centreline was discarded for several reasons especially for its drastic effect to the continuity of the wing structure.

Flying Controls — The tailplane was attached at a considerable dihedral angle near the base of the fin to a bridging structure built in to provide continuity across the fin. It was of tapered section and had a sharply swept leading edge and provided hinge points for four separate elevators. The rudder was divided into three and the ailerons into four sections as mentioned above.

All controls were power operated by universally jointed shafts running in self-aligning bearings, operating through various gear boxes. Each control was driven from a central source of power which consisted of an electric motor driving a hydraulic variable delivery pump. The Boulton Paul power unit for the ailerons was in the top of the hull and those for the elevators and rudder in the rear of the pressurised hull and these were connected to the two pilots' controls by cables for their operation.

Tail Unit — Those in the inboard and central positions consisted of two Proteus coupled together through gear boxes to drive 8-bladed contra-props, 16 ft. 6 ins diameter, made by De Havilland. The outboard power unit was a single Proteus with a directly driven 4-bladed airscrew.

Beaching Gear — Strong points were built into the nose of the hull and the inboard engine nacelles for the attachment of beaching gear. These comprised buoyant twin-wheel units, mounted tricycle fashion, the main units on heavy V-struts being also stabilised to the side of the hull.

Dimensions —		
	Span	209 ft. 6 ins (Floats down)
		219 ft. 6 ins (Floats raised)
	Tailplane Span	77 ft. 2 ins
	Area	5,118 sq.ft.
	Tailplane Area	1,103 sq.ft.
	Length	148 ft.
	Height 24 ft. 3 ins (to top of hull)	
		53 ft. 7 ins (overall)
	Beam	16 ft. 8 ins.
	Draught	8 ft.

Weights — Gross 315,530 lb (141 tons) at take off.
Basic 190,000 lb.

Fuel Tankage — 14,500 gallons

Wing Loading — 61.3 lb/sq.ft.

Design Performance —

Maximum speed		395 mph.
Cruising speed	360 mph at 32,500 ft.	
	380 mph at 37,000 ft.	
Endurance		15 hours
Range		5,500 miles.

Production —
Contract 6/AIRCRAFT II 15/CB.l0(a) dated 7.5.46.

3 aircraft G-ALUN   Built and flown 22.8.52. to June 1954 for a total of 96 hrs 50 mins in 47 flights.

G-ALUO } Built to the stage where they could
G-ALUP } be towed to Calshot for cocooning in 1953.

Saunders-Roe SR.45 Princess. During its trials the first Princess accumulated 100 flying hours before being pulled from the water in July 1954.

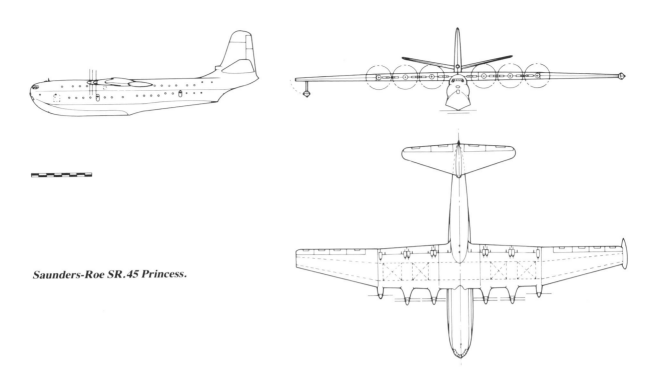

Saunders-Roe SR.45 Princess.

Princess Flight Trial in 1952.

Princess hull being assembled in the stocks in Columbine Hangar in November 1947.

The Bristol Proteus coupled engine units for the Princess.

Princess port wing showing easy access to the engines and the veritable forest of propellers. August 1952.

The vast Columbine Hangar filled by three Princess hulls in January 1951.

THE PRINCESS

PLANNING BOTTOM
1 WATERTIGHT BULKHEADS
2 STEP
3 FRONT-SPAR MAINFRAME
4 REAR-SPAR MAINFRAME
5 BOTTOM STRINGERS, CONTINUOUS BELOW FRAMES (SIDE STRINGERS INTER-COSTAL)
6 BEACHING CHASSIS ATTACHMENT POINTS
7 AIR VENTS (PLANING BOTTOM NOT PRESSURIZED)

MARINE COMPARTMENT
8 PRESSURE BULKHEAD
9 BOW DOOR
10 DOOR TO LOWER DECK
11 HAND-OPERATED WINCH AND HANDLE (STOWED)
12 ANCHOR (STOWED)
13 CLOUD AND COLLISION-WARNING RADOME

LOWER DECK
14 INTERCOSTAL STRINGERS
15 FREIGHT DOOR THRESHOLD (ST'B'D)
16 FREIGHT HATCH
17 FLOOR CONSTRUCTION, FRAMES 8 TO 24 ONLY
18 BELAYING FITTINGS
19 MANHOLES TO PLANING BOTTOM
20 SPIRAL STAIRCASE TO UPPER DECK
21 MAIN ENTRY DOORS
22 ELECTRIC BILGE-PUMPS AND HAND-PUMP

FLIGHT DECK
23 UNDERFLOOR PRESSURE DOME
24 DIRECT-VISION PANEL (EACH SIDE)
25 WINDSCREEN WIPERS

SEATS
26 CAPTAIN
27 FIRST OFFICER
28 NAVIGATOR
29 RADIO OPERATOR
30 FLIGHT ENGINEERS
31 PERISCOPIC SEXTANT MOUNTING
32 RADIO AND RADAR INSTALLATIONS
33 FLIGHT ENGINEERS' THROTTLES AND PANELS

UPPER DECK
34 MAINTENANCE/ESCAPE HATCHES
35 CONTINUOUS STRINGERS
36 STEAMING LIGHT
37 S.T.R. 12c V.H.F. AERIAL IN MAST
38 SUPPRESSED AUTO D/F LOOP AD 7092A
39 PRESSURE HEAD
40 MAIN ELECTRICAL COMPARTMENT
41 FIBREGLASS BLANKET INSULATION
42 INTERIOR TRIM
43 MAINTENANCE LADDER (FIXED)

WING CONSTRUCTION AND INSTALLATION
44 FRONT-SPAR
45 REAR-SPAR
46 WING/HULL MAIN ATTACHMENT POINTS
47 CENTRE-SECTION/INNER-WING JOINT RIBS } MULTI-BOLT
48 INNER/OUTER WING JOINT-RIBS
49 INTEGRAL FUEL TANK END-RIBS
50 SINGLE-SLOTTED FLAPS–THREE SECTIONS EACH SIDE
51 FLAP MOTORS AND SHAFTING
52 FLAP SCREW-JACKS
53 WING-TIP FLOAT OPERATING JACK
54 NAVIGATION LIGHT (WHEN AIRBORNE)
54a NAVIGATION LIGHT (WHEN WATERBORNE)
55 RIDING LIGHT
56 STRINGERS, CONTINUOUS OVER RIBS
57 MANHOLE TO CENTRE-SECTION INTERIOR
58 FIRE SUPPRESSION BOTTLES

ENGINE INSTALLATIONS
59 CONTRA-ROTATION AND REDUCTION GEARBOX
60 ENGINE AIR INTAKE
61 AIR TO OIL-COOLERS 61A
62 DRIVE-SHAFT TO AUXILIARY GEARBOX
63 DRIVE-SHAFT TO AIR-CONDITIONING UNIT
64 126 V 39 KW GENERATORS
64 28 V 6 KW GENERATORS
65 OIL TANKS
   (a) Outer engine (10 gal)
   (b) Centre engine transmission (10 gal)
   (c) Centre engine (two x 7 gal)
   (d) Inner engine transmission (10 gal)
   Inner engine (two x 7 gal) behind spar
66 MAINTENANCE HATCHES
67 LOWER COWLING/MAINTENANCE PLATFORM

AFTER HULL AND TAIL ASSEMBLY
68 REAR PRESSURE-BULKHEAD
69 MANHOLE (LOWER DECK ONLY)
70 MANHOLE TO TAILPLANE TOP SURFACE
71 MANHOLE TO TAILPLANE INTERIOR
72 TAILPLANE MULTI-BOLT ATTACHMENT
73 MAINTENANCE LADDER (FIXED)
74 PLATE AERIAL. AD 94 M/F. H/F. RECEIVER
75 PLATE AERIAL (PORT AND ST'B'D) S.T.R. 15 H/F TRANS/RECEIVER

POWER CONTROLS
76 ELECTRO-HYDRAULIC POWERS-PACKS:-
   (a) To inner section of elevator
   (b) To outer section of elevator
   (c) To upper section of rudder
   (d) To centre and lower sections of rudder
77 SHAFT TRANSMISSION AND SCREW-JACKS
78 SERVO TABS
79 AILERON POWER-PACKS ON CENTRE-SECTION REAR SPAR

AIR-CONDITIONING SYSTEM
A AIR INTAKE
B HOT AIR FROM JET PIPE HEAT-EXCHANGERS
C AIR PRESSURIZING, HEATING, COOLING, REFRIGERATING UNIT
D RECIRCULATION FANS AND MIXING CHAMBERS (UNDER CENTRE-SECTION)
E CONDITIONED-AIR DELIVERY-DUCT (UPPER DECK)
F CONDITIONED-AIR DELIVERY-DUCT (LOWER DECK)
G AIR FLOW-PATH BETWEEN INSULATION AND CABIN TRIM TO:-
H CENTRAL DELIVERY PANELS (UPPER DECK)
   CORNICE DELIVERY PANELS (LOWER DECK)
J RECIRCULATION INTAKES
K CONDITIONED AIR TO FLIGHT DECK
L CABIN PRESSURE-RELIEF VALVES

WING ANTI-ICING
M AIR TO JET PIPE HEAT EXCHANGER
N DISTRIBUTION VOLUTE
P HOT AIR DELIVERY DUCT TO LEADING EDGES
Q INTAKE HEATING TRACT

TAIL ANTI-ICING
R AIR INTAKE
S PARAFFIN COMBUSTION-HEATERS
T HOT AIR TO LEADING EDGES
U AIRSCREW CYCLIC-DE-ICING SHEATHS

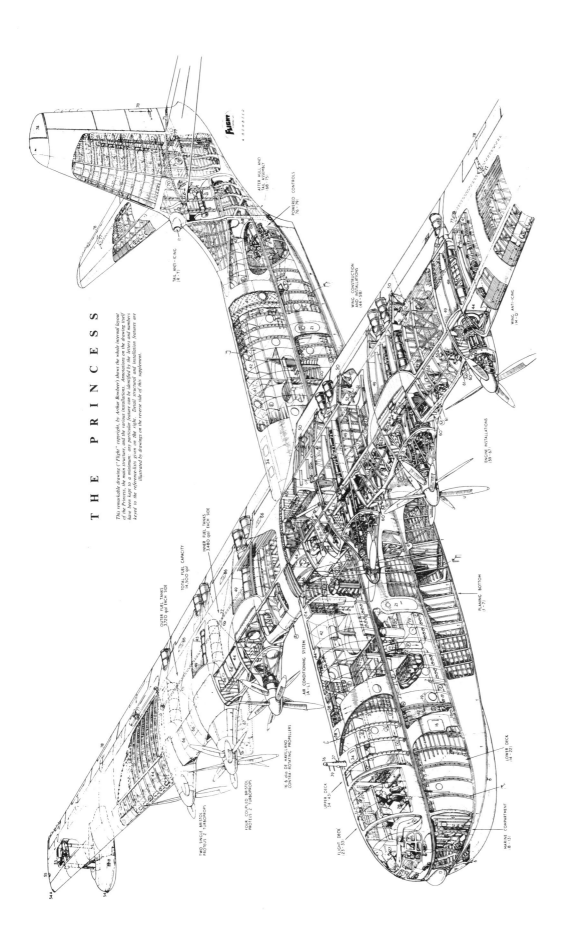

AFTER HULL AND TAIL ASSEMBLY (68–75)

POWERED CONTROLS (76–79)

TAIL ANTI-ICING (R–T)

WING CONSTRUCTION AND INSTALLATIONS (44–58)

WING ANTI-ICING (M–Q)

ENGINE INSTALLATIONS (59–67)

PLANING BOTTOM (1–7)

LOWER DECK (14–22)

MARINE COMPARTMENT (8–13)

FLIGHT DECK (23–33)

UPPER DECK (34–43)

AIR CONDITIONING SYSTEM (A–L)

16 & 6ft 0in DE HAVILLAND CONTRA ROTATING PROPELLERS

FOUR COUPLED BRISTOL PROTEUS 2 TURBOPROPS

TWO SINGLE BRISTOL PROTEUS 2 TURBOPROPS

OUTER FUEL TANKS 3720 gal EACH SIDE

TOTAL FUEL CAPACITY 14,500 gal

INNER FUEL TANKS 3,480 gal EACH SIDE

Saunders-Roe SR.45 Princess. Isometric drawing showing internal structure and installation details.

205

Saunders-Roe SR.45 Princess. The first machine leaving the Columbine Works on 30th October 1951. The tail is held down by water ballast in tanks in the rear of the hull and further clearance under the hangar roof is provided by the omission of the upper fin and rudder.

Saunders-Roe SR.45 Princess. Help from the fire service. Illustrating some of the difficulties of work on large aircraft.

Trial launch of the first Princess. On August 19th 1952 from Columbine Slipway.

Saunders-Roe SR.45 Princess. One of the main beaching gear units being
brought back up the slipway.

Saunders-Roe SR.45 Princess. At rest on the calm waters of the mouth of the Medina.
G-ALUN, lightly laden, rests on her port float with flaps lowered.

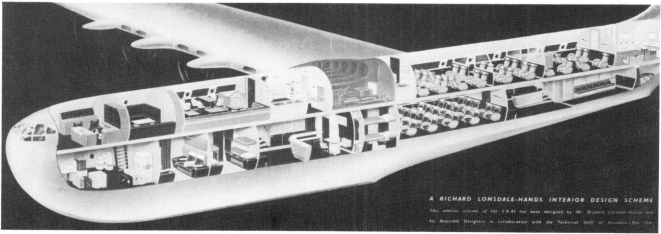

A RICHARD LONSDALE-HANDS INTERIOR DESIGN SCHEME

Proposed interior layout for the Princess Flying Boats on a North Atlantic route.

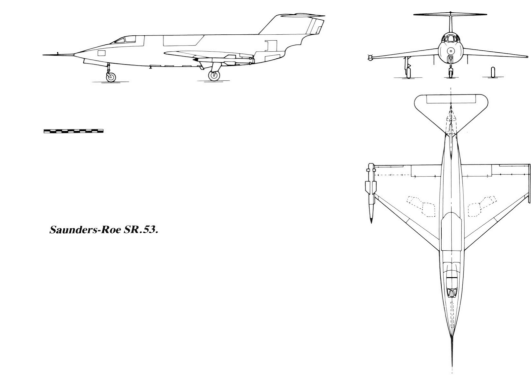

Saunders-Roe SR.53.

The first take-off of the SR.53 at Boscombe Down on May 16th 1957.

Saunders-Roe SR.53. XD145 in flight with the Firestreak guided missiles fitted to the wing-tips. Farnborough 1957.

CHAPTER 14

FIGHTERS, HELICOPTERS AND ROCKETS

The cessation in the demand for marine aircraft resulted in the company spreading its activities into other aspects of aviation and also into space vehicles.

The fighter type, although showing considerable promise, arrived at a time of uncertainty, both operationally and economically and cancellation resulted. The small helicopters developed from Cierva origins, were produced in some numbers until company restructuring transferred them to the Westland parent.

The development of space vehicles was very successfully carried out but was curtailed by changes of national policy.

Alongside all this, Hovercraft were being developed and manufactured and later were to become the main product with which the company became identified. Initially employing aviation technology, Hovercraft have now become more related to marine craft and are outside the scope of this present work.

SR.53 UNNAMED JET & ROCKET   1957 PROPELLED INTERCEPTOR FIGHTER

Type — Single seat short range supersonic fighter for high altitude day interception, to Specification F.138.D.

Engines —
    1 - 1,640 lb thrust Armstrong Siddeley Viper A.S.V.8 turbo-jet.
    1 - 8,000 lbs thrust De Havilland Spectre rocket motor.

Fuselage — The streamlined fuselage was constructed of traditional materials and followed the conventional lay-out for jet fighters with nose wheel undercarriage, pressurised pilot's cockpit with sideways hinging hood. The jet engine was installed centrally above the level of the wing with air intakes on either side of the upper fuselage in removable panels and the jet pipe carried straight aft to exit below the rudder. The rocket motor was mounted below the jet pipe at the extreme rear of the fuselage, access to this being provided by a removable boat-shaped fairing. Dive brakes were mounted on the rear fuselage on either side of the jet pipe.

Wing — The delta-shaped wing 6% TC ratio was constructed in separate halves and was attached by multiple root fittings. The wide-track undercarriage folded inwards to be housed in the inner wing. The entire trailing edge consisted of conventional ailerons and landing flaps; the leading edge was a hinged section which could be drooped to provide additional lift for take-off and landing. The wing tip provided mountings for guided weapons.

Tail Unit — The tailplane was carried at the top of the fin; its delta shape, similar to that of the wing, had

rounded tips and large trim tabs and was power operated for longitudinal control. Construction of the tail units was of conventional materials and design.

Power Plant — The object of the "mixed" power source was to provide the economy of the jet engine with the high thrust obtainable from the rocket. The rocket motor used high test peroxide (HTP) in large quantities and could be switched off for cruising or throttled down to as low as 20% of full thrust to supplement the jet engine for cruising at supersonic speeds. Tanks for both fuels were contained in the lower fuselage.

Dimensions —

Span	25 ft. 1⅛ in.	
Span over missiles	28 ft. 1 in.	
Length	45 ft.	
Height	10 ft. 10 in.	
Wing Area	274 sq. ft.	

Weights —

Gross	18,400 lbs initially	
Basic	7,400 lbs	
Rocket Fuel	10,500 lbs	
Jet Fuel	500 lbs	

Performance —

Maximum speed   Mach 2.0 at 35,000 ft. or more.
Climb to 50,000 ft.   2.2 mins.

Armament —   2 - Firestreak guided missiles on wing tip mountings.

Production —

3 prototypes, only 2 completed -
XD 145   First flight 16.5.57 by Sqn. Ldr. J. Booth. Still in existence at Cosford.
XD 151   First flight 5.12.57. Crashed fatally 5.8.58.
XD 153   Cancelled.

SR.177 DEVELOPMENT OF THE SR.53   1954-57 TO SPECIFICATION F.177.D

A fundamental change was made in the power plant locations, the rocket motor now being the uppermost and the jet engine was now fed by a straight air intake from under the forward fuselage. The after-burning Gyron Junior jet engine was considerably more powerful than the earlier Viper of the SR.53 and the rocket motor had also gained in power by development. The fitment of the powerful AI-23 radar essential for successful interception was the main cause of the considerable growth.

Engines —
    1 - 14,000 lb thrust De Havilland PS.50 Gyron Junior DGJ 101 turbojet.
    1 - 10,000 lb thrust De Havilland Spectre 5A rocket motor.

SR.53. Assembly Bay in the Columbine Hangar.

SR53. Landing at Farnborough with Firestreak air to air missiles fitted and
with wing leading edge slats and fuselage air brakes deployed.

SR.53 Pilots Cockpit. Instrument panel.

Machining a complex fuselage bulkhead at a
wing attachment point.

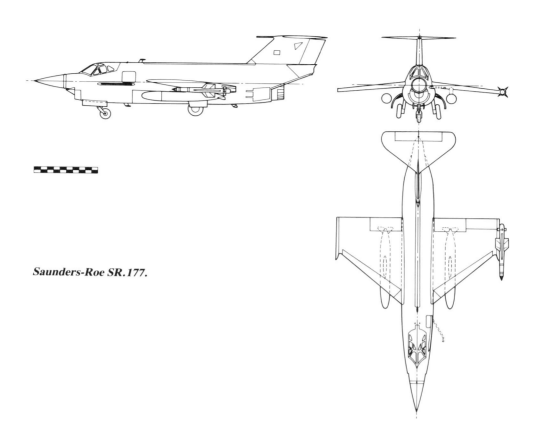

Saunders-Roe SR.177.

SR.177. in German Air Force insignia.

SR.177. Naval version approaching an Aircraft Carrier to land.

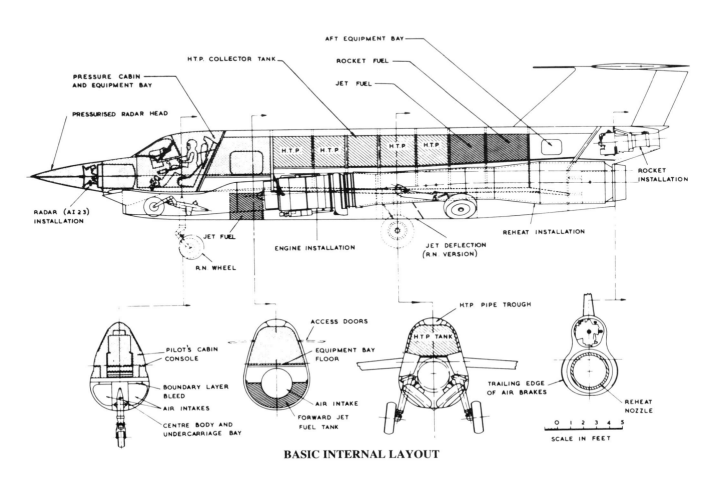

BASIC INTERNAL LAYOUT

Dimensions —	Span	27 ft. 1 in.
	Span over missiles	30 ft. 3⅛ in.
	Length	50 ft. 6 in.
	Height	14 ft. 3½ in.
	Wing area	327 sq.ft.
Weights —	Gross (normal)	25,786 lbs.
	Gross (extended)	28,174 lbs.
	Basic	14,533 lbs.
Performance —	Maximum speed	Mach 2.35
	Climb to 60,000 ft.	3.10 mins.

Armament — 2 - Red Top guided missiles on wing tip mountings.

Production — Contract cover was received authorising production of nine aircraft, as below, with cover up to 27 aircraft with limitations.

XL 905 - 907 Development aircraft.
XL 920 - 922 RAF version.
XL 923 - 925 RN version.

General — Following the withdrawal of the German military interest, the British services also withdrew their support. In order to save the project, proposals were made to build variants of the aircraft for research purposes. A number of schemes of various configurations involving wings of several different types, including W and reversed W planforms were devised, none of which proceeded beyond the early proposal stage.

SAUNDERS-ROE SKEETER 1951 (ORIGINALLY CIERVA W.14 SKEETER)

(Description does not relate to the prototype)

Type — 2 seat light helicopter for military and civil operations.

Engine — See below.

Fuselage — The fuselage consisted of three separate portions. The forward structure, L-shaped in elevation, was constructed of Alclad light alloy sheet frames and longitudinal members and provided a floor to take the crew, controls and equipment. The vertical fore and aft members were the main means of taking structural loads including those from the nose undercarriage back to the centre fuselage, from which the front portion was separated by a steel fireproof bulkhead. The top portion of the front fuselage was a light tubular structure, extensively glazed, and provided with two jettisonable doors. The centre fuselage was a steel welded tubular structure incorporating the power plant and mountings for the rotor drive and main undercarriage. The rear fuselage was a cone with upswept rear end fabricated from Alclad sheet as a conventional monocoque with frames and internal and external stiffeners.

Power Plant — The four cylinder inverted air-cooled engine was mounted transversely in the tubular centre fuselage. The crankshaft on the starboard side drove a

primary gearbox incorporating a clutch and freewheel and through a universally jointed shaft drove a secondary gearbox above the engine. The main rotor drive was taken vertically from this gearbox and the tail rotor drive taken horizontally by suitable gearing and torque shaft. A cooling fan was driven by belts from the primary gearbox, air being provided from an intake on the starboard side. Light alloy cowling panels, most removable, covered the installation. A flexible bag fuel tank holding 23 gallons, increased to 27 gallons on the Mk.4, was contained in a bay behind the crew compartment.

Rotors — The three-bladed main rotor was mounted on a hub with drag and flapping hinges and dampers and was built up on tubular steel main spars with wooden ribs and plywood and fabric covering. Later in production these rotor blades were replaced with ones of all metal type. The original three-bladed light alloy tail rotor was replaced early in the development stage with a two-blade type based on a Hydulignum spar with a plywood skin, balsa wood filled and fibreglass covered with stainless steel leading edge as developed by Hordern-Richmond.

Dimensions —	Rotor diameter	32 ft.
	Length (blades folded)	28 ft. 5 in.
	Width (blades folded)	7 ft. 4½ in.
	Height 9 ft. 10 in. (Skeeter 3)	
	10 ft. 2 in. (Skeeter 6)	
	9 ft. 6 in. (Skeeter 7)	
	Tail rotor diameter	6 ft.
Weights —	Gross (normal) 2,000 lb. (Skeeter 3)	
	2,100 lb. (Skeeter 3B)	
	2,150 lb. (Skeeter 6)	
	2,250 lb. (Skeeter 7)	

Performance —		
Maximum speed	109 mph
Cruising speed	105 mph
Endurance	3 hours at 80 mph
Vertical rate of climb	1,020 ft. per min.
Maximum rate of climb	1,150 ft. per min.
Service ceiling	11,700 - 12,800 ft.

Production — 10 prototype and development machines, 2 originally made by Cierva. 78 production as below.

General — The Cierva Company operating in premises at Eastleigh aerodrome, previously part of Cunliffe-Owen Aircraft, had flown the first version of the Skeeter, designed by C.G. Pullin, on 10th October 1948. The second machine, flown on the 20th October 1949, introduced the monocoque type rear fuselage, new type engine and other changes but required further redesigning to achieve a reasonable performance and to overcome severe problems created by ground resonance which were finally resolved by early 1954. In January 1951, Saunders-Roe took over the design and continued with the development under Project No. P.502, eventually producing versions of the aircraft which were used by the Army, the RAF for pilot training and the Federal German Army and Navy. Army versions were Air Observation Post (AOP) type and doubled for training helicopter pilots for which they were fitted with dual controls. The separate T.13 trainer version was not proceeded with. Civil sales did not materialise. Final deliveries took place in 1960.

The Mk.6 machines G-AMTZ and ANMI were tried for a period with the rocket-booster system NRE.19 developed with Napiers and intended primarily to boost take-off in difficult conditions. A tank was mounted above the rotor hub and fed HTP to the rotor blade tips, where it was burnt to boost rotor speed, increasing the rate of climb significantly from 230 feet per minute to 1,470 feet per minute. This installation was not used on Service aircraft.

One production AOP Mk.12, XM 528, was fitted with a skid undercarriage, developed under project No. P.534, and a D.H. turbo-super-charged engine and conducted tropical trials in Aden but only confirmed the unsuitability of the Skeeter for use in 'hot and high' conditions.

The Skeeter was somewhat limited in this application and was withdrawn from the German services in 1961 and the ten machines were sold to Portugal but were not used again. In Britain the Skeeter remained in use until 1969.

SKEETER PROTOTYPES AND DEVELOPMENT

Man. Mk. No.	Type	Qty	Regn./ Serial No.	Engine	Remarks
1	Prototype Cierva W14/1	1	G-AJCJ	106 HP Jameson FF-1	F.F. 10.10.48. Flown by H.A.Marsh. Scrapped November 1952.
2	Prototype Cierva W14/2	1	G-ALUF	145 HP Gipsy Major 10	F.F. 15.10.49. Flown by H.A.Marsh. Destroyed on ground by effects of resonance 26.6.50.
3 3B	Army W14/3 & 4	2	WF.112-3	145 HP Gipsy Major 8 180 HP Blackburn Bombardier 702	Development and Service Trials 1951-3. To Spec. A13/49
4	Navy W14/5	1	WF.114	180 HP Blackburn Bombardier 702	Development and Service Trials 1951-3. To Spec. A13/49
5	Civil	1	G-AMTZ XG 303 (SR.907)	180 HP Blackburn Bombadier 702/4	F.F. mid 1953. J. Jeffrey. Re-registered from G-AMDC Service serial no. for A & AEE Trials - March 1954.
6	Civil. Dual control trainer version of Mk.4/5	-	G-AMTZ	200 HP Gipsy Major 201	Modified from Mk.5. C of A 21.5.57. Napier NRE 19 rocket booster system installed also ambulance equipment.
6	Development and Service Trials	3	G-ANMH XJ 355 (SR.905)	200 HP Gipsy Major 201 (130)	F.F. 29.8.54. Service serial no. for trials and further development work with S-R/Westland November 1954. To AAC for ground instruction April 1960.
			G-ANMG (SR.904)	200 HP Gipsy Major 201 (130)	C of A 8.6.55. Service serial no. for trials Aug. 1955 and further development work with S-R/Westland to 1960.
			G-ANMI (SR.906)	200 HP Gipsy Major 201 (130)	Service trials Jan. 1956. Reverted to G-ANMI when returned to S-R May 1956. Napier NRE.19 rocket booster system from 5.8.56.
7	Basic type for production	-	G-ANMI	215 HP Gipsy Major 215	Tested from May 1957 until use discontinued in August 1960.
8	Civil	1	G-APOI (S2/5081) (G-APOJ & K not built)	215 HP Gipsy Major 215	Construction of 3 started but only G-APOI completed in 1958. Used for development work until April 1964.
	Total	10			
P.537	Development	-	XM 563 (S2/5118)	250 shp Blackburn Turmo 603	A production Mk.12 aircraft modified for performance improvement and flown in March 1960.

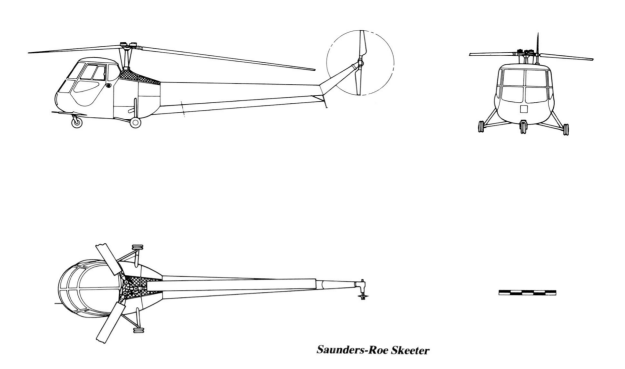

Saunders-Roe Skeeter

Saunders-Roe Skeeter. WF.112 was the first machine built after the takeover by Saunders-Roe and
was used for development and Service Trials of Army requirements.

Saunders-Roe Skeeter. The Mk.6 prototype equipped as an ambulance and fitted with the Napier NRE.19 rocket booster system. Test pilot Ken Reed at the controls flew the machine at Farnborough in 1957.

Saunders-Roe Skeeter. The 1954 S.B.A.C. Show saw the first public appearance of the Mk.6 version G-ANMH was the first of three used later for Service Trials as XJ.355.

Saunders-Roe Skeeter. Evaluating the alternative skid undercarriage and D.H. Turbo-charged engine. Design changes under P.534 were embodied in XM.528 an early production AOP/T.12 for trials. Here being flown by company pilot H. Phillips.

Saunders-Roe Skeeter. The first production AOP/T.12 representative of the type used in largest numbers.

Saunders-Roe Skeeter. Ken Reed running-up the engine of a Mk.51 for the Federal German Navy.

Man. Mk. No.	Type	Service No.	Qty	Serial Nos.	Engine	Remarks
6A	**Army Air Corps** Trials aircraft	AOP.10	3	XK480-82 (S2/3036, 3051 & 3070)	200 HP Gipsy Major 130	
6B		T.11	1	XK479 (S2/3012)	200 HP Gipsy Major 130	
7	**Army Air Corps** 1st batch ordered May 1956		20	XM524-30 XM553-65 (S2/5100 - 5110 5112 -5120)	200 HP Gipsy Major 130	Delivered May 1958 to July 1960. To Spec. H163/P2.
	2nd batch ordered Nov. 1957	AOP & T.12	27	(XL734-40 XL762-72 XL806-14 (S2/5064 - 5099 Intermittent	215 HP Gipsy Major 215	
	3rd batch ordered Jan. 1959		17	XN339-55 (SR/7145 - 61)	215 HP Gipsy Major 215	
7	**Federal German Army**	Mk.50	6	*PC+117-22 Later re-numbered PF+155-160 (S2/5061 - 3, 5073, 5077, 5082	215 HP Gipsy Major 215	Delivered between June 1958 and Jan. 1959.
7	**Federal German Navy**	Mk.51	4	SC501-5 (S2/5065, 5070, 5092)	215 HP Gipsy Major 215	
		Total	78			

* Note: The first Mk.50 PC+117 flew initially with registration G-12-2.

SAUNDERS-ROE P.531 SPRITE (LATER WESTLAND SCOUT AND WASP)   1958

Type — 5/6 seat helicopter for military and civil operations.

Ehgine —
425 SHP (de-rated to 325 SHP initially) Blackburn-Turbomeca Turmo 600 free turbine
650 SHP Blackburn A.129 Nimbus free turbine
650 SHP de Havilland Gnome H.1000 turbine.

Fuselage — The fuselage was a structure of Alclad manufactured in two main sections, the joint being behind the engine. The forward portion comprised the cabin floor constructed of frames and two main longitudinal members. These extended aft, through the tank bay behind the cabin up to the platform carrying a tubular structure for the main rotor mounting. Further aft the fuselage tapered in width and depth but retained a horizontal flat top which was a fireproof platform for mounting the power plant and accessories. The tapered portion provided a baggage and battery bay. The rear fuselage was a cone with upswept rear end similar in construction to that of the Skeeter. A small trimmable tailplane and ventral fin were fitted and on the Naval version the rear section could be folded. A four-wheel undercarriage was used initially and for Naval use but this was changed to a pair of skids for Army use. The cabin top was a light structure glazed with flat glass windscreens and acrylic panels.

Power Plant — The turbine was mounted horizontally on the top of the fuselage and from the primary gearbox at its rear end drove a shaft which extended forward to the secondary gearbox located at the base of the main rotor vertical shaft. An electrical generator was driven direct from the engine and an oil pump for gearbox lubrication

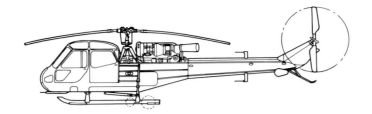

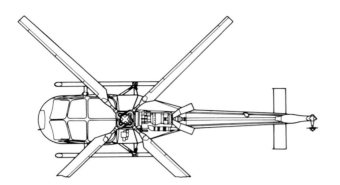

Saunders-Roe P531

Saunders-Roe P531-0 Helicopter. The first machine that was flown in the summer of 1958

Saunders-Roe P.531 Helicopter. XN 332 was originally G-APNV and was progressively modified to the configuration seen here for the evaluation by the Royal Navy in company with two other pre-production machines XN333-4. In service the machine became the Westland Wasp HAS.1.

Saunders-Roe P.531 Helicopter. The lengthened and otherwise modified version of the P.531-2 for use by the Army was for a time known as the Sprite before entering service as The Westland Scout A.H.1.

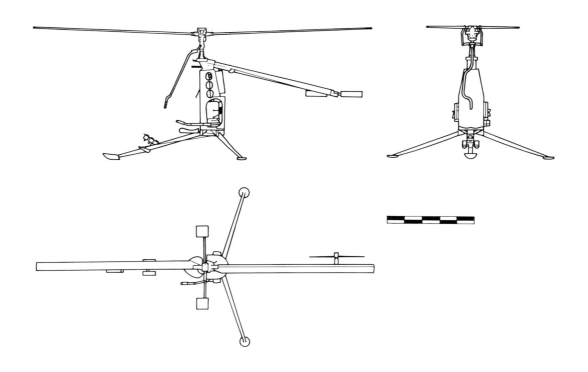

Hiller Rotorcycle

Hiller Rotorcycle YROE-1. Saunders-Roe built ten of these one-man portable helicopters, the first of which flew at Eastleigh in October 1959.

was driven from the secondary gearbox by a lateral shaft. Cooling of the circulated oil was by a twin cooler unit on the port side of the engine through which air was circulated by a fan belt driven from the engine. Fuel was contained in three flexible bag tanks housed in the bay immediately behind the cabin and was fed to the engine by electrical booster pumps in a central collection sump.

Dimensions —	P.531-0	P.531-2
Rotor diameter	32 ft. 6 in.	32 ft. 3 in.
Length (blades folded)	29 ft.	30 ft. 4 in.
Width (blades folded)	8 ft. 6 in.	8 ft.
Height	9 ft. 6 in.	10 ft. 5½ in.

Weights —		
Gross		3,800 lb.
Basic		2,092 lb. (less radio).

Performance —	P.531-0	P.531-2
Maximum speed	120 mph	134 mph
Cruising speed	109 mph	122 mph
Endurance	3.5 hrs	3.2 hrs
With long range tank	5.4 hours.	5.0 hrs

General — At the time when Westland took over in July 1959, Saunders-Roe had been flying prototypes of the P.531 for a year. The first machine, G-APNU, flying initially on 20.7.58 piloted by K.M. Reed, to be followed soon by G-APNV, later adapted to RN requirements and evaluated as XN.332 as part of a batch of three P.531-O/N aircraft XN.332-4 later known as Westland Wasp H.A.S. 1 in service. Further machines were well advanced in manufacture and two P.531-2 development machines, G-APVL with the Blackburn A.129 engine and G-APVM with the de Havilland Gnome, were flying in September at the SBAC Show. Subsequent development was carried out under the Westland name and design responsibility transferred to Yeovil. This was followed by the run down of work at Eastleigh and the closure of the Saunders-Roe Helicopter Division in 1960. Production of the Scout for the Army and Wasp for the Navy was passed to Westland's Fairey Division at Hayes with assembly and test flying taking place at White Waltham. Production terminated in 1972 after manufacture of 148 Scouts. The Royal Navy received 96 production Wasps and a further 35 were exported.

Production — 4 Prototypes and 2 Naval Development machines plus the conversion of one prototype for Naval development work.

A further batch was also in the course of manufacture at Eastleigh, allocated construction numbers S2/8437 - 8447, which were to become aircraft XP165, XP167 - XP.192 and test structures, etc. Only a proportion of this work was carried out at Eastleigh. The remainder was transferred to the Hayes Division.

P.531-0	S2/5267	G-APNU	325 shp Blackburn Turbomeca Turmo F.F. 20.7.58. by K.M. Reed
P.531-1 & O/N	S2/5268	G-APNV (XN332)	425 shp Blackburn Turbomeca Turmo F.F. 30.9.58. by K.M. Reed

P.531-2	S2/5311	G-APVL (XP166)	650 shp Blackburn A.129 F.F. 9.8.59. by K.M. Reed
P.531-2	S2/5312	G-APVM (XR493)	650 shp D.H. Gnome initially fitted. F.F. 3.5.60. by K.M. Reed 650 shp Blackburn Nimbus
P.531-0/N	S2/	XN333	650 shp Blackburn Nimbus
P.531-0/N	S2/	XN334	650 shp Blackburn Nimbus

HILLER YROE-1 ROTORCYCLE   1958-60

Type — One-man portable helicopter.

Engine — 43 HP Nelson H-63B four cylinder two-stroke.

Description — The airframe comprised a rivetted light alloy structure standing on three tapered legs, the engine being mounted with crankshaft vertical at the bottom of the central structure. The drive to the main rotor was taken to a shrouded cooling fan then to a reduction gearbox, clutch and free wheel in cast housings. The tail boom, mounted from the top of the body, enclosed the tail-rotor drive. The main rotor consisted of two main blades, at right angles to which, was a twin-paddle servo-rotor. The main rotor blades were constructed of rolled steel leading edges and channel section spars bonded together and to the plastic trailing edges. The pilot, seated on a saddle-type seat astride the forward leg, controlled the servo-rotor through a "hanging-stick", which in turn tilted the main rotor to produce the effect of cyclic pitch changes, a system known as "Hiller Rotor-Matic" control. The engine was originally started by pull-chord, later replaced by an electric starter, and used a mixture of oil and petrol for which a 12 U.S. gallon tank superseded the original 2.5 gallon tank. By removing 13 pins, one man could fold the machine into a small package 14 ft. 6 in. x 2 ft. 3 in. approximately for transport and air dropping. Re-assembly took only 2 - 3 minutes.

Dimensions —		
	Rotor diameter	18 ft. 6 in.
	Length	16 ft. 6 in.
	Height	7 ft. 4 in.
	Disc area	268 sq. ft.

Weights —		
	Basic	300 lb.
	Gross	556 lb.
	Disc loading	2.07 lb. per sq.ft.

Performance —		
	Maximum speed	70 mph
	Cruising speed	52 mph
	Climb at sea level	1160 ft. per min. max.
	Range	166 miles
	Rotor speed	540 rpm

Production — Contract from Helicop-Air (Hiller European Agents) September 1958.

10 machines	5 for U.S. Marine Corps
	Class 'B' identities G-46-1 to 5
	(S2/7588, 7592-6) allocated
	5 for test and demonstrations
	purposes
	Class 'B' identities G-12-3 and
	G-46-1 applied to S2/7592 and
	G-APYF cancelled 1963

The Rotorcycles were constructed at Eastleigh and the first flew there on 19th October 1959 in the hands of U.S. pilot Phil Johnston.

BLACK KNIGHT BALLISTIC TEST VEHICLE
36 ins. DIA. VERSION   1955-65

Purpose — Initially designed to investigate hypersonic re-entry into the earth's atmosphere in connection with the long-range missile Blue Streak. Subsequently employed for research into re-entry physics and upper atmosphere scientific experiments.

Power Plant — 16,000 lb sea level thrust Armstrong Siddeley Gamma II (later Bristol Siddeley Gamma 201 or 301). (HTP/Kerosene rocket motor consisted of four combustion chambers based on the original Gamma design by the Rocket Propulsion Department, Westcott).

Description — Black Knight was designed as a single stage rocket with a basic diameter of 36 ins. comprising the following main sections:

1. PROPULSION BAY. The main structure consisted of a strong ring frame for attachment to the HTP tank, four longitudinal beams built into the shell which provided mountings for the outer trunnions on which the combustion chambers swivelled and four tubular struts from the top frame to a central casting near the base. This casting carried the inner trunnions and a central spherical spigot for supporting and releasing the vehicle.

   Four fins of rivetted construction employed spars, ribs, stiffeners and skins of light alloy. These were attached to the main shell by lugs at the lower frame and spigots at the front spars. Pods of light alloy construction with steel nose cones provided housings for optical tracking beacon and guidance transponder equipment on two of the fin tips.

2. HTP (OXIDANT) TANK. This housed the HTP in a cylindrical shell forming the skin of the vehicle. It was made of 20 swg light alloy with internal stiffening frames attached by spot welding. The joints in the skins were made by overlapping spot-welds. The tank ends were domed and strong rings provided for attachment.

3. INTER-TANK BAY. This housed the 4000 psi air bottles and control equipment for pressurising the HTP tanks.

4. FUEL TANK. This was constructed in a similar manner to the HTP tank but with a capacity of one eighth by weight of kerosene and was self pressurised.

5. ELECTRONICS BAY. This self-pressurised bay housed the electrical control equipment, command link receivers, autopilot, telemetry transmitters and electric power units using rechargeable batteries. The bay was lagged and provided with equipment for air circulation and cooling.

6. ADAPTOR BAY. This short section provided the means for attaching the various payloads, most of which were required to be detached before re-entry. This was usually achieved by the use of explosive bolts and ejection springs but the two stage versions used a gas jet system to lift and spin up the second stage prior to ignition of the solid re-entry motor.

7. HEAD. Several types were employed for specific purposes and were mainly conical in shape. The shell, which was self- pressurised, was made of a durestos/graphite material or carbon steel with interior heat resistant Refrasil blankets with stainless steel lining. Suitable mountings for instrumentation and various types of equipment were provided. A second stage head was fitted on some later launchers.

Systems — Turbines driven by HTP, one for each combustion chamber, drove pumps for the propellant, also two hydraulic pumps provided power for a 3000 PSI system for operating the control system. Gyroscopes provided constant heading and roll datum, changes and correction of attitude being obtained by deflection of the individual combustion chambers by hydraulic jacks and control valves actuated by electronic signals. The pipes and cables carried externally along the skin of the vehicle were covered by fibreglass fairings.

Dimensions —	Diameter	36 in.
	Basic overall height	32 ft 10 in.
	(varied with type of head fitted)	
	Span of fins	6 ft 0 in.
	Span over pods	9 ft 0 in.
	Kerosene tank	4 ft 0 in. long
	HTP tank	17 ft 0 in. long

Weights —	Take-off weight	12,800 lb.
	HTP 10,138 lb)	
	Kerosene 1,268 lb)	11,406 lb.
	Weight at end of burning	1,394 lb.

TYPICAL PERFORMANCE WITH 200 lb RE-ENTRY HEAD — Vertical climb to 20,000 ft was under manual/-optical ground control then under radar control to the 'all-burnt' height of 375,000 ft continuing to an apogee of 500 miles in 9 minutes 17 seconds. Re-entry at 200,000 ft took place at 17,500 ft per second at 50 - 60 miles down the range after 16 minutes 24 seconds. Data was transmitted throughout the mission by telemetry and recorded on an armoured and insulated tape recorder which survived re-entry.

Second Stage Head — The re-entry physics research programme needed higher velocities at head re-entry this was achieved with a downward firing second stage using a Cuckoo solid propellant motor.

The motor nozzle was enclosed with a nose cone which accommodated the gas jet separation and spin up separation system.

The nozzle nose cone was attached by shear pins which failed under the motor efflux pressure at ignition.

A light alloy fabricated shell structure extended from the Cuckoo base to connect the complete assembly to the 1st stage payload adaptor via explosive bolts.

The re-entry head was housed inside the shell structure, pointing downwards and connected to it via two explosive bolts and a separation sabot. The sabot was powered by eight Imp rockets and detached from the head by an arresting lanyard.

MAIN STAGE

Weights —
Take-off weight	12,750 lb
Weight at end of burning	1,919 lb
(includes second stage)	

Performance —
Altitude at end of burning	325,000 ft.
Apogee for range of 200 miles	315 miles
Velocity at end of burning	9,000 ft per second

SECOND STAGE

Weights —
At separation	624 lb
Payload	100 lb

Performance —
Light-up altitude	325,000 ft.
Velocity at end of burning	17,480 ft per sec.
Altitude at end of burning	230,000 ft.
Flight time - launch to re-entry	12 minutes 50 seconds

54 ins. DIA. VERSION   **1964**

Purpose — To improve the performance, giving greater time at altitude and/or increased payloads, as compared to the 36 ins. dia. version when this had been impaired by separation problems.

Power Plants — Improved thrust Gamma 301 engine and weight reduced. Cuckoo 2 second stage motor.

General Changes — Vehicle diameter increased to 54 ins. and reduced in length by 2 ft. against an equivalent 36 ins. vehicle accommodating more fuel and oxidant. The taper of the fairing from the body to the second stage became more pronounced. A typical vehicle was 37 ft. overall. This version was not manufactured.

BLACK KNIGHT LAUNCH RECORD

Date	Vehicle	Stages	Engine	Mission*	Result
7.9.58.	BK.01			Prove vehicle	Success until near burn-out
	BK.02	1	201	Development, non-flight	
12.3.59	BK.03	1	201	Prove vehicle	Success, cold-thrust at end
11.6.59.	BK.04	1	201	Separate head for re-entry	Success
29.6.59.	BK.05	1	201	Separate head for re-entry	Success, cold-thrust at end
30.10.59.	BK.06	1	201	Repeat 05 plus tape recorder†	Success
24.5.60.	BK.08	2	201	Prove 2nd stage and Gaslight equipment	Success, brief cold-thrust
21.6.60.	BK.09	2	201	Repeat 08†	Success
25.7.60.	BK.07	1	201	Repeat 06†	Success, brief cold-thrust
7.2.61.	BK.13	1	201	Repeat 07†	Success, except for instrumentation
9.5.61.	BK.14	2	201	Repeat 09†	No 2nd stage ignition
7.6.61.	BK.17	2	201	Repeat 14†	2nd stage separated only on re-entry
1.5.62.	BK.15	1	201	No.1 of Dazzle programme†	Success, valuable data
24.8.62.	BK.16	2	301	Dazzle trial, new engine, transistorized controls†	Success (textbook mission)
27.11.62.	BK.18	2	301	Prove engine, and head dynamics†	Success
17.10.63.	BK.11	1	201	Prove Blue Streak range safety	Success
	BK.10	1	201	Backup for BK.11	
11.3.64.	BK.12	2	201	Prove Cuckoo 2 motor	Success, except not clean stage separation
6.8.64.	BK.19	2	301		All flight objectives achieved
6.11.64.	BK.20	2	301		All flight objectives achieved
21.4.64.	BK.21	2	301		Successful - All flight objectives achieved
Not Flown	BK.22	2	301		Science Museum
28.7.65.	BK.23	2	301		Successful except 4 sec short burn on 1st stage
29.9.65.	BK.24	2	301		All flight objectives achieved
25.11.65.	BK.25	2	301		All flight objectives achieved

*The "repeats" may differ in detail.   †Carried scientific experiments.

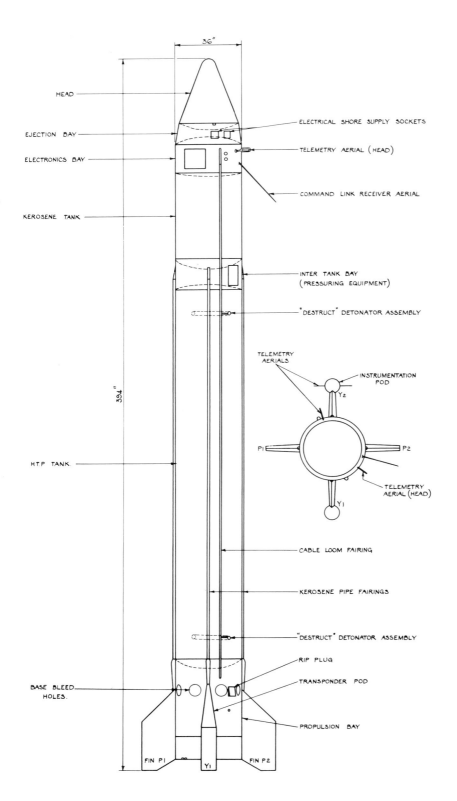

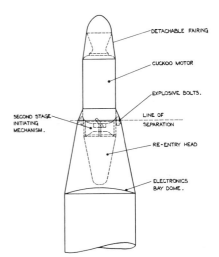

HEAD

EJECTION BAY

ELECTRONICS BAY

KEROSENE TANK

H.T.P TANK.

BASE BLEED HOLES.

FIN P1

Y1

FIN P2

36"

39.4"

ELECTRICAL SHORE SUPPLY SOCKETS

TELEMETRY AERIAL (HEAD)

COMMAND LINK RECEIVER AERIAL

INTER TANK BAY (PRESSURING EQUIPMENT)

"DESTRUCT" DETONATOR ASSEMBLY

TELEMETRY AERIALS

INSTRUMENTATION POD

Y2

P1

P2

TELEMETRY AERIAL (HEAD)

Y1

CABLE LOOM FAIRING

KEROSENE PIPE FAIRINGS

"DESTRUCT" DETONATOR ASSEMBLY

RIP PLUG

TRANSPONDER POD

PROPULSION BAY

DETACHABLE FAIRING

CUCKOO MOTOR

EXPLOSIVE BOLTS.

SECOND STAGE INITIATING MECHANISM.

LINE OF SEPARATION

RE-ENTRY HEAD

ELECTRONICS BAY DOME.

Black Knight. Second stage

Black Knight Ballistic test vehicle.

Black Knight. Being raised into position in an assembly gantry at Woomera.

Black Knight. Exhibited at Farnborough in September 1959.

Black Knight. Numbers BK.13 and BK.14 vehicles on the launchers at Woomera, South Australia.

Black Knight. One of the early vehicles, probably BK.05, rigged for launching at Woomera in 1959. The re-entry head was one of several types which were employed.

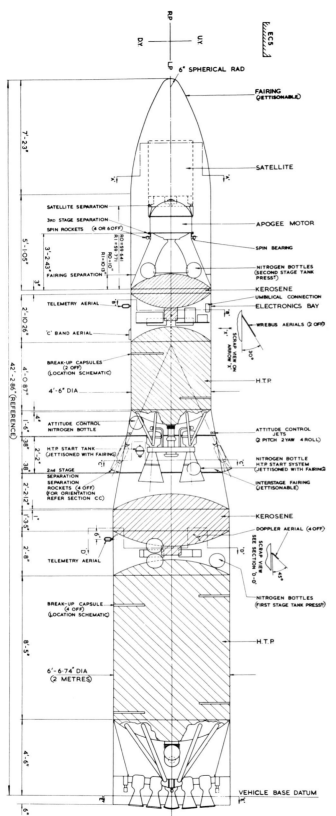

RP

DY UY

LP

EC5

6" SPHERICAL RAD

FAIRING
(JETTISONABLE)

SATELLITE

7'-2.3"

SATELLITE SEPARATION

APOGEE MOTOR

3RD STAGE SEPARATION

SPIN ROCKETS (4 OR 6 OFF)

RO=59.641
RI=59.771
RO=10"
RI=10.13"

SPIN BEARING

5'-1.05"

3'-2.43"

NITROGEN BOTTLES
(SECOND STAGE TANK
PRESS.)

3"

FAIRING SEPARATION

KEROSENE

UMBILICAL CONNECTION

ELECTRONICS BAY

TELEMETRY AERIAL

2'-10.26"

WREBUS AERIALS (2 OFF)

'C' BAND AERIAL

SCRAP VIEW ON
ARROW 'X'

30°

BREAK-UP CAPSULES
(2 OFF)
(LOCATION SCHEMATIC)

H.T.P.

4'-0.87"

4'-6" DIA

ATTITUDE CONTROL
NITROGEN BOTTLE

1'-6"

4"

ATTITUDE CONTROL
JETS
(2 PITCH 2 YAW 4 ROLL)

H.T.P START TANK
(JETTISONED WITH FAIRING)

2'-2"

.38"

NITROGEN BOTTLE
H.T.P START SYSTEM
(JETTISONED WITH FAIRING)

2nd STAGE
SEPARATION
SEPARATION
ROCKETS (4 OFF)
(FOR ORIENTATION
REFER SECTION CC)

.38"

2'-2.12"

INTERSTAGE FAIRING
(JETTISONABLE)

1'-3.5"

1"

KEROSENE

DOPPLER AERIAL (4 OFF)

SCRAP VIEW
SEE SECTION 'D-D'

45°

2'-8"

6"

D

TELEMETRY AERIAL

NITROGEN BOTTLES
(FIRST STAGE TANK PRESS.)

42'-2.86" (REFERENCE)

BREAK-UP CAPSULE
(4 OFF)
(LOCATION SCHEMATIC)

8'-5"

H.T.P.

6'-6.74" DIA
(2 METRES)

4'-6"

VEHICLE BASE DATUM

6"

Black Arrow.

Black Arrow. Mock-up at Farnborough.

226

BLACK ARROW LAUNCH VEHICLE   1966-72

PURPOSE — For use as a satellite launcher, comprising three stages based on the technology developed for the Black Knight.

POWER PLANT

STAGE 1 -   50,000 lb thrust Rolls-Royce Gamma 8 (BS.606) HTP/Kerosene rocket motor.

STAGE 2 -   15,340 lb thrust Rolls-Royce Gamma 2 (BS.625) HTP/Kerosene rocket motor.

STAGE 3 -   6,130 lb maximum thrust RPE Waxwing solid propellent rocket motor. (Manufactured by Bristol Aerojet)

DESCRIPTION — Starting from ground level the vehicle, approximately 43 feet high, comprised the undermentioned main sections constructed generally in a similar manner to the Black Knight.

STAGE 1 — 6 ft 6.74 ins. (2 metres) diameter

1. PROPULSION BAY. Contained the main motor for take-off, a developed Gamma with eight combustion chambers capable of being deflected for guidance of the vehicle. No fins were provided.

2. HTP (OXIDANT) TANK. An enlarged version of that of Black Knight.

3. INTER-TANK BAY. This housed nitrogen bottles and equipment for pressurising the tanks.

4. SEPARATION BAY. This short tapered section integrated the first and second stages. Eight explosive bolts provided the connection and release mechanism.

STAGE 2

5. SEPARATION BAY. A further short tapered section, jettisoned after separation, comprised the connection to the first stage and contained four small Siskin solid propellent motors to separate the stages. These, and the HTP and nitrogen bottles for starting the main motor, were all jettisoned.

6. PROPULSION BAY. This contained the motor for carrying the second and third stages into space and was optimised for operating in a vacuum. As with the main motor, it was gimbal-mounted to deflect the thrust and give control in three axes.

7. HTP (OXIDANT) TANK. A 4 ft 6 in. diameter tank with domed ends.

8. ELECTRONICS BAY. This pressurised compartment contained the main electronics equipment that served the first stage and then continued to control the second stage after separation. In it were housed the batteries providing the sources of electrical power together with the major instrumentation and systems control equipment.

9. FUEL TANK. A shallow tank containing kerosene for the second stage motor.

STAGE 3

10. SEPARATION BAY. The fairings forming the shell of the vehicle were arranged to separate as soon as the vehicle was out of the earth's atmosphere, together with the nose cap. After a period of coasting, four small rockets, named Imp Mk. VI or XV, attached to the apogee motor were activated to spin the combined Waxwing motor and payload prior to separation. Vehicle altitude was maintained during this period by Nitrogen gas attitude control system. At separation a manacle clamp holding the apogee motor to its mounting was released, leaving the Waxwing motor and payload to proceed to orbit.

11. PAYLOAD. The selected payload was mounted on a platform and retained by four attachments with eight springs for separation. A gas cartridge initiated the release operation. Development equipment was mounted initially for proving purposes followed by a Prospero technology satellite.

WEIGHTS —   AUW   40,000 lb
Payload   320 lb (from Woomera)
             400 lb (equatorial launch)

TYPICAL PERFORMANCE

		Height (Miles)	Speed (ft/sec.)	Time	Distance from Launch (Miles)
1st Stage		34	5,469	2 mins 11 secs	26.8
Fairings Jettisoned		68	7,887	3 mins	76.4
2nd Stage		135	16,095	4 mins 7 secs	198.8
3rd Stage:	Ignition	366	13,825	8 mins 30 secs	317
	All-burnt	385	25,459	9 mins 20 secs	348.9

LAUNCH RECORD

Date	Vehicle	Stages	Result
24.7.69	R.0	Stages 1 & 2 live, Stage 3 ballast	Destroyed at +30 secs due to control malfunction.
4.3.70.	R.1	Stages, 2 & 3 live, Payload - boiler plate	2nd stage short burnt due to loss of HTP tank pressure
2.9.70.	R.2	Stages 1, 2 & 3 live. Payload - boiler plate	Payload fairing malfunctioned
28.10.71.	R.3	Stages 1, 2 & 3 live. Payload - Prospero	Successful, with very high orbital accuracy.
	R.4	Not flown	At Science Museum.

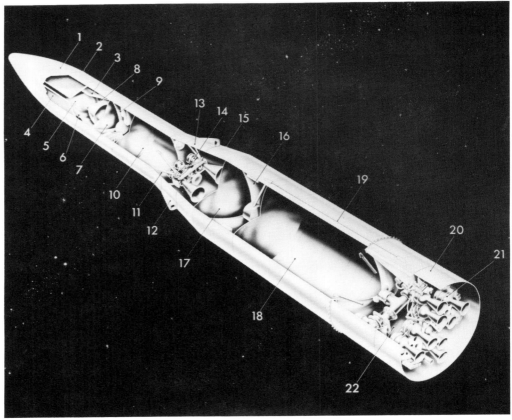

1. Jettisonable payload fairing
2. Payload separation datum
3. 2nd/3rd stage separation datum
4. Satellite
5. Solid propellant Apogee motor
6. Spin rocket
7. 2nd Stage Kerosene
8. 3rd stage mounting bay
9. 2nd stage equipment bay housing 2nd stage control equipment and vehicle attitude reference unit
10. 2nd stage H.T.P.
11. 2nd stage engine mounting bay housing attitude control system
12. Separation rockets
13. Jettisonable interstage structure mounting engine start equipment
14. BSE Gamma motor
15. 1st/2nd stage separation datum
16. 1st stage tank pressurisation and vehicle control
17. 1st stage kerosene
18. 1st stage H.T.P.
19. Kerosene feed line (4 off)
20. 1st stage motor bay
21. BSE Gamma motor
22. Detachable skirt

Black Arrow. Cut-away showing principal components.

Black Arrow. Just prior to lift-off.

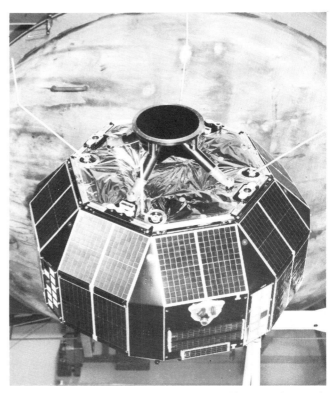

Prospero. Britain's first technological satellite manufactured by Marconi and launched into a near perfect orbit by the Saunders-Roe Black Arrow in 1971.

Black Arrow. Structural assembly bay at Falcon Yard.

Black Arrow. First stage propulsion unit.

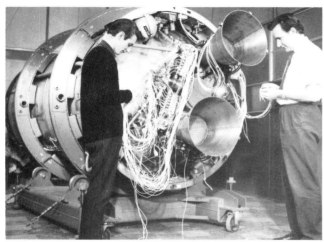

Black Arrow. Second stage propulsion unit.

Black Arrow. The second stage with the third stage fairings.

FALSTAFF LAUNCH VEHICLE 1972-75

Purpose — As an economical means of proving control systems in a space environment.

Power Plant RPE — Stonechat solid fuel rocket motor. (Case produced by Bristol Aerojet).

Description — Falstaff was designed to be mounted at two points on a guide rail which could be moved from horizontal to vertical for launching. It was characterised by its bulbous nose section and large cruciform fins. The following were the main features:-

1. STONECHAT ROCKET MOTOR. 36 inches in diameter, comprised 56 per cent of the overall length of 24 feet and formed the main body. The lower section was increased in diameter to 45 inches and provided mountings for the fins, 14 ft 6 in. in span, positioned diagonally. Between the bases of one pair of fins a hook was fitted as the lower/rear attachment to the launching rail.

2. ADAPTOR BAY. This tapered section was assembled from ring frames and longitudinal members of aluminium alloy with magnesium alloy skin. The lower frame was a substantial machined ring and was bolted to the face of the motor. Ten RPE Imp Mk.X spin rockets were fitted in adjacent bays. An external hook was provided as the upper-forward rail attachment. The upper frame carried the four explosive bolt attachments to the payload separation bay and twenty-four separation spring units.

3. PAYLOAD SEPARATION BAY. This 13 inch section was constructed in a similar manner to the adaptor bay and contained at the lower end the four explosive bolts and two spigots to match the adaptor bay. Inside the structure was the platform and cone of honeycomb construction forming a lightweight mounting for the Attitude Control Unit (ACU) and two Imp VI rocket motors on the cone to assist separation. Four lateral

and two roll jet units were mounted externally together with a sun sensor and magnetometer. Electronic and pneumatic equipment was also mounted in the cone. A heavy triangular-shaped fitting known as the Delta frame was attached to the front face of the assembly and formed a substantial base for mounting the experimental payloads.

4. NOSE FAIRINGS. These were built in halves, split longitudinally, of aluminium and magnesium alloy materials with a steel nose cap. The fairings were located by spigots and retained by gas cartridges until separation, when their release exposed the payload which was then itself separated from the Delta frame by the firing of three explosive bolts, assisted by the simultaneous firing of the two Imp VI retro rockets on the PSB.

Weights —

AUW	14,438 lb.
Standard Head	1,812 lb. At first separation
	1,481 lb. At second separation
	1,200 lb. After final separation

Performance — Subject to considerable variations depending on conditions. Apogee between 30 - 60 miles.

Launch Record — Twelve Falstaff vehicles were built of which six were fired.

F01 - Nonflight

F0 -
F1 -
F2 - } Flew in period 1976-1979
F3 -
F4 -
F5 -

F6 - Built but scrapped at end of programme.

F7 -
F8 -
F9 - } Standby for failure – construction never finalised due to success of F0 through to F5.
F10 -
F11 -

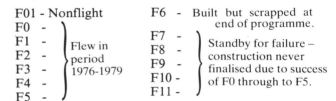

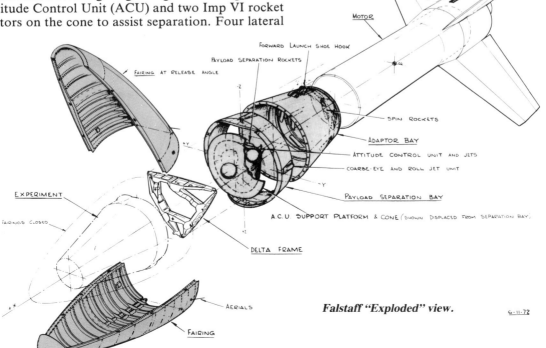

Falstaff "Exploded" view.

6-11-72

Falstaff. Being readied for launch.

The final Falstaff launch . Exhibiting the participating company logos in 1978.

CHAPTER 15

PROJECTS

A famous designer had a saying that in the field of aircraft design it was necessary to have "one on the board, one in the experimental department and one in the shops". Most companies explore various versions of a design by preparing outline schemes of a project, before expending design time on the detail work, which would require many thousands of man hours and so, for every one project that reaches the drawing board, or even the brochure stage, there are many schemes. It is inevitable that the records of these are less precisely maintained than the major designs which proceed into manufacture.

In the early days, S.E. Saunders, with many interests, took out patents on new ideas in various fields of manufacture. (See Appendix 6). Two patented schemes with aircraft interest are those that reveal the concept of a twin-hulled flying boat and, secondly, alternative versions of the float arrangements for high-speed seaplanes in connection with a Schneider Trophy contender in the period 1926-27, both of which remained as projects. The unbuilt version of the Schneider Trophy seaplane designed by F.P.H. Beadle, under S.E. Saunders' direction, did not embody either of the patented schemes, but used the more conventional twin-float arrangement with strut bracing and was not unlike in appearance (except for its tapered wing and tailplane) the wire-braced Supermarine S.5, which eventually won the 1927 contest, for both were based on the use of the Napier Lion racing engine.

The few surviving schemes for later projects in the years prior to the war and in wartime are mainly concerned with marine aircraft and these range from small float-planes to the largest flying boats although some landplane projects, including an early one for Spartan, exist. Certain of the large projects were variations of schemes which started before the war and were developed during and after the war and contributed to the design of the Shetland and Princess flying boats.

In the period when the company was established as Saunders-Roe, project designs covering general arrangement and more detailed drawings were identified by P numbers. In some cases these were major developments of existing types such as the Cloud and Windhover but many were entirely new, few were drawn in great detail, and records of only a few survive. In some cases an identification number was taken out of the range of S numbers - later SR - identifying the company major designs and this indicates that some encouragement to proceed with detail design was present. In post-war years, with the design department re-established at Cowes, the new schemes emerging from the project office re-started at P.100 and continued to P.247 in May 1966 on the establishing of the British Hovercraft Corporation. Many of the drawings in this series remain, covering a wide range of aircraft types, with the main emphasis on large flying boats, culminating in the SR.45 Princess, and marine-based fighters leading to a land-based composite

powered type, which were finally built and flown as the SR.53. The higher project numbers inevitably contain fewer aircraft projects, the emphasis being on hovercraft and advanced marine craft, indicating the changing nature of the company's status and activities.

A summary of the schemes it has been possible to identify which were proposed in these years is included, together with a selection of general arrangement drawings and photographs of models of representative types. The same project number may cover a number of widely different aircraft types with considerable differences of weight and dimensions and alternative engine types. This is inevitable as the project evolved and the drawing included may not necessarily represent the final version. Helicopters were principally dealt with by the separate design team at Eastleigh and projects in this field were identified from P.500 onwards, although not all the projects in this series could be traced. A small number of helicopter-related projects also appear in the main series (P.219-P.222).

PROJECTS PREWAR AND WARTIME

Patent No.	Date	Description
296570	1927	Twin-hulled flying boat.
262579	1926	A high-speed seaplane with twin floats retracting inwards to form a single float.
296594	1927	A high-speed seaplane with central float and hinged wing-tip and floats. A version of alternative construction and with fixed wing-tip floats was also specified.

Project Drg/ Type No.	Date	Description
-	1926	A braced low wing monoplane with 750 HP Napier Lion engine designed by S.E. Saunders and F.P.H. Beadle for the 1926 Schneider Trophy Contest. Span 26 ft 5 in. Length 25 ft 6 in. Height 9 ft 9 in. Wing section RAF 33. Wing area 98 sq. ft. Wing loading 25.33 lb per sq. ft. Maximum take-off weight 2,502½ lb: fuel 437½ lb (62½ gallons), oil 75 lb (7½ gallons), coolant 85 lb (8½ gallons). Power loading 3.33 lb per HP. Patents Nos. 262579 of 1926 and 296594 of 1927 were taken out for retracting floats, neither version of which was employed in this design. Performance: max. speed at sea level 285 mph, landing speed 88½ mph.

Project Drg/ Type No.	Date	Description
P.228	1929	The Severn as a civil aircraft for 21 passengers and three crew.
P.295	1930	Military training version of Cutty Sark with forward and mid-ships gun rings.
P.296	1930	Coastal patrol version of Windhover with forward and mid-ships gun rings.
P.351	1930	Severn Mk.III powered by 2 Rolls-Royce Buzzard Mk.II engines.
P.393	1931	Cloud Mk.II, a three engined biplane version.
P.395	1931	Became the Spartan Cruiser.
P.398	1931	Became the single-engined Cutty Sark.
P.399	1931	Spartan light cabin monoplane with Napier E.97 Javelin engine.
P.463	1932	Became the RAF Cloud.
P.476	1933	Small military flying boat with folding wings for shipboard use. 1 Napier Rapier with tractor airscrew and gun ring amidships.
P.507	1931	Became the London.
P.555	1934	Military version of the Cloud with 2 Napier Rapier engines. Gun rings at forward and mid-ships positions.
P.625		Windhover II passenger amphibian. 2 Gipsy VI engines. Strut-braced high wing with undercarriage housed in balancing floats.
P.713	1938	A strut-braced high-wing monoplane with sponsons. Based on the London Mk.II.
P.714	1938	An alternative to P.713 with balancing floats.
P.792	1936	The final scheme for Spec. R2/33 which became the A.33.
P.937	1939	Identified as Cloud Mk.II but unrelated to the earlier machine. Twin-engined military amphibian with strut-braced high wing and balancing floats.
P.970	1936	Flying boat to Specification R1/36. Became the Lerwick.
P.1029	1939	Projected A.37 a scaled down R5/39. Revised to P.1063 by September 1942 for Shetland trials.
P.1031	1940	See below S.39.
P.1033	1940	A four-engined tank-carrying monoplane.
P.1034	1940	See below. S.39A.
P.1036	1939-41	A single-engined flying boat amphibian monoplane (9,500 lb) identified as Scheme A and powered by a Bristol Mercury XVI. The engine pod extended aft to house a gun turret and to carry the tail surfaces.
P.1037	1939-40	A more conventional central float version of P.1036 identified as Scheme B.
P.1039	1940-41	A single-engined monoplane central float type amphibian powered by a Rolls-Royce Merlin for use for the Fleet Air Arm. Spec.S12/40. AUW 12,000 lb. Span 50 ft. Length 49 ft 9 in. Crew of 5; the observer was housed in the trunk. The rear section of the fuselage, complete with the tail surfaces, folded forward for stowage purposes.
P.1050	1940-41	A single-engined biplane flying boat amphibian with the engine pod extended aft to house a gun turret and to carry the tail surfaces. Spec.S12/40. AUW 12,000 lb.
S.36/C	1939	Mailplane and civil transport versions of the Lerwick. Proposals to Imperial Airways.
S.38	1938-39	Schemes for a large reconnaissance flying boat initially to Spec.R3/38 (53,000 lb AUW) with 4 Bristol Taurus engines later becoming R5/39 (55,000 lb AUW) in May 1939. Later 110 ft span, 70,000 lb AUW. 4 Bristol Hercules engines or Rolls-Royce Griffons and with inward retracting stabilising floats. (The A.37 was a scaled down version of the proposed R5/39).
S.38A	1939-40	The company proceeded on a private venture basis after the specification was terminated in October 1939. By April 1940 Centaurus engines had replaced the Hercules and the armament raised to 20 mm cannon in a Boulton Paul turret. 80,000 lb AUW.
S.39 (P.1031)	1940	Further development of the schemes for large military flying boats to meet Spec.R5/39 and R14/40 from August. Various locations of armament. 4 Bristol Centaurus engines. Span 137 ft. AUW progressively increased 70,000 - 96,000 lb. Bare weight 44,300 lb. Napier Sabre engines as alternative power units.
S.39A (P.1034)	1940	A scheme for a flying boat with retractable bottom.
S.40	1940 (Oct-Dec)	The continued development of the large flying boat to a civil version of current military R14/40 schemes. 31 passengers and 1500 cubic ft of cargo. AUW 82,000 - 112,000 lb. Span 140 ft.
S.41	1941 (Jan)	The large military flying boat finally evolved to meet Spec. R.14/40 for which the Short Shetland was selected. 110,000 lb AUW 3800 miles range. 4 Bristol Centaurus. 3 four gun turrets plus a four cannon tail turret.

Project Drg/ Type No.	Date	Description
S.42 (P.1057)	1942-43	Military flying boat. 4 Rolls-Royce Merlin XX engines using wing of Avro Lancaster. 70,000 lb AUW. 2500 - 3000 miles range.
S.42A (P.1059)	1942-43	Freight carrying version with 4 Rolls-Royce Merlins or 4 Bristol Hercules VI engines. 35,800 lb cargo.

Project Drg/ Type No.	Date	Description
-	1944	Long range transport flying boat with 6 Bristol Centaurus engines.
-	1944	Long range transport flying boat with 8 Bristol Centaurus engines.

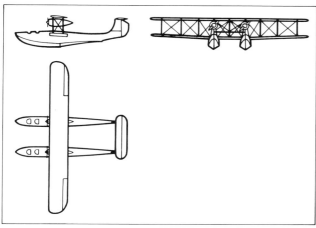

Pat. No. 296570

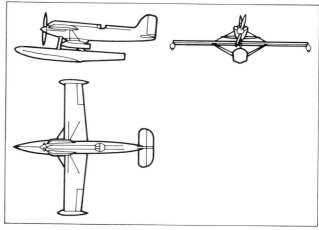

Pat. No. 296594/2

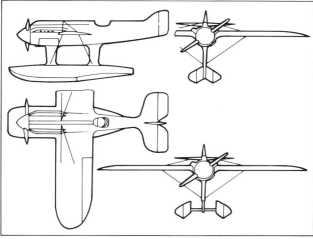

Pat. No. 262579

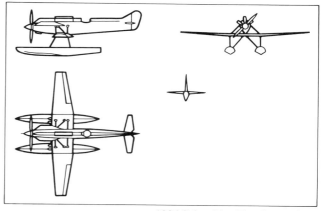

1926 Schneider Trophy Project.

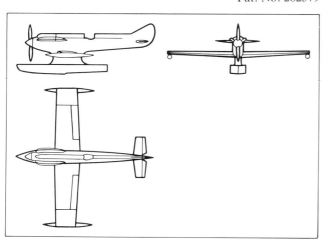

Pat. No. 29655594/1

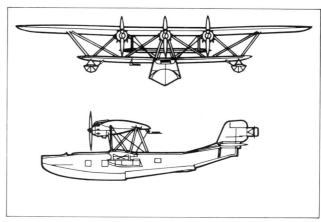

P228

235

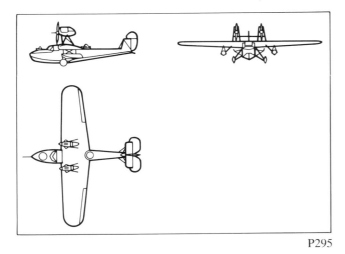

P295

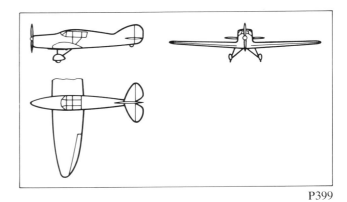

P399

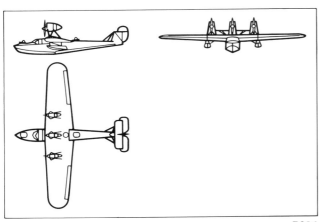

P296

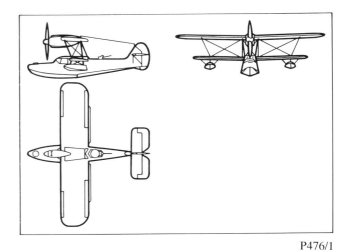

P476/1

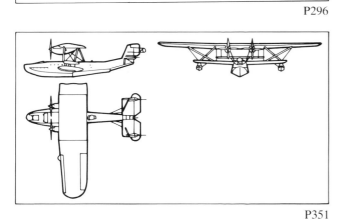

P351

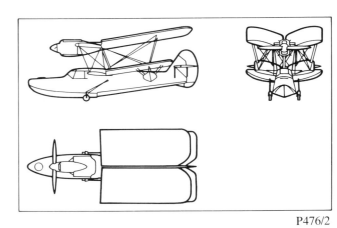

P476/2

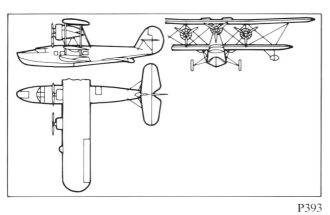

P393

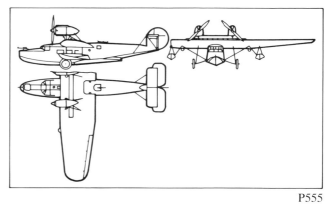

P555

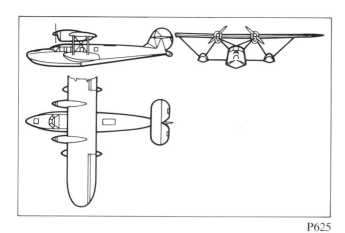

P625

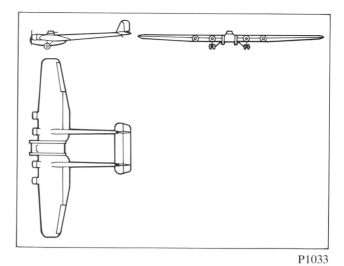

P1033

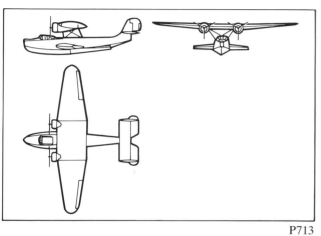

P713

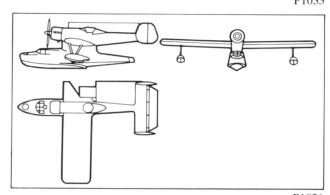

P1036

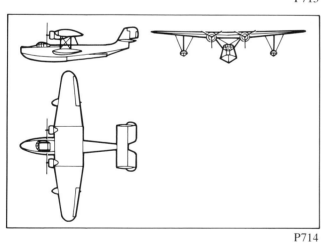

P714

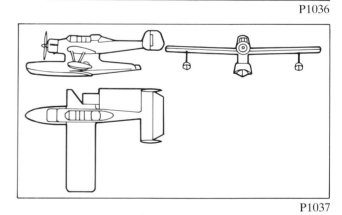

P1037

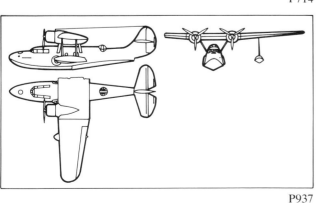

P937

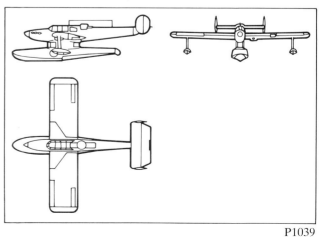

P1039

237

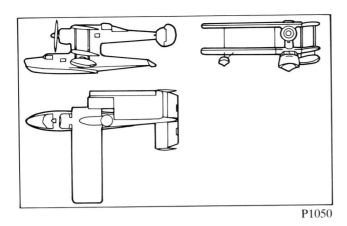

P1050

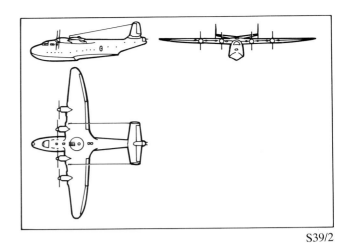

S39/2

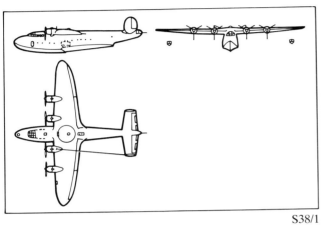

S38/1

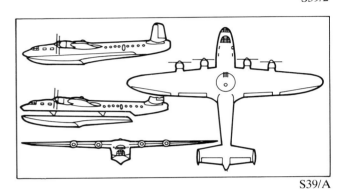

S39/A

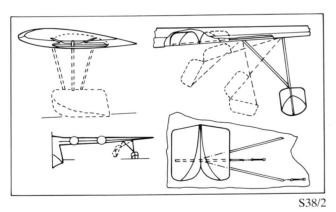

S38/2

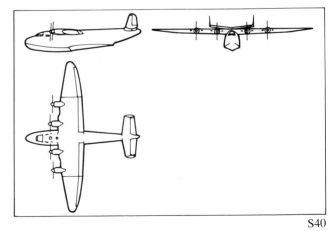

S40

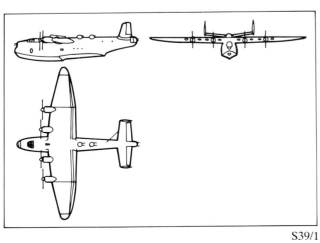

S39/1

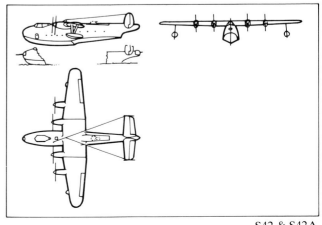

S42 & S42A

PROJECTS POSTWAR

Project No.	Date	Description
P.100	1946-47	Schemes for conversion of the Auster VI and Heston A4/45 AOP to twin-float seaplanes. The Auster scheme was adopted and a prototype was converted and flown at Cowes.
P.103	1947	A swept wing version of the SR.A1 probably with AS Sapphires.
P.104	1948-53	Various schemes of flying boats in connection with MoS Spec.R2/48. 14 versions with weights ranging from 89,900 to 135,000 lb and wing spans from 134 ft to 168 ft included one version based on use of the Britannia wing. Tail units included versions with single fin and rudder, twin fin and rudder and V-type tail. All versions were four engined and included Centaurus Turbo-Griffons, compounded Griffons and Nomad. A retractable radar scanner in the underside was positioned in the nose or alternatively behind the wing.
P.105	1951	50,000 lb military flying boat with pylon-mounted wing. 2 Bristol Centaurus 171. Hull lines and internal layout produced in some detail.
P.106	1949-51	Alternative versions of four-engined military flying boat with mixed power plant of compound piston engines and pure jets permitting high take-off weights and long range on the economic compound engines. First version with conventional hull and V-tail was powered by 2 compounded Rolls-Royce Griffons and 2 Rolls-Royce Nenes, included retractable radar scanner and downward firing rockets. 81,000 lb. 134 ft span. Second version with twin booms and tail floats was powered by 2 Napier Nomad and 2 AS Sapphire engines. 90,000 lb. 135 ft span.
P.108	1949	Two versions of a glider, the hull of which detached to serve as a lifeboat. The Mk.II version was favoured and the hull shape, jettison system and operational technique were investigated in some detail.
P.109		A 100,000 lb flying boat with 6 jet engines, probably Nene or Ghost, buried in a wide chord centre section. Not developed in detail.
P.110	1950	The SR.45 Princess proposed as a reconnaissance bomber.
P.111	1954	The SR.45 Princess proposed as an amphibian.
P.112		A 220,000 lb 215 ft span flying boat in two versions with either conventional or double bubble hull. 6 Napier Nomad driving contra-props.
P.117	1949	A 131,000 lb 162 ft span commercial flying boat with V-tail. Powered by 4 Napier Nomad driving contra-props.
P.121	1949-51	A single-seat swept-wing fighter with AS Sapphire engine with afterburning. Three alternative schemes with retractable bottom, ski undercarriage plus a wheeled trolley and version with wheeled undercarriage.
P.122	1949-50	Development of the SR.A1. A two-seater swept-wing flying boat fighter and a single-seater with straight wing with tapered leading edge. Both with AS Sapphire with afterburning.
P.123	1948-50	Two versions of 120,000 lb 148 ft span flying boat with 4 Bristol Centaurus 663 engines or 146 ft span with 4 Bristol Proteus turbo-props. A smaller version of 98,000 lb and 134 ft span was to be powered by 4 compounded Rolls-Royce Griffons and had twin fins and rudders.
P.124		A light twin-engined amphibian transport for 16 passengers and 2 crew. 2 AS Mamba turbo-props.
P.125	1948	Two versions of a flying boat for freight carrying with either a single hull with twin booms or twin fuselages. The power was provided by 4 Bristol Centaurus engines in coupled pairs driving contra-props.
P.126		A stretched version of the SR.45 Princess for 160 passengers. Increased in length by 26 ft 6 in to an AUW of 360,000 lb.
P.127	1949-50	Three versions of a single-seat flying boat for research purposes powered by a Metrovick Beryl jet engine. The first version with delta wing was followed by swept-wing and straight-tapered wing versions. The last version included schemes with retractable planing plates and undercarriage.
P.129	1949	A 157,375 lb passenger flying boat, 151 ft span, V-tail. 4 Bristol Proteus turbo-props.

Project No.	Date	Description
P.131	1951	The Duchess swept-wing flying boat in long and short range versions with 6 Rolls-Royce Avons or 4 Napier Nomads driving contra-props. The V-tail and Nomad engines were discarded in favour of a swept single fin and rudder. Various versions with Avon engines. including an amphibious version, were schemed providing passenger accommodation varying from 38 to 106 in the troop-carrying version. AUW 150,000 lb. 145 ft span (141 ft in the trooper version).
P.132	1948-49	A landplane passenger transport in two versions in collaboration with Folland Aircraft. The first scheme was for 11 passengers plus pilot based on the use of 4 DH Gipsy Major X Mk.2. AUW 8,500 lb. The second scheme employed DH Gipsy Queen II engines and accommodated 17 passengers and pilot. AUW 12,500 lb.
P.133		A flying boat schemed around the DH Comet wing and DH Ghost engines with afterburning. A landplane project covered by the same number is a basic DH Comet with the addition of 2 DH Sprite rocket motors between the jet engines.
P.135	1950	A six engined swept-wing flying boat on the same lines as P.131 but powered by DH Ghost engines, weighing 130,000 lb with wing span of 135 ft 6 in in the first scheme. Two later schemes were 4 engined machines using Ghosts with afterburning, both were based on an AUW of 107,980 lb with a wing span of 124 ft 6 in for carrying 40 - 70 passengers. One had a conventional swept wing but the alternative was most unconventional and was a canard with forward swept wing.
P.136	1950	A conventional 4 engined passenger flying boat powered by 4 Bristol Hercules 763 engines. AUW 82,000 lb. Wing span 118 ft 6 in.
P.138	1950-52	Versions of the SR.45 Princess with 12 DH Ghost or with 10 Rolls-Royce Avons and 2 RB.93 Jet Packs.
P.139	1950	A passenger landplane for 96 - 104 passengers on two decks, powered by 4 Napier Sabre VII engines. AUW 132,000 lb. Wing span 144 ft.
P.142	1950	Single seat water based fighters. The first a twin jet delta of 50 ft span. The second version, also with hydro-ski, was developed in more detail to show also a carrier based version with undercarriage and upward folding wings. The pilot was housed in a pod on the centre section and twin fuselages housed the 2 Napier E.137 jet engines with afterburning and carried the fins and high-set tailplane.
P.145	1951	A version of the SR.45 Princess with 8 Napier Nomads driving contra-props.
P.147	1951-52	Four versions of the Sea Raider project consisting of a glider housing two motor boats. Weights ranged from 10,000 - 30,000 lb and wing spans from 60 ft to 110 ft. In addition the two motor boats ranged in weight from 8,200 lb to 24,150 lb. Straight and cranked wings were considered but all schemes incorporated V-tails and the main hull incorporated a marine propulsion system for use after jettisoning the wing and tail portions and discharging the motor boats and would be equipped with a gun turret. In the boats 2-125 HP Rover V-6 piston engines were initially employed, later Rover Gas Turbines were proposed.
P.148	1950	A two-seater fighter, land based in two versions and later with an alternative hydro-ski, all using Rolls-Royce Avon RA10 or 14. Initially with a straight wing with tapered leading edge followed by a fully tapered wing and then a swept wing version. Weights varied from 20,400 to 28,000 lb. Pilot and navigator sat side by side and an internal air to air rocket battery was carried. The final version was schemed in some detail and was the subject of a tender to MOS Spec.N114.T.
P.149	1951	Many schemes for a single seat fighter to Spec.ER.110.T which included delta, straight tapered and 60° LE swept wings with side by side engines at 27,000 lb AUW. Variable geometry wings were schemed in some detail, initially at an AUW of 32,000 lb, ranging through a version with stacked engines at 28,000 lb to a preferred scheme with side by side installation. All versions used the Rolls-Royce Avon RA.12 with afterburning.

Project No.	Date	Description
P.151	1951	This covered at least seven schemes for a high performance single seat fighter, including one for carriage to operational height by a turbo-prop aircraft with twin booms and central fuselage pod. Wings were generally tapered on leading and trailing edge but also included delta plan form. Conventional undercarriage, skid and hydro-ski landing gear were considered. A variety of power plants was considered. As many as 6 Rolls-Royce Jet Packs were mounted above the wing or at the wing tips and tail in various combinations. One version employed a Rolls-Royce Avon with 4 Jet Packs and yet others employed additional rocket motors, including the DH Spectre.
P.152	1952	The short and long range versions of the P.131 Duchess were updated with a V-tail but otherwise were similar to the 150,000lb 145ft span machine previously schemed.
P.153	1952	Project for a hydrofoil equipped motor boat.
P.154	1950-52	This was the project which resulted in a proposal being submitted as an Addendum to the tender to MOS for F.124.T finally resulting in the order for the SR.53 by way of further developments under P.167. Various schemes were investigated and these included six delta wing and one swept wing project and a simple skid-landing type with short span tapered wing and propelled by a DH Spectre rocket motor. The designs of these were not developed in any great detail prior to arriving at the scheme proposed to MOS.
P.155		A high performance delta wing fighter on which little detail work was carried out.
P.157		A boat hull.
P.158		A helicopter vibration simulator.
P.160	1952	This covered four versions of a twin-boom freighter or car ferry amphibian aircraft powered by two Bristol Hercules 730 radial engines. P.160/1 & 2 had an AUW of 42,000 lb and P.160/3 & 4 47,000 lb and both offered alternative undercarriages with hydro-ski surfaces or conventional type balancing floats.
P.161	1952	A delta wing fighter with mixed power plant schemed in heavy and light weight versions. The first was powered by 2 Bristol BE.22 gas turbines and 1 DH Spectre rocket motor. AUW 15,300 lb. Span 28 ft. Length 44 ft. Height 12ft 3 in. The second version was powered by 1 Bristol BE.22 and 1 DH Spectre. AUW 8,800 lb. Span 20 ft. Length 34 ft 4 in. Height 11 ft.
P.162	1952-56	Schemes developed for a long-range reconnaissance and anti-submarine flying boat including also a transport version. Ref. P.104. Initially with twin fins and rudders and 4 Bristol Centaurus piston engines, consideration was then given to 4 Nomads, 4 BE.25 with 1 Avon RA.14 in the dorsal fin followed by 4Centaurus with 2 Avons in the inboard nacelles above the piston engines and similar schemes with Nomads. At first retracting wing-tip floats were used but subsequent schemes reverted to fixed floats and a single fin and rudder. AUW varied from 135,000 - 155,000 lb. Wing span from 137 ft to 157 ft. Length 120 ft -126 ft 6 in. The ultimate version used 4 RB.109 turbo-props with bomb-bays below the inboard nacelles. The wing had marked anhedral outboard of the outer nacelles, with retractable wing-tip floats, double slotted flaps and dive-brakes. Watertight doors were incorporated below the forward hull for a retractable ASV radar scanner and a door in the side of the hull at the rear was provided for lowering sonar equipment with the possibility of active sonar lowered through a further aperture with watertight doors behind the step, for a skimming mission with hydro-skis on the tip floats. AUW 148,000 lb. Span 136 ft. Length 114 ft 7 in. Gun armament was varied in type and position as the project evolved and included turret mounted 20 and 30 mm cannon. A crew of 14 was carried.
P.163	1953-54	Started as a project for a 'Mach 2' research aircraft with either 2 Olympus or 2 Avon RA.14 engines mounted on the tips of a short span, broad chord wing, it soon changed to a delta wing with 1 RA.14 and 1 1500 lb thrust rocket motor in the fuselage. Through various changes to its configuration and the addition of AI radar and missile carriage, the design was tendered to MOS to Spec. ER.134.T. Further developed as P.177 the resulting aircraft became the SR.177. A second crew member to operate the radar was considered at one stage.
P.164	1953	Schemes for the Princess with either 10 or 12 Napier Eland coupled turbo-props.
P.165	1953	Schemes for the Princess with either 6 P & W T.34 turbo-props, 4 AS/Wright TP.51A turbo-props based on Sapphire engines or 4 Allison T.40 and 2 Allison T.38 turbo-props.

Project No.	Date	Description
P.166	1953	A 400,000 lb AUW flying boat with 400 seats and clam-shell doors for alternative cargo use. Span 277 ft. Length 183 ft. Height 58 ft with 4 Wright Turbo-Sapphires. An alternative version with 6 Allison T.40 turbo-props had the span reduced to 241 ft.
P.167	1953-54	Further development of P.154 leading to the definitive type SR.53. Schemes using AS Screamer rocket motor and AS Viper jet engine; DH Spectre and either Bristol BE.22 Saturn, DH.PS.31 or Bristol Orpheus jet engines.
P.168	1953	The Auster VI with Hydro-skis.
P.171	1952	A light transport with 2 AS Viper jet engines. AUW 9,000 lb. Span 52 ft. Length 38 ft 6 in. 10 - 14 seats.
P.173	1953-55	This covered a considerable amount of design effort to keep the Princess active. Schemes for alternative engine installation, 6 Bristol BE.25, 6 Bristol Proteus 705 or 755 and 6 Rolls Royce RB.109, together with a proposal to extend the forebody with a matching increase in the height of the fin and rudder; also a rearward extension of the planing bottom. Internal schemes for the accommodation of between 130 and 264 passengers and freight carriage were investigated. A military version as an early warning radar station and fighter carrier was proposed. This carried two SR.53 type fighters under the wings and was based on the version with the extended hull.
P.175	1953-54	The Australian GAF Jindivik and Pika piloted target aircraft modified by the fitment of hydro-skis and buoyancy chambers for water landing. Several retractable types of skis were investigated.
P.176	1953-55	A twin-engined medium range flying boat maritime patrol aircraft for New Zealand requirements. 2 Rolls-Royce RB.l09 turbo-prop. engines. 117 ft wing span. AUW 70,000 lb. A modified version for the RAF for North Atlantic operations at an AUW of 93,000 lb with wing span increased to 124 ft included 4 Rolls-Royce Soar turbo-jet engines in addition for use at take-off. This project had started with 4 Bristol Hercules piston engines followed by a variety of power plants which included 4 Centaurus, 4 RB.109s, 4 Darts, 4 Elands or Mambas before the final configuration was reached. AUW varied from 70,000 to 110,000 lb with wing spans of 107 to 130 ft.
P.177	1954-58	Became the SR.177. See Chapters 7 and 14.
P.178	1954	Two versions of a twin-jet swept-wing naval strike aircraft with crew of two side-by-side. 2 DH Gyron Junior PS 37 engines mounted above the rear fuselage or alternatively above and forward of the wing at one-third span. Wing span 95 ft. AUW 50,000 lb.
P.179	1954	Single-seat strike fighter with Bristol Orpheus or 8,000/10,000 lb thrust DH.PS.37 jet engine. Delta wing of 26 ft 6 in span. AUW 12,500/15,700 lb. A version with hydro-skis was also projected.
P.180	1954	Single-seat supersonic interceptor with one DH.PS.37 8,000/10,000 lb thrust jet engine. Delta wing of 26 ft span. AUW 15,300 lb.
P.186	1955	Adaptation of P.163 for an Australian requirement.
P.187	1955-56	Mach 2 all-weather fighter to Spec. MOS F.155T. After three schemes based on a straight tapered wing, the design evolved into a delta wing type with 2 DH PS.52 jet and 4 DH Spectre rocket engines carrying 2 Red Dean and 4 Blue Jay missiles with a crew of two. Span 48 ft. AUW 107,500 lb. The nose cone could be raised for max. performance and lowered for forward vision.
P.188	1955	VTO schemes to Spec. ER.156.T with 16 or 18 Rolls-Royce RB.121s mounted in line in the wing or stacked at the wing-tips or 4 RB.122 engines mounted two at the wing-tips and two on the fuselage. AUW 180,000 lb - 210,000 lb. Length 181 - 195 ft. A version with a delta wing and end plate fins with 18 RB 121s was also schemed.
P.189	1955	Further investigation of the hydro-ski applications to fighters and to an Auster AOP.9. (Ref. P.168).
P.190	1955	Investigation of a 4% steel wing. The Bristol 188 resulted from the official requirement.
P.192	1956	A long-range passenger/cargo flying boat of 1,500,000 lb weight and 313 ft wing span, fitted with 24 Rolls-Royce Conway by-pass turbo-jet engines. The aircraft could accommodate up to 1,000 passengers on four decks in similar accommodation to a luxury liner. A version with T tail and 16 Bristol BE.25 turbo-props was also prepared.

Project No.	Date	Description
P.193	1956	Known as a Combat Information Centre, this was an AEW version of the Princess with extremely long range. Also suitable for adaptation as a flight refuelling tanker or troop transport. 6 - 8 Bristol BE.25 turbo-props.
P.194	1956	Floats and chassis for Scottish Aviation Twin Pioneer.
P.195	1956-57	Four versions of a turbo-jet VIP transport for 7 passengers including crew. 2 x 2,400 lb ST Rolls-Royce RB.108, later 2 x 2,000 lb ST Armstrong-Siddeley Vipers. Engines were positioned in pods below the wings on the high wing version and on the sides of the rear fuselage and the tips of the tailplane on a low-wing version. The fourth version had engines buried in the fuselage and these could be tilted to assist take-off.
P.196	1957	A missile target. Four unmanned and one manned version based on the SR.53. (See Chapter 14). Early schemes employed various power plants. Both manned and unmanned versions used 2 AS Vipers on the wing-tips with an AS 9/3 rocket motor in the rear fuselage. One target version used 1 Bristol Orpheus 1 DH Spectre and 4 Bristol 18 inch Ramjets positioned on the wing tips and rear fuselage. The type illustrated has the Orpheus and Spectre with 2 - 25 inch Ramjets on the wing-tips.
P.199	1957	Landplane freighter version of the SR.45 Princess with six nacelle-mounted Rolls-Royce Tyne engines. Schemes for conversion from the existing Princess flying boats at Cowes including means for floating them to a suitable airfield were prepared in some detail. (See Chapter 6).
P.200	1957	Schemes for a 30 ft long hydrofoil assault vessel to be carried and guided by a mother-ship. The craft was driven by a single turbo-prop and was based on a channel section hull with missiles carried in the cavity.
P.201	1957	Various versions of an executive aircraft for 10 passengers plus crew based on the SR.177. Schemes with two AS Viper or Bristol Orpheus engines.
P.202	1957	A Mach 1.8 executive aircraft for 8 rearward facing passengers plus 3 crew. 3 tail-mounted Bristol Orpheus BOR 12 engines. AUW 50,000 lb. Length 71 ft. Span 36 ft. Based on SR.177.
P.203	1958	Investigation of the use of 4 Rolls-Royce Tyne and 2 Pratt & Whitney T.57 engines in the SR.45 Princess. (See Chapter 6).
P.204	1958	Light agricultural monoplane - six schemes including schemes for carrying a second and third man.
P.205	1958	Skeeter development including 3 seater and Continental engine.
P.206	1958	Various schemes for panto-based and floatplane versions of the HDM 106 (Hurel-Dubois Miles).
P.207	1958	The HDM.106 which was used as a basis for a light twin-engined transport similar to the Short Skyvan.
P.208	1958	A twin-engined flying boat Maritime Patrol aircraft to NATO requirements built round advanced submarine detection equipment. 2 Rolls-Royce Tyne 11 turbo-prop. engines. 150 ft wing span. AUW 73,000 lb. A retractable hydro-ski was embodied in the hull. A 65 passenger civil version was considered.
P.209	1958	Various schemes to develop the SR.53 with twin DH Spectre and Rolls-Royce Soar engines including the carriage to altitude on a Valiant bomber.
P.210	1958-65	Hovercraft. Various types including SR.N1 and SR.N2.
P.211	1958	Anti-submarine project. Initially schemed as a STOL four-engined float seaplane, finally developing into a V/STOL four engined amphibious flying boat with tilt-wing. 120 ft span, 100,000 lb AUW. 4 Rolls-Royce Tyne turbo-props of 5500 HP. An intermediate scheme known as a Hover-Air-Craft incorporated hovercraft technology in the hull of a flying boat of 120,000 lb AUW with a tapered wing of 162 ft span which could fold upwards at the approach to the landing. Power was supplied by 1 Rolls-Royce Tyne engine and either 2 Rolls-Royce Avon RA.29 or Conway CO.11. The central pod-mounted engine was used for propulsion only. The outer engines operated in ducts and provided power for both lift and propulsion. Alternative versions with cranked delta wings of 120 ft span with foldable outer sections were also schemed.
P.212		Submarine cargo vessel. Length 604 ft. Max. diameter 72 ft. Displacement - submerged - 50,000 tons. Dead weight 28,000 tons.

Project No.	Date	Description
P.213	1958-59	Studies of nuclear-powered flying boats. Two versions of a 1,000,000 lb, 310 ft span machine powered by 2 indirect-cycle reactors driving 6 power turbines with or without 4 intermediate compressor turbine sets. Two similar versions of a 600,000 lb, 250 ft span machine plus an alternative twin hull version. Schemes included proposals by GEC for a direct-cycle reactor in conjunction with T.57 engines.
P.214	1959	Scheme to fit Rolls-Royce Tyne engines in the Martin Marlin P5M-2 flying boat.
P.215		Meter rating tank.
P.216		Towed flexible tank (Flecon).
P.217		Submersible hydrofoil craft (in conjunction with Miles).
P.218		Hydrofoil landing craft. Alternatives with airscrews or marine propulsion.
P.219	1959	Helicopter-assisted airship - Skeeter or P.531.
P.220	1959	Autogyro studies. An 8,000 lb single rotor machine. Twin engines on a high stub wing. A similar machine but with twin rotors mounted on the tips of an extended wing. Several versions of an autogyro based on the P.531 helicopter with single and twin propellers also shortened tail versions of both types. An entirely new design with 475 HP Artouste seating pilot and 4 passengers using the P.531 rotor. Conventional tractor propeller and a 30 ft span tapered cantilevered low wing.
P.221	1959	Hover-fly jeep 8,000 lb AUW.
P.222	1959-60	Various helicopter studies based on the Westminster and Wasp including a 5 seat Autogyro.

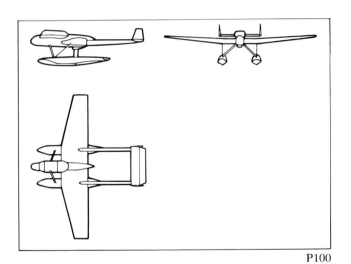

P100

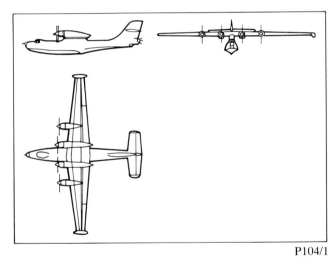

P104/1

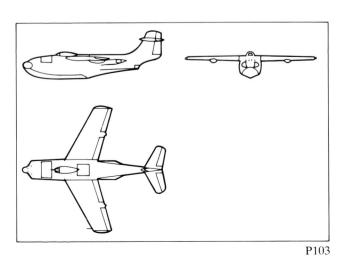

P103

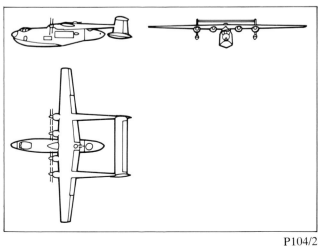

P104/2

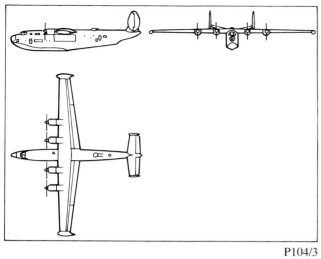

P104/3

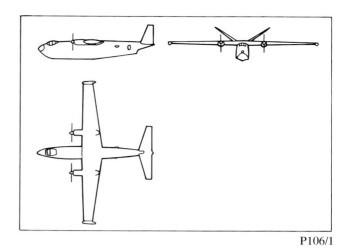

P106/1

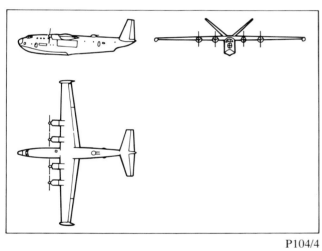

P104/4

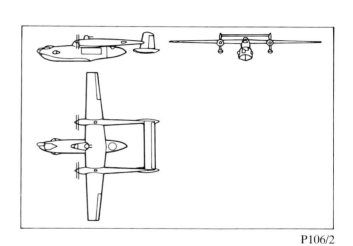

P106/2

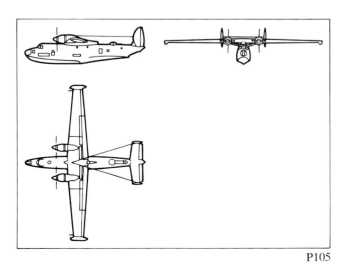

P105

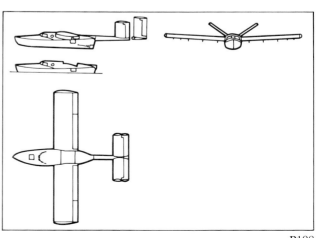

P108

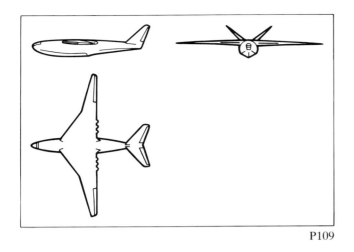

P109

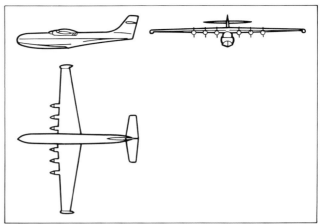

P112

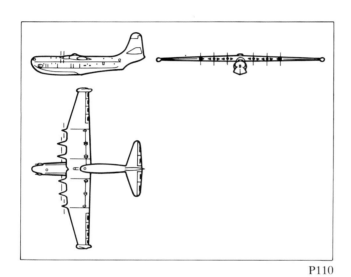

P110

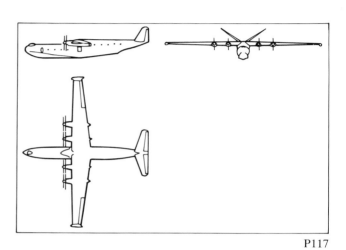

P117

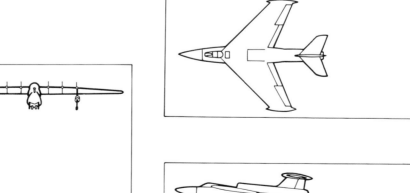

P121/1

P111

P121/2

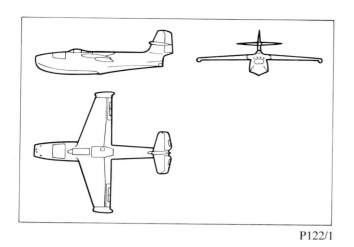

P122/1

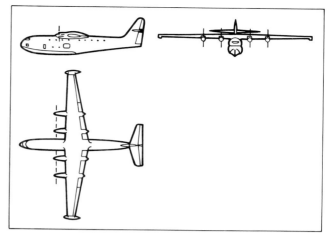

P123/2

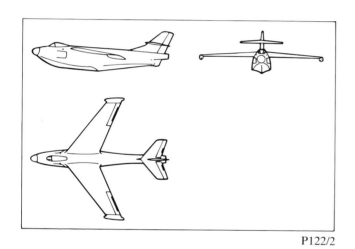

P122/2

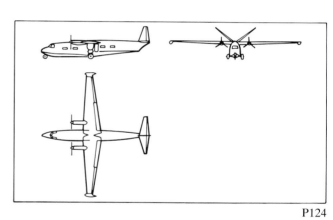

P124

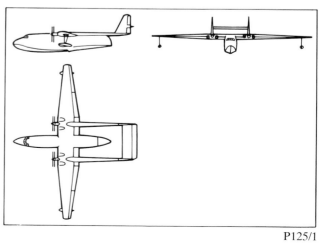

P123/1

P125/1

247

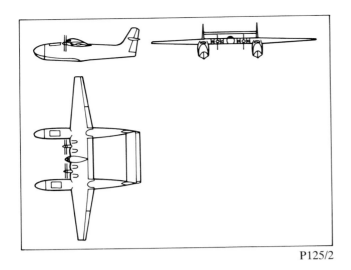

P125/2

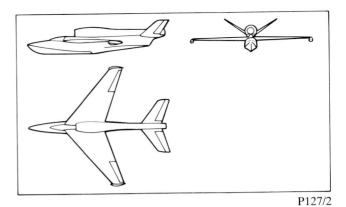

P127/2

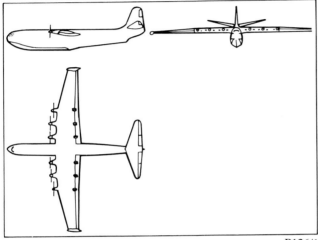

P126/1

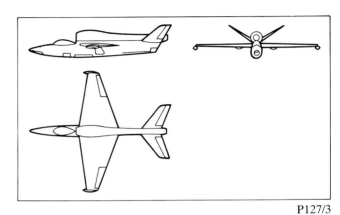

P127/3

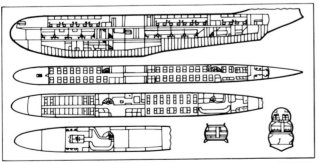

P126/2

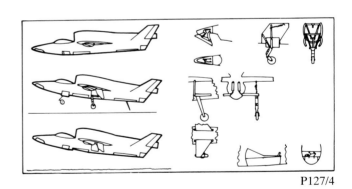

P127/4

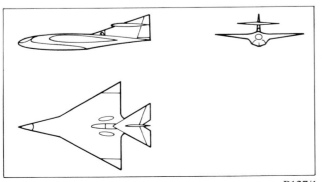

P127/1

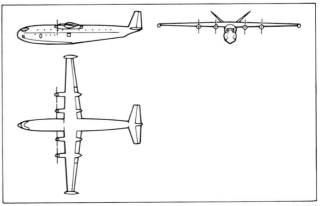

P129

248

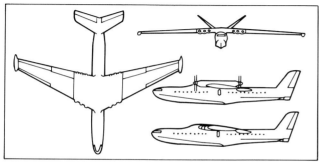

P131/1

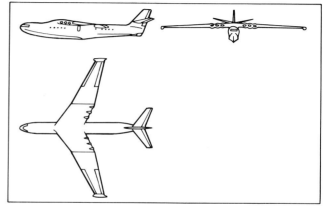

P135/1

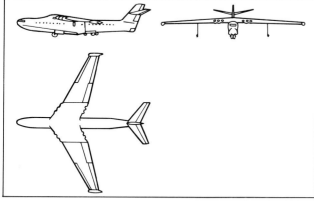

P131/2

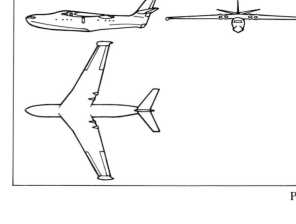
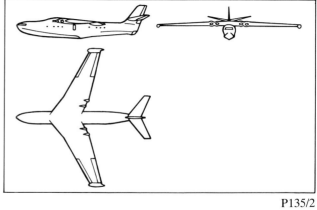

P135/2

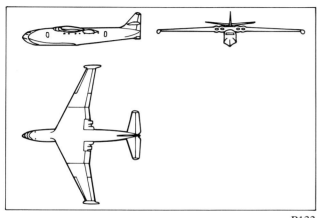

P132

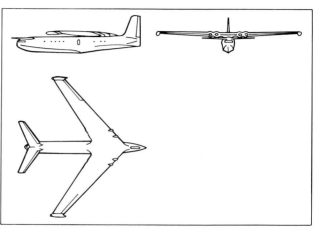

P135/3

P133

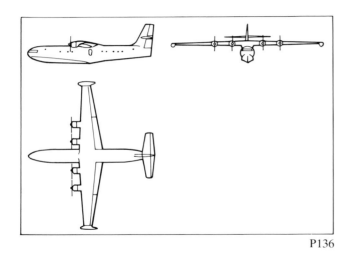

P136

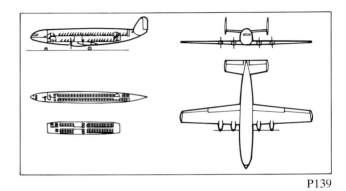

P139

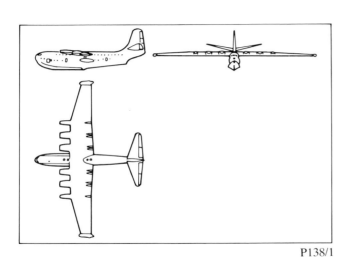

P138/1

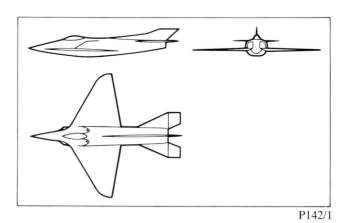

P142/1

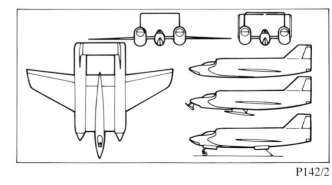

P142/2

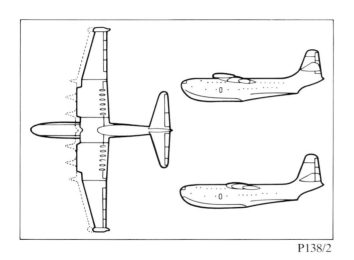

P138/2

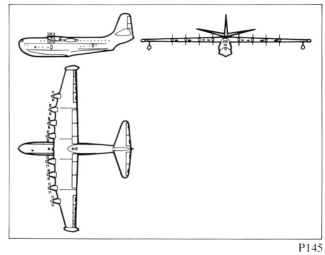

P145

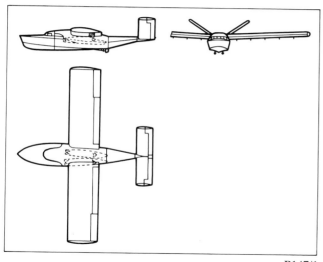

P147/1

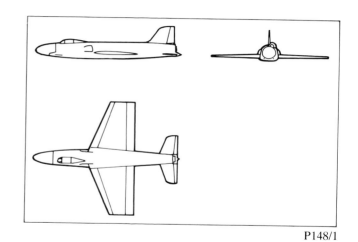

P148/1

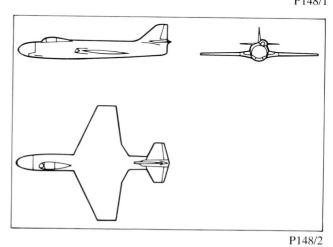

P148/2

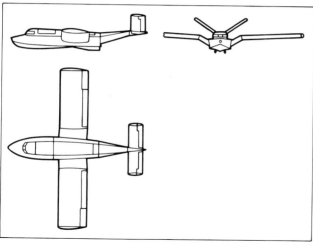

P147/2

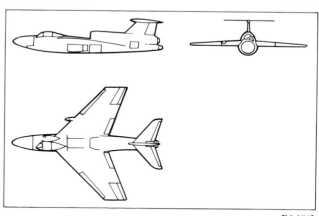

P148/3

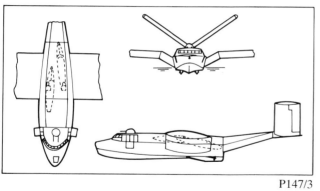

P147/3

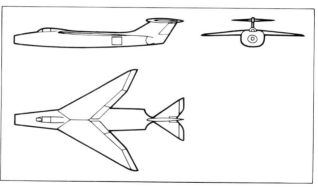

P149/1

251

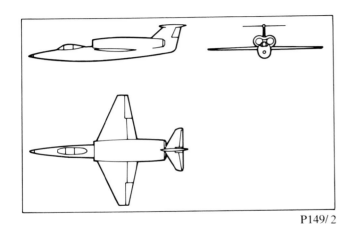

P149/ 2

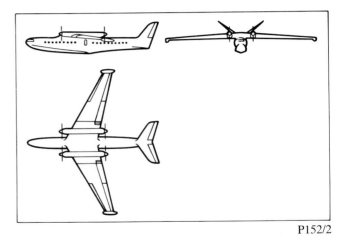

P152/2

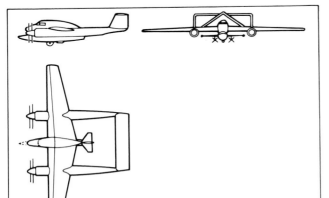

P151/1

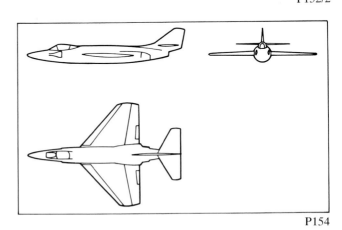

P154

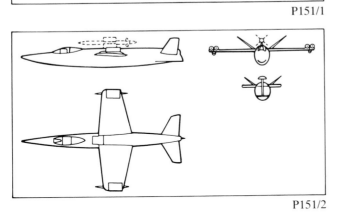

P151/2

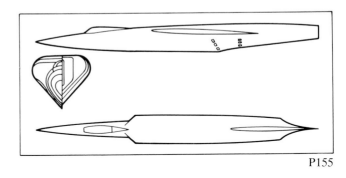

P155

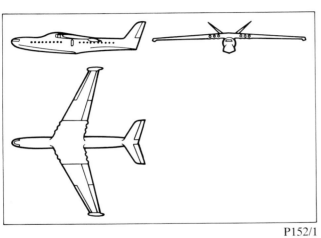

P152/1

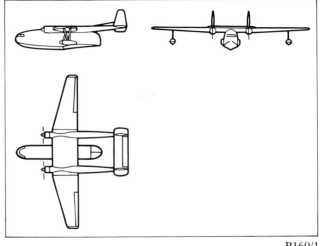

P160/1

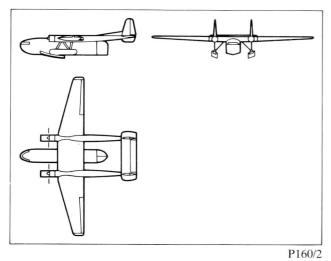

P160/2

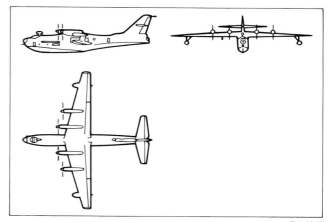

P162/2

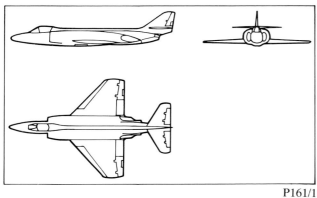

P161/1

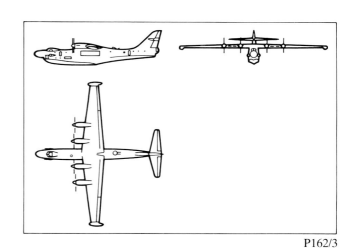

P162/3

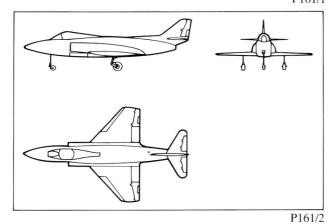

P161/2

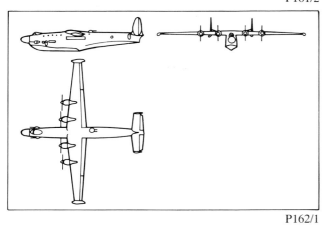

P162/1

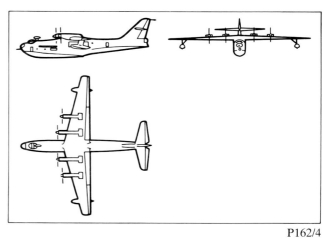

P162/4

253

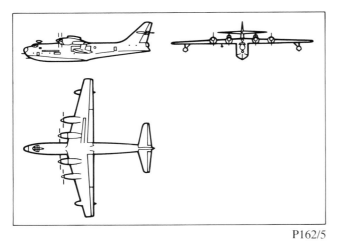

P162/5

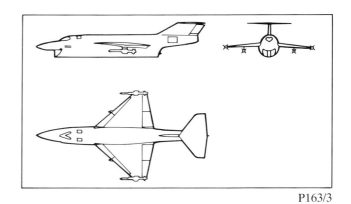

P163/3

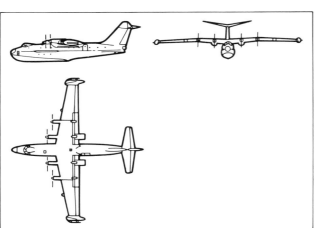

P162/6

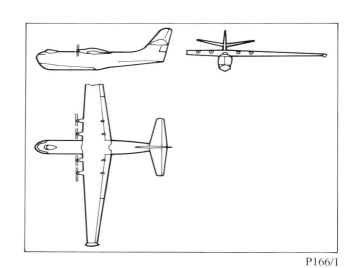

P166/1

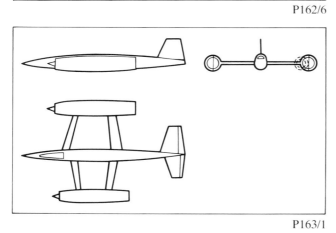

P163/1

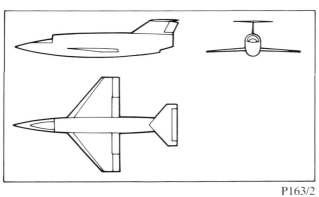

P163/2

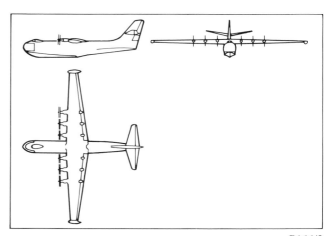

P166/2

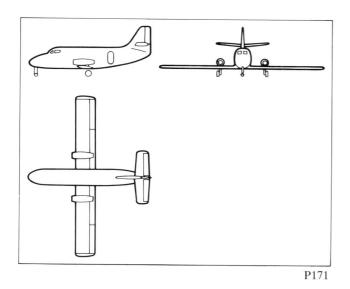

P171

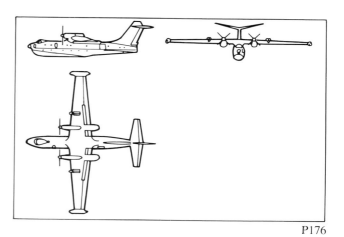

P176

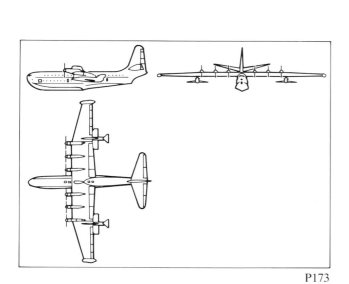

P173

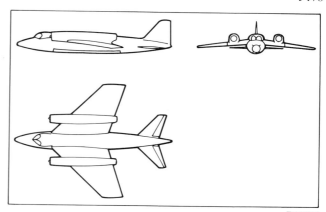

P178/1

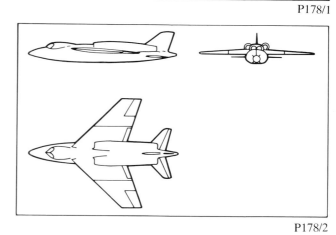

P178/2

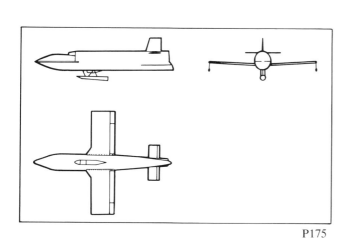

P175

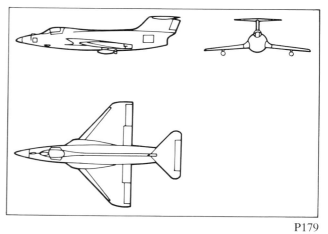

P179

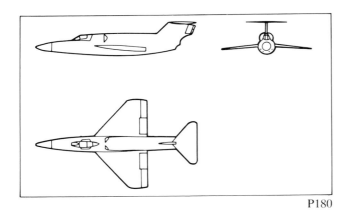

P180

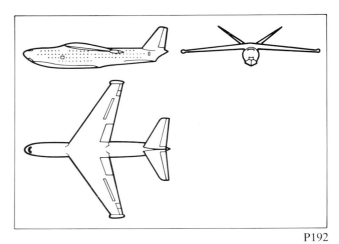

P192

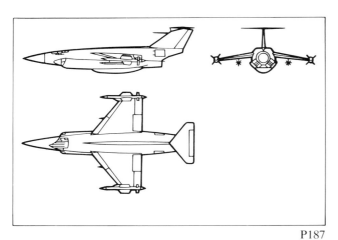

P187

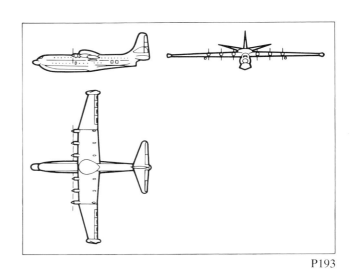

P193

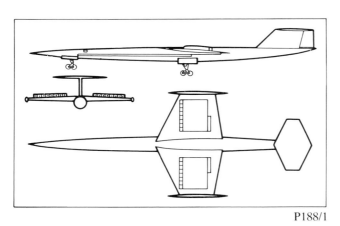

P188/1

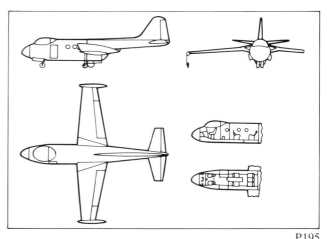

P195

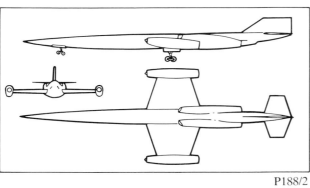

P188/2

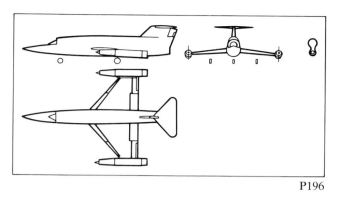

P196

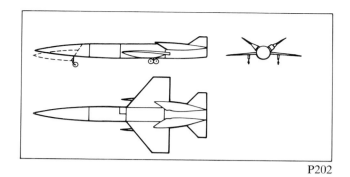

P202

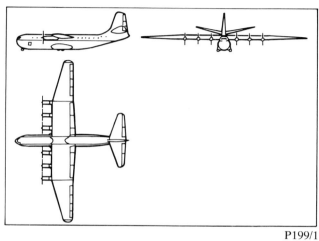

P199/1

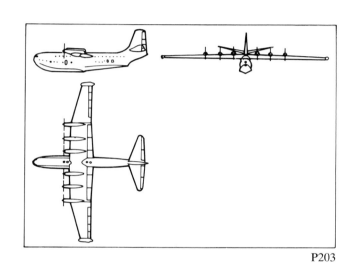

P203

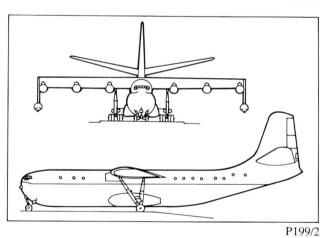

P199/2

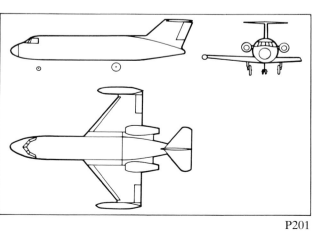

P201

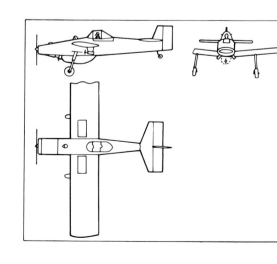

P204

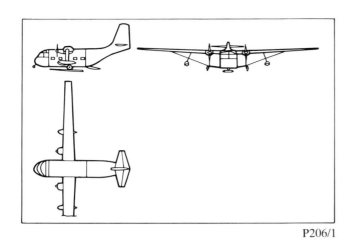

P206/1

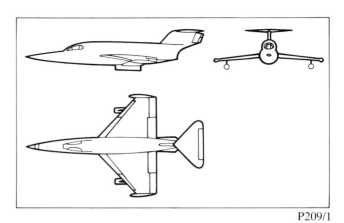

P209/1

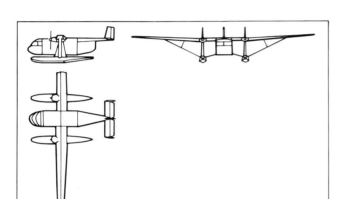

P206/2

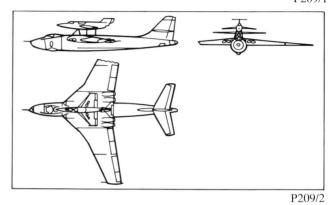

P209/2

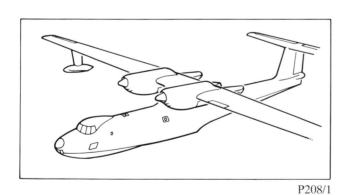

P208/1

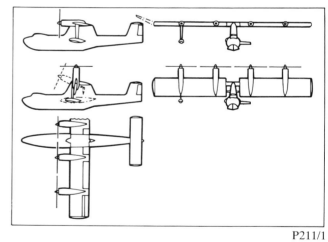

P211/1

P208/2

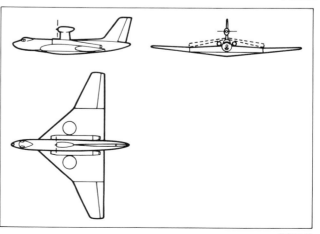

P211/2

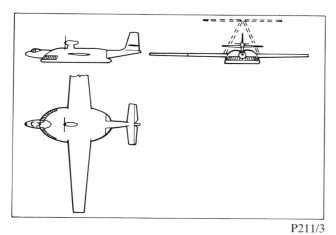

P211/3

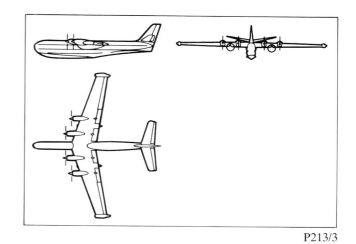

P213/3

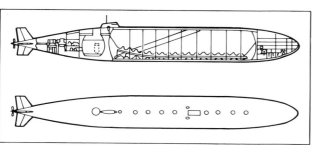

P212

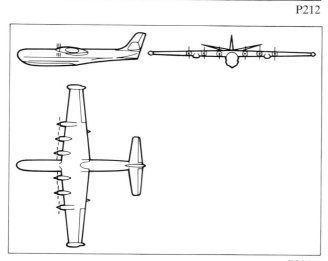

P213/1

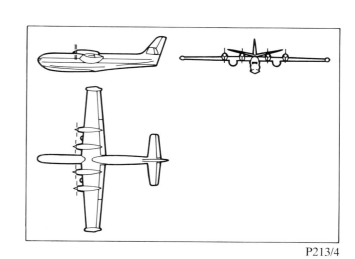

P213/4

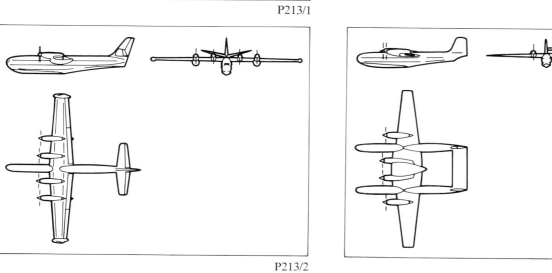

P213/2

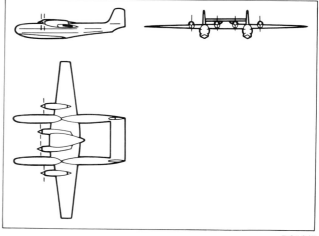

P213/5

259

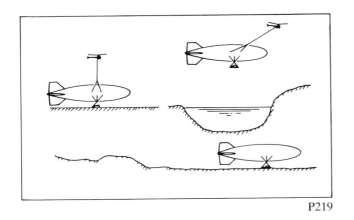

P219

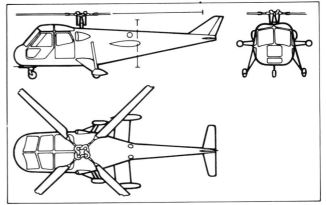

P220/3

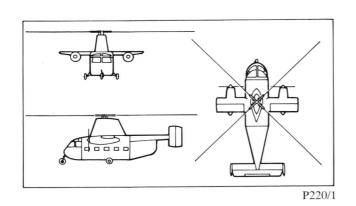

P220/1

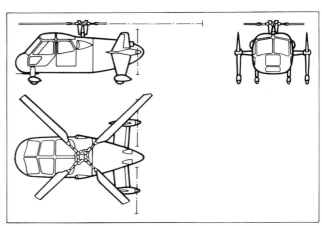

P220/4

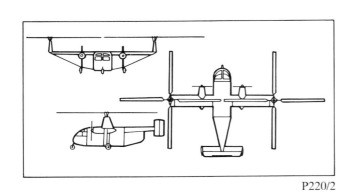

P220/2

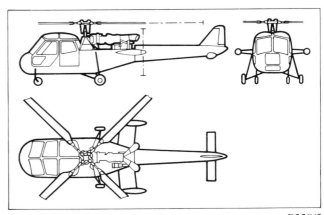

P220/5

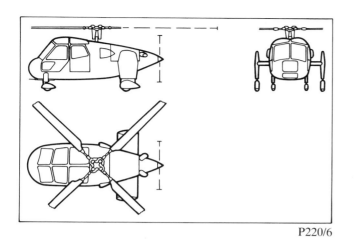

P220/6

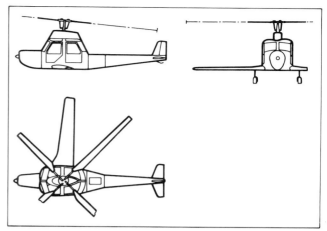

P220/7

PHOTOGRAPHS OF MODELS OR
ARTISTS IMPRESSIONS OF AIRCRAFT PROJECTS

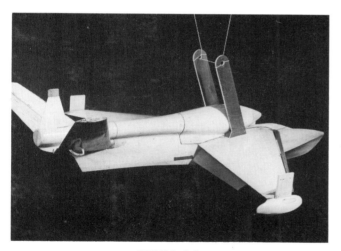

P127 Model

P131 Artists impression

P148 Model

P148 Artists impression

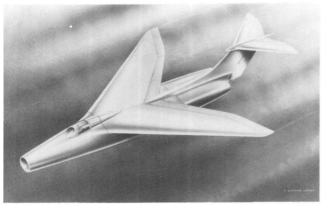

P149 Artists impression

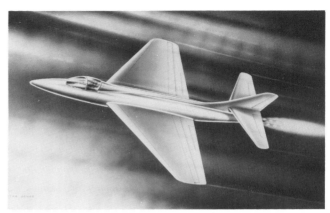

P154 Artists impression

P162 Artists impression

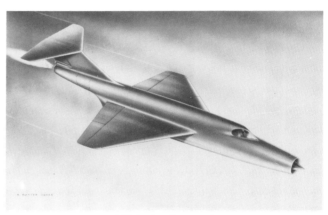

P163 Artists impression

P187 Model

P187 Model

262

P192 Artists impression

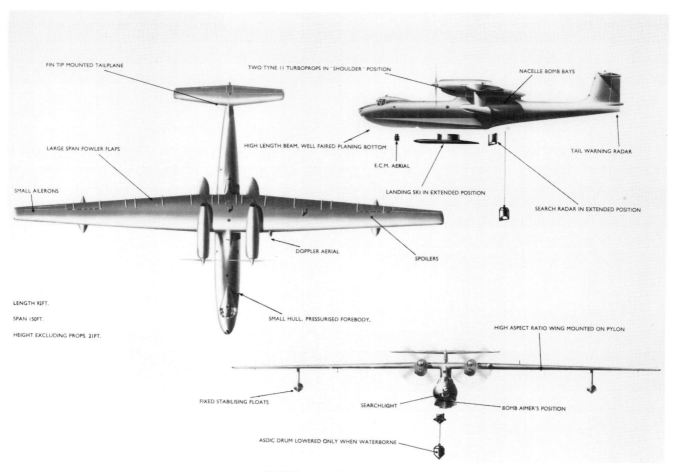

FIN TIP MOUNTED TAILPLANE

TWO TYNE II TURBOPROPS IN 'SHOULDER' POSITION

NACELLE BOMB BAYS

LARGE SPAN FOWLER FLAPS

HIGH LENGTH BEAM, WELL FAIRED PLANING BOTTOM

E.C.M. AERIAL

TAIL WARNING RADAR

SMALL AILERONS

LANDING SKI IN EXTENDED POSITION

SEARCH RADAR IN EXTENDED POSITION

DOPPLER AERIAL

SPOILERS

LENGTH 92FT.

SPAN 150FT.

HEIGHT EXCLUDING PROPS. 21FT.

SMALL HULL, PRESSURISED FOREBODY.

HIGH ASPECT RATIO WING MOUNTED ON PYLON

FIXED STABILISING FLOATS

SEARCHLIGHT

BOMB AIMER'S POSITION

ASDIC DRUM LOWERED ONLY WHEN WATERBORNE

P208 General Arrangement

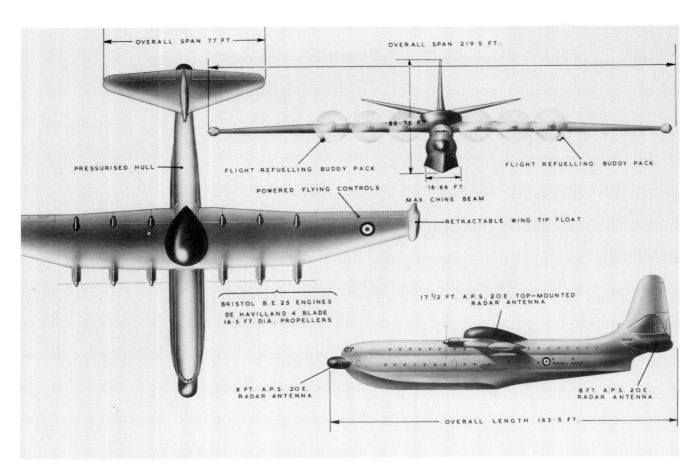

P193 General Arrangement
AWACS In 1956!

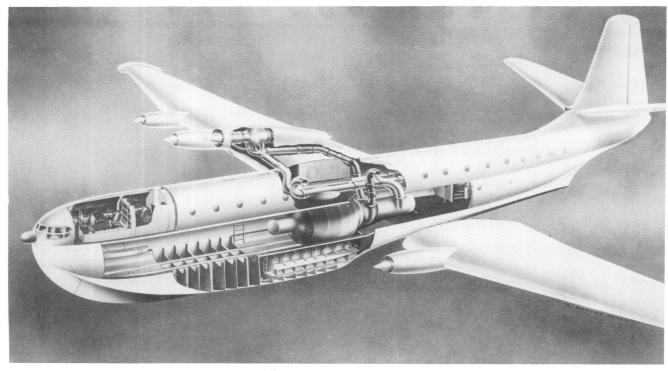

P213 Nuclear Reactor Layout

HELICOPTER PROJECTS AT EASTLEIGH

Project No.	Date	Description
P.500	1951	Medium size pod and boom type helicopter with twin piston engines mounted on a low wing. Tip driven three blade rotor propelled by pulse-jets. Twin fins and rudders.
P.502	1951-59	Development of the basic Skeeter to final Mk.12 form, including trial installations of the rocket-boost installation and casualty evacuation equipment.
P.507	1953	Light two-seat reconnaissance helicopter to MOA Specification HR.144T. Two blade rotor tip-driven by 2 Saunders-Roe 8½ inch pulse-jets. 360° vision. AUW 1500 lb.
P.508-1	1953	Light pod and boom type helicopter with tail rotor. Twin gas turbines on high stub-wings driving three-blade main rotor.
P.514	1953	'Rotorcoach'. Large twin-engined twin-rotor passenger helicopter with centrally mounted low wing for 50 passengers. Design study to MOS Specification 7/Policy/242/RD(H).
P.519 P.521 P.529 P.530	1954-57	Various schemes leading to the P.531.
P.531	1957	The project which reached production as the Westland Scout and Wasp.
P.534	1960	The Skeeter with skid undercarriage.
P.537	1959-60	The Turmo powered Skeeter XM.563.

Project No.	Date	Description
P.538-2	1964	Light two seat reconnaissance helicopter to replace the Skeeter with 350 shp Turbomeca Astazou (de-rated from 550 shp). AUW 2600 lb.
P.539	1967	Vectored slipstream VTOL/STOL type aircraft. Two 1500 shp DH Gnome gas turbines mounted on a high wing with limited tilt and large double nesting flaps.
P.540-1	1960	Ground reconnaissance vehicle with airborne capability based on the Champ road vehicle powered by a Coventry Climax engine. A 980 shp Blackburn Nimbus gas turbine drove a four blade main rotor and a tail rotor on a foldable rear extension for airborne use.
P.540-2	1960	Ground reconnaissance vehicle with obstacle jump and swimming capability using the ground running gear of the Champ vehicle. Maximum jump to 17 ft high over 75 ft at AUW of 6750 lb was obtained by means of a contra-rotating ducted fan with four blades of 7 ft 6 in diameter ballasted for energy storage. Power for all operations was provided by a 300 hp Lycoming six cylinder horizontally opposed air-cooled engine restricted to 90 hp for ground use.
P.541-1	1960	A five-seat passenger helicopter powered by two 800 shp Blackburn Turmo 603 gas turbines. Conventional configuration with transmission and four-blade main rotor and tail rotor making use of P.531 components. Twin Turbomeca Astazou engines also under consideration.

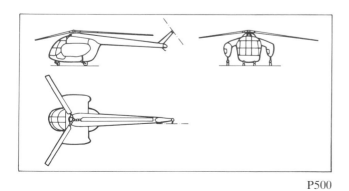

P500

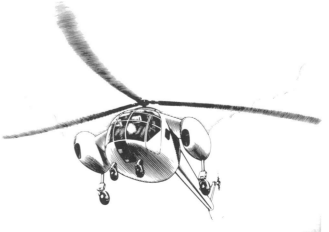

P500-1

265

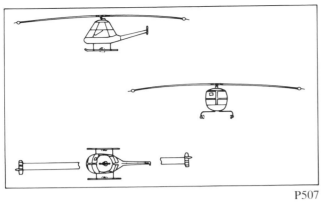

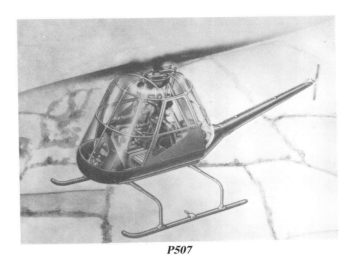

P507

P507

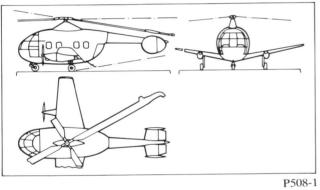

P508-1

P508-1

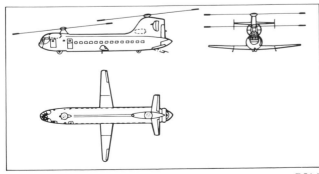

P514

P514

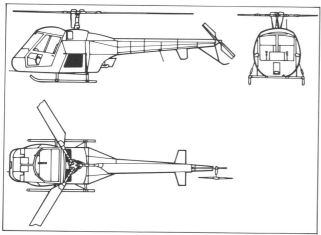

P538-2

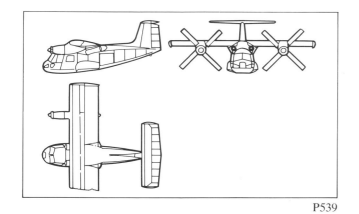

P539

P539

P540-1

P540-1

P540-2

P540-2

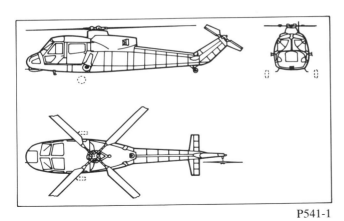

P541-1

P541-1

SELECTED LIST OF RACING BOATS BUILT BY S.E. SAUNDERS AND SAUNDERS-ROE

Name	Date	Length ft	BHP	Motor	Speed kts	Remarks
Durandel	1903	30	40	IMMC	19.5	Competed in British International Trophy at Queenstown, Ireland.
Napier Minor	1904	35	70	1 Napier	21.0	Won Gold Cup Kiel Regatta and British International Trophy.
Yarrow Napier	1905	40	70	2 Wolseley	23.0	Won races at Monaco; also 1st in BIT Race at Arcachon, France.
Napier Bulb	1905	40	70	1 Napier	23.0	2nd in BIT Race at Arcachon, France.
Fiat San Giorgio	1906	40	280	4 Yarrow Napier		Destroyed by fire on trials. Built near Genoa, Italy.
Legru Hotchkiss	1906	40	160	2 Hotchkiss	27.5	In 1906 highest speed in the world. Built on Seine near Paris.
Flying Fish	1907	40	140	2 Wolseley	23.0	Won Pearl of Mediterranean at Palmero.
Wolseley/Siddeley	1908	40	360	2 Wolseley	30.25	Won Prix de Monte Carlo Race at Nice, and Pearl of Mediterranean at Palmero.
Ursula	1909	49	720	2 Wolseley	35.3	Won Coupe de Nations at Monaco on 4 successive years, also Flying Kilometre and big races at Kiel.
Columbine	1910	26	80	1 Wolseley	32.0	Won 14 firsts and 2 seconds out of 18 starts at British motor boat meetings.
Pioneer	1910	40	360	1 Wolseley	40.0	Second boat in BIT races in America - was leading by a lap when her engine overheated and the carburettor caught fire.
Maple Leaf IV	1912	40	760	2 Austin	49.0	Won BIT races in America in 1912 and in England in 1913. World Record Holder 1912.
Rip III	1912	22	60	1 Vauxhall	31.0	Fastest boat in the Motor Yacht Club 22 ft Hydroplane Class.
Angela II	1913	20.5	44	1 Wolseley	27.0	Most successful BMBC 21 ft Class Racer.
Maple Leaf V	1919	40	1600	4 Sunbeams	57.5	Sea mile record holder.
Maple Leaf VI	1919	30	1100	2 Rolls Royce		Competed in B.I. Trophy contest.
Maple Leaf VII	1920	24	1800	4 Sunbeams	80	Competed in B.I. Trophy.
Ardenrun I	1923	20	70	1 Wolseley	36	Fastest 3 litre class racer of that season.
Ardenrun II	1924	17	60	1 Sunbeam	34.17	Won 100 kms races at Cannes in 1½ litre class.
Newg	1926	18	60	1 Sunbeam Super-charged	35	Won Duke of York's Trophy on Thames in 1½ litre class.
Puma	1926	30	240	Puma	45	Many racing successes. Several built for private owners.
Leumas	1927	18	60	1 Sunbeam	37	Sister craft to Newg. Competed in Duke of York's Trophy.
Jack Stripes	1928	78		4 Napier Lions		50 tons multistep hydroplane. Later known as Voodoo.
Miss England II	1930	36	3500	2 Rolls-Royce R-Type	98.76	Mr F. Cooper's design. Saunders built. Record speed 120 mph one run.
Bluebird	1937	23	2000	Rolls-Royce R.37	126.3	Mr F. Cooper's design. Sir Malcolm Campbell's record speed on Lake Maggiore.

AIRCRAFT TYPES BUILT BY S.E. SAUNDERS LTD
FOR OTHER MANUFACTURERS 1910-1914

Firm	Name	Type	Remarks	Date	Qty
Ravaud	Air-Hydroplane	Surface Skimmer	Complete Construction	1910-11	1
Sopwith Aviation Co.	Bat-Boat Type 1	Amphibian	Hull & Erection	1912-13	1
Wigram Flying Boat Ltd.	-	Flying Boat	Construction not Completed	1913	1
Perry, Beadle & Co.	-	Flying Boat	Hull & Erection	1914	1
Bass, Paterson & Co.	Bat-Boat	Flying Boat	Destroyed by Fire before Flight	1914	1
				Total	5

OTHER FIRMS' DESIGNS BUILT FOR THE BRITISH GOVERNMENT 1913-21

Contract No.	Serial Nos.	Type	Remarks	Contract Date	Qty Built
—	469	B.E.2	70 HP Renault	1913	1
CP.65070/14	1228-35	Curtis H.4	2 - 100 HP Anzani in conjunction with Aircraft Manufacturing Co.	1914	3* (8)
A.3123	2890-939	Avro 504A	80 HP Gnome. Majority to RFC. 2929, 2933-4 to RNAS	June 1915	50
CP.71756/15	8001-30	Short 184	225 HP Sunbeam	June 1915	30
—	7740	Avro 504A	80 HP Gnome. Additional Aircraft ex Avro Contracts	1916	1
87A/317	A.412-61	Avro 504A	80 HP Gnome	1916	50
	A.3355-3404	Avro 504A	80 HP Gnome	1916	50
	A.9763-9812	Avro 504A/J	80/100 HP Gnome Mono-Soupape	1916	50
AS.10065	N.1140-49	Short 184	240 HP Renault	1916	10
AS.10495	N.1600-24	Short 184	240 HP Renault (21 A/C) 260 HP Sunbeam (4 A/C)	1916	25
AS.10495	N.1760-74	Short 184	260 HP Sunbeam	1916	15
AS.22028	N.2500-23	Norman Thompson NT.2B	200 HP Sunbeam Arab At least 14 were completed	1917	14* (24)
AS.14154	N.4080-99	Felixstowe F.2A	2-360 HP R.R. Eagle VIII Delivered late July 1917	1916/18	20
AS.14154	N.4280-309	Felixstowe F.2A	2-360 HP R.R. Eagle VIII Delivered from mid Nov. 1917	1916/18	30
AS.4498/18	N.4430-79	Felixstowe F.2A	2-360 HP R.R. Eagle VIII Delivered from Oct. 1918	1916/18	50
AS.24911 38A/550/C.563)	N.4580-629	Felixstowe F.5	2-360 HP R.R. Eagle VIII Not completed	1916/18	0* (50)
AS.17670	N.124-6	Vickers Saunders Valentia B.S.1	2-650 HP R.R. Condors Vickers built super-structure. Flew 1921	1918	3
				Total	402
—	J.8096-225	D.H.9A	Rebuild of Aircraft from this Range	Post War	18

( ) Quantity on Contract. *Additional quantities to those built were partly completed.

SUMMARY OF SAUNDERS/SARO AND SPARTAN AIRCRAFT TYPES

Type No.	Name/Specification	Type	F/Flight date	No. built
T.1		2 seat tractor biplane. Land or seaplane for shipboard use.	1917	1
-	KITTIWAKE	Twin engined 7/8 seater biplane amphibian civil flying boat.	1920	1
-	FELIXSTOWE F5	Built to test Saunders' patented tunnel type hull	1925	1
A.3	VALKYRIE	3 engined military biplane flying boat.	1929	1
A.4	MEDINA	Twin engined 10 seater civil biplane flying boat.	1929	1
A.5	VICKERS-SAUNDERS VALENTIA	Twin engined military biplane flying boat.	1921	3 (not counted in total)
A.7†	SEVERN	3 engined military biplane flying boat.	1930	1
A.10†	F20/27 F10/27	Single seat fighter biplane. Single seat 4 gun fighter biplane. }	1929	1
A.14	HULL FOR SOUTHAMPTON	Experimental - first metal hull by firm.	1929	1
A.17†	CUTTY SARK	Twin engined 4 seat monoplane amphibian civil flying boat. Limited military use.	1929	12
A.19/29	CLOUD	Twin engined 10 seat monoplane amphibian civil and military flying boat.	1930	21
A.21	WINDHOVER	3 engined 4 seat monoplane amphibian civil flying boat.	1930	2
A.22	SEGRAVE METEOR I	Twin engined 4 seat monoplane.	1930	1
A.24	SPARTAN MAILPLANE (originally SARO-PERCIVAL)	3 engined long range monoplane.	1931	1
A.24M	SPARTAN CRUISER	3 engined 6/8 passenger monoplane.	1932	16
	SPARTAN CLIPPER	2 seat light cabin monoplane.	1932	1
A.27	LONDON	Twin engined military biplane flying boat.	1935	31
A.29	CLOUD MONOSPAR	Experimental version of A.19 Cloud with monospar wing for trials in connection with A.33.	1934	1 (conversion not included)
A.33	R2/33	4 engined military monoplane flying boat.	1938	1
S.36	LERWICK	Twin engined military monoplane flying boat.	1938	21
A.37	SHRIMP	4 engined research monoplane flying boat.	1939	1
S.35 } S.40 }	WING FOR SHETLAND 1 & 2	Joint design with Shorts including power plant for 4 engined military/civil flying boat.	1944	2 (not counted in total)
SR.A1 (Orig. SR.44)	E6/44	Twin engined jet-propelled flying boat single seat fighter.	1947	3
SR.45	PRINCESS	10 engined 100 passenger monoplane flying boat. (1 flown, two not finally assembled)	1952	3

Type No.	Name/Specification	Type	F/Flight date	No. built
SR.53	F.138.D	Single seat interceptor fighter, jet and rocket propelled.	1957	2(3)*
SR.177	F.177.D	Development of SR.53, cancelled after manufacture had commenced.	-	0 (27)*
-	SKEETER	Single engined military or civil helicopter based on Cierva W.14.	1951	79
P.531	SPRITE	Single engined military helicopter developed as the Westland Wasp.	1959	6
				209

†These types, initially Saunders, became known under the Saunders-Roe name, generally abbreviated to Saro.

( ) Quantity on contract.   *Additional quantities to those built were partly completed.

SPACE VEHICLES

Name	Type	F/Flight date	No. built
BLACK KNIGHT	Liquid fuel rocket launcher for re-entry and upper atmosphere experiments. Single and two stage versions were constructed	1958	25
BLACK ARROW	Three stage satellite launcher based on Black Knight.	1969	5
FALSTAFF	Single stage solid fuelled rocket for testing control systems in space.	1976	12

SUMMARY OF OTHER FIRMS' AIRCRAFT BUILT BY SAUNDERS-ROE FROM 1929

Design Organisation	Name	Type	Remarks	Date	Qty
FIXED WING TYPES					
BLACKBURN	BLUEBIRD IV	Light 2-seater biplane	Production batch. Not all completed.	1929-31	55
SPARTAN	ARROW	Light 2-seater biplane	Production batches of variants previously made by Simmonds/ Spartan prior to absorbtion by Saunders-Roe	1930-31	13
SPARTAN	3-SEATER MK.I	3-seater. Rear pilot's cockpit		1930-31	19
SPARTAN	3-SEATER MK.II	3-seater. Front pilot's cockpit		1932	7
SUPERMARINE	WALRUS I & II	Single engined military amphibian	Pre-war and wartime sub-contracts and direct M.A.P. contracts	1939-44	461
SUPERMARINE	SEA OTTER	Single engined military amphibian	Direct M.A.P. contracts	1943-46	290
*BRITTEN-NORMAN	ISLANDER TRISLANDER	Twin-engined and three-engined light transports	Sub-contract from Britten-Norman	1968-73	363 (Plus 29 kits)
				Total	1208

*NOTE: Production in the BHC period.

ROTARY WING TYPES					
ISACCO	HELICOGYRE	Helicopter	British Government order for research at Farnborough	1929-32	1
*HILLER	YROE-1 ROTORCYCLE	One-man collapsible helicopter	For U.S.M.C.contract through Helicop Air, Paris. (Hiller European Agent)	1959-60	10
				Total	11

*NOTE: Production partly in the Westland period.

HOVERCRAFT TYPES

Type No.	Name or Registration No.	Type	F/Flight date	No. built
SR.N1	G-12-4	Experimental	1959	1
SR.N2	G-12-5		1962	1
SR.N3	XS.655		1963	1
SR.N4	MOUNTBATTEN CLASS	Became Saunders-Roe Division of Westland Aircraft Limited and later British Hovercraft Corporation products.	1967	6 (2 lengthened)
SR.N5	WARDEN CLASS		1964	12
SR.N6	WINCHESTER CLASS *		1964	57
BH.7	WELLINGTON CLASS		1969	7 (to date)
AP.1-88	-		1982	8 (to date)

* Including lengthened and twin propellor craft.

PERSONALITIES

FOUNDERS AND MANAGING DIRECTORS

SAMUEL EDGAR SAUNDERS FRSA, MRINA
(1857 - 1933)
Member of the Institute of Naval Architects and Chevalier of the Order of St. Charles of Monaco. Fellow of the Royal Society of Arts. Holder of a Royal Warrant as motor-boat builder to King George V. Between the years of 1880 to 1928 he took the lead in running the Syndicate and the Company until he withdrew in 1928 on the formation of Saunders-Roe Limited, then continuing in the honorary position of President until his death.

SIR ALLIOTT VERDON-ROE, OBE, FRAeS
(1877 - 1958)
Famous pioneer airman and founder of the company that bore his name which he sold in 1928 to acquire a major share in S.E. Saunders Limited, then reconstituted as Saunders-Roe Limited. Joint Managing Director with John Lord and director of subsidiary companies, he became the President in succession to S.E. Saunders in 1933.

JOHN LORD, FRAeS (1877 - 1936)
First associated with the Roe family in 1910, he became a director of A.V. Roe Limited during the 1914-18 war. He joined with Sir Alliott in the acquisition of the old S.E. Saunders company and the formation of Saunders-Roe Limited. As Joint Managing Director he undertook the major share in organising and developing the new company and contributed greatly to its improved circumstances until his early death in harness at the age of 59 in January 1936.

HAROLD EDGAR BROADSMITH FRAeS, MRINA
(1890 - 1959)
A senior member of the Avro design staff from 1912-19, leaving for a period in Australia. On his return in 1928 he re-joined Avros but in 1929 transferred to Saunders-Roe as a director and General Manager and later Technical Director of the Spartan subsidiary. In this position he took responsibility for the Cruiser development when Percival withdrew and for the design of the Clipper. In January 1935, with the ending of the Spartan company, he was elected Technical Director of Saunders-Roe and and Joint Managing Director with Capt. Clarke in December 1939, being responsible for development and design. He continued as a director throughout the war but progressively relinquished his responsibilities and retired in 1945. He continued to act as a part-time consultant until 1956 when he retired completely through illness.

CAPTAIN EDWARD D. CLARKE, CBE, MC
(1897 - 1966)
Born in Finland he won his MC in the 1914-18 war as a pilot in the Royal Flying Corps. He took part in the initial sorties to develop techniques of attacking German Zeppelin airships during raids in the East Anglia area. Joined the company in March 1937 in a senior position to deal with commercial and administrative matters. Appointed to the board and from December 1939 became Joint and subsequently Managing Director, holding this position until the take-over by Westland Aircraft Limited in 1959 when he became a director of Westland but retired a few months later.

SIR ARTHUR GOUGE, FRAeS, MIMechE, FIAeS
(1890 - 1969)
Vice-Chairman and Chief Executive from 1943 to 1959. A leading authority on flying boat design with the experience of 28 years with Short Brothers Limited, where he was responsible for the design of many large machines, mainly flying boats, which included the outstanding Sunderland and the later Shetland, jointly built with Saunders-Roe.

SIR DAVID CHARLES COLLINS, CBE, Hon. DSc, CEng, FIMechE, FIProdE, FRAeS (1908 - 1983)
Joined Westland Aircraft Limited as Works Director in 1951 and was appointed Managing Director in 1965. Appointed Managing Director of British Hovercraft Corporation on its formation in 1966. Appointed Chairman in 1968 remaining a director until 1977 when he retired from the Westland Group.

RICHARD STANTON-JONES, MA, FEng, FRAeS, MRINA (1926 -)
Born in India, educated in England, he joined Saunders-Roe in 1949 as an aerodynamicist. Appointed Chief Designer in 1959. On the formation of the British Hovercraft Corporation in 1966, he was appointed Technical Director and Deputy Managing Director. In 1968 he was appointed Managing Director, a post he held for fourteen years to 1982. He retired from the company in 1984 to set up his own consultancy business.

ANTHONY VERNON NELSON REED, CBE, BSc(Tech), CEng, FRAeS (1927 -)
Joined the Westland Group in 1971 as Commercial Director of Westland Helicopters Limited after twenty years at Bristol Aero Engines and Rolls Royce. Appointed Managing Director of British Hovercraft Corporation in 1982, retiring in 1985.

CHRISTOPHER CLARK GUSTAR, MBIM (1946 -)
Joined Saunders-Roe Limited in 1962 as an engineering apprentice. His subsequent career, until 1984, was primarily concerned with technical and commercial management of the Experimental and Electronic Laboratories division of the company. In 1984 the division became a limited company, EEL Limited, with Mr. Gustar as its Managing Director. When the Westland Group was reorganised late in 1985, he was appointed Managing Director of Westland Aerospace Limited which combined British Hovercraft Corporation Limited and EEL Limited.

Note: In the period 1959 to 1966 there was no Managing Director of the Cowes facilities of the Westland Group as it had purely divisional status and was known as the Saunders-Roe Division of Westland Aircraft Limited.

Harold E. Broadsmith, FRAeS, MRINA.
(1890 – 1959)

Captain Edward D. Clarke, CBE, MC.
(1897 – 1966)

Sir Arthur Gouge, FRAeS, MIMechE, FIAeS
(1890 – 1969)

Richard Stanton-Jones, MA, FEng, FRAeS, MRINA.
(1926-   )

Christopher C. Gustar, MBIM
(1946 –   )

Maurice J. Brennan, BSc, CEng, FRAeS, FIMechE.
(1913 – 1986)

Tadeus L. Ciastula, Dipl.Ing, FRAeS, FIMechE.
(1909 – 1979)

Raymond Wheeler, MSc(Eng) DIC, CEng, FRAeS,
FRINA, FRSA. (1927 –   )

CHIEF DESIGNERS

H.H. THOMAS
Responsible for the design of the T.1, he died in the influenza outbreak at the end of the war. The small office of 3 draughtsmen, 2 office boys and a tracer was then disbanded.

F.P. HYDE BEADLE
He had several periods of association with Saunders but only one aircraft bearing the company name was built to his designs. This was the Kittiwake of 1919-20. His earliest design, which the company largely built, was the Perry-Beadle when he was a partner in that concern and in 1926-7 he prepared the design of the Schneider Trophy project which was not built.

BERNARD THOMSON
Joined the company to form the revived Aircraft Department in 1923 with previous experience in the Air Department of the Admiralty and H.G. Hawker Engineering Company. Responsible for the design of the F.5 Channel Hull conversion and the Valkyrie and Medina.

HENRY KNOWLER, FRAeS, AMICE   (1894 - 1978)
Chief Designer from 1926 to 1952, when he was appointed technical Director, holding this position until his retirement in 1956. He had been a director since 1942. Prior to joining the company he had been a designer with Vickers Limited and the English Electric Company which included work on flying boats particularly at the latter concern. The design of the Valkyrie was mainly his work and, with the departure of Thomson, he then became responsible for all types from the Severn onwards culminating in the design of the Princess.

MAURICE J. BRENNAN, BSc, CEng, FRAeS, FIMechE
(1913 - 1986)
Joined the company in 1936 from Hawker Aircraft Limited and held various appointments in the design department. Assistant Chief Designer in April 1951 and promoted to Chief Designer in November 1952 on the appointment of Henry Knowler as Technical Director. Consequent to this appointment helicopter design was made a separate function. Responsible for the SR.53, SR.177 and Black Knight designs. Resigned in March 1959 to join Vickers-Armstrong (Aircraft) Limited.

TADEUS L.CIASTULA, Dipl.Ing, FRAeS, FIMechE
(1909 - 1979)
Appointed Chief Designer of the Helicopter Division in January 1957. An officer in the Polish Air Force, came to Britain in 1940 and was posted to the R.A.E. Farnborough. Joined Saunders-Roe Design Department in 1948, transferring to helicopter design in November 1952. Responsible for the Scout and Wasp designs.

RICHARD STANTON-JONES, MA, FEng, FRAeS, MRINA   (1926 -)

Chief Designer from 1959 to 1966. See Managing Directors.

RAYMOND L. WHEELER, MSc(Eng), DIC, CEng, FRAeS, FRINA, FRSA   (1927 -)
Chief Designer from 1966 to 1985. Joined Saunders-Roe in 1945 as an apprentice studying part-time at Southampton University for a degree in aeronautics. Winner of a Spitfire Mitchell Memorial Scholarship, which enabled him to complete his degree and spend three years as a post-graduate at Imperial College. Progressed through the company as Chief Stressman, five years, Chief Structural Designer, one year, becoming Chief Designer in 1966, the year in which British Hovercraft Corporation was formed. Responsible for the design of the SR.N4 Mk.3, BH.7 and AP.1-88 hovercraft and Black Arrow and Falstaff space launchers. Appointed Technical Director in 1972, retaining the post of Chief Designer until 1985 when Westland Aerospace was formed and he was appointed Business Development Director, a post he holds at the present time. One of the authors of this book.

TEST PILOTS

In the early lifetime of S.E. Saunders Limited there were no established test pilots. In wartime the aircraft, mainly of proved types, were cleared after ground tests by the resident A.I.D. inspector and then accepted by a visiting R.F.C. or R.N.A.S. pilot who would check for airworthiness to their own satisfaction before departing. During the time of Avro 504 production, the amount of testing demanded the presence of a pilot permanently and this resulted in the secondment of 2nd Lieut H.S. Stevens in July 1917, who remained with Saunders until the end of the war. Among these pilots collecting Avros was Capt. Leslie S. Ash, R.F.C., who joined the company post-war. The Saunders T.1 was flown by Lieut. W.H. Sayers, also by Major Evans who, with civilian Marcus D. Manton, flew machines for the other Isle of Wight firm, J. Samuel White at Somerton.

Flying of new types in the years following the 1914-18 War was limited and very intermittent, so free-lance pilots were engaged when needed.

Norman Macmillan Ex-Captain R.F.C., flew the Kittiwake on its first flight on 19th September 1920 during which damage occurred resulting in an emergency landing.

F. Warren Merriam Ex-Commander R.N.A.S., carried out later flights of the Kittiwake.

Frank L. Courtney Ex-Lieutenant R.F.C. Tested the A.3 Valkyrie in the summer and the A.4 Medina in the spring of 1926. More than a decade later he was employed in 1938-9 to fly the initial trials of A.33 and Lerwick types.

Edward Chilton Flt. Lieut. R.A.F. (later Air Marshal Sir Edward), carried out the initial flights of the Cutty Sark.

L. Cole Ex-Captain R.F.C., was flying Cutty Sark in 1931.

Edgar W. Percival Ex-Captain R.F.C. Tested the Mailplane during its initial trials.

Louis A. Strange Ex-Lt. Col. R.F.C. A director of Spartan, flew these machines for test and demonstration purposes.

Hubert S. Broad Flew the first flights of the A.10 fighter. Mainly known for his flying of de Havilland aircraft from 1925 for more than 20 years.

Established Test Pilots from 1931

Stuart D. Scott Ex-Flt. Lieut. R.A.F. (Capt. R.F.C.). Chief test pilot from 1931 to 1938. Carried out much flying of the Severn, Cutty Sark, Cloud, Windhover and London including initial flights of the types.

Leslie S. Ash Ex-Lieut. R.F.C. Joined the company as a draughtsman in 1924. Acted as flight test observer and a part-time test and demonstation pilot flying all types from the A.10 to the Lerwick including the Spartan Cruiser. He carried out the initial trials of the A.37 at both Cowes and Beaumaris before it was sent to M.A.E.E. In wartime transferred to Beaumaris as Chief Test Pilot before retiring in 1946.

Flt. Lieut. Lamb R.A.F. Flew Walrus aircraft at Addlestone. Killed with flight mechanic Ron Conway in 1943 in a take-off accident to one of these machines. Assisted Leslie Ash in test flying the Lerwick aircraft.

Geoffrey Verdon-Roe Youngest son of Sir Alliott, commenced test flying on the Lerwick and continued flying through the war mainly on the Walrus and Sea Otter. Became Chief Test Pilot at Cowes and Addlestone when L.S. Ash transferred to Beaumaris. Post-war Director of the subsidiary plywood company and later the shipyard in Anglesey.

Geoffrey A.V. Tyson Ex-Flt. Lieut. R.A.F. Joined Saunders-Roe as chief test pilot in December 1946 after test flying with Shorts since 1940. In the period to the end of 1955 when he retired he carried out the flight trials of the SR.A/1 and Princess flying boats.

John O. Lancaster, DFC Apprenticed to Armstrong-Whitworth in 1935, he joined the RAF in 1937 and served throughout the war in Bomber Command and with later appointments at Boscombe Down and with ETPS. He was a test pilot with Boulton Paul for six months before joining Saunders-Roe in July 1946. He flew Sea Otters and the SR.A1 before leaving in December to join Armstrong-Whitworth at Baginton as a test pilot.

John S. Booth Ex-Sqn. Ldr. R.A.F. Joined as deputy to Tyson from Shorts in February 1949 and took over as chief test pilot in January 1956. Flew the prototype SR.53 on its initial flight at Boscombe Down on 16th May 1957 but was killed in a take-off accident to the second machine on the 5th June 1958.

J.R.S. Overbury Ex-Lieut. Cmdr. F.A.A. Joined in 1956 to assist Booth on the test flying of the SR.53. Resigned in 1959.

Peter M. Lamb Ex-Lieut. Cmdr. F.A.A. Joined in 1958 with considerable service and test flying experience. Carried out test flying of SR.53 after the death of John Booth. Undertook the development trials of hovercraft until 1973.

Helicopter flying was carried out at Eastleigh by pilots with service experience and specialised in this work.

Kenneth M. Reed Ex-Lieut. Cmdr. F.A.A. Joined the company in 1952 and appointed senior helicopter pilot in 1958.

John J.M. Jeffery Ex-Lieut. F.A.A. A helicopter test pilot with the company from 1950 onwards.

Harry Phillips Ex-Lieut. Cmdr. F.A.A. Joined the company in 1958 retiring in 1971. Following the company's purchase by Westland became hovercraft pilot.

Geoffrey A.V. Tyson.

Peter Lamb.

PATENTS

The list of patents appended here is included to illustrate the wide range of subjects investigated by S.E. Saunders and his associates from the early days to the late 1920s. There may be other applications not identified but the significant patents are included and of these one of particular importance to the growth of the company was undoubtedly No.222 covering Consuta which is included here complete, together with further information on the subject.

CONSUTA PLYWOOD

LATIN FOR 'SEWN TOGETHER'

The use of laminated plywood for boatbuilding had commended itself to Sam Saunders as a means of securing lightness and stiffness in the construction of boat hulls. Contemporary glues were not suitable for immersion in water and with the precedent of the birch-bark canoes of the North American Indians, several methods of stitching using waxed thread were employed with reasonable success on light sculling and sailing craft.

Miss Ethel Saunders, daughter of Sam Saunders, generally assisted her father in the firm and was directly involved with the development of the sewing techniques. Her death from meningitis at the age of 33 in 1913 at the White House was a great loss to her parents, particular her father who placed great reliance on her help.

From this early work were evolved various combinations of layers and thicknesses of Consuta plywood, typical of which might be a four-ply laminate held together with 16 SWG copper wire used as individual stitches or continuously or a combination of these methods. In these more substantial forms the construction of larger, power driven craft with significant weight advantages became an attractive proposition and was brought into prominence by the first vessel, an umpire's launch named Consuta built in 1898 and used many times at Henley Royal Regatta and later by the B.B.C. for radio and T.V. coverage of the Universities Boat Race. Further evidence of the merits of Consuta is provided by the continued existence of the launch at the time of writing, currently being enthusiastically rebuilt at Kew. This launch was followed by many other power boats of superior quality including many race winners and world record holders. The use of Consuta in marine aircraft and to a degree in landbased aircraft also followed naturally as aviation developed in the period before 1914 and lasted for a decade until superseded by aluminium alloys or improved adhesives where wood construction continued.

The techniques employed for boat hull construction improved with experience. The hulls were generally built upside down on a mould and initially were sewn with waxed thread in parallel lines about 2 inches apart let in on the outside surface to be under-flush enough to be puttied up. Wire-sewn hulls had grooves cut in the outer layer (the thickness of which was sufficient to allow for this) to take the wires which were punched in with a chisel-like punch. Special tools, one with a cutter on a flexible shaft like a dentist's drill for cutting the grooves and a wire-puller with a springloaded hinge to return it in the open position, were developed. A typical hull would have a line of wire at each timber (rib) and perhaps two rows between. In some designs ribs were eliminated and reliance placed on the use of longitudinal stiffeners pulled to the skin by the wires. Whichever form of construction was employed, the shell of the hull was built up by the successive application of the skins with intermediate layers of canvas, solutionised with linseed oil for waterproofing. Generally four layers of wood were used and these could be applied in strips along the length of the hull or in a diagonal manner with successive strips at an angle. Problems of splitting of the outer ply were overcome by a staggered pattern of stitching and one boat (Angela III) was stitched with a pattern of stitching in the form of a letter T, diagonally on its side.

Various developments including the use of sewing machines and stapling of flat sheets took place throughout the useful life of the material.

Mahogany and cedar were the woods mainly employed, with cedar preferred for aircraft use for its weight advantage.

At the end of 1918, Vickers were granted a licence to manufacture Consuta but material produced at Weybridge was criticised by purchasers and sales discouraged. However, late in 1920 the Joyce Green management reported to the board unfavourably on Consuta, claiming that Haskelite could be obtained at half the cost. This led to comparative testing, the results of which are not recorded. Vickers later used an alternative material named S.C.T. in some of their Vulture amphibian hulls.

No.	Title	Application	Accepted
222	Building Boats, Carriages, Panels etc. (Consuta)	4.1.1898	31.12.1898
3,640	Construction of Boats, Carriages, Panels, etc.	13.2.1912	5.12.1912
3,853	Flexible Shaft Couplings	15.2.1912	13.2.1913
10,774	Improvements in Clutches	7.5.1913	7.5.1914
12,376	Folding Row-lock Carring Frames for Boats	7.8.1890	13.6.1891
15,545	Hydro-Seaplanes	1913	Abandoned
17,297			Abandoned

No.	Title	Application	Accepted
17,486	Seaplanes	1915	Abandoned
18,055	Motor Launches and Other Self-Propelled Vehicles	6.9.1905	16.8.1906
18,741		1909	Abandoned
19,405		1904	Abandoned
19,516	Improvements in Aircraft	7.9.1914	27.5.1915
20,428	Construction of Mechanically Propelled Vessels	29.9.1908	23.9.1909
21,030	Construction of Boats, Launches and the like	22.9.1906	20.6.1907
21,223		1903	Abandoned
23,333	Construction of Cylindrical or other Hollow Bodies	12.10.1909	6.10.1910
23,735		1902	Abandoned
27,441	Wood Framework	1906	Abandoned
28,875	Receptacles for Mustard, Icing Sugar, etc.	12.10.1910	7.12.1911
101,434	Improvements in Aircraft	31.1.1916	21.9.1916
105,412	Manufacture of Ply Boards or Sheets	15.4.1916	16.4.1917
113,295	Construction of Framing, Planes, etc.	13.1.1917	13.2.1918
115,260	Landing Runners for Airships	28.4.1917	29.4.1918
115,704	Improvements with Aeroplanes	24.5.1917	23.5.1918
119,375	Improvements to Air Cooled Radiators	17.1.1918	3.10.1918
120,298	Improvements in Airships	19.12.1917	7.11.1918
121,032	Improvements in Turnbuckles	5.2.1918	5.12.1918
121,047	Improvements in Concrete Vessels	2.3.1918	15.12.1918
122,506	Improvements in Stays or Tension Members	5.2.1918	30.1.1919
123,374	Improvements in Hollow Wooden Struts, etc.	16.2.1918	17.2.1919
124,037	Improvements in Pulleys	11.3.1918	11.3.1919
125,159	Improvements in Seaplanes	21.6.1916	17.4.1919
125,469	Improvements in Propeller Drive Mechanisms	18.8.1916	24.4.1919
126,872	Improvements in Hollow Spars	15.8.1918	22.5.1919
129,453	Propelling and Steering Mechanism	15.7.1918	15.7.1919
129,705	Improvements to Aircraft Alighting Gear	30.11.1917	24. 7.1919
130,725	Laminated Propellers for Aircraft	19.2.1919	14.8.1919
135,338	Improvements in Aircraft	11.12.1918	27.11.1919
137,411	Interplane Struts for Aeroplanes	20.2.1919	15.1.1920
151,677	Improvements in Sewing Machines	31.5.1919	30.9.1920
152,510	Construction of Motor Car Bodies	7.10.1919	21.10.1920
157,541	Improvements in Dwelling Houses	15.10.1919	17.1.1921
163,853	Variable Camber Wings or Control Surfaces	18.3.1920	2.6.1921
176,965	Improvements in the Construction of Boats	18.1.1921	23.3.1921
178,168	Improvements in Aeroplane Wings	31.12.1920	31.3.1922
179,607	Steering and Propelling of Ships	3.2.1921	3.5.1922
180,470	Improvements in Sewing Machines	18.3.1921	1.6.1922
181,959	Improvements in Outboard Motors	8.6.1921	29.6.1922
191,612	Hulls for Flying Boats, High Speed Launches, etc.	12.1.1922	18.1.1923
200,553	Variable Camber (105,412 referred to)	16.3.1922	
210,208	Improvements in Panellings	14.11.1922	21.1.1924
215,626	Hulls for Flying Boats, High Speed Launches, etc.	7.7.1923	15.5.1924
229,409	Apparatus for Landing Flying Boats	26.11.1923	26.2.1925
230,196	Construction of Hulls and Metal Structures	13.12.1923	12.3.1925
234,303	Improvements in Pontoons and Vessels	25.6.1924	28.5.1925
236,300	Circular Saw Guards	10.4.1924	20.8.1925

No.	Title	Application	Accepted
244,520	Metal Hulls for Flying Boats, Launches, etc.	17.9.1924	17.12.1925
244,606	Cementing Plys or Layers of Wood, etc.	26.1.1925	24.12.1925
248,916	Seaplane Float Structures	2.3.1925	18.3.1926
254,820	Racing Motor Boats, Hydroplanes, Floats, etc.	18.4.1925	15.7.1926
255,653	Improvements to Hulls of Boats	11.8.1925	27.9.1926
256,743	Aeroplanes Having Folding Wings	15.6.1925	19.8.1926
258,151	Improvements to Door Knobs and Handles	28.1.1926	16.9.1926
261,979	Construction of Hulls of Boats	7.4.1926	16.9.1926
262,579*	Improvements in Aeroplanes (Retracting Floats)	21.11.1926	16.12.1926
268,135	Improvements in Fasteners or Paper Clips	29.3.1926	31.3.1927
278,544	Propelling and Steering Mechanisms for Vessels	20.11.1926	13.10.1927
278,996	Improvements to Baking Tins or Pans	2.7.1927	20.10.1927
289,245	Gun Mountings for Flying Machines	1.4.1927	26.4.1928
289,640	Aircraft Wing Rib Construction Improvement	4.5.1927	3.5.1928
294,713	Flying Boat and Seaplane Improvements	4.5.1927	2.8.1928
296,570*	Improvements in Flying Boats - Twin Hulls	29.9.1927	6.9.1928
296,594*	Retracting Floats	9.11.1927	6.9.1928
302,137	Aircraft Rudder Bar Improvements	15.9.1928	13.12.1928
303,946	Flying Boat Structure Improvements	2.11.1927	18.1.1929
305,399	Flying Boat Structure Improvements	17.3.1928	7.2.1929
305,514	Flying Boat Structure Improvements	2.11.1927	4.2.1929
305,865	Aircraft Heating	26.3.1928	14.2.1929
306,676	Flying Boat Structure Improvements	28.1.1928	28.2.1929
310,576	Improved Metal Plate Joining	2.2.1929	2.5.1929
314,148	Improved Radiator Cooling	4.4.1928	27.6.1929
316,751	Improved Boat Hull	7.7.1928	8.8.1929
317,958	Improved Boat Structure	14.7.1928	29.8.1929
338,078	Waterproofing of Hulls	5.2.1930	
339,886	Waterproofing of Hulls	24.2.1930	
411,925	Aircraft Bomb Loading Gear	3.12.1927	26.11.1928
411,926	Aircraft Bomb Loading Gear	12.3.1929	23.1.1930

*See Chapter 15 for diagram.

N° 222

A.D. 1898

Date of Application, 4th Jan., 1898
Complete Specification Left, 4th Nov., 1898—Accepted, 31st Dec., 1898

PROVISIONAL SPECIFICATION.

Improvements in Building Boats, Carriages, Panels, and other Articles.

I, SAMUEL EDGAR SAUNDERS, of Springfield Works, Goring-on-Thames, in the County of Oxford, Boat Builder and Engineer, do hereby declare the nature of this invention to be as follows:—

My invention relates to the building of boats, carriages, panels or other articles
5 wherein a series of layers or strips of wood or other material are laid crosswise or diagonally of each other and united together, and the object of my invention is to provide improved means for uniting these layers.

In carrying out my invention I place the several layers one upon another in the usual manner and temporarily secure them together and then I form several
10 series of holes through which wire is threaded or laced, grooves being preferably formed between the several pairs of holes to receive the wire so that the latter shall be flush with or below the exterior surfaces of the articles.

The wires also serve for securing strips, battens or the like to the surfaces according to requirements without the use of nails.

15 My invention is of especial advantage in connection with launch building as I am enabled to obtain great strength with little weight and to dispense with the use of the usual ribs.

Dated the 4th day of January 1898.

G. F. REDFERN & Co.,
20 4, South Street, Finsbury, London, Agents for the Applicant.

COMPLETE SPECIFICATION.

Improvements in Building Boats, Carriages, Panels, and other Articles.

I, SAMUEL EDGAR SAUNDERS, of Springfield Works, Goring-on-Thames, in the
25 County of Oxford, Boat Builder and Engineer, do hereby declare the nature of this invention and in what manner the same is to be performed, to be particularly described and ascertained in and by the following statement:—

My invention relates to the building of boats, carriages, panels or other articles wherein a series of layers, veneers or strips of wood or other material are laid
30 cross wise or diagonally of each other and united together, and the object of my invention is to provide improved means for uniting these layers.

In carrying out my invention I place the several layers one upon another in the

[Price 8d.]

Price 5s. 6d.

usual manner and temporarily secure them together and then I form several series of holes through which wire is threaded or laced, grooves being preferably formed between the several pairs of holes to receive the wire so that the latter shall be flush with or below the exterior surfaces of the articles.

The wires also serve for securing strips, battens or the like to the surfaces **5** according to requirements without the use of nails.

To enable my invention to be fully understood I will describe the same by reference to the accompanying drawing, in which :—

Figure 1 is a view in elevation illustrating my invention; and,

Figure 2 is a section on the line 2—2 Figure 1: **10**

Figure 3 is a view similar to Figure 1 but shewing strips or battens secured upon one surface of the material; and,

Figure 4 is a section on the line 4—4 Figure 3:

Figure 5 is a view similar to Figure 1 but shewing the holes and grooves for the wires: **15**

Figure 6 is a section on the line 6—6 Figure 5; and,

Figure 7 is a sectional view illustrating a slight modification.

Figures 5, 6 and 7 are drawn to a larger scale than Figures 1 to 4.

a, b, c, d indicate four layers of wood which are to be secured together in accordance with my invention the said layers being arranged so that the grain **20** of one layer crosses or is at an angle to the grain of the adjacent layer or layers. In some cases, for instance when my invention is to be applied for the building of boats, I advantageously arrange between the layers of wood other layers of waterproofed canvas or other fabric. The several layers having been temporarily secured together have rows of holes e, e, Figures 5 and 6, formed through them **25** through which a copper or other wire can be threaded to secure the several layers together, as indicated in Figure 2, grooves g, g being formed between the pairs of holes at opposite sides of the combination board or the like in which the wire will lie so as to be flush with or below the external surfaces of the outer layers.

In practice the rows of stitches are preferably arranged so that they are **30** transverse to the grain of the outer layers and the wires are so threaded that the wire loops of one row will alternate with the spaces between the wire loops of the adjacent row. Instead of using a continuous wire f short wires may be used, for instance as shewn in Figure 7, the ends of the said wires being suitably connected together. **35**

When strips, battens or the like are to be secured to the surfaces such battens are laid on before the wire binding is applied and then the wire is passed over the said strips as clearly indicated in Figures 3 and 4.

My invention is of especial advantage in connection with launch building as I am enabled to obtain great strength with little weight and to dispense with the use **40** of the usual ribs. I prefer when applying my invention for this purpose that the several layers of which the boat is composed should extend over as large a surface of the boat as possible and that they should be moulded or set to conform to the shape of the boat during their application so that when the several layers, which are temporarily united during their application, are permanently united **45** according to my invention the boat will possess great rigidity.

Also for most purposes it will be found advisable to unite the several layers after they have been shaped and placed in the position which they are to permanently occupy.

In some cases it will be found advisable that, after the wire has been applied **50** to bind the several layers together, the grooves and holes should be filled with suitable putty or stopping and the whole surface then cleaned off to make it flat and even.

Although I have described my invention in connection with four layers of material it is to be understood that a greater or less number of layers may be used **55** according to requirement. The outer layers, however, should be of such thickness that the grooves g, g in which the wires lie will not unduly weaken the material,

Having now particularly described and ascertained the nature of my said invention and in what manner the same is to be performed, I declare that what I claim is :—

    1. The combination of a series of layers or veneers of wood or other material,
5 holes formed through the said layers, grooves in the outer layers connecting the said holes and wires for uniting the several layers together the said wires being inserted through the said holes and having those portions which run along the surfaces of the material lying in the said grooves, substantially as described.

    2. The method of uniting a series of layers of wood or other material together
10 consisting in inserting wires through holes in the said material the portions of the wires which extend between the said holes lying in grooves formed in the outer layers, substantially as described.

    Dated the 4th day of November 1898.

G. F. REDFERN & Co.,

15   4, South Street, Finsbury, London, Agents for the Applicant.

Redhill: Printed for Her Majesty's Stationery Office, by Malcomson & Co., Ltd.—1899.

A.D. 1898. Jan. 4. N°. 222.
SAUNDERS' Complete Specification.

SHEET 1.

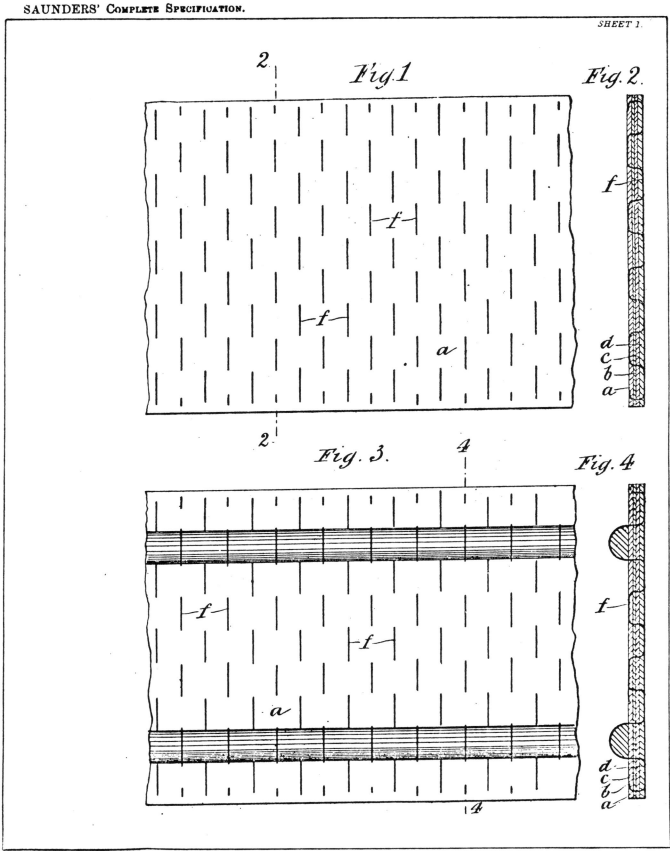

Fig. 5

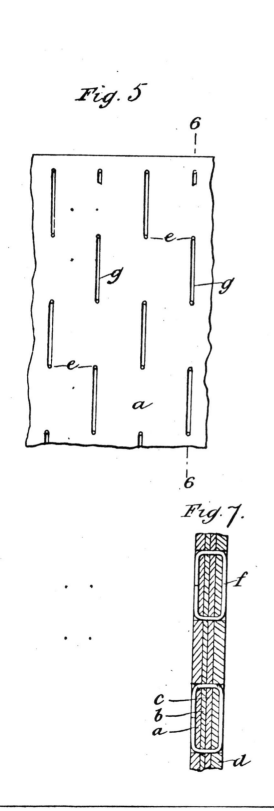

Fig. 6

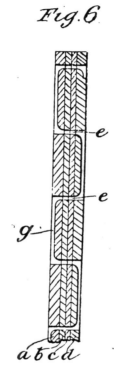

Fig. 7.

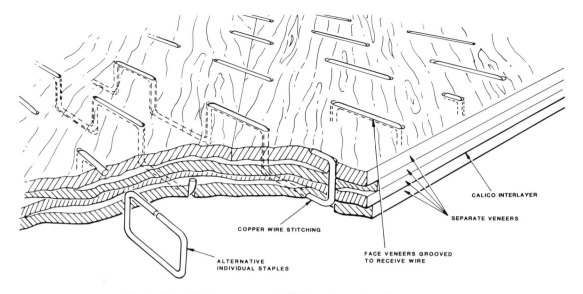

Typical detailed arrangement of Consuta construction.

CALICO INTERLAYER

SEPARATE VENEERS

COPPER WIRE STITCHING

FACE VENEERS GROOVED
TO RECEIVE WIRE

ALTERNATIVE
INDIVIDUAL STAPLES

Closely sewed the bark
together
Bound it closely to the
framework
That the water may not
enter
That the river may not
wet me.

HIAWATHA'S SAILING

An amusing cartoon of Sam Saunders and his Consuta construction
appearing in the Motor Boat dated March 2nd 1911.

Consuta
The Super-Plywood

The Finest Material yet evolved for Aircraft Construction.

"CONSUTA," the Super-Plywood, is actually **sewn together.** The layers are first cemented together with waterproof material and then **stitched through** in parallel rows about $1\frac{1}{4}$ inches apart.

This gives a rigidity and resilience unattainable by any other method. Weight for weight, it is the strongest material yet evolved.

"Consuta" is used for the cabins of the commercial type of Vickers "Vimy" bombers, entirely dispensing with the use of cross-bracing wires. It is now being used for the whole covering of flying boats—the largest type yet built. Its uses are limitless.

The sheets are made to any desired size and shape up to 8 feet wide by 60 feet long, and from $\frac{1}{8}$ inch to $\frac{5}{8}$ inch thick, thus eliminating waste in conversion.

We shall be pleased to quote for your requirements.

Patentees and Sole Manufacturers:

S. E. SAUNDERS, LTD.,
EAST COWES, I.O.W.

When communicating with advertisers, mention of "Flight" will ensure special attention.

A typical advertisement for Consuta construction appearing
in Flight of August 5th 1920

Summary table of the location and use of Company Premises from 1830 to the present day.

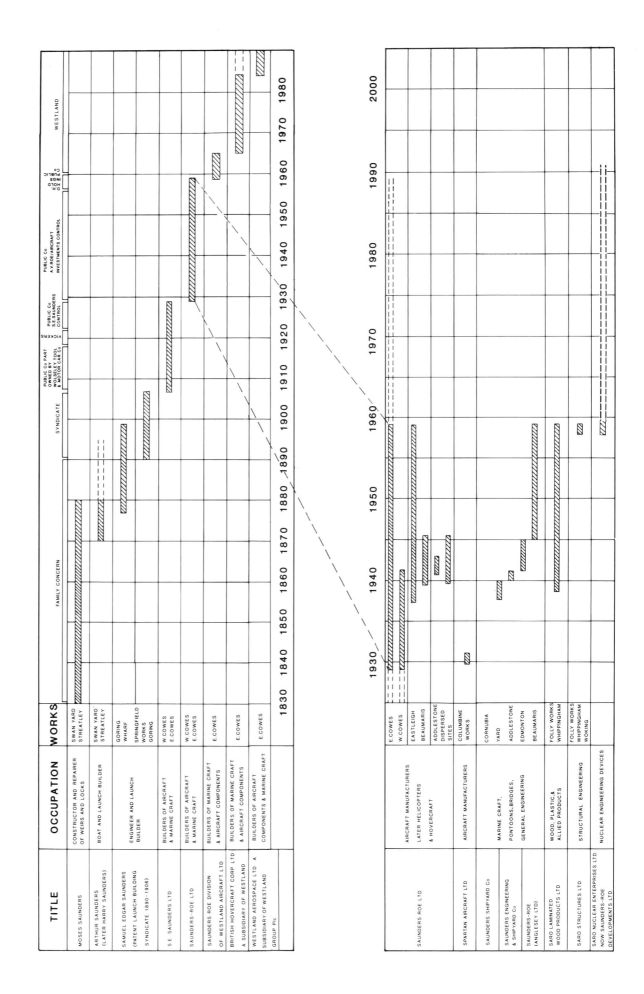

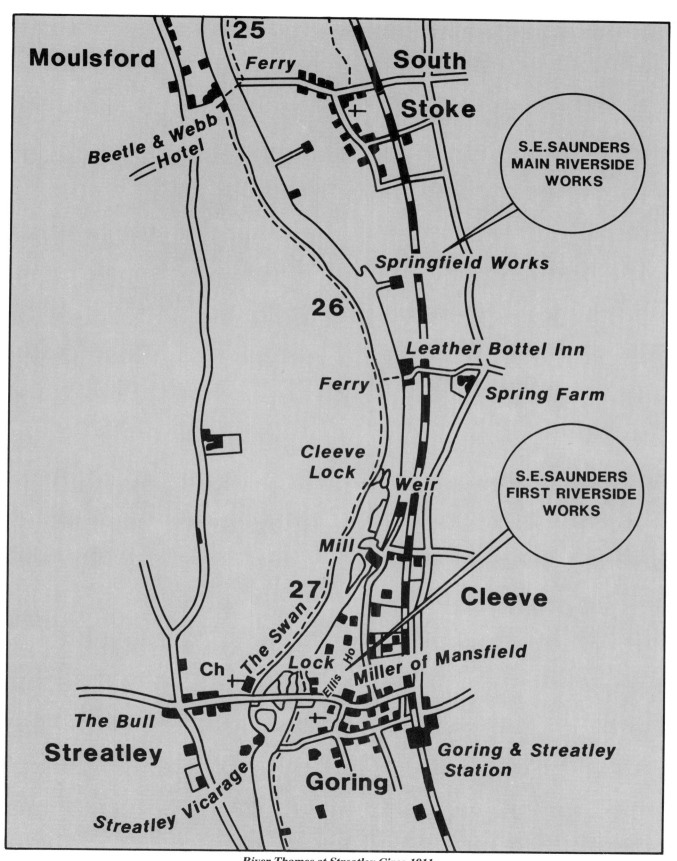

Location of the first premises of Sam Saunders in the Streatley/Goring area
of the River Thames in the late 18th century and early 19th century.

River Thames at Streatley Circa 1911
(from Salters guide to the Thames)

PREMISES IN THE ISLE OF WIGHT (W denotes West Cowes / E denotes East Cowes)

Name	Location		Period of Use	Purpose	Remarks
Alexandra Hall	Birmingham Road	W	1909		Original Premises - Wesleyan Chapel
Solent Works	Medina Road	W	1916 - 4/5 May 1942	Assembly and operation of marine aircraft	Housed Schneider Contest Competitors in 1919 and 1923. Destroyed by air raid when in use for Walrus production.
Victoria Hall	Medina Road	W	Early to late 1920s	Mould Loft	
Old Lifeboat Shop	Albany Road	E	1914 - 1944	Manufacture and assembly of aircraft components.	Burnt down accidentally. Replaced by Albany Works.
Maresfield Works	Old Road/ Maresfield Road	E	1914 to present	Press Shop, Sheet Metal, Coppersmiths, etc.	Extended in 1927.
Seaholme Building	Junction High Street/ Medina Road	E	1910 to present	Offices incl. Head Office.	Still in use.
White House	Medina Road	E	1909 - 1934	S.E. Saunders' House	Demolished.
Green Shed	Union Street	E			These premises demolished to make way for new Columbine Works.
Old Stables	Union Street	E	1910 - 1935	Aircraft assembly.	Old premises. Previously Liquid Fuel Engineering Co. (LIFU).
Sunbeam Yard	Medina Road	E			
Columbine Yard	Medina Road	E			
Columbine Works	Castle Street	E	1935 to present	Marine aircraft assembly.	New. Occupied most of land between Castle Street and Medina Road which then extended from Seaholme to Albany Road.
Esplanade Building	Attached to original Columbine Works	E	1910 to present	To Spartan 1931	Retained after rebuild of Columbine Works. Became Executives' Dining Room and now offices.
Medina Shop	Adjacent to Columbine Works	E	1910 - 1939	Originally the Prototype Shop	Dismantled and moved to Whippingham.
			1939 to present	Re-built for Lerwick production.	Now overload building.
Cornubia Yard	Clarence Road	E	1914 - 4/5 May 1942	Boatyard. Built Miss England, Bluebird and other famous boats.	Destroyed by air raid when in use for Walrus repair.
Victoria Barracks	Albany Road	E	Purchased in 1961, to present	Works Engineering Dept., etc.	Initially used as manufacturing area for Skeeter rotor blades.

Name	Location		Period of Use	Purpose	Remarks
Osborne Yard	Near Whippingham	E	From Jan. 1911	Seaplane Sheds. Housed Ravaud, Sopwith Bat Boat, Circuit of Britain aircraft.	Original sheds destroyed by gale 16.3.14. Rebuilt May/June 1914. Wooden sheds with curved corrugated iron roof. 2 sheds 6,000 sq. ft.
Folly Works	Whippingham		1919 - 21 Jan. 1960	Short Seaplanes, Cutty Sark wings. Manufacture of plywood and plastic products.	Burnt down accidentally. Rebuilt works for subsidiary company later sold.
Osborne Stables (Formerly the Naval College)	York Avenue	E	1945 - 6 April 1987	Design Office	Design of Princess, SR.53/177, Black Knight/Arrow and all hovercraft. Floor area approx. 60,000 sq. ft.
Osborne Works	Whippingham Road	E	1941 to present	Test Tanks and Model Making. Mock-up of Princess. Apprentice training. Tensile Testing. Electronics.	Site where EEL Limited had its origins. Electronics design and production moved to Kings Building in 1983.
Albany Works	Between Albany and Maresfield Roads	E	1955 to present	Aircraft assembly area. Valiant components. Skeeter helicopter. Now Machine Shop.	An enlarged building on the site of the Old Lifeboat Shop.
Parkhurst Forest	Parkhurst I.W.		May 1942 - 1965	Aircraft repair works. Later Machine Shop, etc.	Dispersal site after bombing.
East Medina Aerodrome	Nr. Padmore Farm	E	1917 - 1918	Flight Test Avro 504s	Aerodrome in fields adjacent to Folly Sheds. Area 40 acres.
Carisbrooke Brick, Tile and Pottery Works	Gunville and Afton, I.W.		1930 - 1937	Manufacture of high class pottery, bricks, tiles, etc.	Operated by Hubert (Peter) Saunders, Sam's son, on his behalf.
Kings Building	Castle Street	E	1960 - Present	Production Engineering and Tool Design Office. Now EEL Limited design and production.	Originally the only East Cowes cinema.
West Wight Aerodrome	Somerton	W	1925 - 1946	Flight Test A.10, Spartans, Bluebirds, etc.	Originally owned by J.S. White Ltd. Now mainly industrial site.

293

Name	Location	Period of Use	Purpose	Remarks
Falcon Works (Formerly J.S. White Ltd)	East Cowes	E 1966 - present	Manufacture of aircraft and space components and hovercraft skirts.	Formerly J.S. White & Co. Ltd., ship yard for ship and submarine hull construction. Also used as hovercraft development operating base. Floor area approx. 215,000 sq. ft.
High Down	Nr the Needles	1956 - 72	Rocket development	Two test stands for static testing of rocket motors and systems for Black Knight, etc.

After the bombing in World War 2, considerable dispersal took place into garages, shops, and other premises, mainly in the Isle of Wight, in Ryde, Cowes, Newport, Totland, Bembridge and Freshwater. Approved premises are listed below, these were retained in use until circumstances had improved.

LIST OF SAUNDERS-ROE LIMITED PREMISES APPROVED BY THE AERONAUTICAL INSPECTION DIRECTORATE DURING THE 1939 - 45 WAR

Correct to Amendment List No. 14 April-May 1943

	LOCATION	APPROVAL NUMBER
1.	East Cowes.	489394/24
2.	Tarrants, High Road, Byfleet, Surrey.	Ext. of 489394/24
3.	New Barn, New Barn Road, East Cowes.	Ext. of 489394/24
4.	Osborne Hall, Osborne.	Ext. of 489394/24
5.	Osborne Shops (Old Holiday Camp), Osborne.	Ext. of 489394/24
6.	Melchet Court, Sherfield English, Romsey.	Ext. of 489394/24
7.	The Round Chapel, Hersham, Walton-on-Thames.	Ext. of 489394/24
8.	The Tin Chapel, Addleston Road, Weybridge.	Ext. of 489394/24
9.	Weybridge Trading Estate, Addleston Road, Weybridge.	Ext. of 489394/24
10.	The Old Power House, Riverside, Newport, I.W.	Ext. of 489394/24
11.	Crabbe Stores, East Street, Ryde, I.W.	Ext. of 489394/24
12.	Reflex Photo Co., East Street, Ryde, I.W.	Ext. of 489394/24

	LOCATION	APPROVAL NUMBER
13.	Read's Garage, Simeon Street, Ryde, I.W.	Ext. of 489394/24
14.	Redman's Garage, Station Approach, Winchester.	Ext. of 489394/24
15.	West Cowes.	B.117229/40
16.	Bembridge Hangar, Bembridge	Ext. of B.117229/40
17.	Somerton Aerodrome, Cowes.	Ext. of B.117229/40
18.	Cornubia Works, East Cowes.	Ext. of B.117229/40
19.	Osborne Garage, East Cowes.	Ext. of B.117229/40
20.	Fountain Garage, Northwood, Cowes.	Ext. of B.117229/40
21.	No. 1 & 2 Hangars, Park Green, Nr. Newport, I.W.	Ext. of B.117229/40
22.	Hall's Garage, Totland, I.W.	Ext. of B.117229/40
23.	Pink's Garage, Totland, I.W.	Ext. of B.117229/40
24.	St. Joseph's, Totland, I.W.	Ext. of B.117229/40
25.	Vittlefields No. 1 & 2 Hangars, Nr. Newport, I.W.	Ext. of B.117229/40
26.	The Airport, Southampton.	747400/38
27.	Fryars, Beaumaris, Anglesey.	542/41

The above titles for premises are those entered into the Aeronautical Inspection Directorate records!

Saunders-Roe group factory facilities 1955.

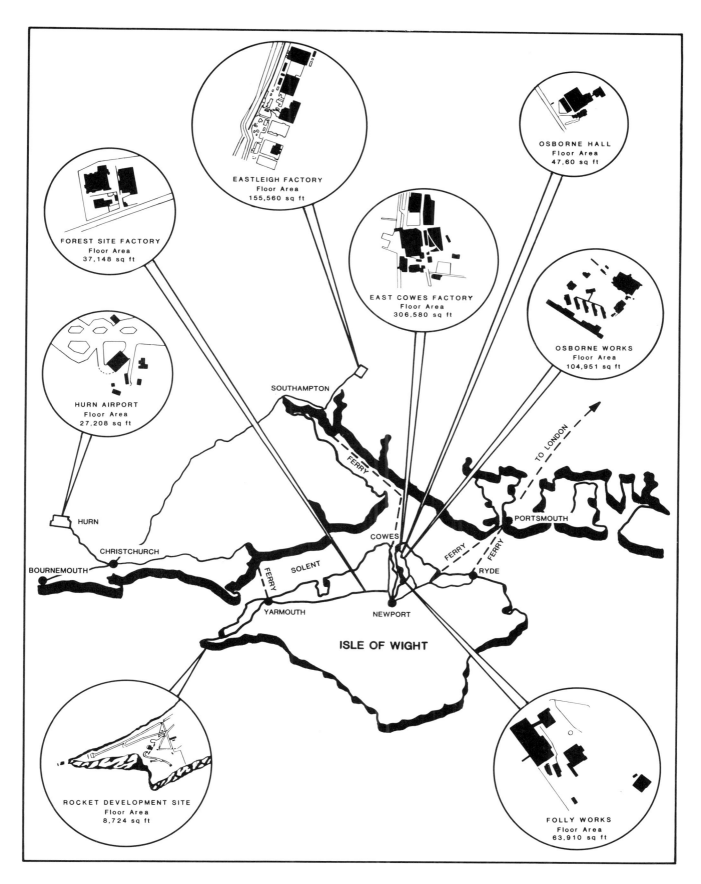

FOREST SITE FACTORY
Floor Area
37,148 sq ft

EASTLEIGH FACTORY
Floor Area
155,560 sq ft

OSBORNE HALL
Floor Area
47,60 sq ft

EAST COWES FACTORY
Floor Area
306,580 sq ft

HURN AIRPORT
Floor Area
27,208 sq ft

OSBORNE WORKS
Floor Area
104,951 sq ft

SOUTHAMPTON

TO LONDON

FERRY

PORTSMOUTH

HURN

CHRISTCHURCH

COWES

FERRY

FERRY

BOURNEMOUTH

RYDE

FERRY

SOLENT

YARMOUTH

NEWPORT

ISLE OF WIGHT

ROCKET DEVELOPMENT SITE
Floor Area
8,724 sq ft

FOLLY WORKS
Floor Area
63,910 sq ft

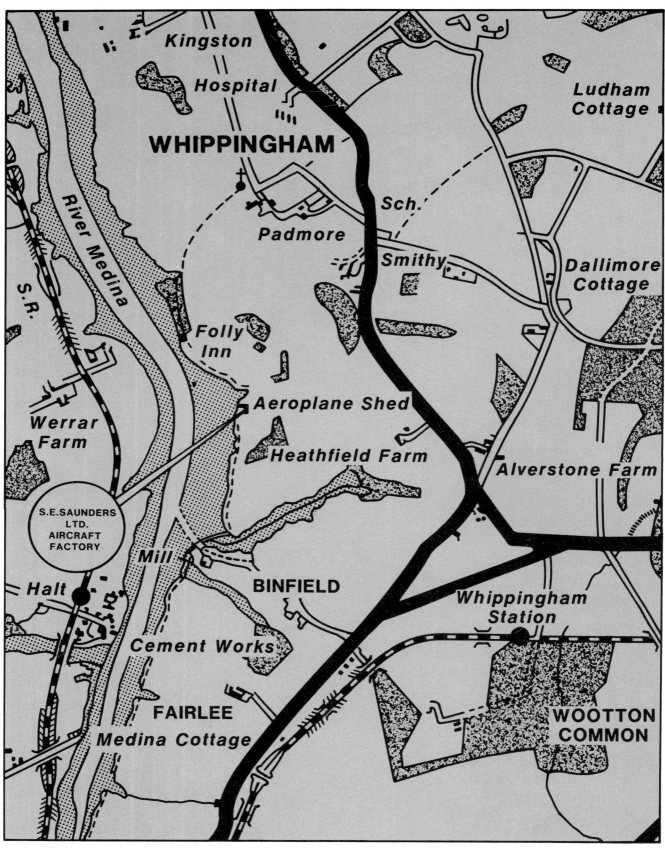

Ref. Ordnance survey sheet 142 1919
with minor corrections 1928.

SAUNDERS-ROE PREMISES OUTSIDE THE ISLE OF WIGHT

Name	Location	Period of Use	Purpose	Remarks
Fryars Bay	Beaumaris, Anglesey	1940 - 1945	Design Department. Repair and over-haul facility for American aircraft.	Dispersal from Cowes in Wartime.
Addlestone Works	Addlestone (Weybridge Trading Estate), Surrey	1940 - 1944	Production of Walrus amphibian aircraft.	Aerodrome on adjacent Chertsey Meads. Factory handed over to Fairey Aviation on completion of Walrus production. Works 150,000 sq. ft. Office 20,000 sq. ft. Tarrants, Byfleet leased for 3 years from 2.9.40 and Round Chapel, Hersham.
Luton Works	Adamant Engineering Co. Ltd., Luton	1936 - 1937	Manufacture of flying boat components originally under sub-contract to Adamant in 1935	Adamant taken over by Saunders-Roe in July 1936. All work transferred to Eastleigh Works in 1937.
Eastleigh Works	Eastleigh Aerodrome, Southampton, Hants.	1937 - 1959	Parachute release mechanisms. Lerwick tail units and Spitfire rudders. Component manufacture and structure assembly work. Helicopter design and manufacture.	Factory space increased by 20% with take-over of Cierva Company. Produced Skeeter helicopter, Wasp helicopter design, Viscount wings, one man helicopters and outboard motors.
Melchet Court	Romsey, nr Southampton	1941 - 1945	Main company offices controlling contracts, production and repair at all sites except Beaumaris.	Dispersal from Cowes in Wartime.
Hurn Airport	Nr Bournemouth	1956 - 1958	Intended flight test centre for SR.53.	One hangar and seven small buildings leased.
London Office	Bush House, Aldwych, WC2	Pre-war		
	45 Parliament Street, Westminster, SW1	Post-war		
	York House, Queen Square, WC1.	Jan. 1955 to Feb. 1958	Design Office	Opened for design of SR.177. Closed when contract terminated.
Cheltenham Office	Within Gloster Aircraft complex	Dec. 1956 to Feb. 1958	Sub-contract liaison.	Opened for liaison with sub-contractors of ancillary equipment for SR.177 in the Cheltenham area.

Note: The premises used by the company have been many and varied and it is not possible to record the areas in use at any given time, however, it is recorded that in January 1957 the overall area was 1,135,000 sq.ft. The outlying sites then in use have since been disposed of and with consolidation at East Cowes and the Osborne Works, the area available is currently in the order of 400,000 sq.ft.

Site of the Beaumaris factory on the Isle of Anglesea

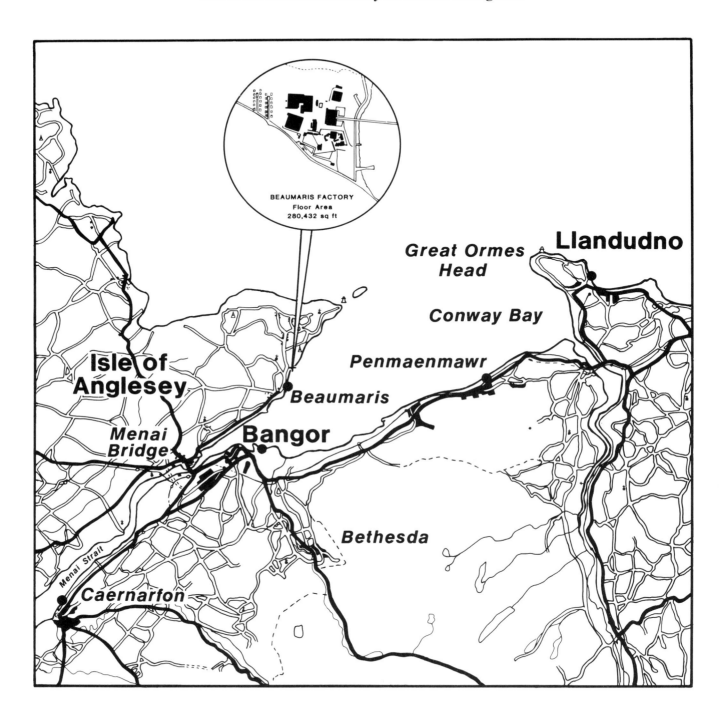

BEAUMARIS FACTORY
Floor Area
280,432 sq ft

Great Ormes Head

Llandudno

Conway Bay

Penmaenmawr

Isle of Anglesey

Beaumaris

Menai Bridge

Bangor

Bethesda

Menai Strait

Caernarfon

Saunders-Roe works Weybridge trading estate, Addlestone

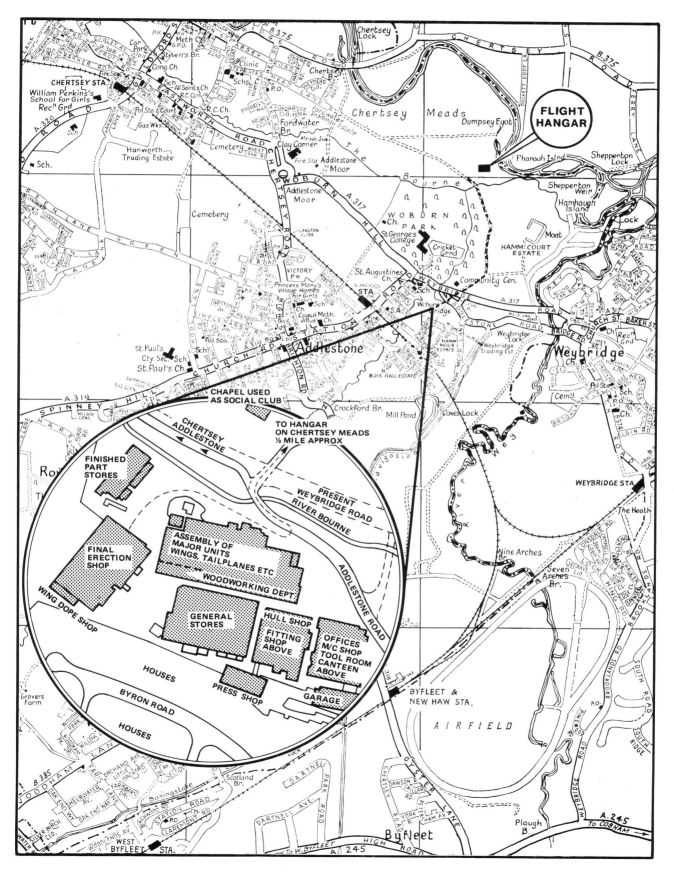

DIVERSIFICATION IN THE PERIOD 1945 TO 1960

The following products were made at various company establishments during a highly active diversification programme in the period between 1945 and 1960. The companies involved were:

Saunders-Roe Aircraft and Electronics Divisions
Saunders-Roe (Anglesey) Limited
Saro Laminated Wood Products
Saro Structures Limited
Saro Nuclear Enterprises Limited

1. BUS BODIES

During the years immediately after the war a very large number of bus and trolley bus bodies, single and double decked, were designed, manufactured and assembled on varying types of chassis to suit customers' requirements. They were operated in many parts of the British Isles as well as in foreign countries including Australia, Burma, Canada, South Africa, New Zealand, Cuba and China.

2. MARINE CRAFT

Marine craft of many types were designed and built for the British Admiralty and for other governments, including Burma, Finland, Japan, Canada, Argentina, Brazil, Portugal, Holland and Uruguay.

An indication of the range of craft can be obtained from the following selection:

Motor Torpedo Boats
The first aluminium alloy boat for the Royal Navy designed and launched on 22nd April 1949 with a top speed of 42 knots.

Fast Patrol Boats 'Dark Class'
Length 71 ft. 4in. Two Napier Deltic 2500 HP engines. Built for the Royal Navy and many other foreign countries.

Inshore Minesweepers
Length 105 ft. 4 in. Beam 20 ft. 6 in.

Marine Launches and Tenders
Length 30 to 50 ft.

Fibre Glass Launches

Airborne Lifeboats for use on Shackleton aircraft
Length 32 ft. Beam 7 ft. Range 1,000 miles. Material -Light Alloy

Auxiliary Motor Yacht Morag Mhor
Length 72 ft. Launched June 1954. Built of light alloy for the British Aluminium Company. The first marine application of argon arc welded aluminium alloy.

Hydrofoil Craft Bras d'Or
The research, design, and some manufacture was carried out at Cowes. The craft was built, equipped and tested at Anglesey. This was a specialised craft for the Royal Canadian Navy, with the British Admiralty co-operating on the research on foils. Launched on 29th March 1957. Length 60 ft. Engines 2 Rolls-Royce Griffons.

Water and Land, Reconnaissance Unit, Survey (WALRUS)
A novel amphibious prototype built for the Ministry of Defence in 1960. The light alloy hull 18 ft 4 in long and 4 ft 4 in beam was driven by two 16 ft long, 1 ft dia. mild steel drums which had welded helical leaders over their full length at 1.8 ft pitch. The blades increased in depth from zero at the forward end to six inches at the stern. The craft weighed 3000 lb empty, was powered by a Coventry Climax engine. Speed over land 2 mph. Speed over water 7.5 knots.

Barges
Length 80 to 90 ft. Built at Beaumaris for clients such as British Transport.

3. GENERAL ENGINEERING

Two 350 ft high free standing radio towers for British Somaliland.

Light alloy roofs of conventional type.

Light alloy circular domed roofs.

H.T.P. Storage tanks of various sizes.

H.T.P. refuelling tankers carrying 1,800 gallons of H.T.P. and 360 gallons of water as well as suitable pumping equipment.

Light alloy recompression chambers for the Admiralty.

Pontoons and bridge units in wood and light alloy.

Radar scanners and mountings

Torpedo tubes in light alloy.

Bomb Carriers

Rotary Dispensers in large quantities over a long period.

Stabilizers for small ships developed in co-operation with William Denny and Brothers Limited and Brown Brothers.

Assault Boats and Launches of various sizes.

Aircraft refuelling tankers with pumping equipment up to 10,000 gallons capacity.

Equipment for the U.K. Atomic Energy Authority.

Trolleys and crates for electronic equipment.

Plywood flush doors and decorative panelling.

'Medina' outboard engines for small boats.

Golf club and axe handles, field and ice hockey sticks, snow skis.

Industrial washing machines, draining boards and prams.

Sarolite and Saropane translucent corrugated roofing sheets of high strength manufactured from polyester resin reinforced with fibreglass.

Sar-Rez plastic finish supplied as a liquid and as a particularly hard wearing surface which was easily cleaned.

Saroy thermoplastic sheet produced by extruders in large quantities for home and foreign markets.

Fibreglass components of intricate shapes were manufactured, such as air conditioning and pressure ducts, radar transparencies, tools for drop hammers, 18 ft. launch, swimming pool panels, ducts, crates, light alloy deck hatches, etc.

4. ELECTRONICS

Production of strain gauges of various types suited to particular purposes. The design and manufacture of such specialized equipment as Analogue Computers, Ship Motion Recorders, Control Simulators, and a variety of electronic equipment and electronic test sets associated with guided weapons, etc.

5. NUCLEAR ENGINEERING

Beta lights - Self powered light sources using very low nuclear devices.

Industrial nucleonic instruments for measurement of thickness and density of a wide variety of materials from steel to tobacco.

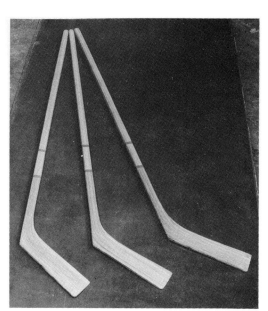  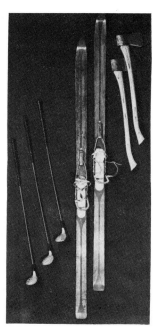

Sports equipment and axe handles made at Folly Works.

A Saro Bus on the slipway outside the Columbine Hangar at Cowes.

Flying Boat floating maintenance pontoons. Designed and built at Beaumaris following the 1939-45 war.

Veneered panelling finished with Sar-Rez liquid plastic at Folly Works.

Large analogue computers were built for many customers in the 1950's. These included The Ministry of Supply, and Imperial College.

Rotary dispenser designed and built at Cowes fitted to a Gannet.

A Flight Simulator for the SR.53. Designed and built at Cowes.

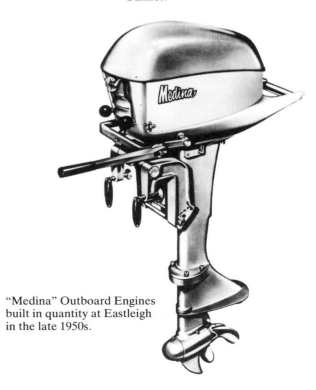
"Medina" Outboard Engines built in quantity at Eastleigh in the late 1950s.

Motor Torpedo Boat on trials in 1950.

'Dark' Class fast patrol boats built at Beaumaris for the Admiralty. Five of these were built.

Seven 106 ft long inshore Minesweepers were built for the Royal Navy at Beaumaris.

41½ ft Welded aluminium general purpose launch built at Beaumaris in 1958-9.

Airborne Lifeboat, built at Beaumaris, slung beneath an R.A.F. Shackleton Aircraft.

'Morag Mhor'. Built at Beaumaris with an all-welded aluminium hull.

'Bras dOr'. A hydrofoil research craft designed at Cowes and built at Beaumaris for the Canadian Defence Research Board.

Stern view of WALRUS hull showing the unusual helical screw propulsion. Designed and built at Cowes in 1959/60 to a concept of Naval Intelligence Dept.

Bow view of WALRUS hull and propulsors. Craft being lowered into the water for watertightness checks.

Barges buillt at Beaumaris for British Transport in 1959.

WALRUS. Undergoing static propulsor thrust checks.

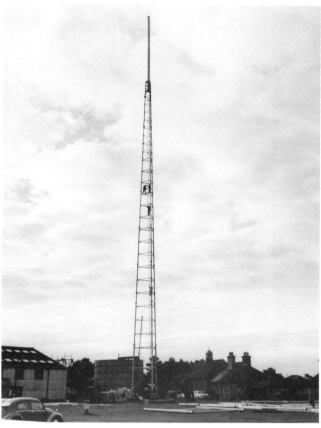

A trial erection of one of two 350ft high free standing radio towers, constructed of aluminium alloy tubes, built at Cowes for British Somaliland in 1959.

Hamilton Dome at Manchester Domestic & Trades College Built in 1959 (Span 77ft)

An aluminium alloy modular construction roof being erected.

Hazardous fluid transporter designed and built at Beaumaris in 1956.

High test peroxide toad tanker designed and built at Beaumaris in 1956.

Their wartime production experience in building thousands of bridging pontoons for the army, enabled Saunders-Roe (Anglesey) Ltd. to co-operate closely with the Military Experimental Establishment in designing and building prototypes of new post war equipment in aluminium alloy.

CONSTRUCTORS' NUMBERS AND CLASS 'B' IDENTIFICATIONS

No records exist of the company construction numbers prior to the Kittiwake (C/N 101) hopefully starting a period of production of civil aircraft which did not materialise. When the new series of type numbers began, commencing with the A.3 Valkyrie, the individual aircraft were identified by a stroke number as a suffix (e.g. A3/1) which included the Spartan Cruisers and this system was perpetuated to 1939. The Spartan biplanes followed the system already started by Simmonds and the machines constructed by Saunders-Roe came within the range 53 to 107. The sole example of the little Clipper monoplane bore C/N 201. Blackburn Bluebirds built at Cowes came within a series of SB (Saro Bluebird) numbers between 200 and 254.

Wartime numbering of production Walrus and Sea Otter aircraft conformed to Ministry requirements in which major components were individually identified using numbers in the S2 range. This system continued with production type Skeeters and the P.531 helicopters starting at S2/5000. Prototype and development Skeeters were identified as SR900-7 for identification during construction prior to registration.

Class 'B' identification has been a requirement of the appropriate government department since 1929 to identify aircraft prior to certification to enable test flying under certain restrictions to be carried out. The system employed has been changed at different periods, the L and S identities being pre-war allocations to Saunders/Saro and Spartan respectively. The wartime system was not applicable to the company, but post-war, G-12 identified Saunders-Roe built aircraft, helicopters and some hover-craft. G-46 was introduced later for the helicopter division.

CLASS 'B' IDENTIFIED AIRCRAFT

Saunders-Roe

L.1	G-AAIP	A.17/1	Cutty Sark
L.2	K.1949	A.10	Fighter
L.3	-	A.17/3	Cutty Sark. Retained L.3 in New Zealand.
L.4	G-ABCJ	A.19/1	Cloud
L.5	G-AETI	A.17/8	Cutty Sark

Spartan

S.1	G-ABMK	Arrow Seaplane. For trials at Felixstowe.
S.2		Allocation not traced.
S.3	G-ACEG	Clipper.

Saunders-Roe/Westland

G-l2-1 TG.263	SR.A1 Jet Flying Boat Fighter.
G-12-1 SC.501	Skeeter Mk.51 Helicopter (for Federal German Navy) S2/5065
G-12-2 PC + 117	Skeeter Mk.50 Helicopter (for Federal German Army) S2/5061.
G-12-3 G-APYF	YROE-1 Hiller Rotorcycle S2/7592
G-12-4	SR.N1 Hovercraft
G-12-5	SR.N2 Hovercraft (under Westland name).

Saunders-Roe (Helicopter Division)

G-46-1 U.S.M.C.4021	Hiller YROE1 Rotorcycle S2/7588
G-46-1 G-APYF	Hiller YROE1 Rotorcycle S2/7592
G-46-2	Hiller YROE1 Rotorcycle S2/7593 (crashed at Eastleigh 8.5.61)
G-46-3	Hiller YROE1 Rotorcycle S2/7594
G-46-4	Hiller YROE1 Rotorcycle S2/7595
G-46-5	Hiller YROE1 Rotorcycle S2/7596

BIBLIOGRAPHY AND SOURCES OF REFERENCE

A.V. Roe	**Lanchbery** E.	Bodley Head	1956
Adventure with Fate	**Penrose** Harald	Airlife	1984
Aeromarine Origins	**King** H.F.	Putnam	1966
Part 1 In the Shadow of the Eagle's Wing Part 2 An Aeronautical History of the Cumbria, Dumfries and Galloway Regions	**Connon** Peter	St. Patrick's Press	1984
The Aeroplanes of the R.F.C. (Military Wing)	**Bruce** J.M.	Putnam	1982
Aircraft of the R.A.F. since 1918	**Thetford** O.	Putnam	1958
Aircraft of the 1914-18 War	**Thetford** O. & **Riding** E.J.	Harborough	1944
Blackburn Aircraft Since 1909	**Jackson** A.J.	Putnam	1968
Boats of the Air	**Wragg** David	Hale	1984
British Aeroplanes 1914-18	**Bruce** J.M.	Putnam	1969
Bristol Aircraft since 1910	**Barnes** C.H.	Putnam	1964
British Aircraft 1909-1914	**Lewis** P.	Putnam	1962
British Aviation - The Pioneer Years	**Penrose** Harald	Putnam	1967
British Aviation - The Great War and Armistice	**Penrose** Harald	Putnam	1969
British Aviation - The Adventuring Years	**Penrose** Harald	Putnam	1973
British Aviation - Widening Horizons	**Penrose** Harald	H.M.S.O.	1979
British Aviation - Ominous Skies	**Penrose** Harald	H.M.S.O.	1980
British Civil Aircraft since 1919 Vols 1, 2 & 3	**Jackson** A.J.	Putnam	1974
British Flying Boats	**Duval** G.R.	Bradford Barton	1973
The Challenging Sky	**Ludovici** L.J.	Jenkins	1956
Combat Aircraft Prototypes since 1945	**Jackson** R.	Airlife	1985
Curtiss - The Hammondsport Era 1907-15	**Casey** L.B.	Crown	1981
The Dragonflies	**Jackson** R.	Barker	1971
Felixstowe	**Kinsey** G.	Dalton	1978
First Through the Clouds	**Merriam** F.W.	Batsford	1954
Helicopters and Autogiros	**Gablehouse** C.	Scientific Book Club	1970
J'ai Vu Naitre L'Aviation	**Fabre** H.	Guirimand	1980
The Motor Balloon 'America'	**Mabley** G.	Stephen Greene	1975
Nine Lives Plus - Record Breaking on Land, Sea & In the Air	**Bruce** The Hon. Mrs Victor	Pelham Books	1977
Outlines	**Bateson** R.P.	I.S.O.	1985
Pictorial History of the R.A.F. (Vol. 1)	**Taylor** J.W.R. & **Bowyer** C	Allan	1980
The Schneider Trophy	**Mondey** D.	Hale	1975
Schneider Trophy Aircraft	**James** D.N.	Putnam	1981
The Schneider Trophy Races	**Barker** R.	Airlife	1981
Shorts Aircraft Since 1900	**Barnes** C.H.	Putnam	1967
The Solent Sky	**New** P.T.		1976
Sopwith Aircraft 1912-20	**King** H.F.	Putnam	1981
Sopwith - The Man and His Aircraft	**Robertson** B.	Air Review	1970
The Speed Seekers	**Foxworth** T.G.	Macdonald & Jane's	1975
Supermarine Aircraft Since 1914	**Andrews** C.F. & **Morgan** E.B.	Putnam	1981
Vickers Aircraft	**Andrews** C.F.	Putnam	1969
World Flying Boats	**Duval** G.R.	Bradford Barton	1975

The Public Records Office at Kew contains many records with some relevance to the subject including the reports of testing carried out by M.A.E.E. at Felixstowe and Helensburgh and by A. & A.E.E. at Martlesham Heath. The following are some of the reports held in the files to which reference has been made.

FELIXSTOWE REPORTS

		DATE	REF.
F/A/8	F.5 Saunders Channel Hull	April 1924	AVIA19/254
F/A/9	Saunders Pontoon Chassis	January 1925	255
F/A/22	Saunders Collapsible Dinghy	July 1926	267
F/23	Saunders A.3 Valkyrie N186	April 1927	501
F/45	Saro A.17 Cutty Sark G-AAIP	September 1929	518
F/A/47	Saunders Bilge Pump Mks. I & II	February 1928	292
F/60	Saro A.19 Cloud G-ABCJ	August 1930	525
F/63	Saro A.14 Hull (Southampton) N251	October 1930	
F/69	Saro A.17 Cutty Sark Sl575	February 1931	532
F/73B	Saunders A.7 Severn and		
F/76A	Short Singapore II comparative trials		
F/81	Saro A.19 Cloud G-ABHG	July 1931	538
F/88	Saro A.19/29 Cloud K2681	April 1932 - March 1934	539
F/92	Saro A.17 Cutty Sark (1 Lynx IVC) G-ABVF	March 1932	543
F/113	Saro A.19 Cloud K2894	May 1933	561
F/129	Saro A.27 London I K3560 and K5258	1935 - May 1937	1251
F/185 F/186 F/187 F/188	Saunders-Roe SR.45 Princess Trials G-ALUN	Jan. - April 1955	

HELENSBURGH REPORTS

H/158	Saro A.37 Trials G-AFZS	March 1941	598
H/163	Supermarine Walrus II Tests W.7280	November 1942	603

MARTLESHAM HEATH REPORTS

M.543/2/C2	Saro A.10 Trials	September 1930	AVIA18/1095
M.583/CA	Saro A.21 Windhover Trials	July 1931	1098

Articles in contemporary issues of these magazines and newspapers provided sources of reference:

Aero
Aeroplane
Aerospace
Air Pictorial
Aircraft Engineering

Flight
Popular Flying
Propliner 79
Isle of Wight County Press

The New Slipway
Saro Progress } Saunders-Roe House Magazines

Aeroplane Monthly, a more recent publication, has dealt with various aspects of Saunders-Roe activities. In particular, the following issues contain excellent articles by Alec Lumsden, Bill Gunston and Philip Jarrett summarising their research into the backgrounds of individual aircraft types and are recommended for more detailed study:

November 1973 SR.A1
April 1974 SR.45 Princess
July 1974 SR.53 and SR.177

May 1977 A.10
March 1978 Shetland
January 1979 S.36 Lerwick

Flight of 26th September 1952 contains a detailed description of the SR.45 Princess and includes the outstanding line drawing by Arthur Bowbeer.

ILLUSTRATION ACKNOWLEDGEMENTS

The authors are very pleased to acknowledge the following sources of photographs, drawings and diagrams-

1. Companies and Organisations
   Westland Aerospace Limited, Beken of Cowes Limited, the G.S. Leslie and J.M. Bruce collection, Aeroplane magazine, the Autocar magazine, British Aerospace plc, the Daily Mail, Flight magazine, the Imperial War Museum, the Isle of Wight County Council Cultural Services Department, the Oxford Public Library, the R.A.F. Museum, Rolls Royce plc, the Royal Aerospace Establishment, the Royal Scottish Museum, Short Brothers Limited, Sport and General magazine, and Vickers Limited.

2. Individuals:
   C. Bowyer, H. Busteed, P.T. Capon, S. Cribb, M.H. Goodall, J. Garrett, T.R. Hiott, F. Hubert, S.D. Hunt, G. Kinsey, J. and N. Nicholls, Harald Penrose, K. Turner, and E. White. Together with numerous other past and present employees of the Company.

The publishers have endeavoured to observe the legal requirements with regard to the rights of suppliers of photographic material.

INDEX

Bold page numbers indicate illustrations.

310

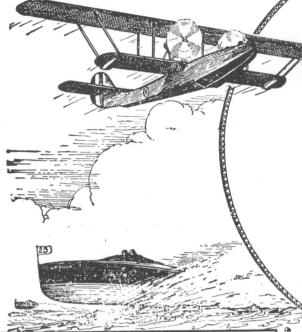